BOUDICA
to
RAEDWALD

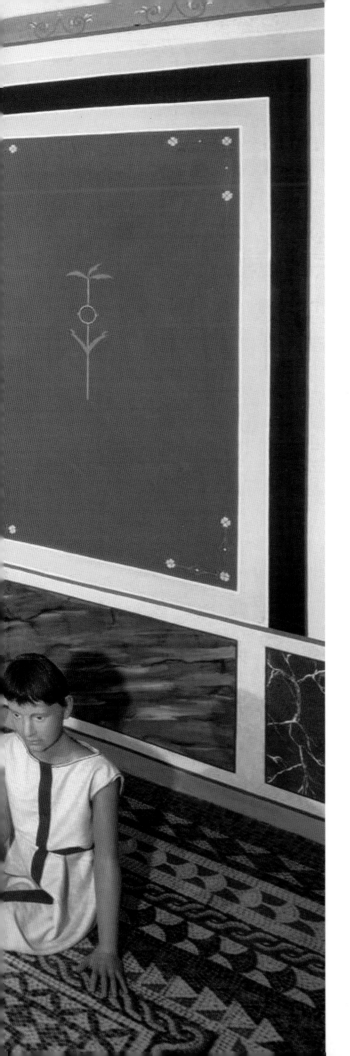

BOUDICA

to

RAEDWALD

East Anglia's relations with Rome

JOHN FAIRCLOUGH

MALTHOUSE PRESS, SUFFOLK, 2010

Published by Malthouse Press, Suffolk
17 Reade Road, Holbrook, Ipswich IP9 2QL

ISBN 978 0 9539680 3 9

© John Fairclough 2010

British Library Cataloguing-in-Publication Data

A catalogue record for this book is available from the British Library.

Designed by Robert Malster
Typeset by John Walton
Printed in Great Britain by Print Wright Ltd, Ipswich

Contents

Footnotes: the following abbreviations are used.
Archaeology of Roman Suffolk: Moore, I.E., Plouviez, J. & West, S.E., *The Archaeology of Roman Suffolk*, Suffolk County Council, 1988.
EAA: East Anglian Archaeology. A series of publications with more than 100 produced over the past thirty years: for current details see www.eaareport.org.uk.
PSIAH: Proceedings of the Suffolk Institute of Archaeology and History.
RIB: Collingwood, R.G. & Wright, R.P., *The Roman Inscriptions of Britain*, Vol. I, new edition, Tomlin, R.S.O., Alan Sutton, 1995; nos. 2401 ff. vol. II in fascicles, 1990-95.
SROI. Suffolk Record Office, Ipswich branch.

Introduction

Boudica and Raedwald are two of the greatest characters in the early history of East Anglia, separated by over five and a half centuries of activity during which our region did not always conform to the national pattern. Earlier experience of contact with Rome in the days of Julius Caesar helps us to understand the background to Queen Boudica's rebellion. How close did she come to driving the Roman army out of Britain within twenty years of the Claudian invasion?

The best surviving monuments of the army's activities in Suffolk and Norfolk are the main roads they imposed across an agricultural landscape. As the Roman Empire exploited the natural resources of this part of Britannia, we must look for its impact on the farming and industrial economy. The towns and great houses of the first centuries AD remain elusive in a region where the only truly Roman town was the colonia at Colchester, itself strictly outside modern East Anglia, but the clues are worth interpreting. As the Empire became less secure some settlements apparently declined, but there was a new, or renewed, emphasis on coastal defences which has left visible consequences.

A few local residents became very wealthy and some, at least, became Christians, although we cannot say how many adopted the new religion. How far their faith survived the end of Roman rule is unclear, as the evidence for the response of local communities in the last years of Roman government and the immediate aftermath of its collapse is limited. Its interpretation remains controversial. Were the incoming Anglo-Saxons a massive horde, or relatively few soldiers and warlords with their families? How many Britons just carried on farming the land as their ancestors had done? Once we have grasped the impact of Rome it is difficult to close the story without noting the Roman elements in seventh-century kingship and specifically in the contents of the great ship at Sutton Hoo that was almost certainly the last resting place of King Raedwald. How strong was the thread of continuity through these centuries of change?

Genio Loci – to the Spirit of the Place

M(arcus) FAVONI(us) M(arci) F(ilius) POL(lia tribu) FACILIS C(enturio) LEG(ionis) XX VERECVUNDVS ET NOVICIVS LIB(erti) POSVERVNT H(ic) S(itus) E(st)

Marcus Favonius Facilis, son of Marcus, of the Pollian tribe, Centurion of the Twentieth Legion, lies here. Verecundus and Novicius, his freedmen, set this up.

Tombstone of a Roman centurion, Marcus Favonius Facilis, from Colchester. He commanded eighty men of the Twentieth Legion, and was probably still a serving officer when he died. He and Longinus (see page 36) were buried beside the main road from London and St Albans.
© Colchester and Ipswich Museum Service

Acknowledgements

First I must record my debt to Adrian Sherwin-White of St John's College, Oxford, who encouraged me to argue about Ancient History in the 1960s, and to Stan Stanford, who instructed me in the practical skills of archaeology on the hillforts of the Welsh Marches. Since coming to Ipswich I have learned much from Elizabeth Owles, Judith Plouviez, Bob Markham, Stanley West, Norman Scarfe, Keith Wade, Edward Martin, Steven Plunkett, Sam Newton, John Newman, Stuart Boulter, and many others. Students on various courses have added fresh ideas, including Sue Toomey, Tony Greenacre, Adrian Donaghey, Rob Steerwood and Richard Newman.

Mike Hardy introduced me to the pleasures of tramping across muddy fields in search of tiny scraps of pot, and has always generously shared his knowledge and the results of his own extensive field walking. Bob Malster and Pete and Val Cundy have accompanied me on long walks in pursuit of elusive Roman roads. Judith Plouviez and Edward Martin commented on the draft text. I have benefited from their expertise, but they are not responsible for occasions when I have failed

Looking into the guardroom at one side of the Balkerne Gate in Colchester, part of the walls of the Roman town of Camulodunum.

The Mildenhall Treasure, found by a ploughman during the Second World War, is one of the finest survivals from the Roman period in Suffolk. Among that hoard is this silver plate showing Pan playing his pipes and a dancing Bacchic reveller.
© Trustees of the British Museum

to accept their views. Stephen Schwarz of Expression worked his magic on my attempts to create clear maps and illustrations.

For permission to use illustrations I am grateful to the Trustees of the British Museum which contains so many fine objects from the region, Colchester and Ipswich Museum Service, Suffolk County Council Archaeological Service, the Vatican Library, University of Cambridge Air Photograph Library, Colchester Archaeological Trust and Peter Froste, Sam Newton and Stella Goodsir, Aldeburgh and District Local History Society and Herring Bone Design, and Steven Plunkett.

I thank them all and apologise to the many others I have failed to mention. This book is built on their work and that of previous generations, but interpretations that are controversial and conclusions that some will question are entirely my responsibility. I have tried to ensure the factual information is accurate and apologise for any surviving errors. I hope others will feel encouraged to search for more evidence, as we still have much to learn about the early story of East Anglia and why its people so often do different. This book would never have been completed without the support and encouragement of Jo Batley and Bob Malster.

Boudica's rebellion

ALMOST a hundred years before Boudica's revolt Julius Caesar brought a Roman army into Britain. He conducted only brief campaigns here in 55 and 54BC because in the following years he had to defeat a major rebellion in France and then was involved in civil war in Italy. In 54BC he defeated King Cassivellaunus, who led much of south-east Britain in its resistance to the Romans. Cassivellaunus' home was north of the Thames, and apparently he had aroused hostility from other states before they agreed to accept his leadership against Caesar. We are told that Caesar guaranteed the freedom of the Trinovantes against any interference by Cassivellaunus, who had threatened their independence.

We know the Trinovantes lived in Essex and their territory probably extended over the River Stour into south Suffolk, just as today that part of Suffolk tends to look towards Colchester. In the north were the Iceni. They were probably the "Great Ceni" (Cenimagni) who, along with four others – Segontiaci, Ancalites, Bibroci and Cassi – sent delegates to offer their submission to Julius Caesar in 54BC[1]. Almost certainly the text should be read as the Latin word "magni", meaning "great" or "strong", qualifying the tribal name "Ceni", although the loss of an initial I or E (coins generally appear to show "ECEN") is unexplained. It could be how Caesar heard the name or an error by a later scribe copying an unfamiliar name. However as there are references to Cenoman(n)i in Gaul some prefer to see Cenimagni as the tribal name, which might or might not be a version of Iceni. The Iceni were certainly the main power in Norfolk, and in the Roman period their capital was at Caistor by Norwich. There might have been a settlement at Caistor before the conquest but its status is unknown, so the capital might be a new Roman creation.

The extent of Icenian rule is unclear: it is very likely to have included the southern side of the Waveney valley, as even today that part of Suffolk generally relates as naturally to Norwich as to Ipswich. Edward Martin has made a detailed study of the evidence, particularly from coin finds, and suggests that the boundary between Iceni and Trinovantes might have varied at different times during the Iron Age. He thinks the division was broadly based on the high ground north of the Gipping valley in the east and on the valley of the River Lark in the west.[2] The other four states named by Caesar are not mentioned after the Roman conquest in AD43, so we can only say they are likely to have been located in eastern England and might have been absorbed before the conquest by the Iceni or the Trinovantes. Given the activities of Caratacus in what is now Wales and the possibility considered below that Boudica planned a migration to the west, is it possible that the Roman name Segontium for Caernarvon does preserve a reference to the Segontiaci as exiles from East Anglia after the conquest?[3]

We know nothing of the earlier history or evolution of the people known to the Romans as Trinovantes and Iceni. Some authorities have tried to explain the differences between them by claiming the Trinovantes were

1 Caesar *Gallic War* V.21.
2 for details see Martin, E., "Suffolk in the Iron Age" in Davies, J. & Williamson, T., *Land of the Iceni*, Norwich, 1999, p.83 ff.
3 I owe this suggestion to Adrian Donaghey.

Opposite page: *Boudica as portrayed in Ipswich Museum. She wears a gold torc and her long flowing hair is conspicuous after she has dismounted from her chariot in this imaginative image of the "warrior queen" leading the rebellious Iceni into battle against the Romans.*
Ipswich Museum

Belgic immigrants from France. They have based this on Caesar's statement that people from Belgic Gaul, that is roughly Belgium and part of north-western France, invaded Britain. However Cunliffe[4] makes a good case for seeing a limited area of Belgic immigration in Hampshire where Roman Winchester was later called *Venta Belgarum* (the market of the Belgae). They were joined later by another Belgic group led by Commius that became the Atrebates centred on Silchester near Reading. It is likely that in other parts of Britain, including East Anglia, the indigenous people adopted some of the customs and material culture of their continental neighbours.

The Trinovantes did adopt more of the pottery styles and burial practices typical of Belgic peoples in France and Belgium, using wheel-turned Belgic type pottery made in Britain and importing fine red and black Gallo-Belgic cups and platters made near Rheims. However both Iceni and Trinovantes were probably descendants of the people who had lived here and farmed the land for thousands of years through the New Stone Age and the Bronze Age. Increasing evidence of continuous management of the land through these periods strengthens this case.

No doubt they were always influenced by travellers coming from overseas, either directly from the Rhine valley or up the coast from the Channel, opening up opportunities to exchange ideas and goods with foreigners, some of whom probably married and settled here. Finds from Icenian territory in Norfolk include an Etruscan bridle bit and several Early Hallstatt type brooches which presumably arrived from the continent centuries before Caesar.[5] While the core population was indigenous there is no need to see them as isolated or unchanging.

Links between Britain and the continent were well known to Julius Caesar when he was campaigning in Gaul in 56BC.[6] He found the Veneti on the Brittany coast had the largest fleet of ships "in which they sail to Britain" and controlled shipping in the area, imposing tolls on traffic. When the Veneti opposed Rome they gathered support from other coastal peoples including the Morini and Menapii, which means their interests on the continent extended as far as the area of the present Netherlands, and from Britain itself. Caesar does not specify which British peoples took part, but for a major conflict they might have called on East Anglia. Caesar had a fleet of Roman warships (navis longas) specially built on the River Loire and also gathered some from his Gallic allies.

Caesar describes the different construction of the Gallic ships: they had flatter bottoms than the Roman ships and high bows and sterns, so were good in heavy seas. They were built of oak for strength, crossbeams were fixed to timbers a foot high with iron nails as thick as a thumb, they secured the anchors with chains instead of ropes and used fine leather instead of linen for sails. Most significantly, they were too strong to be damaged by the rams of Roman ships. Sean McGrail[7] compares this description to a group of excavated vessels which he calls Romano-Celtic. In particular he notes three seagoing ships of this type, one from the Thames in London (Blackfriars I, c.AD150), one from Guernsey (St Peter Port I, c.AD275) and one from the Severn estuary (Barland's Farm, c.AD300), which were built frame first, by building up the frame from the keel plank and then nailing on the planks, which is quite different from either the Mediterranean or Nordic traditions in which the shape of the hull was first built up from planks nailed together and

4 Cunliffe, B., *Iron Age Communities in Britain*, ed.3, Routledge, 1991, p.108.
5 Dennis, M., "Silver of the Iceni", *Current Archaeology 217* (April 2008).
6 Caesar, *Gallic War* III.8.
7 McGrail, S., *Ancient Boats and Ships*, Shire Archaeology 31, 2nd ed. 2006.

then the framing was inserted into it. This "Celtic" technique reappears in the great ships of the fifteenth and sixteenth century explorers. One of the Rhine barges of the first to second century AD from Zwammerdam was of "Romano-Celtic" design, but two others were in the Mediterranean style. The late Roman ship from the Thames at County Hall (excavated in 1910) was carvel built with planks joined by mortises and tenons in Mediterranean fashion.

Caesar makes the point that the one advantage the Romans had was the ability to use oars, while the Gauls depended totally on sails. Once Caesar had assembled his fleet it faced 220 enemy ships and developed the tactic of using grappling devices to catch the Gallic rigging and then rowing away, snapping the halyards and bringing down the yards so as to immobilise the ships. In this way his fleet gained total victory over the Veneti after fighting all day. This ended Veneti control of seaborne trade with Britain, giving control, and ability to tax the trade, to the Romans.

Certainly Rome had gained control of the south side of the Channel and its ports, but we do not know how many ships were sailing out of independent Britain, including East Anglia with its access to the open waters of the North Sea. They could trade with continental ports north or south of the Roman frontier on the Rhine. Caesar went on to make a brief and inconclusive attack on the Morini and Menapii which brought him to the Channel coast east of Boulogne and so into the North Sea.

That is the only reference to the Romans fighting a serious sea battle in northern waters, but the long coastlines of Gaul and Britain were always

The medieval divisions of the southern part of Suffolk might have originated from pre-Roman kingdoms. Ipswich (1) and Stoke (2) were probably part of the original "Wicklaw".

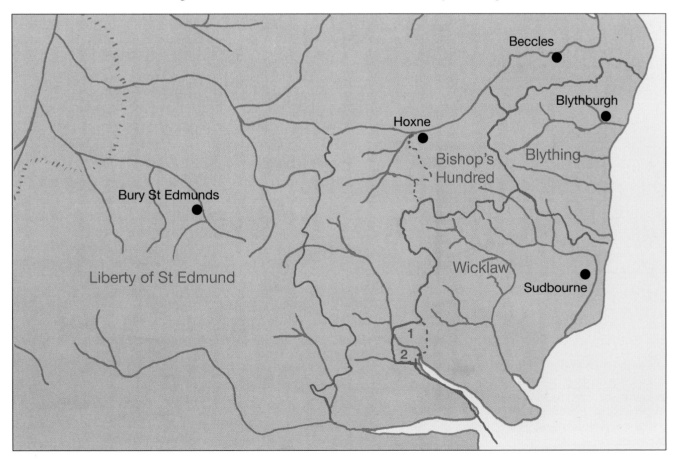

The Iron Age enclosure at Burgh by Grundisburgh. The massive ditch system, enclosing a large area on the valley side, is clearly visible on this air photograph. Clopton church is in the right foreground and Burgh church stands among trees inside the enclosure.
© Cambridge University

exposed to threats from foreign states or from individual pirates. Although classical sources make few references to naval activities the Roman authorities must always have maintained a fleet or fleets to patrol the Gallic coast and also the coast of Britain after it became part of the empire. Presumably this was part of the duties of the Classis Germanica ("the German fleet"), based on the River Rhine, augmented later by the Classis Britannica ("the British fleet") based at Boulogne.

Philip Crummy has presented strong arguments[8] based on finds of Iron Age material that the stronghold of Cassivellaunus attacked by Caesar in 54BC was Colchester, rather than Wheathampstead as proposed by Mortimer Wheeler. Clues in Julius Caesar's account of the taking of Cassivellaunus' stronghold are even more supportive of Colchester as its location than Philip Crummy argues. While the "man-made" defence fits the rampart and ditch of the first great dyke in the complex series south of Colchester, the "natural" defence was surely the woods and marshes of the valleys of the River Colne and its tributaries.

Caesar tells us he got his knowledge of the stronghold when the five tribes surrendered to him. We have identified the first named, the Cenimagni, as the "Great Iceni" of northern East Anglia, who always seemed rather remote from Wheathampstead but make perfect sense if Caesar was heading north-east through Essex. Edward Martin[9] has suggested we might look for the other four who are otherwise unknown (Segontiaci, Ancalites, Bibroci and Cassi) in East Anglia. All we can gather from Caesar is that the representatives of these five states were able to tell him where to find the stronghold, and they did not come from Kent as the four kings of Kent were still taking orders from Cassivellaunus.

There can be no certainty about the four named states, but in the west of Suffolk the land that looks towards the Fens and rivers feeding into the Wash,

8 *Current Archaeology* 208 (March 2007).
9 Martin, E., "Suffolk in the Iron Age" in *Land of the Iceni* ed. Davies, J. & Williamson, T., Norwich, 1999, p.90.

later the Liberty of St Edmund which became the county of West Suffolk, might have had a separate identity. On the coastal side of Suffolk two later administrative units could have originated as independent states. One is the valley of the River Blyth behind Blythburgh, which later formed a distinctive single hundred. The other is the Wicklaw, the group of five and a half hundreds which lay east of, and originally included, Ipswich. The Wicklaw includes the distinctive Iron Age earthwork at Burgh by Grundisburgh,[10] which might have been its focus. The size of the enclosure is only visible on air photographs. Being sited on a terrace on the side of a valley just above the stream it is no defensive "hillfort". It is more likely to have contained the residence of a local ruler combined with some religious centre. This interpretation of the Wicklaw gives added interest to the burial of the six Ipswich gold torcs close to a Holy Well which was a marker in the tenth-century bounds of Stoke by Ipswich[11] and remains part of the current boundary of Ipswich Borough. It might have marked the south-west limit of the Wicklaw kingdom at its closest point to Colchester.

Philip Crummy describes Cassivellaunus' men escaping from Caesar's two-pronged attack by withdrawing north-east, which would take them towards the Wicklaw. On this argument it had already submitted to Caesar, so presumably they were not welcomed. In any case the Roman troops took possession of large numbers of cattle gathered in the stronghold and killed or

10 Martin, E., *Burgh, Iron Age and Roman Enclosure*, EAA 40 (1988), p.72.
11 Fairclough, J., "The Bounds of Stoke and Ipswich", *PSIAH* vol. 40 part 3 (2003).

The Iron Age enclosure beside the river Stiffkey at Warham in north Norfolk. This is an impressive earthwork, but like Burgh it is on the side of the valley close to the river, so cannot properly be called a "hillfort".

captured many of the fleeing Britons. It is no surprise that Cassivellaunus himself then made terms with Caesar, agreeing to give hostages and pay tribute because his allies had defected. He had nowhere to go after Colchester.

There is an additional point if Caesar was proceeding from a Thames crossing, perhaps at or near London, towards Colchester. This took him through the heartland of the Trinovantes, who gave him hostages and supplies as he marched through their territory. It is likely that his route would be through Chelmsford. Perhaps its distinctive name as Caesaromagus, "the market town of Caesar", recorded the place where Trinovantian leaders (legati) met Julius Caesar to make formal submission to him, gave him forty hostages and provided him with corn for his army. They negotiated his support for Mandubracius, whom he allowed to join them as their ruler. Mandubracius had fled to Caesar on the continent when his father, the king of the Trinovantes, was killed by Cassivellaunus.

When Caesar left Britain he gave Mandubracius as king of the Trinovantes special protection against Cassivellaunus, so they would have seen the place where negotiations took place as special and properly to be associated with Julius Caesar. If the Trinovantes had not joined the Boudican rebellion it is possible that Caesaromagus would have become their capital. I believe that in the aftermath of the rebellion they probably lost their favoured status and possibly their identity, while their territory was split between the restored colonia at Colchester and the new provincial capital at London.

Six Iron Age gold torcs were found at Ipswich during the building of the Chantry estate, close to the site of a holy well recorded in the tenth century. Were they deposited at an ancient sacred site?
© Trustees of the British Museum

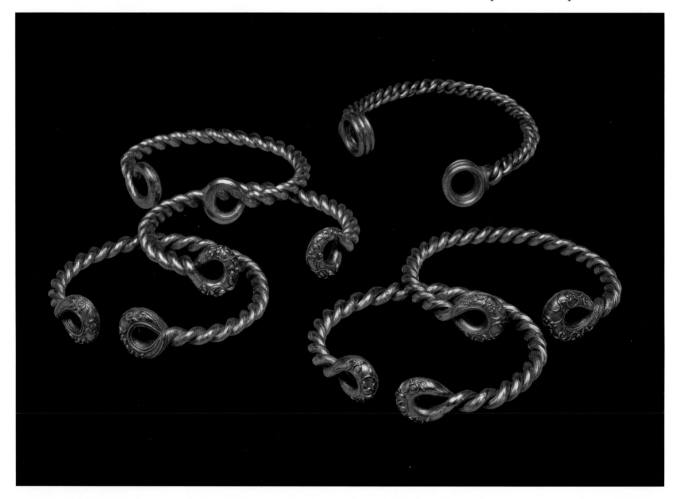

Beauvais in Gallia Belgica was Caesaromagus Bellovacorum, so presumably if it had not been for the Boudican revolt Chelmsford would have become Caesaromagus Trinovantium.

We do not know whether the Britons went on paying the annual tribute after Caesar's departure. Continuing contact changed the Roman view after the time of Cicero, whose brother served here with Caesar. He wrote to his friend Atticus that in Britain there was not even a tiny amount of silver and no hope of booty except slaves, "none of whom I think you foresee being learned in letters or in music".[12] Strabo later described Britain exporting grain, cattle, gold, silver, iron, hides, slaves and hunting dogs,[13] but stressed the value to Rome of export and import taxes, so he doubted if it would be worth conquering Britain. He said some British rulers had by their embassies and deference gained the friendship of the emperor Augustus[14] and dedicated offerings in the temple on the Capitol at Rome, so practically made the whole island Roman property. British merchants were trading with the Roman market, bringing Britons into contact with the political and commercial world of Rome at the time when it was turning from Republic to Empire.

Silver head of the Roman emperor Augustus on a medallion buried in the Lexden tumulus at Colchester. The emperor's head was cut from a cast of a coin struck between 18 and 16 BC. It suggests that the ruler of Colchester at the time had some friendly contact with Rome. © Colchester and Ipswich Museum Service

Some British states maintained friendly relations with Rome. We know that in later years some British princes appealed to Rome and called on the emperor himself for help when expelled from their homes. One of these was Dubnovellaunus, apparently at one time ruler of the Trinovantes, who fled to Augustus. Later Adminius, a son of Cunobelinus expelled by his father, fled to Claudius.

Coins help us to discover something of what was happening in our region during this period. It is often said that Iron Age coins were not really used for trade, but I find it difficult to believe there was no commercial use of coins that were minted with symbols that confirmed their authenticity and were manufactured to a remarkably consistent weight of silver. Although some very large hoards of Icenian coins, including those from Freckenham[15] and Lakenheath, represent the wealth of individuals, considerable numbers have now been found in scattered locations that defy the possibility that all come from hoards of bullion used in gift exchange. It is now realised that Icenian silver coins were issued in huge numbers. We should not underestimate the sophistication of these people. However, it is notable that while at Colchester Cunobelinus was producing large numbers of bronze coins that must have represented the small change of true commerce, the Icenian rulers issued nothing other than gold and silver coins, presumably suited only to relatively high value transactions. Some ninety different types of Icenian coins are now known, and some have gold and silver examples struck from the same die. This and the use of fractional units confirms that they were used for trade.

12 Cicero *ad Atticum* IV 16.7
13 Strabo, *Geography* 4.5.2-3
14 Emperor until his death in AD 14.
15 More than 90 gold Icenian coins found in 1886 : Allen, D.F., "The Coins of the Iceni" *Britannia* vol.1 (1970) p.7.

Most of the Icenian gold coins show the familiar Gallic and British design with a horse on the reverse. One type, known as the British J stater, or "Norfolk wolf", is distinctive because it shows a wolf-like animal with fearsome jaws, so we are left to wonder why the Iceni chose this wolf. Centuries later we find kings of East Anglia favouring the "wolf and twins" design on their coins and deriving their family name of Wuffings from the wolf. Was this partly due to some enduring affinity with the wolf? However, given the strong Roman connection of this image with the legend of Romulus and Remus it might also have been part of a claim that the kings were descended from the Roman emperors. Another kind of sophistication is revealed by the presence of forged coins of bronze plated with a thin covering of gold or silver. These were hardly appropriate in the context of gift exchange, but forged coins remain a feature of commercial transactions.

Late in the first century BC rulers put their names on coins, showing their command of Latin letters. Tasciovanus issued many coins inscribed Ver or Verlamio showing his power over Verulamium (St Albans), centre of the Catuvellauni. This places them in Hertfordshire, but their territory probably reached the Wash. He inscribed a few Camu for Camulodunum, presumably

Some of the 825 Iron Age gold coins, mostly Icenian, found buried in a pot at Dallinghoo near Wickham Market in 2008. This must have been a very substantial amount of money. These coins from the heart of the Wicklaw territory, with the torcs from its southern boundary at Ipswich, suggest it had rich Icenian rulers in the early part of the first century AD.
© Suffolk County Council
Archaeological Service

because he had taken control of Colchester, despite Caesar's declaration protecting the Trinovantes of Essex from interference. However, the distinctive nature of the evidence from Colchester, including the later burials at Stanway, suggest that it might always have been a Catuvellaunian centre, even if it was in the land of the Trinovantes. Perhaps both Colchester and St Albans were always Catuvellaunian centres.

In the early years AD we find Cunobelinus inscribing coins Tascio F, as the son of Tasciovanus (Tasciovani filius), so presumably he was a Catuvellaunian. He too inscribed some Camuloduno, indicating his capital was at Colchester (abbreviated to Camu on many issues, with Cuno as the short form of his own name). By showing a head of barley on many of his coins he was presumably emphasising a key source of his wealth. In fact Cunobelin seems to have dominated most of south-eastern Britain until his death some time between AD40 and 43, shortly before the Claudian invasion.

Extensive issues of coins in northern East Anglia show common features that imply all were Icenian, but several different designs were used. Some carry the tribal name in the form "Ecen" or "Ece" and some apparently followed the Roman practice of putting the name of the ruler on coins. There

These ditches at Thetford are part of a massive Iron Age fort that dominated the point where the Icknield Way crossed the rivers Little Ouse and Thet. Still impressive today, the ditch was originally much deeper and the bank much higher.

The great gold torc from Snettisham. The most magnificent from a remarkable collection of torcs deliberately buried in pits, it provides some indication of the considerable wealth of the Iceni.
© Trustees of the British Museum

16 Chadburn, A., "Tasking the Iron Age" in Davies, J. & Williamson, T., *Land of the Iceni*, Norwich, 1999, p.166.
17 Davies, J., "Patterns, Power and Political Progress" in Davies, J. & Williamson, T., *Land of the Iceni,* Norwich, 1999, p.40.
18 Williams, J., "New light on Latin in pre-Conquest Britain", *Britannia* vol. 38 (2007), p.1.

were mints at Needham on the Norfolk bank of the Waveney, at Saham Toney in Norfolk, at Thetford beside the Little Ouse on the border between Norfolk and Suffolk, and at West Stow[16]. Another mint further south at Haverhill was probably outside Icenian territory. On the basis of the coins and other archaeological evidence John Davies[17] suggests that even Norfolk itself was not a single political entity in the Iron Age but rather was an area of social and political diversity. Perhaps the Iceni were a confederation of states which retained some individuality. While many of their coins use abstract or stylised designs the so-called "Bury" type shows a life-like clean shaven head with a band round the hair and the "Norfolk god" type has been interpreted as the horned head of the god Cernunnus. Some later Icenian silver coins have a Roman imperial style bust and the inscription "Prasto". This has been interpreted as an abbreviation of the British version of the king called by the Romans Prasutagus. Recent finds suggest the full inscription on the two sides of the coin is a sophisticated use of Latin giving "sub Esuprasto, Esico fecit", meaning "under Esuprastus, Esico made it".[18] British rulers were using Latin for their own purposes. We do not understand how this came about, but presumably it was already seen as the language of authority.

Strabo notes British exports of gold and silver, in which trade the Iceni might also have been involved, even though they had no natural deposits of these in their own territory. An enigmatic clue is offered by the group of five lead ingots "stamped ICENES or similar" out of 271 ingots (22 tonnes) from a shipwreck from Sept Iles off the coast of Armorica, France, dated as Gallo-

Roman from the presence of tegulae roof tiles made from Armorican clay. Other ingots being stamped Brigantes suggest a cargo from varied sources.[19] Were the Iceni actually processing lead, perhaps to extract the more valuable silver, or were these, as David Mattingly[20] suggests, really marked as destined for the Iceni? Were the Iceni making an income from metalworking? The greatest surviving sign of their wealth is the collection of gold torcs and other valuables found at Snettisham in north-west Norfolk. This is the very area where we shall see (in chapter three) evidence of extensive iron working in the Roman period.

If the Iceni had mastered the new skills of working iron in the early part of the Iron Age ahead of their neighbours and kept the lead in exploiting this technology they would have earned their title "Great Iceni". They could have used their achievement to exchange iron for gold and silver, which were not present naturally in East Anglia. Using an electron microprobe Megan Dennis has studied the mix of silver, copper and other metals in Icenian "silver" coins. She concludes that as early as the middle of the first century BC, the time of Caesar's visits, the Iceni were melting down continental and Roman coins to provide metal for their new issues.[21] She finds that for their later issues they were adding more copper to make the silver go further, an example of sophisticated economic planning.

The artistic standard of the designs on their tiny silver coins is very high. Some were based on Gaulish or Roman coins but others followed a native British abstract style. All had to be finely engraved on a very small space, smaller than a modern 5p piece. Confirmation of their skill in working different metals to produce fine ornament can be seen in the collection of decorated bronzes found at Ringstead, which is close to Snettisham. They include a pair of bridle bits with the same designs found on some of the gold torcs.[22]

Presumably the torcs found at Snettisham represented the reserve wealth of Icenian leaders. They were carefully buried in groups in a series of pits within an enclosure which is likely to have been under some religious protection. We might compare the ancient Greek practice of using temples as banks where wealth could be deposited under protection of the gods, but could be recovered on payment of a fee to the gods through their priestly agents. Possibly the location of these Icenian deposits was only known to a limited group who were killed in the rebellions or remained bound by religious oaths to conceal the knowledge. Similar circumstances presumably explain the select group of six solid gold torcs buried at a sacred spring, later sanctified by the Christian Church as a holy well, on the edge of Stoke by Ipswich.

The distribution of Iron Age coins in the Waveney valley is presumably the result of trade between neighbours. The vast majority of Iron Age silver coins found in the valley were minted by the Iceni, but a significant number of Trinovantian gold coins have been found there as well. Coin moulds for the production of Icenian coins found at Needham, which was presumably the site of a mint,[23] suggest the Waveney was within Icenian territory, but high-value Trinovantian coins were also in circulation. If so, the eight Roman silver coins found at Needham might have been the pay of a Roman soldier stationed in the southern part of Icenian territory in the last years of its independence. They include three Republican coins issued before 62BC and

Two of the Dallinghoo gold coins. Many Icenian coins include this crescent design and most show the horse, of which this is a particularly fine example.
© Suffolk County Council Archaeological Service

19 Chadburn, A., "Tasking the Iron Age" in *Land of the Iceni*, Davies & Williamson, UEA, 1999, p.165.
20 Mattingly, D., *An Imperial Possession, Britain in the Roman Empire*, Allen Lane, 2006, p.508.
21 Dennis, M., "Silver of the Iceni", *Current Archaeology* 217 (April 2008).
22 Clarke, R.R., "A Hoard of Metalwork … from Ringstead", *Proceedings of the Prehistoric Society*, 1951, p.214; Robinson, B. & Gregory, T., *Celtic Fire and Roman Rule*, Poppyland, 1987, p.15.
23 Chadburn, A., "Tasking the Iron Age" in *Land of the Iceni*, Davies, J. & Williamson, T., UEA, 1999, p. 168.

24 *Diss Mercury*, 15 January 1993.
25 B.L. Harleian MS 52 A.49.
26 Martin, E., "Suffolk in the Iron Age", in *Land of the Iceni*, Davies, J. & Williamson, T., UEA, 1999, p.90.

five from Julius Caesar, Augustus, Tiberius and Nero, the latest being minted in AD60 just before the Boudican revolt, which could have prompted the soldier to conceal his savings.[24]

One piece of evidence from the reign of Henry III may be a clue to the boundary between the Iceni and the Trinovantes/Catuvellauni. A thirteenth-century document[25] refers to a Grim's Ditch in Thornham Parva 'in campo qui vocatur Grimisdich' ("in the field which is called Grimsditch") and this field name of 'Grimsditch' still appeared on nineteenth-century maps to the south of Howe Lane. This highway comes from the direction of Mellis and might follow the line of a sunken lane south of Thornham Parva churchyard and continue east across the A140 towards the swampy margins of the River Dove at Eye.

In Anglo-Saxon times earthworks of unknown origin were often attributed to Grim (an alternative name for the god Woden), just as later people called such things "the Devil's work". This may record the line of an ancient ditch marked out by Cunobelinus to define his enlarged kingdom after taking over the Trinovantes. This would define his boundary with the Iceni in the same way that an article in *Current Archaeology* 163 suggests Aves Ditch and Grim's Ditches in Oxfordshire marked his western boundary. In his discussion of the evidence regarding the boundary between the Trinovantes and the Iceni, Edward Martin suggests the Black Ditches at Cavenham might mark part of an Iron Age boundary.[26] We might note that one of the defensive ditches at Colchester itself is called Gryme's Dyke, and this has been dated by Philip Crummy as having been constructed in the Roman period, probably

This lane beside Thornham Parva church probably preserves the line of Grim's Ditch, which was being cited as a boundary in the Middle Ages. Without excavation it is impossible to say whether it was once a deep ditch in front of a high bank, as we might expect.

soon after the Boudican revolt.[27] Unfortunately we do not as yet have any evidence for the date of construction of the Thornham Grim's Ditch. It may be relevant that about three miles further up the A140 a location, now marked by a petrol station at the junction with the road to Diss, is called "The Devil's Handbasin", suggesting that here as well an unexplained feature in the landscape was being attributed to the devil.

This was a busy landscape long before the Roman army entered it. The Britons living in eastern Britain included accomplished farmers and skilled craftsmen. They had wealthy rulers who appreciated ornate jewellery and imported wines. They traded with the Roman Empire, which then reached the northern coast of France, known to the Romans as Gaul, and the mouth of the River Rhine. Some Britons had probably even seen the pomp and splendour of imperial Rome itself. The brightest of them probably knew as well as Claudius himself that Virgil, the great epic poet of the early empire, in the opening book of the *Aeneid* had Jupiter, Father of the Gods and Men, declare before Rome itself was founded that he placed no limits of territory or time on the empire of the Romans. The power of their future emperor would extend to the outer Ocean and his fame would reach the stars. This was the mission statement for a Roman Empire that claimed the right to rule all the known world and to impose its authority everywhere by military force. As an island set in the Ocean that was believed to encircle the world Britain could be seen as the most westerly component of this ambitious vision.

Current evidence suggests that most, if not all, of East Anglia was a managed agricultural landscape long before the Roman invasion. It has been argued that the higher areas of boulder clay between the river systems are lands least likely to have been farmed at that time and that they might have been left as natural woodland. However, extensive field walking and metal detecting in north-east Suffolk have revealed significant activity on the high ground above the Waveney and Dove valleys extending into the high plateau between the Waveney and Gipping/Orwell systems. If these areas were being farmed there is no reason to exclude any land in the region as unsuitable. Only systematic field surveys of other areas can confirm the extent and nature of agricultural activity. From ancient times down to the present day local variations in the types of soil have caused farmers to make different choices. Climate changes and market forces have also affected their decisions over time. When Strabo[28] wrote about the geography of Britain before the Roman conquest he listed grain among the major exports to the empire. It is reasonable to think that East Anglia was one of the areas producing much grain at the time. It probably also contributed to the cattle, hides and hunting dogs that Strabo lists among the exports. The evidence from field walking suggests a scatter of small sites occupied during the Iron Age that were presumably farmsteads. Where excavation has been possible, as at West Stow and Foxhall, it has revealed a group of substantial roundhouses within a ditch that presumably separated the farmyard from the fields. There is some evidence for the land being divided into fields defined by ditches; these probably accompanied hedges, as in more recent times, but it is only the ditches that can be identified by archaeology. Such a field system was found buried under the Saxon cemetery at Sutton Hoo.[29]

Where Roman roads appear to have been cut across existing field boundaries we can see evidence of systematic planning in divisions of the

Two sides of a gold coin of Cunobelinus (CVN) issued at Colchester (CAMV for Camulodunum). It shows an ear of corn, perhaps to emphasise the source of his wealth, and a horse, which often appears in similar style on Iron Age coins.
© Colchester and Ipswich Museum Service.

27 Crummy, P., *City of Victory*, Colchester, 1997, p.90.
28 Strabo, *Geography* 4.5.2.
29 Carver, M., *Sutton Hoo*, Society of Antiquaries Research Report 69, 2005, p.451.

The ard was a very simple form of plough. The share that cut into the ground was a separate piece of wood, sometimes with an iron tip, so that it could be replaced when worn down by use. The ploughman controlled the handle to the left and the draught animals, probably oxen, were harnessed to the yoke on the right.

land, some of which survived to be recorded on the maps of the Ordnance Survey. At least some of our landscape has been farmed for many generations within field boundaries created before the Roman conquest and lasting into the early twentieth century. This intensive use of land, whether for arable fields producing grain or for grazing land for cattle and sheep, implies that the limited areas of woodland must have been managed to produce both the timber for buildings and the underwood for fuel.

If land between the river valleys was being ploughed to grow grain it would require some method of draining to prevent waterlogging, which remains a problem on this land today. Where this clay land is flat it holds the water and was probably better used to grow grass for cattle or for managed woodland. This was certainly true in more recent times; sloping land could be ploughed as long as there was some drainage.[30] In addition to the open ditches carrying water into the river systems it is possible that bush drains were in use, as Fussell suggests there might be a reference as early as the writings of Cato the Censor in the second century BC to the Roman use of "hollow drains".[31] It seems that standard Roman practice was to grow cereal crops in fairly small fields that were ploughed several times with oxen yoked to a plough. Pliny the Elder[32] describes the ploughman working first in straight furrows, then slanting ones, to produce ground on which it is impossible to tell which way the share went without the need for harrowing. We cannot be sure if this was done in Britain nor whether the plough was a simple ard type that just scratched the surface or a more elaborate wheeled plough with coulter and mouldboard capable of turning the earth as it cut the furrow. Peter Reynolds has pointed out that even an ard can cope with heavy clay land if the wooden spike is protected by an iron sheath,[33] so Iron Age and Romano-British farmers could have worked any land without needing the heavy wheeled plough. He suggests that given a suitably matched and trained pair of cattle to pull the plough a field of about 0.13 hectares (about a quarter of an acre) could be worked in a day. Like all productive work in the ancient world it was labour intensive. Interestingly Reynolds points out from observation in Spain that the tool carried by the ploughman in some illustrations and generally interpreted as a goad was in fact a stick to free the earth from the point of the ard at each headland.[34] Pliny in the passage above recommends that the share should be cleaned from time to time with a stick tipped with a scraper. Those who have walked across our clay fields will recognise the same problem that requires scraping clay from one's boots to avoid them becoming impossibly

30 Martin, E., "Regionality in East Anglian field Systems" in *Wheare most Inclosures be*, East Anglian Archaeology 124, 2008, p.198.
31 Fussell, G.E., *The Classical Tradition in West European Farming*, David and Charles, 1972, p.22.
32 Pliny, *Natural History* xviii, 177-9.
33 Reynolds, P., *Iron Age Farm*, British Museum, 1979, p.51.
34 Reynolds, P., *Iron Age Farm*, British Museum, 1979, p.17.

heavy. No doubt such a simple scraping tool was an essential part of the ancient ploughman's equipment.

Presumably the farmers of both the Iron Age and Roman periods in East Anglia were producing significant quantities of grain. In addition to two substantial round houses six metres and ten metres in diameter, Stanley West draws attention to groups of post holes in the Iron Age farm at West Stow that might represent four-post rectangular structures.[35] They range from 1.6m to nearly 4m square and he suggests these might have been raised granaries comparable to those found by Stanley Stanford, excavating on the Welsh borders. Stanford found rows of these structures within the hillfort at Croft Ambrey and notes others at the Breidden, Moel Y Gaer and the Wrekin, and as a few appeared to contain hearths he suggests some might have been dwellings but interprets others as granaries or stores.[36] We cannot be certain, but these structures at West Stow might have held quantities of grain produced from the surrounding fields.

Edward Martin has examined the evidence for thirteen likely Iron Age roundhouses in Suffolk.[37] They vary in date and in structural details. Most have curving ditches, some of which appear to have held timber walls, while others are seen as gullies to collect rainwater from the thatched roofs of roundhouses supported by large internal posts. We know little about the inside of these houses, although in some cases internal hearths have been identified. Diameters seem to range between five and thirteen metres, although we do not always have a complete ground plan.

At Foxhall a large roundhouse stood inside a substantial ditched enclosure which also contained one or two possible four-post granaries.[38] Two smaller roundhouses were found within an Iron Age field system adjoining the enclosure. Although this farm was not in use during the Roman period the land was still being farmed, as the ditches of a Roman field system were identified nearby and there were new buildings there in Saxon times.

35 West, S.E., *West Stow, the Prehistoric and Romano-British Occupations*, EAA 48, 1990, p.109.
36 Stanford, S.C., *The Archaeology of the Welsh Marches*, ed. 2, Ludlow, 1991, p.60; cf. Cunliffe, B., *Iron Age Communities in Britain*, ed.3, London, 1991, p.376.
37 Martin, E., "Suffolk in the Iron Age" in *Land of the Iceni* ed. Davies, J. & Williamson, T., Norwich, 1999, p.63.
38 John Newman in "Archaeology in Suffolk", PSIAH vol. 37 (1992), p.386.

Peter Froste's painting shows what the legionary fortress at Colchester probably looked like soon after the Roman invasion. It housed the 5,000 men of the Twentieth Legion for a period after the conquest.
© Colchester Archaeological Trust

An artist's interpretation by Herring Bone Design of the round house that stood on an island in the River Alde at Barber's Point near Aldeburgh. This house was lived in during the Roman period when the island seems to have been involved in the salt making industry on the tidal river. The combination of a traditional roundhouse and rectangular structures is common on Roman sites in East Anglia.
© Aldeburgh and District Local History Society

Thus long before it came under Roman government most of the East Anglian landscape was already managed as productive farm land. There were planned arrangements of fields reached by a complex of trackways, some of which survive today as roads and footpaths. Some of these tracks appear to extend over long distances, with one leading from the Ipswich area to the crossing between the head of the Rivers Waveney and Little Ouse, while others may simply have served to link local fields to facilitate the movement of grazing livestock. Waterways also played an important role in the settlement pattern and presumably had a significant part in the communication system over both long and short distances. Boats of various sizes could carry goods up and down rivers, round the coast and across to the continent.

Ninety-seven years after Caesar's last visit and seventeen years before Boudica launched her rebellion the full force of Roman military might was employed to impose imperial authority on south-eastern Britain. Claudius, emperor of Rome, and adoptive great-grandson of Julius Caesar, entered Colchester in AD43 at the head of a Roman army of about 20,000 legionary soldiers, accompanied by elephants and auxiliary cavalry troops, a total of some 40,000 men if all the invasion force was present. He had defeated Caratacus the son of Cunobelin who, with his brother Togodumnus, had ruled much of southern Britain.

Colchester was turned into a Roman fortress for the Twentieth Legion (legio XX) and a Thracian cavalry unit. The legion was a unit of 5,000 men, and the Twentieth was one of the four legions that were the core of the

In Colchester the "Hole in the Wall" public house stands on the remains of the Roman entrance known today as the Balkerne Gate. The stretch of town wall on the right with its distinctive tile courses leads up to the projecting guardhouse of the Roman gate.

invasion force and became part of the permanent garrison in Britain. It was based previously on the Rhine at Cologne. Each legion was made up of Roman citizens who were professional soldiers and was commanded by a legionary legate who had held the office of praetor at Rome, so was experienced in both military and political matters. Legionary soldiers were not only fighting men, they had among them considerable skills as builders, engineers and craftsmen so they could build their own camps and fortresses, assemble ships, make weapons and vehicles and build roads.

The Thracian unit was part of the auxiliary forces whose personnel were not Roman citizens but qualified for citizenship if they completed their period of service. As the legions were essentially infantry forces with only a small number of mounted troops the auxiliaries provided cavalry and other specialist skills. In the invasion force and the later garrison organisation there were probably about equal numbers of legionary and auxiliary soldiers, making a total of about 40,000 troops. There were also an unknown number of ships with military crews supporting the land forces. The Romans classified the men serving in their fleets as soldiers, but we have little information about the composition of crews and number of ships involved.

After taking Colchester Claudius received the surrender of eleven British kings,[39] but unfortunately neither they nor their kingdoms are named in our sources. Presumably they included the Iceni, who enter the record in AD47 as a client kingdom bound by treaty to accept some Roman authority. Whatever the situation before the Roman conquest, it is likely that as the new Roman province of Britannia was given its formal structure southern Suffolk

39 recorded on an arch at Rome, ILS 216.

The inside view of the remains of Colchester's Balkerne Gate, presumably spanning the original main road to London. The arch on the left is the entrance to the guardhouse and that on the right is the surviving pedestrian entry. The two carriageways, blocked later in the Roman period, are under the "Hole in the Wall" to the right.

A gold aureus of the emperor Tiberius found in north Suffolk. It might have been brought by a soldier after the Roman conquest or the result of local contacts with Rome before the conquest.
© Suffolk County Council Archaeological Service

was initially included, along with Essex, in the land of the Trinovantes. The northern part of the county, along with Norfolk, was probably within the client kingdom of the Iceni. It is possible that after sending their embassy to Julius Caesar the Iceni, assuming they were the "Cenimagni", had kept up contact with Rome, perhaps avoiding the area under the domination of Cunobelinus by using the direct sea route to the continent. In any case they were accorded special recognition by the conquering emperor who made them a client kingdom. This meant that as allies bound by treaty to Rome they enjoyed greater independence than the Trinovantes who were incorporated in the new province.

The new province of Britannia was placed under a senior Roman citizen of the senatorial class who had already held the high office of consul. There were only two consuls each year, and in the old days of the Republic they were the ruling magistrates. This recognised Britannia as one of the most important provinces whose governor commanded an army initially of four legions, later reduced to three. Governors were senior politicians but also experienced military commanders, and the first governor was Aulus Plautius who had commanded the invasion force. At the end of his term of office in AD47 some Britons from the unconquered part of Britain broke into the province before the new governor, Publius Ostorius Scapula, took over.

Ostorius moved rapidly to defeat the invaders, and then planned to make his province more secure by disarming all those within it. This was normal practice within the empire, where only members of the army were permitted to carry weapons, except for hunting. Law and order was maintained by the army under the authority of the emperor, not by private individuals. However, Ostorius included the Iceni under this order. As a powerful and unconquered client kingdom, they took exception to this. They gathered support from some of their neighbours and challenged the Romans from a base enclosed by a rustic mound with an entrance too narrow to be attacked by cavalry.[40] A number of sites have been suggested: one possibility is in the Fens at Stonea Camp, near March, where the wet conditions would have prevented a cavalry attack. Ostorius deployed auxiliary infantry and dismounted cavalry to storm the rampart at a number of points. There was a fierce fight in which the Iceni were defeated. For the moment Ostorius had secured this part of his province without having to fight a pitched battle.

Remarkably the Iceni retained their status as a client kingdom. Perhaps those in the east of their large territory had chosen to stay away from Stonea and it might have been a smaller kingdom that was ruled over by king Prasutagus for the next thirteen years. As a client of the Roman emperor he could govern his territory and no doubt maintain his own wealth as long as he was seen to be loyal to Rome. Tacitus says he was celebrated for his long and prosperous reign.

If there was a division between eastern and western Iceni the dividing line might be marked by Peddars Way. This road, running in a straight line along the watershed and constructed to the monumental width of about 36ft, double the width of many major roads, looks like a frontier or demarcation line. As the Roman army took control of the province it constructed a number of major roads, but among these Peddars Way stands out as more than just a highway. It runs from Stanton outside Ixworth to Holme-next-the-Sea on the edge of the Wash. Presumably there was a ferry crossing from there to give

40 Tacitus, *Annals* xii, 31.

access to Lincoln; the terminal quay must have been destroyed by coastal erosion long ago.

Even when as a green lane it has acquired a deep layer of soil from many seasons of dead leaves and grass, modern vehicle ruts reveal solid metalling. Although some stretches have been lost, the line of the road is very clear and even for a Roman road it runs remarkably directly. There can be no doubt that it was an official creation imposed on the landscape, and it must have been seen as a massive symbol of Roman authority, as conspicuous as any building. It strikes a clearly perceptible line along the watershed between the rivers running west into the Wash and those that feed directly into the North Sea through the Great Estuary at Yarmouth.

It often lies a little west of the actual watershed, so crosses several streams heading for the Wash, but it would be difficult to find a straight line that more closely defined the division between the river systems. It seems superfluous as a communication route as much of its northern line runs parallel to and close beside the Icknield Way. The latter could simply have been "improved" to Roman highway standards, as seems to have been done along at least part of its route through East Anglia, whatever might be argued about its function as a prehistoric link to Salisbury Plain.

Some people have questioned whether there was a continuous track. However, the Icknield Way does seem to have existed even before the Iron Age as a link from the northern edge of East Anglia on the Wash to central England and possibly on to the vicinity of Stonehenge. Looking at Peddars Way I am reminded of the Fosse Way, which probably marked the first temporary frontier within Roman Britain, and the Stanegate that preceded

The restored Iron Age ditch of Stonea camp. This fortified island in the Fens is a good candidate for the site of the decisive battle in the first Icenian revolt against the Romans.

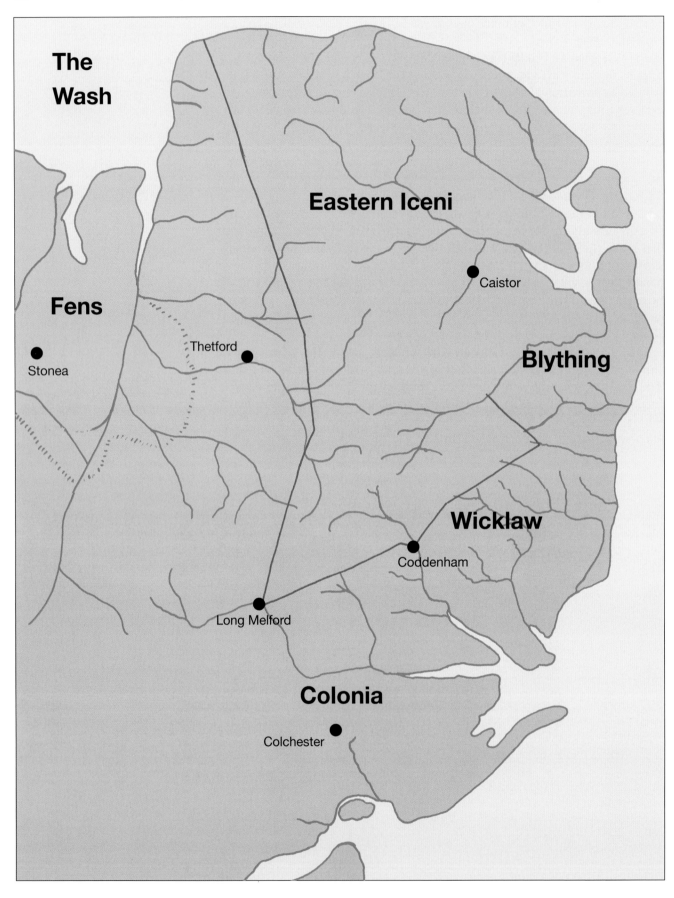

The Wash

Eastern Iceni

Fens

Caistor

Blything

Stonea

Thetford

Wicklaw

Coddenham

Long Melford

Colonia

Colchester

Hadrian's Wall. The deliberate line along the watershed and the very straight route suggest that Peddars Way was meant to create a boundary between two territories. One early Roman fort is known on this road at Saham Toney (sometimes called Threxton or Woodcock Hall) which could have provided a base for cavalry to patrol the boundary. The division would have separated the people of the Fens, and those looking towards them, from the inhabitants of lands drained by the Wensum and Waveney systems who look east towards the North Sea. It would not be surprising if the Roman authorities made this division after the first Icenian rebellion in AD47. It split the group centred on Caistor-by-Norwich (Venta Icenorum) from those looking towards the Wash, who perhaps had an administrative centre at Thetford or in the Fens at Stonea.

We have already noted Stonea as the likely location of the decisive battle in the rebellion, and we shall find it became an administrative centre under Roman rule. At Thetford, a key location where the Icknield Way crossed the River Little Ouse, Tony Gregory found a remarkable enclosure on top of Gallows Hill (Fison Way industrial estate).[41] On this dominant site, apparently some time between AD43 and 60, an acre of land enclosed by deep ditches was itself enclosed by an outer ditch creating an eleven-acre area that was filled with timber posts. We cannot tell the purpose of this artificial forest of posts. The inner enclosure contained three large round houses without much sign of occupation debris.

This elaborate arrangement suggests either a ceremonial royal residence or a massive temple. Perhaps it combined both functions, and the religious

Opposite: *Perhaps these particularly straight Roman roads marked the boundary of the territory defined as the civitas of the Iceni after the Boudican revolt. The eastern end of the boundary would be the River Waveney.*

41 Gregory, T., *Excavations in Thetford, 1980-1982 Fison Way*, East Anglian Archaeology 53, 1991.

This air photograph taken by Bob Carr identified the Iron Age rectangular enclosure on Fison Way, Thetford, that some regard as Boudica's palace. It was certainly proved to be an elaborate construction when excavated by Tony Gregory.
© Suffolk County Council Archaeological Service

one might be supported by the later building of a Roman temple about 50 yards away, where a great gold and silver treasure was found. It might be significant that a later group of wealthy villas on the edge of the Wash, west of Peddars Way, is different from the general pattern of known Roman housing in Norfolk. Did this western group prosper more than their eastern neighbours because they avoided involvement in Boudica's revolt? Did they benefit from the economic opportunities offered by access to waterborne trade through the Wash combined with iron working in an area with good natural supplies of ironstone?

Whatever the extent of the client kingdom of the faithful and prosperous king Prasutagus, the Iceni suffered from another intervention by arrogant Roman officials. The king died in AD60, leaving instructions in his will that his two daughters and the emperor were to be his co-heirs. It is notable that he did leave a will that was recognised, even if ignored, and was presumably written under Roman official guidance in Latin. It was not uncommon for wealthy Romans to make the emperor co-heir in an effort to ensure that their will was carried out and that their heirs retained some independence. In Petronius' novel *The Satyricon*, written in the time of Nero, the freedman Trimalchio became extremely wealthy because he inherited his master's estate as co-heir with the emperor. It turned out otherwise for the family of Prasutagus, because the Roman historian Tacitus tells us that the kingdom was plundered by Roman officers and the household by slaves as though they had been taken in a war.[42] The king's widow, Boudica, was flogged and her daughters raped, presumably because they resisted these depredations.

They were not the only victims, as the leading Iceni were deprived of their ancestral properties and the royal family were treated as slaves. At this time the governor, Gaius Suetonius Paulinus, was leading the army on a campaign in Wales and responsibility for these events lay with the second most powerful official in the province, the procurator Catus Decianus. He was responsible for the financial affairs of the province and presumably saw an opportunity to increase the funds in his treasury.

He might also have been influenced by a matter reported by Dio, who says that the procurator, presumably acting on orders from the new emperor Nero, was demanding that British leaders repay money lent to them by Claudius.[43] At the same time Seneca, one of Nero's closest advisers, was also demanding repayment of large loans he had made to Britons. Some have suggested the Britons did not understand these were loans rather than gifts, but this probably underestimates the sophistication of British leaders. More likely they were simply infuriated and perhaps embarrassed by demands for premature repayment of long-term "development" loans on which they were said to be paying high rates of interest.

We are left wondering what these loans were used for. Did they fund improvements in agriculture, new roads or ships? Did they fund new houses for the leaders, or an extravagant lifestyle? Were Nero and Seneca unhappy about how the money was being used, or was the demand for repayment caused by the financial crisis at Rome attributed by Suetonius to Nero's chronic extravagance?[44] Our sources do not tell us.

Whatever the causes of discontent among the Iceni, Boudica led her people in a rising against the Romans. No doubt they were infuriated by the arrogance of the imperial officials. They were joined by the Trinovantes.

42 Tacitus, *Annals* xiv 31.
43 Dio, *Roman History* lxii.
44 Suetonius, *Nero* 32.

Tacitus tells us the Trinovantes were particularly discontented because of the behaviour of the retired soldiers who had been settled in a new Roman town at Colchester. This new "colonia" replaced the military fortress when the troops were moved to newly conquered parts of the province. These retired soldiers were not just given houses in the new town but also land to provide them with an income. They were seen as driving the Britons from their homes and treating them as slaves, presumably because they kept the original occupiers working the land while the new owners took the profits and lived well on the proceeds.

The Trinovantes were also infuriated by demands that they fund the great temple to the dead Claudius who was treated as a god after his death. Its foundations survive under the keep of Colchester Castle to reveal the massive size of this alien structure. They saw it as a symbol of Roman authority imposed on them and an excuse to take money from them to fund the religious

A model of the great Temple of Claudius at Colchester, where the Roman colonists made their last stand against Boudica's army. The foundations of this temple can still be seen below Colchester Castle keep. Religious ceremonies centred on the altar in front of the temple.
© Colchester and Ipswich Museum Service

Iron Age enamelled fittings for chariot harness found at Westhall provide further evidence of ostentatious display, perhaps designed to impress the enemy faced by fast moving and brightly coloured vehicles of war.
© Trustees of the British Museum

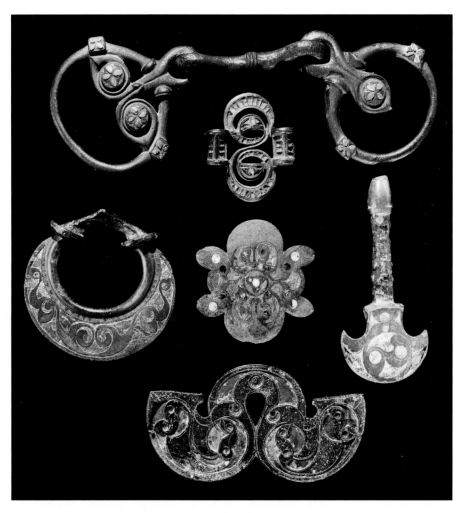

ceremonies. This probably affected many in south Suffolk as they would be close enough to Colchester to fall within its "territorium".

It seems that most, if not all, of East Anglia supported Boudica and her followers when they completely destroyed Colchester. Archaeological evidence points to massive devastation of the new town, which had been left without defences when the colonists demolished the ramparts of the fortress to expand their settlement. Tacitus records that the residents made a desperate but doomed last stand in the temple. The rebels defeated a detachment of the ninth legion, whose commander escaped with his cavalry. He had probably come in haste from the military base at Longthorpe, outside Peterborough. They went on to devastate London and St Albans, two significant Romanised towns. Tacitus claimed that 70,000 Roman citizens and their allies were killed.

Boudica had a huge army and might have put an end to the new province. Perhaps she had heard the story that Nero had thought of withdrawing the army from Britain, and only retained the province because it had been conquered by his adoptive father Claudius.[45] However, the main Roman army now returned as fast as it could march from Wales. She could not defeat almost 10,000 highly trained Roman soldiers in a pitched battle at a site in the midlands chosen by Suetonius to suit his tactics. He had the whole of the fourteenth legion, part of the twentieth and a number of auxiliary units,

45 Suetonius, *Nero* 18.

but it still seems to have been a hard fight against Boudica's large force. Dio claims the British numbered about 230,000 fighting men.

It was a hard-fought battle. One feature of the British attack was the presence of large numbers of chariots which seem to have been much used in East Anglia. Ornamental bronze fittings from chariots are a feature of local finds, including terret rings which were fixed as guides for the reins. A particularly fine one was found at Weybread in the Waveney valley. The chariots were light vehicles that could move warriors rapidly across the battlefield while providing an elevated fighting platform from which to wield a heavy spear, although they were vulnerable to Roman archers. Romans claimed 80,000 British dead against 400 Romans.

Many British were unable to get away after the defeat because their baggage wagons obstructed the escape routes. Whether this battle was fought at the site near Mancetter in Staffordshire suggested by Graham Webster or elsewhere on the route to the west, we are left wondering why Boudica was leading her army away from home in this way. It has been suggested that she was not deliberately looking to fight the Romans head on.

Perhaps this great army complete with its wagon train and all the families was a massive migration from East Anglia moving out of Roman territory to settle in a new location in the west, perhaps in Wales or in the north-west. We might recall that Caratacus, son of Cunobelin, fought in Wales after Colchester fell and tried to stir up the Brigantes to the north, so there had been contact with areas still free from Roman government.

There is also a suggestion the Iceni might have been involved in the precious metal trade, perhaps through their use of Welsh gold and a possible connection with silver works to the north. This explanation looks plausible. It would explain their failure to plant crops, which is documented, and their total destruction of eastern towns. They did not intend to return to the east and suffered the effects of famine when the Romans forced them back home after defeating them. The migration does make sense of that wagon train. Otherwise it is difficult to see why Boudica moved into "foreign" territory. She could have stayed in the east and waited to fight on her own territory against a Roman army exhausted by the long forced march from the west.

Instead the Romans faced the task of stopping a substantial population from deserting East Anglia and creating a new hostile community in unconquered territory. The people of East Anglia had come near to ending Roman rule and had destroyed the new Roman towns so completely that the evidence at Colchester and London still survives in the ground as an unusually recognisable layer of debris. This may not have quite ended the affair, as Tacitus records all too briefly that when Suetonius was removed from office a little later it was because he lost a few ships and their crews on the coast. Did the East Anglians have one last fling at destroying the Roman fleet?

Tacitus tells us that the reprisals by Suetonius and his troops were brutal. A gladiatorial practice helmet found at Hawkedon in Suffolk might be an item of loot or armour used in the revolt but discarded after the defeat.[46] As found in 1965, the helmet had been damaged by the plough and it was only in 2001 that the broken brow guard was recognised in a garden shed and reunited with the helmet in the British Museum. The guard is attached across the front of the helmet, creating a heavy protective ridge above the face. The bronze helmet had been tinned so that it would have shone like silver. Kenneth Painter

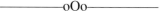

BOUDICA PREPARES

The Icenian queen mounted her chariot and was driven to the front of her great army. The gold torc shone at her neck, red hair tumbled to her waist, her tunic showed many bright colours. The enamel mounts shone red, yellow and blue on the chariot. Leather and wood were brightly polished. An attendant slipped a large hare into the ample folds of her dress. She thanked him and gripped the hare: "When I release him the goddess of victory will give us the sign of good luck to encourage our warriors. We shall drive the enemy from our lands for ever." As the hare ran before the army to the correct side, she raised her sword to catch the sun. Men cheered loudly. All the chariots moved forward towards the Roman line.

——————oOo——————

46 Painter, K.S. in PSIAH 31 (1967), p. 57, found at TL 793545; now in the British Museum.

Roman military harness decorations buried at Holbrook, seen here before they received conservation treatment. These ornate silvered bronze decorations, still attached to some surviving leatherwork, were found by a metal detector user in 2004.
© Suffolk County Council Archaeological Service

47 Tacitus, *Annals* iii, 43.
48 now in the British Museum.
49 Sealey, P., *The Boudican Revolt Against Rome*, Shire Archaeology 74, 1997.
50 *Ipswich Evening Star*, 11 December 2007.

pointed out that this is an unusually heavy helmet with a wide neckguard, stamped with a maker's mark suggesting it was made in Italy, so was suitable for use by gladiators. He noted that gladiators in training, who were slaves, had joined the revolt by the Treveri and Aedui in Gaul under Florus and Sacrovir in AD21, when Tacitus commented that their heavy metal armour made them impregnable against attack, but too clumsy to fight effectively.[47] Perhaps slaves from Suffolk were being trained for combat as gladiators at Colchester soon after the conquest and turned on their masters.

If the bronze head of Claudius found in 1907 by a boy fishing in the river Alde at Rendham[48] was looted from Colchester at this time it would not be surprising if the once proud looter quickly offered it to the river god before Roman soldiers searched his property. Paul Sealey[49] argues that a slight backward tilt of the head suggests the statue showed the emperor on horseback. He refers to a find at Ashill in Norfolk of the knee of a horse, hollow-cast like the head of Claudius, and made from the same rare alloy. This has a low lead level (he notes that lead was usually added to bronze to make it flow more easily) so perhaps came from the same statue. There is no certainty that the statue did stand in Colchester; it might have been set up at Combretovium, Baylham House in Coddenham parish, where air photographs reveal forts of two different periods beside the river at the junction of several Roman roads. Presumably this was the origin of the magnificent "Barking" statuette of Nero.

A set of Roman cavalry officer's horse harness might have been buried at Holbrook at this time. Thirty ornate silvered bronze decorations on some surviving leatherwork were found by a metal detector user in 2004 and are now in Ipswich Museum.[50] As local pottery and a clay loomweight were buried with them, they are likely to have been collected as trophies by a

The remains of a Roman helmet found at Hawkedon. The heavy helmet with a wide neckguard, a gladiator's practice helmet, was perhaps used or looted in the Boudican revolt and discarded after the defeat.
© Trustees of the British Museum

This head of the emperor Claudius found in the river at Rendham, near Saxmundham, came from a figure of the emperor on horseback that was larger than life size. It was probably looted during the Boudican rebellion and consigned to the god of the river when the rebels were defeated.
© Trustees of the British Museum

51 Cf. Sealey, P., *The Boudican Revolt Against Rome*, Shire Archaeology 74, 1997, p.45 ff.

Briton. It is generally accepted that some hoards of coins which include very late Icenian issues were probably buried in AD60, and at least one does include a coin of Nero. A large hoard from Lakenheath contained one Icenian gold coin of Antedios, two Catuvellaunian gold coins of Cunobelinus, 410 Icenian silver coins and 67 Roman silver denarii, the last of them being issued by Gaius Caligula in AD37. Other groups of metalwork are more difficult to date, but could also relate to this period. A bronze saucepan and a spouted bowl with strainer to remove solids from drink, together with a wooden pail were found under a bronze cauldron suitable for brewing beer at Brandon. Across the river at Hockwold at least seven Roman silver wine cups had been reduced to bullion ready for recycling. Groups of bronze chariot fittings from Westhall in north Suffolk and Saham Toney in Norfolk and a mixed collection of metal from Santon in Norfolk are all of similarly uncertain date.[51]

The long-term effects of the revolt are more difficult to judge. The

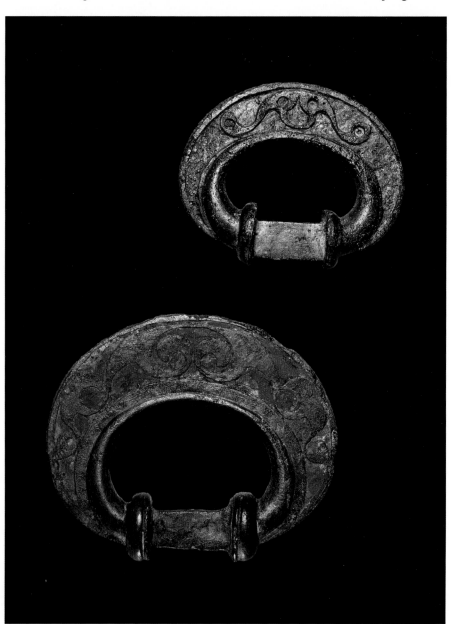

Enamelled Iron Age rings to guide chariot reins, found at Westhall. Chariots were certainly used in warfare in this region and we can see they offered an opportunity to display the skills of the metalworkers.
© Trustees of the British Museum

Romans did not withdraw but rebuilt Colchester as the only truly Roman town in our region. They surrounded it with a massive stone wall 2,800m long that was probably built soon after the revolt,[52] and they provided new earthwork defences, Gryme's Dyke, and a revised version of the Iron Age Sheepen Dyke. The Iceni preserved their identity because the small town from which they administered their territory was called Venta Icenorum, "the market place of the Iceni". But it appears to be by far the smallest and least Romanised of all the regional capitals and, although presumably they were fully incorporated in the province of Britannia under the direct authority of the governor and procurator, their territory does not appear particularly prosperous nor specially Romanised. This is particularly true of the eastern part, centred on Venta.

Those living in north-western Norfolk, the area now centred on King's Lynn and looking towards the Wash, seem to have been more prosperous, and many of the late Icenian coin hoards come from the area west of Peddars Way. John Talbot has made a detailed study of the individual coin types resulting in a strong case for a significant number of these hoards having been assembled by Icenians about the time of the Boudican revolt. It is very possible that they, having been the probable rebels of AD47, kept out of this revolt and flourished accordingly. Perhaps they had even been detached from the official civitas of the Iceni. Could they have been attributed to the Catuvellauni, or become a separate unit whose name eludes us? After all, it is generally accepted that the Romans divided up the former kingdom of the Atrebates in the south, and our knowledge of the tribal or civitas territories generally is far from complete. Perhaps at some date these western Iceni became part of a new civitas based on the large town of Durobrivae, Water Newton near

52 Crummy, P., *City of Victory*, Colchester, 1997, p.89.

Silver wine cups buried at Hockwold, perhaps loot intended for melting down. At least seven Roman cups had been squashed ready for recycling.
© Trustees of the British Museum

Burned debris from the destruction of Roman Colchester by Boudica's army, part of a burnt barrack block in Culver Street. The red block is distinctive evidence of Boudica's destruction of the first Roman town at Colchester. Similar debris is found in excavations at various places throughout the colonia.
© Colchester Archaeological Trust

Peterborough. We know that civitates were established as the local administrative units within the province of Britannia and some at least had a council drawn from the wealthiest families. They had only such powers as the Roman governor chose to delegate to them, and the Romans may not always have respected existing British tribal boundaries.

The Trinovantes do not appear in later records, although it can be argued that Chelmsford, given the prestigious name Caesaromagus, "Caesar's market", was intended to be the capital of their civitas. It shows no sign of appropriate development, and this scheme might have been scrapped after they joined the Boudican revolt. I believe a good case can be made for suggesting that the Romans were the more indignant that the Trinovantes whom they had, as they saw it, favoured as recipients of Roman culture had joined the rebellion. Archaeological evidence from Gosbecks and Stanway near Colchester suggests that this area immediately south of the colonia was reserved before the rebellion for some high status Trinovantes who prospered under the new regime.

The Iceni, on the other hand, were perhaps just seen as the "usual suspects". In reorganising the area after the rebellion the northern part of Trinovantian territory, including south Suffolk, was probably directly attached to the refounded colonia of Colchester to serve as its territorium. As an important colony Colchester would have needed a considerable area of land to support the retired soldiers living there. Tacitus tells us that they drove Trinovantes from their homes, seized their lands and treated them as slaves. The description by Tacitus suggests land was not allocated according to any proper centuriation system and there is no firm evidence for the location of these lands.[53]

The original territory of the colonia may have been mostly north of Colchester. Ian Richmond suggests the number of good villas in the Colne valley might indicate this was part of the territorium.[54] However, this valley alone was insufficient for a large colonia. The territory might have extended north of the River Deben as a hoard of first century AD silver denarii coins found at Sutton near Woodbridge would make most sense as the surviving balance of the lump sum savings of a retired legionary soldier, that is a 'colonist'.[55] They appear to have been buried a little before or very soon after the Boudican revolt.

We have very little evidence for the territories of colonies in Britain and Gaul, but Sherwin-White notes that all the lands of the Allobroges in Gaul between Lyons and Geneva were administered by the magistrates of the colonia of Vienne on the river Rhone.[56] As a result the Allobroges disappear from inscriptions and all dedications in their towns are made to the magistrates of the colonia. The boundary stones of the "territorium" have been found 60 kilometres from an active legionary fortress on the continent.[57]

The southern part of the former Trinovantian territory, modern south Essex, was probably given to the expanding town of London, which was being turned into the administrative centre for the province and would need land to be allocated to its residents. Presumably at that time the effective capital of the province was moved from Colchester to the new town of London sited on the tidal highway of the Thames.

If this was done then we can see the new Roman governor Petronius Turpilianus and the new procurator Julius Classicianus working to create a secure base for the province. They had seen that Roman authority could not be imposed on western and northern Britain if East Anglia was able to assert its independence. Tacitus notes that one consequence of the rebellion was a famine because the British had failed to sow their crops before setting out for battle. If the losses were anywhere near those reported there would have been a shortage of people to work the land when the fighting was over. If the Romans did rely on the rich farmlands of East Anglia to feed their army, then the first priority must have been to get the farms back to producing food, not only for the Britons but for the conquering Romans as well.

Presumably a new group of retired soldiers with the full rights of Roman citizens were installed at Colchester with a brief that included bringing the farms in the territorium back into full productivity. Meanwhile soldiers and administrators faced the task of incorporating into the province the territory of the Iceni, now ordinary provincial subjects with no special rights. It became one more civitas within Britannia.

We do not know where army units were stationed at that time. It is very likely that the headquarters of the ninth legion was at Lincoln with a detachment in the fortress at Longthorpe near Peterborough. The commander of this legion was probably responsible for enforcing Roman law in eastern Britain, so both legionary and auxiliary units were deployed in our region under his authority. One such unit was probably based at Pakenham near

A bronze mirror with a cover showing a fine head of Nero on one side and a general addressing troops on the other. It was found with a cremation burial in a pottery vessel at Coddenham. The owner probably died while serving as a soldier based in the Combretovium fort.
© Trustees of the British Museum

53 Tacitus, *Annals* 12.32 and 14.31.
54 *VCH Essex*, vol. 3, p.22.
55 personal comment Judith Plouviez.
56 Sherwin-White, A., *Roman Citizenship*, Oxford, 1973, p.369.
57 *EBURACUM, Roman York*, RCHME, 1962, p.xxxv refers to ILS 2454 and 2455 and Petrikovits *Das Romische Rheinland*, p.63-7.

Ixworth where an excavation by Judith Plouviez suggested that the fort, a parallelogram protected by three ditches, was used for only a short period and was part of the programme that followed the Boudican revolt.[58]

The other known military site in Suffolk is marked by two superimposed forts at Baylham Mill, Coddenham, which are visible on aerial photographs within the area of the town of Combretovium. These have not been excavated, but it is most likely that one was constructed soon after the initial conquest and the other after the Boudican revolt, although we cannot be sure of this. They would have controlled an important junction of roads and dominated the river crossing.

Perhaps the magnificent statuette of Nero with decorative inlay said to

A statuette of the emperor Nero found near Coddenham. Standing twenty-two inches high and inlaid with silver and black silver sulphide, it might have come from the shrine of the standards in the Roman fort at Combretovium.
© Trustees of the British Museum

have been found nearby at Barking in the eighteenth century was taken from the sacellum, the shrine of the standards, in the centre of the fort during the revolt.[59] This is a high quality figure 22in high inlaid with silver and niello (black silver sulphide). It shows the emperor in a Hellenistic pose typical of figures of Alexander the Great. This figure was one of the earliest objects from Roman Suffolk to be published, as it was engraved by James Basire on five plates in 1807, while it was in the possession of the Earl of Ashburnham at Barking Hall. These were bound together in the fourth volume of *Vetusta Monumenta* produced by the Society of Antiquaries in 1815. A cremation burial in a pottery urn found in 1823 outside the fort, forty or fifty yards west of the Roman "Pye Road",[60] might be the remains of one of the garrison. It was accompanied by a small bronze circular mirror decorated with a fine head of Nero on one side and a general addressing his troops on the other.[61]

These are the only known military structures in Suffolk, as a single stretch of ditch with a rounded corner at Stuston, near Diss, which was noticed on an aerial photograph as possible evidence of a marching camp[62] has since been shown by excavation to be part of a group of pre-Roman ditches.[63] In Norfolk some forts have been identified, although presumably a number remain undetected in both counties. Large triple ditches outside the later walls of Caistor-by-Norwich have been interpreted as two sides of a large early fort covered by the later Roman town, but so far no dating evidence has been obtained. Smaller forts are known at Threxton,[64] Ashill, Swanton

59 on land of the Earl of Ashburnham, who presented it to the British Museum in 1813.
60 *Gentleman's Magazine*, 1825 part 1, 291, 293.
61 Now in the British Museum (38.3-31). Fox, G.E., "Roman Suffolk" in *Archaeological Journal* vol. 57 (1900), p.140.
62 Edwards, D., in *Norfolk* EAA 5, 1977, p.236.
63 Ashwin & Tester, *Scole Report*, EAA forthcoming.
64 sometimes referred to as Saham Toney or Woodcock Hall.

The Roman fort excavated by Judith Plouviez at Pakenham on the edge of Ixworth. This outline plan shows the position of the fort in relation to the modern bypass south of Ixworth.
© Suffolk County Council Archaeological Service

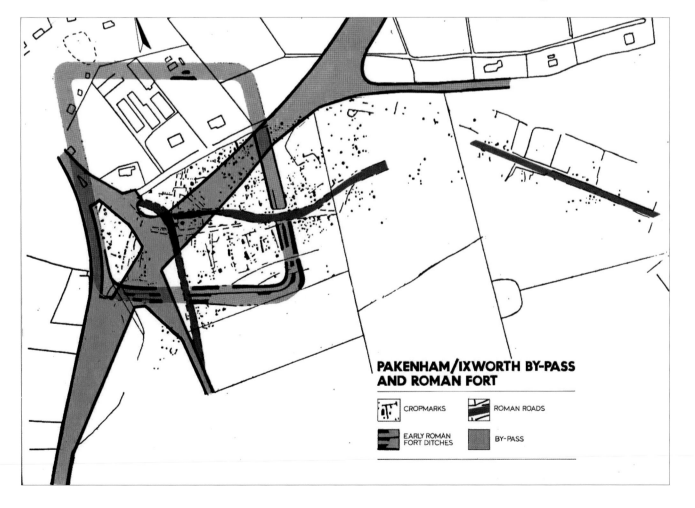

PAKENHAM/IXWORTH BY-PASS AND ROMAN FORT

CROPMARKS   ROMAN ROADS

EARLY ROMAN FORT DITCHES   BY-PASS

Tombstone of an auxiliary cavalryman, Longinus Sdapeze, found in Colchester. An officer of the First Squadron of Thracian Cavalry, he had served for fifteen years and was aged forty. The tombstone was found in 1928, but the head was recovered from the same place in 1996.
© Colchester and Ipswich Museum Service

Morley and Horstead. The forts, when occupied, would each have housed between 500 and 1,000 troops.

Judith Plouviez points to the presence at Pakenham, Long Melford and Burgh by Grundisburgh of early Roman pottery, "Lyon Ware", which seems to have been used by the military. This is supported by quantities of early South Gaulish Samian ware and of "Hod Hill" type brooches which indicate an early military presence. Items of military equipment have been reported as stray finds at a number of places in Suffolk, but these may only represent the presence of military patrols on policing duties in the area. One recent find from Long Melford is a long military sword, probably a *spatha* carried by a cavalryman. Uniformed Roman soldiers, whether members of the legionary or auxiliary forces, would have been a regular reminder of the authority of the imperial government.

The Roman army introduced to Britain surveyors and engineers who could plan and construct main roads that ran on straight alignments over very long distances. They used skills of measurement and calculation to lay out these roads and the military camps and forts required for the troops. No doubt they used these skills in other applications, so we should expect to find evidence of precise measurement and the use of right angles where the Britons seem to have preferred curves and circles, as seen in their round houses and curvilinear decorations.

The Roman army was also responsible for keeping the peace throughout the province and enforcing the rule of law, as only professional soldiers were allowed to carry weapons other than those used for hunting or personal protection. We should recall that it was the Roman order to surrender their weapons in accordance with this law that led to the first revolt by the Iceni. These policing duties meant that the army would always require that the roads were kept in good order, as would the administrators who used the Imperial Post when travelling on official duties.

As part of their campaign to convert the British to Roman ways in the first century AD the authorities introduced schools for the sons of the nobility.[65] We do not know of their impact on East Anglia, but Demetrius, a Greek schoolmaster from Tarsus, carried out a survey of islands around

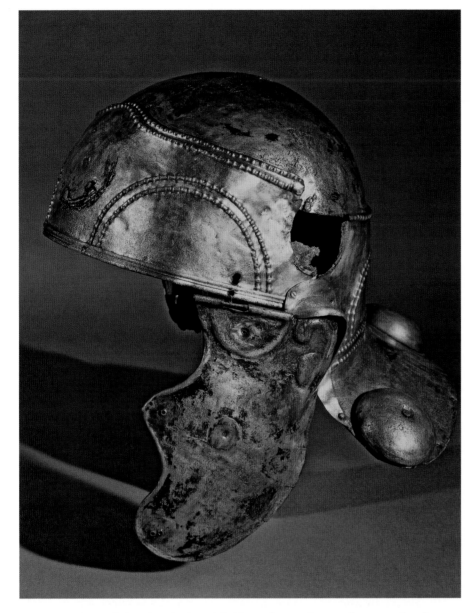

First century cavalry helmet found at Witcham near Ely. It was made from iron and bronze with a silvery coating of tin on the dome, neckguard and cheek pieces. It has lost some parts, including the holder for its crest.
© Trustees of the British Museum

Britain on imperial orders before AD83, perhaps after setting up schools.

The administrative language of the western Roman Empire was Latin, but the language of culture, literature and intelligent thought was Greek, and there can be little doubt that all who aspired to become educated needed to be fluent in both these classical languages. They would also use the local British language, which was presumably a variety or dialect of Celtic. Unfortunately we do not have any known Greek inscriptions on stone from Suffolk, but the corpus of *Roman Inscriptions in Britain* contains only one entry for the whole county (the Mars statue base from Martlesham) so this is not significant. A fair number of Greek monumental inscriptions are known from other parts of Britain.

However, a gold ring with a central uncut sapphire, found at Stonham Aspal, has an inscription in Greek "OLYMPEI ZESAIS", meaning "Life to Olympis!" which is presumably a token of love expressed in the language of love.[66] A silver ring said to come from somewhere near Brandon is also

65 Tacitus, *Agricola* 21.
66 Henig, M., *The Art of Roman Britain*, London, 1995, p.72: diameter of ring 2.5cm. It is in the Ashmolean Museum at Oxford.

67 *Britannia* vol. 9 (1978) 481, no.66.
68 Parsons, P., *City of the Sharp-nosed Fish*, London, 2007 p. 131.
69 Tacitus, *Histories* 1.70.2.
70 Tacitus, *Agricola* 29.2.

inscribed in Greek "SYNELTHE", "Marry me".[67] More esoteric is the Greek name on the backs of two of the silver plates in the Mildenhall Treasure, "eutheriou", which K.S. Painter suggests might mean they once belonged to Eutherios, a senior official under the emperor Julian in 360.

The Romans seem to have been surprisingly open to those from other cultures, including Africa, but still expected those who aspired to becoming civilised to speak Greek. The Romans had taken over from the Greeks the habit of referring to foreigners as barbaroi, which meant simply those who were so uncivilised that when speaking they made "bar, bar" noises instead of using the Greek language, the mark of the civilised person. When Christianity entered our region it was probably linguistically more Greek than Latin, with the Greek bible, use of the "chi-rho" symbol and such concepts as "ecclesia" for the community of Christian people. So far we cannot tell how many East Anglians welcomed this element of inclusion in a wider cultural environment or whether there was resentment against the imposition of the languages and lifestyle of the Roman Empire.

We should think of several distinct groups at this time. Roman soldiers maintained order and imposed Roman law on behalf of the emperor. These were men in uniform with official authority who had been born in distant lands. Administrators acting on behalf of the central government in Rome were also likely to be foreigners. Britons from local wealthy and powerful families might have sought classical education and adopted Roman clothing and lifestyles, even going on to obtain full Roman citizenship and taking an appropriate tripartite name which concealed their ethnic origin. They might join the council of the civitas.

The majority of the local British population who followed the customs of their ancestors as farmers, craftsmen, fishermen, etc. accepted or resisted the new Roman rulers as they saw fit. Many are likely to have become tenants or employees of the incomers. The retired soldiers in the new colony at Colchester must have had a specific impact as they were allotted land which they might farm themselves or lease back to British farmers, while they lived comfortably in Romanised Colchester, drawing rent from the farms. They had served over twenty years as professional soldiers, so they were not experienced farmers but were used to giving orders. They were probably glad to instruct the Britons to use their local knowledge to farm the land efficiently and pay over the profits.

A papyrus from Oxyrhynchos in Egypt reveals how a centurion could ask a district governor to protect one of his tenant farmers from being compelled to perform onerous services in his village.[68] A military officer expected the support of a government official in opposing local impositions. This was a very diverse population and there must have been uneasy relations at times between the native Britons and incoming Roman citizens. Some Britons chose to join the Roman army, as we find British auxiliary soldiers serving on the continent in AD69,[69] while Agricola deployed some during his campaign in Scotland against Calgacus in AD84.[70]

Roads and waterways

THE MAJOR ROADS that survive are the most enduring legacy of Roman rule in East Anglia and are a remarkable monument to imperial activity. The roads described here as Roman roads are main routes taking direct lines across the countryside in a way that suggests they were constructed by the army for military and administrative communications. Surveyors attached to the original Roman invasion force probably defined the primary routes to suit the advancing army.

Modifications were no doubt needed after the defeat of the Boudican Revolt and the establishment of the provincial capital at London. Once the area had been accepted as part of the province of Britannia it would be more difficult to ignore existing boundaries and established properties: thereafter we should expect to see only minor changes and necessary repairs.

Josephus describes the emperor Titus leading his army through hostile territory in Palestine with "road makers and camp constructors" immediately behind the advance guard and ahead of the legions marching six abreast.[1] For a single legion the column must have extended to over 800 ranks. Presumably this stage of roadmaking involved no more than clearing a route for the troops, and the work would be consolidated later as time allowed. The new roads clearly ignored existing property boundaries and land ownership in a way that was only possible for a conquering power with absolute authority conferred by the emperor.

These roads were laid out in remarkably straight alignments, generally keeping to high ground over long distances, although they sometimes changed from these alignments to cope with difficult hills or valleys. They must have been seen by the Britons as massive symbols of Roman authority cutting across their landscape. Most of them ignored existing tracks, which no doubt continued to serve local traffic, although some main roads do seem to have been created as improvements of existing tracks, particularly on parts of the Icknield Way. There are places where a straight road deviates to respect an ancient burial mound, but generally they cut across the existing pattern of the landscape in a ruthless way that was not seen again until the creation of the railways.

They were engineered to create a solid base with good drainage. The key feature in their design was to provide a suitable route and surface for the rapid movement of marching troops and mounted cavalry, engaged in truly military tasks or as part of the policing of the province, as well as facilitating efficient travel for officials. Where military supplies could not be transported by water they presumably had to be carried by pack animals or carts on the roads. Use by civilian travellers and traders would be incidental to official use, and they might well have been encouraged to use the existing tracks as far as possible. Some roads seem to have originated as borders or demarcation lines dividing different territories.

First class roads can be about 27ft. wide, and where it is possible to estimate the agger of Peddars Way it varies between 30 and 36ft. wide,

1 Josephus, *The Jewish War* 17, 267.

Opposite page: Eastern England in the Roman period, with probable Roman roads marked in red. While the coastline cannot be mapped precisely as so much of it has been lost to the sea, the changes in the Orwell and Yare estuaries and in the Wash are based on evidence discussed in the text. Elsewhere as much as two miles might have been removed by erosion.
● Roman towns
■ Roman coastal forts

2 Vitruvius, *On Architecture* 7.1.3.
3 for more details see Dilke, O.A.W., *Greek and Roman Maps*, London, 1985.

A section across the Roman road at Otley, excavated by Elizabeth Owles in 1967. The road, part of the road from Combretovium to Hacheston, was twenty-five feet wide with a surviving thickness of eight inches of rammed gravel in the centre. The ditches were four feet wide and two feet deep from the present ground level.
© Suffolk Institute of Archaeology and History

indicating that it was a major road indeed. Many lesser roads were built with a carriageway of 16ft. or 12ft. The raised mound or agger usually had a gravel surface on top of layers of larger stones or rammed chalk to provide a strong surface, and ditches on either side carried off the rainwater. A reference by Vitruvius describing four layers of material has been taken as a formula for laying roads, but in fact relates to the floors of buildings.[2] No ancient source describes the detailed structure of roads.

Sometimes a wider corridor was marked out by additional ditches some distance from the roadway, but running parallel to it. Keeping this strip clear made the road safer for travellers. The long alignments of the main roads must have depended on accurate maps prepared by military surveyors attached to the advancing army, but it is often possible to see how shorter stretches could be laid out between sighting points on high ground.

Some have questioned the use of maps by the Romans, but this is only because none have survived. Clearly the survey of the world by Ptolemy of Alexandria, written in Greek in the second century, accompanied a map, and he refers to the preceding work of Marinus.[3] An earlier map of the empire was carved on a wall at Rome in the time of the first emperor Augustus, based on the work of Agrippa.

The professional Roman land surveyors, the agrimensores, were trained to create detailed plans for new colonies and other official allocations of land. The army must have surveyed captured territories at an early stage, and even if early versions started as "sand table" exercises laid out on a clear floor these must soon have been copied on to tablets or parchment scrolls that could be used in the field.

Although the surface of the gravel was cambered to shed water and the solid base prevented the roadway subsiding, the roads would still need regular maintenance to keep the surface in good condition and to ensure the ditches were kept clear and did carry rainwater away effectively. It is not clear whether this remained a military responsibility, but the roads would be essential to the army responsible for maintaining order throughout the empire, as civilians were forbidden to carry arms.

There is a tendency to ignore this aspect of Roman government, but keeping the peace and maintaining the rule of Roman law was a military matter throughout the provinces. The road system remained a vital communication link for the army in its policing role as much as for civilian administrators.

Once the Roman army had built the main roads they provided direct routes to all parts of the empire. They were used by the Imperial Post that transported officials and official messages rapidly between Rome and anywhere within the empire. Augustus had initiated the service by placing relays of runners along the highways to the provinces, but later replaced this

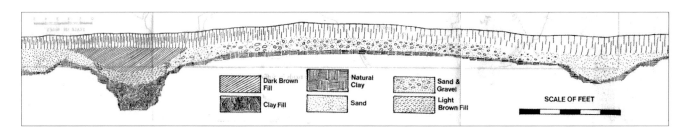

| | Dark Brown Fill | | Natural Clay | | Sand & Gravel |
| | Clay Fill | | Sand | | Light Brown Fill |

SCALE OF FEET

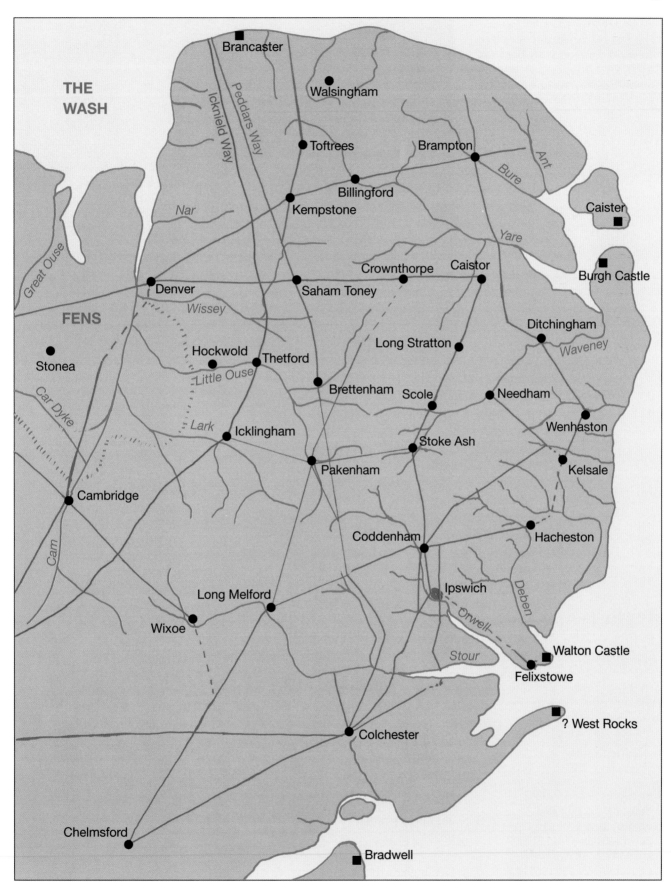

THE
WASH

Brancaster

Walsingham

Peddars Way

Icknield Way

Toftrees

Brampton

Ant

Bure

Billingford

Caister

Kempstone

Nar

Yare

Denver

Crownthorpe   Caistor

Burgh Castle

Great Ouse

Saham Toney

FENS

Wissey

Ditchingham

Stonea

Hockwold

Thetford

Long Stratton

Waveney

Little Ouse

Brettenham

Scole

Needham

Lark

Car Dyke

Icklingham

Stoke Ash

Wenhaston

Pakenham

Kelsale

Cambridge

Coddenham

Hacheston

Cam

Ipswich

Deben

Long Melford

Wixoe

Orwell

Walton Castle

Stour

Felixstowe

? West Rocks

Colchester

Chelmsford

Bradwell

At Thetford where the Icknield Way forded the rivers Little Ouse and Thet, narrow bridges named Nuns Bridges carry modern traffic over the crossing, still a busy route today.

with light carriages based at posting stations so that a single messenger travelled all the way and could be questioned about the news rather than just delivering the written message.[4]

The carriages were also used by those travelling on official business. The Imperial Post (cursus publicus) was an official service that could only be used by those who had a valid permit from the emperor. Pliny the Younger, as governor of Bithynia, did feel able to use a permit for his wife when her grandfather died, and this was approved by the emperor Trajan.[5] Pliny makes it clear that Trajan was very strict about control of permits (diplomata) to use the post.[6] It provided changes of horses (at mutationes) and rest centres (mansiones) at regular intervals. Travellers might be on horseback, but for long journeys officials and messengers rode in the light carriage (raeda) and might then be carried at speed. It is suggested the average speed was probably 50 miles a day, but the emperor Tiberius once covered 200 miles in 24 hours. We might compare the effort of Lieut. Lapenotiere in 1805 when he carried news of Trafalgar from Falmouth to London, 271 miles by post chaise, in 37 hours.

Apart from these main roads there were many minor roads, not engineered to such high standards. Most will have been existing tracks used by the local population from ancient times, although some were improved by Roman engineers. This seems to be the case with the Icknield Way, which is generally held to be a prehistoric route providing a long-distance link to Salisbury Plain via the Chilterns. The section that runs up the edge of the Fens north from the crossing of the River Cam at Great Chesterford to the north coast of Norfolk seems to have been given straight Roman alignments rather than being left to a sinuous course more typical of ancient tracks.

A deed of about AD1250 refers to a highway (regia strata) in Dersingham as Ykenildestrethe,[7] suggesting the name was in use then for the

4 Suetonius, *Augustus* 49.
5 Pliny, *Letters* 10.120-1.
6 Pliny, *Letters* 10.46.
7 Lewton-Brain, C.H., "The Icknield Way" in *Norfolk Archaeology* vol.33 (1965) p.408.

road in Norfolk. Some argue that its name is derived from Iceni as the route that led from the south-west to the territory of the Iceni, but this is disputed. The name as Icenhylte appears in a charter of 903 marking a boundary at Princes Risborough in Buckinghamshire,[8] so apparently it was recognised then. "Icenhilde Way" appears as a boundary in a charter for Compton Beauchamp in 955.[9] Sarah Harrison rejects the existence of the Icknield Way as a through route because she cannot find it on any maps for the area between Royston and Newmarket produced between 1600 and the middle of the nineteenth century,[10] but the absence of the name from tithe and estate maps is not conclusive. She suggests the name was given currency by Henry of Huntingdon who gave it as one of the Four Highways of Britain (along with Watling Street, Fosse Way and Ermine Street) which were protected by special laws. She takes this as explaining its appearance in thirteenth and fourteenth-century documents as far afield as Warwickshire (perhaps through confusion with Ryknild Street) and the road from Salisbury to Dorchester in Dorset (this could be a westward extension to complete the "national" system). She dismisses the idea that it was a trade route, and her argument has some force, but she fails to consider it as a religious pilgrimage route to Salisbury Plain. I do not think it unreasonable to believe the Iceni wanted access to Stonehenge and other features of the "sacred landscape" on Salisbury Plain. That the route retained the name of the Iceni seems eminently reasonable.

Certainly many of our long meandering tracks, some now tarmac roads, others green lanes or farm tracks, appear to be older than the Roman roads and have remained in use right up to the present day. Many lesser routes had been developed generations before to meet local needs, and these continued unchanged or were improved to carry heavier Roman traffic. Such ordinary roads were by far the greater in number, and while they are impossible to date, it is safe to assume that many in use today are much older than those we recognise as Roman. Where the two systems of roads do meet it often appears that the local lanes ignore the Roman roads, and this suggests that they were already there when the Roman engineers cut through them.

Local lanes would have been linked to the new Roman highway, providing access to the existing network. Some of these lanes and minor roads could be remnants of long-distance routes that were in use long before the Roman conquest. Debenham History Society have suggested one such route started from the large Iron Age ditched enclosure at Burgh by Grundisburgh, near Woodbridge, taking the line of the present B1079 to Helmingham.[11] Then it becomes a lane past Bocking Hall and a footpath to Winston Green, continuing past Poplar Hall, in 1361 "Cattenhaugh", to the springs at the head of the Deben (TM158636) above Debenham. Then it goes by a way north described in 1621 as a processional way to Old Hall, after which the precise route is lost through Wetheringsett but picked up as "Deadmans Way" through Stoke Ash. It crosses the River Dove at Waterhouses and follows the alignment of the present village street of Thornham Magna, continuing as a private drive to the Hall, where it becomes Cowpasture Lane. This leads to Mellis Green; then extends by Stonebridge Lane and Bugg's Lane in Burgate to the market at Botesdale. From here it arrives at the watershed between the rivers Waveney and Little Ouse. They suggest the route continued north-west

Today at the entry to Cowpasture Lane from Mellis Great Green we find a sign banning even horse-drawn vehicles from this ancient routeway that was probably in use long before the Roman conquest.

8 British Library, *Stowe Charters* 22 (Sawyer 367).
9 Eadred's Charter S 564 of AD 955.
10 Harrison, S., "The Icknield Way – Some Queries", *Archaeological Journal* vol.160 (2003)
11 information per David Aldred.

12 Davies, J. & Williamson, T., *Land of the Iceni*, 1999, p.35.
13 Preliminary report in PSIAH vol.41 (2007), p.365.

to Swaffham, in which case it would form a fairly direct route to the Fen edge and the northern section of the Icknield Way from the east coast at Felixstowe. It could survive as the modern road down the valley of the Lark from Burgh to Martlesham. From there on the direct route through Brightwell parts of the nineteenth-century road might preserve the line. Although impossible to prove, it could be that this was a major alternative way, providing a cross-country alternative to sailing round the coast of Norfolk. This route would cross the major Iron Age site at Saham Toney which John Davies points out has produced a notable number of non-Icenian coins.[12]

Long before the Romans arrived East Anglians could have created artificial carriageways if necessary. An excavation close to the River Waveney in the Town Marshes near Beccles[13] revealed a prehistoric timber causeway of several phases where a narrow brushwood trackway across marshy ground had been replaced by a solid timber structure based on three parallel rows of oak posts. This used large timbers from managed woodland felled in spring 75BC. A similar wooden causeway supported by timber posts at Barsham is dated about seventeen years either side of BC/AD.

When noting the stretches of Roman roads and ancient tracks that still survive, we can see this as a sign that they have remained in continuous use even through the so-called Dark Ages. Had they not remained in use they would soon have been overwhelmed by natural growth or destroyed by

An Iron Age timber trackway across the marshes of the river Waveney at Beccles. Dendro-chronology gives a date of 75BC for a major phase in its construction, so it was built long before the Roman invasion.
© Suffolk County Council Archaeological Service

agricultural activity. This is confirmed by the way that even strongly-built modern roads disappear when they go out of use. An obvious example is the way that two long stretches of the Roman road from Coddenham to Hacheston survive as a busy road, but are lost where the modern road turns away at one end to reach the current town at Needham Market and at the other takes a less direct route into Wickham Market. In the middle it disappears for a short distance where the modern road takes an easier route across the steep-sided valley at Otley.

The general framework of main Roman roads in our region was identified by I.D. Margary and published in his *Roman Roads in Britain*, with his system of numbering. Local research has since modified the picture and filled some gaps in the system to show evidence of a fairly complete network of main roads. Results of more recent work can be found in *The Archaeology of Roman Suffolk*,[14] which lists additional roads referred to as Suffolk A to E. For Norfolk the booklet in the Norfolk Origins series provides some additional details.[15] Gaps remain where the line might simply have been followed by later roads. This may be the case up the Gipping valley north-west of Coddenham towards Pakenham, and down the Colneis peninsula to Felixstowe. There is scope for further research to identify missing roads: denser strips of flint or gravel across a field, crop marks on aerial photographs, significant stretches of hedges or parish boundaries can all offer clues.

When I told Stanley West I was looking for more examples he very wisely urged me to remember that not all Roman roads are straight and not all straight roads are Roman. Straight alignments and signs of a solid raised agger are good indicators, while early maps can help us to eliminate those straight roads that result from recent enclosure schemes or modern highway improvements. We can sometimes explain the loss of the direct line where the road has been diverted to create a park in the Middle Ages (as with Framlingham Great Park) or more recently. Chalk or gravel pits and golf courses are also good at eliminating all traces.

The individual routes will be considered separately, but it is apparent from a look at the map that many roads converge on the town (Combretovium) at Baylham House, Coddenham. The main one came from Colchester and continued north to Venta Icenorum (Caistor-by-Norwich). One from Long Melford continued to Peasenhall and another ran east to Hacheston (Margary 34a and b and 340). Another ran south-east through Ipswich to Felixstowe. There might also have been a route up the Gipping valley on the line of the A14 beyond Combretovium to reach Pakenham.

This meeting of roads might well explain its Roman name of Combretovium, which means "a confluence" and more often refers to a meeting of rivers. However, we should not leave the river out of account as part of the transport system at this point. No doubt small vessels could use the River Gipping to reach Combretovium even without the eighteenth-century works that created the Gipping Navigation from Ipswich up to Stowmarket. Roman river traffic might have continued well above Combretovium. I see no need to doubt that some of the stone for the great abbey at Bury St Edmunds was carried up this river all the way to Rattlesden in the Middle Ages.

John Speed in his Tudor map of Suffolk shows this as the main stream and names the whole river, now the rivers Rattlesden, Gipping and Orwell, as the River Orwell.[16] Rhodri Gardner has raised the possibility that there was

The sharpened point of one of the oak posts from the Beccles trackway.
© Suffolk County Council Archaeological Service

14 Moore, Plouviez & West, *The Archaeology of Roman Suffolk*, Suffolk County Council, 1988.
15 Robinson, B., & Rose, E., *Roads and Tracks*, Norfolk Origins 2, Poppyland, 1983.
16 Speed, J., *The Counties of Britain, A Tudor Atlas*, ed. British Library, 1995, p.166.

In Ipswich this artificial channel of the Gipping continued to the right as the Alderman Canal. It probably originated as a Roman canal entering the River Orwell at Stoke Bridge, while the cut in the immediate foreground was dug in the eighteenth century to form a direct link between the Gipping Navigation and the tidal Orwell.

Roman management of the stream that flowed into the Orwell in Ipswich below Brook Street.[17] Also in Ipswich the artificial channel of the "fresh water" Gipping, now known as the Alderman Canal, created by the dam at Horseshoe Weir, might be a Roman creation as it existed before AD970.[18] The Romans certainly used waterways to transport heavy goods, and even passengers, when possible and when speed was not essential. When Strabo (4.1.2) describes Gaul, modern France, he emphasises the value of the navigable rivers for transportation from the Ocean (the North Sea) to the Mediterranean, known to Romans as "Our Sea", with cargoes being carried for only short distances by land. He says that was easily achieved through plains so that most of the way they used rivers to travel between the seas and the interior.

When Pliny the Younger described his Tuscan estate at Tifernum he emphasised that the River Tiber was navigable through his lands.[19] It carried his produce to Rome in winter and spring, although not during the summer when its bed was so dry it lost its claim to be a great river until restored by the autumn rains. No doubt some Suffolk landowners had to accept this seasonal nature of water transport.

In more recent times some of the most serious problems in navigating the lower reaches of our rivers have been the result of the embanking of marshes, because this has prevented the tides washing in over wide areas and creating a large current of water on the ebb tide. A strong flow on the ebb tide removes silt from the river and keeps the channel clear for ships. When William Chapman reported to a Committee of Subscribers for the Improvement of the Port of Ipswich at the end of the eighteenth century on the condition of the Orwell, he said the river had been in better condition "in memory of man" before the Corporation Marshes had been embanked. Perhaps the river had been a good deal better in Roman times.

17 PSIAH vol.41 (2006), p.251.
18 Fairclough, J., "The Bounds of Stoke and Ipswich", PSIAH vol.40 (2003), p.266.
19 Pliny, *Letters* 5.6.

There is still no certain evidence as to whether the Romans used some type of lock to move boats into the higher reaches of rivers as proposed by Raymond Selkirk for northern Britain.[20] His arguments have been disputed[21] but not disproved, and in the gentler landscape of East Anglia simple flash locks could have made many of our smaller streams accessible. When rivers were dammed to provide a head of water for watermills a flash lock or staunch would sometimes be created by having a set of removable planks or a single pair of gates in the centre of the weir so boats could pass through on a "flash" of water. On some rivers these devices were used in the Middle Ages and were not replaced by pound locks until the twentieth century. They were certainly familiar in the Fens.

Early records show that in more recent times barges on rivers were often pulled upstream by teams of men when they could not proceed under sail.[22] When progress by water became impossible it was worth using labourers to tranship goods to pass obstacles in the river rather than put heavy vehicles on the roads over long distances. It has been suggested that this was the way the Car Dyke in Lincolnshire was used, and the Romans were certainly using canals for transport in the Fens, including the Cambridgeshire Car Dyke, the Aylmer Hall canal in Norfolk and part of the Fen Causeway route.[23] The remains of the Car Dyke are still visible where it left the River Cam at Waterbeach, although the Roman canal is now much reduced by silting.

The distribution of finds suggests that several lodes in Cambridgeshire, particularly the one leading to an inland port at Reach, were constructed as Roman canals. These canals and rivers in the eastern area of the Fens would have provided access to the west of East Anglia for boats entering from the Wash or transporting goods to and from the hinterland to the west and north accessible by rivers and canals. Thus the River Lark would be navigable at Icklingham, giving that town access to the Ouse and so to all the Fenland waterways. Colin Pendleton points out that the amount of pottery recovered from dredging suggests that the very straight channel of the Lark from Mildenhall Fen all the way down to Prickwillow was the result of Roman engineering.[24]

While large seagoing vessels were confined to the estuaries of the Orwell/Stour, Deben and Waveney/Yare, it would be simple to provide small barges or simple logboats or rafts to move goods far up the rivers. The towns at Combretovium on the Gipping, Hacheston on the Deben, Scole on the Waveney, probably Stoke Ash via the Dove, and Wenhaston on the Blyth could all have been accessible by boat. On the Stour small boats could have reached Long Melford and even Wixoe.

On the amount of water in this river we might note that when first we have records of such matters, in the seventeenth century, between Haverhill and Wixoe there was a large lake of twenty acres on the river. This Stoure Meare gave its name to the Essex village of Sturmer (it can be seen on Speed's map of Suffolk). In Norfolk Caistor St Edmund (Venta Icenorum) could be reached by the Yare and the Tas, Brampton by the Bure and Hockwold and Thetford by the Little Ouse.

Places where roads cross navigable rivers offered the opportunity for interchange. In considering the communication links provided by roads we must not ignore the coastal seaways and rivers, which remained widely used until the coming of the railways. The railways so changed the ability to move

The silted channel of the Car Dyke near the River Cam at Waterbeach. This Roman canal was probably the start of a route that reached as far as the Trent and Humber without facing the perils of the open sea.

20 Selkirk, R., *The Piercebridge Formula*, Cambridge, 1983.
21 Anderson, J.D., *Roman Military Supply in North East England*, BAR 224, 1992.
22 Hadfield, C., *British Canals, an illustrated history*, Phoenix House, 1950, p.16.
23 Hall, D. & Coles, J., *Fenland Survey*, English Heritage, 1994, pp. 108-9; also *Roman Routeways across the Fens*, EAA Occasional Paper 10, 2002.
24 personal comment.

heavy goods by land that we have almost forgotten the extent to which transport by water was a vital economic factor until the middle of the nineteenth century. Unfortunately little hard evidence has so far been found to confirm the manner in which rivers were used in the Roman period, and we should take every chance to examine possible sites of quays or staithes.

In discussing the situation on the Thames Gustav Milne argues that on the available evidence Roman London should not be seen as a port developed by merchants but as a town with important administrative functions for the province and a flourishing population, serviced by the quays along the Thames.[25] He suggests that trade through these quays was providing for the needs of the residents of London and that items exported from Britain to other parts of the empire were better handled by the coastal ports more conveniently situated for this traffic. While cross-Channel traffic might have been concentrated in ports on the south coast such as Dover and Richborough, it is likely that trade with the Rhine valley was handled in the Orwell estuary and the Great Estuary of the Yare. At both Orwell and Yare estuaries goods for export and import could be transhipped between river boats and seagoing vessels in the vicinity of the Shore Forts, below Walton Castle at Felixstowe and behind Caister-on-Sea (see chapter five).

We shall consider in chapter three the evidence for trade in pottery between Britain and the Rhine valley from the ports at Domburg and Colijnsplaat near the mouth of the Rhine. This might have included pottery from the Waveney valley kilns[26] as well as continental exports to Britain and Julian's grain supplies to the Rhine garrisons, which probably originated in East Anglia.

In considering the sophistication of Roman navigation we might note that Vitruvius describes a device for measuring distances travelled at sea in miles, whether the ship was rowed or sailing.[27] It used a paddle wheel attached to a device similar to the odometer he describes for measuring distances travelled by a carriage on land. We do not know how widely it was used, but we should recognise the practical skills of the Romans.

Roads in East Anglia feature in two of the routes listed in the Roman road book known as the Antonine Itinerary. It is thought that this book was originally prepared for a tour of the empire by the emperor Marcus Aurelius Antoninus (Caracalla), AD198-217, but modified for use by officials perhaps as late as the fourth century. This might explain the different forms of the names of Colchester and Caistor-by-Norwich in the two routes below. I have kept the spelling of names here in the form used in the surviving version of the Itinerary.

Route 5 is a long itinerary from London to Carlisle via Lincoln and York, which includes a section from Colchester (Colonia) to Villa Faustini, the location of which between Stoke Ash and Scole is argued below. It continues to Caistor-by-Norwich (Icinos), then Camboricum, which is probably Icklingham, and Durolipons, which is believed to be the walled town at Cambridge.

25 Milne, G., *The Port of Roman London*, Batsford,1985, p. 147.
26 one wonders if there is any evidence of Waveney pottery at continental sites.
27 Vitruvius, *On Architecture* 10.9.5.

Colonia (Colchester) to Villa Faustini (Stoke Ash/Scole)	35 Roman miles
to Icinos (Caistor by Norwich)	18
to Camboricum (?Icklingham)	35
to Durolipons (Cambridge)	25

The Roman mile (mille passus) was one thousand paces, but the Roman pace was two strides (left foot, right, left) making five feet (pedes, where one pes is 11.65 inches) so rather less than two English yards of six feet. This makes the Roman mile about 1,618 yards (1,480 metres) as opposed to the English mile of 1,760 yards.

It has been suggested that Villa Faustini might be Stanton Chare, near Ixworth, on Peddars Way, but it seems too far from Caistor. Camboricum might be Hockwold, but it is too far from Cambridge.

Route 9 runs from Caistor-by-Norwich (Venta Icinorum) to London by way of Sitomagus, which is probably the settlement at Kelsale East Green, Coddenham (Conbretovium), Ad Ansam, which might be in East Bergholt rather than Stratford St Mary, and Colchester (Camulodunum).

Venta Icinorum (Caistor-by-Norwich)	to Sitomagus (?Kelsale)	32
	to Conbretovium (Coddenham)	22
	to Ad Ansam (?East Bergholt)	15
	to Camulodunum (Colchester)	6

There has been much discussion about the location of Sitomagus, the name of which might be more correctly given in the Peutinger Table as Sinomagus, which could be derived from Senomagus, meaning "old market". The Peutinger Table is a medieval copy of a diagrammatic Roman map. Its interpretation is made more difficult because it was only designed to show road links, much as the London Underground Map only shows the stations and lines between them without reflecting the surface geography of the city. As a further complication the copy was made from an original on which the British section was apparently torn, leaving some names incomplete, where they survived at all.

The best compromise based on current evidence, although that evidence is admittedly limited, supports the placing of Senomagus at Kelsale East

The canal known as Reach Lode was probably created in the Roman period. It linked the edge of the Fens to the Ouse river system and through the Wash to the open sea.

Green (see chapter four) rather than Knodishall, which is more likely to be a country house, or Dunwich, which does not fit the distances. There is no positive evidence for a Roman town at Dunwich, although a town there might have been totally destroyed by coastal erosion. Ptolemy in his Geography refers to a promontory south of the Yare, but this could as easily be the extension of the Naze beyond Walton in Essex to the West Rocks (see chapter five) or some other projection lost to erosion. When listing eastern towns Ptolemy only gives Venta in the land of the Iceni and Colchester in the land of the Trinovantes, so adds nothing to our knowledge of East Anglia.

The Roman road from Colchester to Caistor-by-Norwich took a fairly direct line as the key highway in the area. Colchester, the Roman Camulodunum, was a major fortress at first and then had the high status of a colony founded to house retired legionary soldiers with full citizen status, and was the only really Roman town in East Anglia. Caistor-by-Norwich, as Venta Icenorum, became the official administrative centre for the Iceni and later received massive defensive walls, but remained relatively small, as if the Icenian way of life was predominantly rural and never absorbed the urban attitudes of Roman society.

Two of the main routes out of Colchester superimposed on a 1946 Ordnance Survey map, that on the left bound for Hitcham and on to join Peddars Way (see map on page 62) and that on the right heading for Combretovium and on to Venta Icenorum. It seems that both of them avoided the sacred area at Stratford St Mary.
© Crown copyright

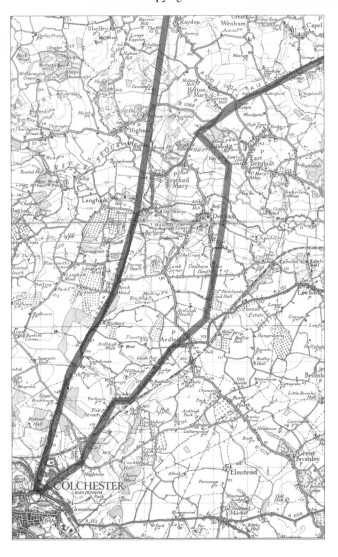

From Colchester Margary regarded the route as his 3c, which was aligned direct from the crossing of the River Colne to cross the River Stour at Stratford St Mary which has been claimed as "Ad Ansam". It seems surprising that the rest of 3c does not run more directly towards Combretovium at Baylham House, Coddenham, as this first alignment out of Colchester appears to head directly towards it.

However this appearance is misleading, as the surviving clues suggest that the Roman road followed by the present-day A12 from Colchester towards Stratford St Mary, after actually crossing the river Stour on the edge of Higham, turned north-west up the east side of the Brett valley towards Hitcham. The most direct route to Combretovium appears to run through Ardleigh, Dedham and East Bergholt before picking up the classic straight stretch of the A12 from Capel St Mary to Copdock.

South of Capel St Mary at Lattinford Bridge the straight road line of the A12 is a result of modern engineering where the old road (now Old London Road) wandered drunkenly up the hill. At some point the road had to turn from the alignment used at Capel in order to cross to Dedham. It also had to cross the deep valley now seen at Lattinford Bridge and probably kept to the high ground between East Bergholt and the Four Sisters cross roads on the A12. However, there is no sign of a link from this point to the Stratford crossing. If one did exist it probably kept to the higher ground as far as possible before dropping to the river, and this might well have been a Roman adaptation for use when flooding made the valley impassable between Dedham and East Bergholt.

Our confusion appears to be the result of all roads across the Stour falling out of use. The likely explanation is that after the collapse of Roman administration in AD410 all the lands north of the Stour valley quickly fell under the control of Angles and in due course became the kingdom of the East Angles. Meanwhile the Stour valley became the northern limit of the reduced territory of Colchester, which lasted much longer as an enclave dominated by a Roman elite before it fell under East Saxon rule to become part of Essex. For some time there was no desire to cross the border. In considering the possible river crossings at Stratford St Mary it might be relevant that the present A12 at TM048343 cuts through an apparent Neolithic "sacred landscape" as crop marks here have been interpreted as a small cursus and a possible henge or mortuary enclosure.[28] It is possible that in the Roman period standing earthworks here were still regarded as sacred and so to be avoided. Certainly the most likely Roman roads run close to the east and west boundaries of the parish.

Apparently three Roman roads headed north-east from Colchester after leaving the East Gate and crossing the River Colne. One became the A12 as far as Stratford St Mary (see below for its route to Hitcham). Another headed towards the presumed port at Mistley and a possible crossing of the Stour near Wrabness (for details see Appendix 4). The very direct single alignment from Colchester to Mistley suggests an early military road linking the Colchester fortress to a port with deep water anchorage on the Stour. The third is the most likely route to Venta Icenorum via Combretovium. It is first apparent as two lengths of the A137 Harwich Road through Fox Street and Trap Street, which were noted by M.R. Hull as likely to indicate a Roman road.[29] They are linked by the short stretch that negotiates the steep Johnnyboys Hill.

Beyond Trap Street the modern road leaves the Roman alignment at TM044289, apparently as a consequence of the owner of Ardleigh Hall moving the highway from his front door to the other side of the church. The Roman line survives on the map as a footpath at TM054297, but this is ploughed out and only becomes visible at TM056300 where it changes alignment to lead directly into the road to Dedham. The modern road makes a spectacular kink where Good Hall has clearly been built on the agger. It is lost beyond the crossing with Long Road, but the precise alignment takes it straight down a spur of high ground where it might be marked by a field boundary and two gates. Then it becomes a field boundary and footpath at TM062323 heading directly to the bank of the Stour, before which Pound Farm stands on the agger. This line would cross the river near Fen Bridge and the point where the modern navigable river diverges from the original Dedham Old River, close to the boundary between East Bergholt and Stratford St Mary.

In 1878 Dr. Raven placed the crossing in this area, saying that "early in 1877 a man digging a hole for a post came on a ridge of hard gravel presenting all the appearance of a road. Near this spot were found several cinerary urns … In the meadows between Stratford and East Bergholt stands a stone much resembling a "milliarium"[a Roman milestone] which is thought to indicate the position of a disused road".[30] It is likely that the road looped round on a spur west of East Bergholt (between TM 062345 and 059357) to pick up the line near the Four Sisters mentioned above.

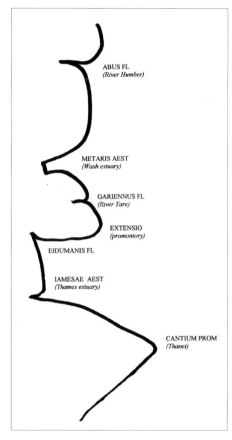

An attempt to show the relative positions of places named by Ptolemy, who compiled his Geography in Greek in the second century. He gave latitude and longitude for the features marked here, so we have an idea of their relative positions. We cannot be sure of their accuracy which was presumably dependant on his maps which have not survived, so we can only make an informed guess at the actual line of the coast.

28 PSIAH vol.35 (1982), p. 141: National Monument Record Nos. 1056952 and 1056949.
29 Hull, M.R. *Roman Colchester* , Society of Antiquaries Research Report 20 (1958), p.11 note.
30 Raven, J., "Roman Roads in the East of England" in *Archaeological Journal* vol.35 (1878), p.80 ff.

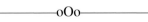

NAMING OF PLACES

The governor looked closely at the map his engineer had unrolled across the table. "That fort where all those roads meet and cross the navigable river is obviously a confluence, so write there *Combretovium*. Before that on the way out of the *colonia* the crossing of the first river is quite difficult so we should have a posting station on the north side, so note *mansio* there."

"Yes sir, the Brits call that river Stour."

"Write that on the map then, but we still need a name for the *mansio*." At that moment his slave placed a fresh jug of wine on the table, and the governor said "Look, that curve up the spur of high ground before your long straight is just like the handle of my jug, so the *mansio* is at the handle. Write *Ad Ansam*."

"Yes, sir."

The governor poured wine into their cups before looking for more places in need of names.

———————oOo———————

31 SROI: FB 191/A8/1 *"A Survey of the Parish of East Bergholt …"* in 1731 by William Brasier for Sir Henry Hankey, Alderman of London.

The line could be marked by a double line of trees to the edge of the flood plain close to the parish boundary, although there is no sign of an agger on the spur above, where a great deal of gravel is apparent. At the crest of the slope the road ditch might have been adapted to form Dead Lane, which later becomes a hollow way, suggesting the road material had been removed to create the predecessor of the modern A12. Remarkably, the lane survives as a footpath.

Using this route, we might be looking for Ad Ansam somewhere in the area of East Bergholt near the Four Sisters. To the south east of this crossroads a cropmark might be a villa, but it looks remarkably like a mansio. Taken with finds of metalwork in this area and towards Lattinford, this suggests that we might be looking at the site of Ad Ansam, at the head of the loop in the road. Perhaps the loop in the road was the "ansa" which strictly means the handle of a jug. It has been widely explained as a bend in the River Stour, but there is no obvious "handle" in its course, so more likely it was the curving line of the road dictated by the geography of the valley. This becomes more probable if we note that Combretovium is generally explained as the confluence of roads rather than waterways.

If the Roman route made a sharp turn eastward at the summit where Dead Lane joins the A12, it would cross the deep valley a little downstream from Lattinford Bridge. Beyond Bradfield Farm on Old London Road the change of alignment to head for Copdock is marked by a faint ridge in a paddock at TM089371, and a pit in the corner might have been a source of road material. The line continues past Boynton Hall as part of Old London Road, now closed to the public through Bush Farm.

There might have been an alternative line out of the Stour valley staying east of the stream at Fishpond Wood and Vale Farm to pick up the The Street of East Bergholt at TM069346. A large eighteenth-century map[31] shows the straight Street but also a feature south of it that appears to preserve the line downhill as far as Tainter Field. Unfortunately subsequent landscaping has destroyed this feature, and nothing is visible on that slope.

A new alignment from TM072354 would pick up a ditch and wood bank along the edge of Hustlers Grove to cross the stream from Lattinford at TM087360. From here a straight footpath shown on old maps preserves the line that becomes the straight stretch of the A12 from the top of Old London Road, Capel St Mary, to Copdock (Margary 3c). The footpath was visible in a growing crop in the spring of 2006 as a lighter green strip across the field, cutting across any lines created by the cultivation of the field.

North of Capel St Mary the line of the Roman road is very straight, although it is not clear exactly where it crossed the Belstead Brook at Washbrook. Then the presumed route (Margary 3c) changes line near Copdock to run directly up the river valley on the line of the modern road through Sproughton to Great Blakenham. However, on the way the route of the present main road straight past Bramford is a modern change (Loraine Way), but is it on the Roman line? The road was probably diverted in the eighteenth century to improve the prospect from Bramford Hall which White described as "commanding a delightful view". If so, our main road has been restored to the Roman line. The modern village is below the crest of a spur and so would be invisible from the hall. The alignment apparently continues on to cross the River Gipping at Sharnford below Baylham Mill and so enters Combretovium.

Does the light strip across a field show the line of the Roman road, long preserved as a footpath but now ploughed out? This view looking from near the agreed main road at Capel St Mary towards East Bergholt is one of those inconclusive clues that puzzle those seeking Roman highways.

The A140 north from Coddenham to Caistor-by-Norwich is often referred to by its medieval name The Pye Road, or locally The Great Road, and is numbered 3d by Margary. The *Gentleman's Magazine* recorded in April 1825 that "three years ago on opening some ditches on the property of Sir Wm. Middleton, on the West of the present turnpike road from Ipswich to Scole (the Pye Road) and near the seven mile stone, the labourers came to a solid artificial stratum of stone and gravel about six or seven yards in breadth – evidently an ancient road, British or Roman. This has since been satisfactorily traced in nearly a straight direction to the River Gyppen where there was formerly a ford. It is remarkable that the meadow next the river on the North side still retains the name of Sharnford, q. d. the Causeway Ford, and that adjoining the river on the South is now called Causeway Meadow."[32]

Hamlet Watling noted the "paved road" directly north of the river in 1878 as a strip 30ft. wide visible in the growing crop, with evidence of the foundations of buildings visible on both sides. In 1935 the line was marked by a swathe of wilting sugar beet, so Ivan Moore helped Guy Maynard, curator of Ipswich Museum, to expose the road. It was, he says, 18ft. "in diameter" with fragments of late first and early second century pottery in the ditches.

As we now know from aerial photographs, just north of the river crossing the road ran through the ditched enclosure of the two forts, one superimposed on the other, which have never been excavated. North of the forts the road was sectioned by Stanley West in the 1950s.[33] The road was 32ft. wide with a raised carriageway, the agger, 1ft. 6in. high made of rammed sand and gravel. It was reported that "Near Baylham House ... a section cut to

32 *Gentleman's Magazine* 1825 part 1, pp.291, 293.
33 West, S.E., "A Roman Road at Baylham, Coddenham", *Antiquaries Journal* vol.35 (1956) p.73 and PSIAH vol. 27 (1954), p.42.

the north of Mill Lane showed the road well preserved, of gravel 18 inches thick, apparently 23 feet wide at first, but later widened on the west side to 32 feet above a pit containing Claudian pottery dated to about AD50. From the absence of silting it was obvious that the pit cannot have been long closed before the road was constructed." Another description said that "work of Ipswich School … assisted by Mr. S.E. West of Ipswich Museum … found road width of 22-26 feet rammed sand and gravel 1 foot 6 inches thick. Samian ware of Claudian date was found in a pit below the road and a coin of AD77-8 was stratified in the road make-up."

The authors of *The Archaeology of Roman Suffolk* in 1988 suggested the construction date of the Pye Road as about AD70. Why? Even at that date the coin recorded by West has to be a later intrusion which either worked down into the road or was lost during repair work. It seems more likely that this military highway was constructed towards the Iceni soon after the initial conquest and extended to Venta once the Iceni were fully incorporated in the province.

The road takes only two alignments to reach Caistor-by-Norwich, with a change at the north side of Stoke Ash. Route 5 of the Antonine Itinerary features a location called Villa Faustini, meaning the Estate of Faustinus. It is worth remarking that although archaeologists use the term "villa" for a Roman-style house its use in Latin, the language of the Romans in which the Itinerary was written, usually refers to a country estate and not just the house of the estate's owner.

Arguments have been put forward at various times suggesting that either Scole or Stoke Ash is the Villa Faustini. The suggestion that Villa Faustini might be the large villa site at Stanton Chare north of Ixworth[34] seems much less likely. The use of a villa name in the Itinerary is not unique, since one is listed in Italy and no fewer than seven in Africa. The central building of the villa estate was not necessarily beside the road, and the record could well refer simply to a road-station dependent on it which might have been developed by the estate owners to take advantage of the passing traffic. The Roman author Varro, writing in the first century BC, had suggested that for a villa estate near a road it was a profitable sideline to own an inn.[35]

There is a problem about the actual distances listed in the Itinerary. The total mileage for the whole of Route 5 from London to Carlisle is an accurate sum of the individual stages, but the distance allowed between Colchester and Caistor is inadequate and this affects Villa Faustini. A detailed study of this problem was made by Leo Rivet,[36] who concluded that there are two acceptable textual emendations which are easy errors for a later copyist to make, either changing the figure of xxxv (for 35 Roman miles[37]) from Colonia (Colchester) to Villa Faustini to xxxx (40 miles) so that it falls at Scole, or changing the xviii (18 miles) from Villa Faustini to Icinos (Caistor St Edmund) to xxiii (23 miles) it becomes Stoke Ash.

There is a possible alternative based on the suggestion[38] that the routes were compiled from the milestone survey prepared when each road was built, and that these were measured from a fort or the capital of a civitas, that is the local administrative unit generally based on the pre-Roman people. In Iter V Caistor-by-Norwich is named as Icinos, presumably using the name of the people of the civitas, as is often found on the continent, rather than the

34 Rodwell, W., *Britannia*, vol.6 (1975), p.76.

35 Varro, *Rerum Rusticarum* I.ii.23.

36 Rivet, A.L.F. & Smith, C., *The Place-names of Roman Britain*, London, 1979, p.163.

37 The Roman mile was 1,000 paces (mille passus) based on a pace of two strides, giving about 57 or 58 inches, so the Roman mile was 1,618 yards or 1,480 metres. The Roman foot (pes) was 11.2 inches.

38 Rivet, A.L.F., & Smith, C., *The Place-names of Roman Britain*, London, 1979, p. 153.

individual name of their main town which is given as Venta Icinorum (Market of the Iceni) in Route 9. If the road was originally constructed soon after AD43 and measured north from the fortress at Colchester to the northern limit of the territory of the Trinovantes directly governed as part of the new Roman province this would give the figure of xxxv miles to Stoke Ash. After the Boudiccan revolt this probably became the northern limit of the territorium of the colonia of Colchester, if the whole of the northern part of the territory of the Trinovantes was attributed to the colonia, and the southern part to Londinium so that the Trinovantes lost their independent existence.

When the Iceni were incorporated into the province the new section in Icenian territory was measured north from the River Waveney at Scole to Caistor-by-Norwich, giving the correct distance of xviii miles. Thus the two distances of xxxv and xviii are correct, but the property of the estate (villa) of Faustinus is excluded. This omission may have arisen because this was a large estate extending for some five Roman miles along the road, and of unknown extent to either side, although it could have included Eye and Hoxne. Perhaps it was not included in either the territory of the colonia of Colchester or the civitas of the Iceni, so that it was missed from the milestone survey. The actual measuring might have been done mechanically as Vitruvius describes an odometer to measure distances in miles, based on a toothed drum attached to one wheel of a four-wheeled carriage.[39]

Possibly the owner of the estate maintained the main road through his land, but it is more likely that this was part of the land in this region that was made into an imperial estate in the personal ownership of the emperor. It may then have been sold or leased to Faustinus.

Rivet and Smith may not find the inclusion of Villa Faustini in the itinerary surprising, but it is unique in the British routes, suggesting a large and important estate that might have been established in the border territory. This is particularly interesting if Grim's Ditch in Thornham Parva was the northern boundary of Trinovantian territory.

It is notable that Stoke Ash marks the only major change of alignment in this road and that there was a significant pre-Roman settlement, equivalent to a small market town, here at Stoke Ash/Thornham close to the border between the Trinovantes and the Iceni. It is worth recalling a nineteenth-century comment by J. Raven[40] that "From Stoke Ash a gravel road goes northward by Scole, Dickleburgh and Long Stratton to the great camp Ad Taum at Caistor, near Norwich. Those who work at the pick and shovel on this road say that there is a great difference in its character north and south of Stoke White Horse."

Until the end of the nineteenth century the main road made a curious deviation north of the crossroads along the curving route now marked by Chapel Lane. It is possible that there was some post-Roman obstruction of the direct route, but perhaps here, as is found elsewhere, the Roman road was diverted to avoid a large burial mound (a tumulus), perhaps of Bronze Age origin. A number of apparent Bronze Age burials are recorded below in the Dove valley. If so, this mound would have been a conspicuous feature of the landscape, marking the last resting place of some hero from the past.

It is only possible to study the structure of the road where the modern route deviates from it. Thus in 1936 Rainbird Clarke tried to trace the road to Caistor from the point where the A140 leaves it at Swainsthorpe and

39 Vitruvius, *On Architecture* 10.9.
40 Raven, J., *History of Suffolk*, 1895, p.41.

41 Clarke, R.R., "Roman Norfolk
since Haverfield" in *Norfolk
Archaeology* vol. 30 (1952), p.142;
(*Norfolk Archaeology* vol.26
(1937), pp.120-1 and 161-2); C.H.
Gale in *PSIA* vol.22 (1936), p.267
and *JRS* vol.27 (1937), p.239.
42 Rogerson, A.,"Excavations at
Scole 1973" in *Norfolk*, EAA 5,
1977, p.222.

suggested it was laid out about AD70. He says the road was examined in 1936 by Thrower and Long west of Scole Bridge across the River Waveney a few yards beyond the county boundary. It was 21ft. wide and made of packed flints, with a ditch on its west side containing fragments of Roman pottery, and was making for a ford across the Waveney, of which traces still existed.[41] Roadside ditches recorded on the Suffolk side of the river show that the Roman road ran on or close to the same line as the modern A140.

Portions of three other roads, probably Roman, may connect with the main road at Scole. The first runs north and south on Stuston Common, with a surface of compact gravel with good camber 18ft. wide. The second runs south-east from the bridge towards Oakley, having a gravel surface 11ft. wide, and appears to follow the edge of the flood plain. The third was recorded at Waterloo in Scole parish as 12ft. wide, also made from gravel, running south-east towards Scole Bridge. Later observations show it formed part of an east to west road north of, and roughly parallel to, the Waveney which may have run from Needham to Brettenham, although it is not recorded outside Scole.[42] South of this road at Waterloo, Gale found wooden piles with struts and horizontal timbers which he interpreted as a wharf with wooden and flint buildings. It would presumably have been easy for small barges to travel this far up the river in the Roman period.

The modern crossroads at the White Horse in Stoke Ash might well echo a road junction from the Roman system, as there is evidence of a road going west to Pakenham. So far there is no trace of a continuation eastwards to the market town at Wenhaston in the valley of the River Blyth near the east coast. The road going west from here links the line of towns at Stoke Ash on the Pye Road, Pakenham on Peddars Way and Icklingham on Icknield Way (for details see Appendix 7).

Returning to the north end of the straight length of A12 from Capel St Mary, it is likely that another road took the route of our modern road into Ipswich from Copdock. It ran down Crane Hill, crossing the river at Handford Bridge and entering the area of significant Roman activity beside Handford Road between Cullingham Road and Alderman Road. The line of Handford Road might have continued straight up to the Cornhill, until it was broken by the construction of Ipswich Castle on a site bounded by the curve of Elm Street, when traffic was diverted up London Road to enter the town by the West Gate.

South of Ipswich the straight line of Wherstead Road probably represents an alternative route north from Colchester (see Appendix section 4, Colchester to Westerfield). Crossing the river where there was certainly a medieval ford, it would make one key feature of the street grid of the Anglo-Saxon town of Ipswich, the straight line of Brook Street, a Roman creation. Perhaps it was based on adapting the brook itself to follow this line. St Matthews Street, Westgate Street, Cornhill and Fore Street would also be based on Roman routes. Norwich Road might follow the general line of a Roman road from Baylham House into Ipswich and on to Felixstowe. The Castle Hill "villa" complex of Roman buildings stands just north of this line, but the Roman road could have reached this point by keeping to the higher ground.

From Long Melford a very straight alignment heads towards Combretovium (part of Margary 34a). Although only short stretches survive there is a direct alignment from Long Melford via Washmere Green and Brent Eleigh to Bildeston. The first part out of Long Melford might follow Bull Lane but is then lost climbing the hill through more recent sand pits. The main alignment starts as a solid green lane but then makes a curving diversion southwards before resuming the line at Slough Farm. Perhaps this name is indicative and the road curved to avoid a great boggy slough. The line continues as a field boundary to School Farm, which actually stands on the agger, and then becomes the lane to Washmere Green. Part of this stretch Norman Scarfe identifies as "the paved road" in his account of the tenth-century bounds of the estate of Balsdon in Acton, described in the will of Aelfflaed and still serving today as part of the Acton parish boundary.[43] It is lost until a short stretch of lane at Monks Eleigh Tye.

At Chelsworth it seems the road had already gone out of use by the time its boundary was recorded in 962[44] as the stretch on the line of the road is recorded as along "wealc hurst" (Welsh wood). A reference to "straet" appears to be the ordinary road from Hadleigh to Lavenham in an area where the modern map shows many "street" and even "stone street" names, apparently unrelated to the Roman system. Then a substantial stretch survives north-east of Bildeston as a footpath before being destroyed by Wattisham airfield. It re-appears as a stretch of road beyond the airfield and here[45] it was

43 Scarfe, N., *The Suffolk Landscape*, ed.3, Phillimore, 2002, p. 99.
44 Hart, C.R., *The Danelaw*, Hambledon Press, 1992, chap. 15.
45 *Archaeology of Roman Suffolk* p. 31: section at TM032513: SMR: RGL 006 and BCG 004.

Amid the various contemporary changes to Ipswich docks just below Stoke Bridge the three small gables at right angles to the waterfront mark the line of the Roman road leading north from the ford across the Orwell, heading for the original line of Brook Street.

46 SMR: BRK 078 and 079 at TM 05605227.

sectioned at Great Bricett to reveal "paving" 16ft. wide between flanking ditches 40ft. apart (unpublished). It then appears lost for a short distance during which it crosses one known concentration of Roman finds,[46] but then survives as a solid farm road through Middle Farm, Barking Tye. Lower Farm, Barking Tye, encroaches on the road, causing a slight diversion, but the line is then marked by the ditch along the north-west side of the Tye.

The actual road line is probably the very solid headland of the field outside the Tye, as the green area of the Tye is very swampy. If so the first cottage at the eastern end of the Tye is on the actual line and a short row of older cottages beyond is aligned directly beside the Roman road. Across the modern road (B1078) a public footpath near the line looks like a diversion past modern houses and then round the edge of a large "prairie" field. Two large fields either side of a valley have removed any trace up to Swingen's Wood. The stretch through Priestley Wood and to Bottys Plantation appears to be lost in woodland of considerable age which has clearly been managed by coppicing, destroying any evidence. Beyond Priestley Wood the whole area as a very large field appears to be the result of major landscape changes almost

The Roman road from Coddenham to Pettaugh running through Crowfield. A classic long straight road that is still a highway, although now only used by local traffic.

revealed a Roman farm at the head of a small valley draining towards the Orwell.[8] The living area was enclosed by a ditch about two metres deep with a gated entrance. Material from the ditch had formed a bank that was apparently still visible in the nineteenth century when J. Wodderspoon in his *Memorials of the Ancient Town of Ipswich* (1850) mentions an earthwork on the way to Tuddenham. Some of the complex of ditches here might have been divisions between animal enclosures as well as providing very necessary drainage on the heavy clay soil. All traces of buildings had disappeared, but occupation here seems to have ended late in the third century or early in the fourth. At Martlesham, in the angle between the Rivers Deben and Fynn, crop marks indicate a field system, probably of the Roman period, on spurs above the valley with tracks which might have taken sheep up to the heathland on higher ground.

Field walking surveys of the arable fields in north-east Suffolk have shown that most of the land in this region was already being farmed long before the Roman invasion, even on the higher clay lands which have been viewed traditionally as least suited to agricultural use.[9] Here too demand might have led to increased production under the Roman administration as the population during the Roman period seems to have been significantly higher than during the preceding Iron Age or the following Saxon periods. In addition the Roman government was demanding production of food for its armies in Britain and on the Rhine. A survey of some 29,000 acres of land provided evidence of 116 sites of Roman activity on farmsteads and larger settlements. There are 85 in the Elmham area of the Waveney valley and 31 on the Thornham Estate near Eye, all surrounded by land on which a thin scatter of abraded pottery indicates manuring of the fields with the rotted remains of household waste in addition to animal dung.

The evidence suggests that each farmstead was working about 200 to 250 acres of land, which is reasonable if they were tenanted farms on large estates. The farms are generally sited to include a mixture of soil types, with the buildings on rising ground above a reliable source of water. Finds from these sites suggest a prosperous economy, doubtless producing significant quantities of grain and meat, with evidence of efficient butchery. Dairy products and wool were being processed. Some sites involved industrial activity including pottery and tile manufacture, leatherworking, metal work, furniture production and brewing.

The presence of coins on the larger settlements and on most farmsteads implies the production of surpluses for sale either on the open market or to contractors supplying the army. This prosperity seems to extend throughout the Roman period in most of the parishes studied with the exception of Metfield, where there is a marked decline in the fourth century.

Only one extensive stretch of land on the Thornham Estate has failed to produce any evidence of Roman or other early activity despite repeated field walking, which suggests that, being on notably high and wet land, it was maintained as woodland, no doubt managed for the production of both timber and fuel. In the Roman period there is evidence of activity right up to the edges of watercourses, while in the Iron Age people seem to have avoided occupying those areas close to the water and liable to flooding. Indeed, there are signs that in the Roman period watercourses were being actively managed.

The distribution of sites in the region where Roman pottery is found

8 PSIAH vol.37 (1992), p.387, Ipswich Archaeological Trust Newsletter 34.
9 Fairclough, J., & Hardy, M., *Thornham and the Waveney Valley*, Heritage Marketing, 2004, chapter three.

suggests that the majority are individual farms, or small farming communities, situated about half a mile apart. Where they can be related to known or likely main Roman roads they are set back from the line of the road as we might expect farm buildings to be. There were also farms on the high plateau in Mendlesham where Roy Colchester has identified fifteen Roman sites, showing that the clay lands between the Waveney and Gipping valleys were also being farmed. Similar patterns are indicated by the results of less thorough studies in a number of other parishes across the region.

Sometimes actual farm tools have been found. A large group of iron tools found at Worlington in 1955 included the metal shoe from a wooden spade, a number of small reaping hooks and large combs for carding wool. Carding combs have also been found at Icklingham and Great Bricett. Spindle whorls, circular pottery or stone weights that kept the spindle turning evenly, are frequent finds throughout the region. There must have been many areas for grazing sheep, and preparation of the woollen thread took place on the farms, although the thread may have been taken to larger centres for weaving.

Presumably the basic farming practice was a mixture of pastoral and arable, with animals being essential to manure the land for corn growing. Indications of dairy farming come from the number of cheese presses recovered, and this is supported by the presumed use of scythes to provide hay for winter feeding. Milk might have been obtained from cattle, ewes or goats, probably from all three. Sheep bones at Hockwold on the Fen edge and from sites in the Fens are largely those of older animals, so these were being kept in

Probably used to harvest grain, these typical Roman reaping hooks were also strong enough to clear undergrowth or trim hedges. These were standard tools for the countryman; similar ones were still in use in the twentieth century.
© Trustees of the British Museum

This Roman bronze figure of a ploughman at work, found at Piercebridge in County Durham, is one of the few original representations of Roman farming in Britain.
© Trustees of the British Museum

significant numbers for milk and wool rather than being killed young for meat. This does not tell us how many sheep were kept, nor whether the manufacture of woollen cloth was a significant local industry, as it certainly was in the Middle Ages. We do know the "Byrrus Britannicus", apparently a type of hooded woollen duffle coat made in Britain, and "Tapete Britannicum", a woollen rug, were among items of which the price was controlled by an edict of Diocletian at the start of the fourth century. Unfortunately a reference to the manager of a woollen mill at "Venta" does not tell us whether this was Caistor-by-Norwich or Winchester.

A more controversial find from Worlington was a group of long curved hollow tines, which might have come from a vallus, a type of reaping machine that Pliny the Elder described as being used in Gaul on large estates.[10] He says it was a frame on two wheels with toothed edges which was pushed through the crop by oxen so that the ears of corn were ripped off and fell into the frame. Perhaps in the Roman period, as in more recent times, East Anglian farmers adopted the latest advances in mechanisation. Generally, he says, corn was harvested with a sickle.

Peter Reynolds testifies to the advantages of using a small sickle to cut just below the ear, because only ears of wheat and no weeds are gathered. The ears can be dropped into sacks worn as aprons.[11] The Worlington finds are in the Cambridge Museum of Archaeology, which also has a large group of iron items found in 1948 just over the Essex border at Great Chesterford. It includes wheel tyres, a plough coulter, the vertical knife that cut through the ground ahead of the ploughshare, suggesting a sophisticated type of plough rather than a simple ard, and very large scythe blades with steel edges that would be effective tools for mowing hay. There are also very long napping shears that would have been used in the final stages of making cloth, so presumably weaving was being carried on there. The iron stone-spindle designed to carry the runner stone of a mill implies the presence of a watermill. Locks show concern for security, while portable anvils and tools show that some working of metal was taking place.

Iron hinges and a padlock case were identified among a hoard of iron

10 Pliny, *Natural History* xviii, 296.
11 Reynolds, P., *Farming in the Iron Age*, Cambridge, 1976, p.38.

The elaborate gridiron found at Icklingham is an unusually ornate example and might have been intended for some special purpose rather than being a simple cooking utensil.
© Trustees of the British Museum

objects from Lakenheath that also included a magnificent cauldron chain that would have suspended a large cauldron over the communal cooking fire, a feature of Iron Age life that continued through to Saxon times.[12] Other cooking equipment includes an iron tripod to support a cooking pot on a hearth found at Sicklesmere.[13] A gridiron from Icklingham has an ornate design and includes a suspension ring for hanging it up when not in use.[14] Also from Icklingham is a very neat iron frying pan with a folding handle; its body had been repaired carefully with two bronze patches secured by rivets.[15] Nina Crummy points out that gridirons, and tripods, are rare finds from Roman Britain and are generally found in hoards of metal objects, several with military connections, so perhaps they were not widely used.[16] The Sicklesmere hoard is a mixed group including a set of ankle shackles and handcuffs incorporating a padlock (presumably to restrain either a criminal or a runaway slave), an iron lamp and a protective iron shoe for a horse. This group, which was apparently buried together at some depth, has no obvious logic; most of the components are only seen as Roman because they were found with the others. Perhaps we are simply failing to recognise much Roman ironwork, particularly as rusty iron is heavy and unattractive.

Despite the use of quite sophisticated metal tools, worked flints have been recovered from many Iron Age and Roman period sites, but these are not products of the early prehistoric styles. They are poor quality flakes roughly struck and crudely worked to produce scraping and cutting tools suitable for simple tasks on Iron Age and Romano-British farms. Even today farm workers will often use a freshly struck flint to cut binder twine rather than looking for a knife. They remind us that the basic technology of using stone tools has never entirely disappeared.

Aerial photographs of parts of south-east Suffolk do reveal cropmarks

12 British Museum PRB 1882. 2-6.13, 14, 15.
13 in Ipswich Museum.
14 British Museum PRB 1844. 2-23.21.
15 British Museum PRB 1844. 2-23.22.
16 Crummy, N., "The mixed grill over-egged" in *Journal of Roman Pottery Studies* vol.12 (2005).

that show the ditches that marked ancient field boundaries, but even when we can identify the shape of early field systems it is difficult to determine their date. However comparison with other areas and a few datable finds suggests that many are Late Iron Age or Roman. The system of fields buried under the Saxon cemetery at Sutton Hoo was found to have been in use throughout the Iron Age and Roman periods. Boundaries of some fields have been recorded by geophysical survey on the edge of the surveyed town at Icklingham, and soil marks on aerial photographs reveal an extensive field system that might be Roman at Eriswell, between Icklingham and Lakenheath. Scatters of small abraded fragments of pottery found in the forest area near Icklingham look like the remains of rubbish carried out with manure to fertilise arable fields. This suggests that even land usually considered unsuitable for arable farming was being ploughed and manured to produce grain for some time during the Roman period. However, this activity is confined to land close to the town at Icklingham. Elsewhere in Breckland evidence gathered along the line of a main water pipe is very sparse, with on average only one sherd of Roman pottery for every two and half kilometres. This suggests that perhaps the higher dry ground was used only for grazing sheep, while people lived in the river valleys close to water.

Some rectilinear patterns in the Lothingland area of north-east Suffolk have also been studied, but so far it has not been possible to tell which of them

A rural scene reconstructed in Ipswich Museum. The Soay sheep is the breed closest to those kept in Iron Age and Roman Britain. In the background the building site for the bath house shows how Roman roof tiles were used.
© Colchester and Ipswich Museum Service

belong to the Roman period. Studies by the team working on the National Mapping Project in Norfolk of aerial photographs from a range of sources do appear to reveal a Roman field system replacing an Iron Age one with a very different pattern of fields at Hopton-on-Sea, not far from Burgh Castle. Could the new rectilinear system relate to allocations of land to support the Saxon Shore fort later in the Roman period? The Flegg to the north of Caister-on-Sea also shows dense systems of fields and enclosures. Indeed, there is a very dense pattern of tracks and enclosures in a number of areas of Norfolk. Some have long linear trackways, suggesting they might be part of extensive "co-axial" systems, and there are many enclosures with rounded corners. Clearly these are not forts, and they give the lie to attempts to identify Roman forts on the basis of a single ditch with a rounded corner.

Behind Reedham in the peninsula between the rivers Yare and Bure a dense system includes 184 small enclosures that might be homesteads. At Heacham in north-west Norfolk a rectangular enclosure contains three round buildings, suggesting a farmstead, but this cannot be dated from the crop marks as we know that in some places round houses were still being lived in well into the Roman period. At nearby Snettisham excavation in advance of the bypass revealed round houses within an area of high density activity occupied from the first century AD through the second century but fading in the third. This appears to be part of a pattern for this particular area, with a farming and craftwork settlement of British style in each valley relating to a large Romanised villa at the head of the valley, and trackways leading down to the saltmarsh on the Wash. At Watlington, six miles south of Kings Lynn, excavation is gradually confirming that one area of fields was in use only during the Iron Age and Roman periods but saw many changes within that time. We should not assume that any one system always applied throughout the Roman period.

By examining nineteenth-century and earlier maps Tom Williamson has demonstrated that certain lengths of the Pye Road (the Roman road that is now the A140) in Suffolk and Norfolk apparently cut across the pattern of fields that survived into the nineteenth and twentieth centuries.[17] This only makes sense if that field system was already in place before the Roman road was created. Flinders Petrie recognised this significance when studying the roads of Kent in the nineteenth century.[18] He saw that when new roads were constructed, at any time, across open downs or woods the fields were laid out at right angles to them as the easiest way to divide up the land, creating hedges conformable to the roads. If the land being crossed had already been divided up then the new road either wound round the existing properties or cut across in a nearly straight line, regardless of the hedges. The latter is typical of roads constructed by the Roman army across existing fields and produces what Petrie called roads unconformable to hedges.

On this basis the landscape north of Grim's Ditch in Thornham Parva towards Yaxley appears to be a pre-Roman field system cut by the Roman road. Williamson argues that this may be part of an ancient "co-axial" field system in which fields are defined by parallel but slightly sinuous lanes and boundaries, and have few prominent continuous features running in a transverse direction. This type of system is described as Bronze Age on Dartmoor, where the boundaries are called Reaves. The evidence in East Anglia is not so clear and merits further research, because some field

17 *Historical Atlas of Suffolk*, 1999 edition, Suffolk County Council, p.48.
18 Flinders Petrie. W.M., "Notes on Ancient Roads", a lecture recorded in *The Archaeological Journal*, 35 (1878), p.169-175.

boundaries certainly do appear to be earlier than the Roman road, which would mean that elements of the Iron Age field system survived into modern times. South of the apparent line of Grim's Ditch those boundaries that can be identified seem to be aligned on the Roman road, and it is likely that these result from later changes in the field pattern.

Edward Martin does not accept that there is a large-scale co-axial field system in the region.[19] He suggests the main axes running roughly at right angles to the watercourses were created by the prehistoric long-distance trackways, probably devised for moving livestock between grazing areas. The fields were then aligned on these tracks, which set a general pattern for the field boundaries. He thinks these probably do reflect a prehistoric pattern but specific areas of fields have varied at different times, so it is impossible to tell which specific boundaries are pre-Roman except by large-scale excavation.

One area of regular field patterns on the same alignment as a Roman road through the Ilketshalls and the Elmhams in north Suffolk has attracted much interest. Oliver Rackham suggested it might have originated in the Bronze Age,[20] but it is difficult to believe his view that the Roman road was "insinuated along one of the axes" of the existing field system. It seems more likely that here the fields were laid out after the Roman road had been constructed. Some have suggested it is an example of Roman centuriation or "limitatio" but that was a very precise method of land division carried out by Roman surveyors working to precise right angles and exact distances which are well documented.

Despite the efforts of some researchers to impose such patterns there is nothing in our region that fits the precision and specific dimensions of professional Roman surveyors operating across an undeveloped landscape. The surviving evidence suggests some local changes based on stretches of Roman road but constrained by the existing pattern of fields. Clearly the areas where this continuity is visible from Roman times to the last century never adopted the rigid three-field system of the Midlands during the Middle Ages. In fact we know that in East Anglia some areas kept enclosed fields, while others combined them with irregular open fields, but few if any changed to the three open fields which have been put forward as the medieval "standard system" based on Laxton. Probably our soils were too variable and our farmers too independent for that style of farming.

P.J. Drury, writing on the later Iron Age and Roman landscapes,[21] points to work by Warwick Rodwell[22] establishing long sinuous boundaries in the Roding Valley which are cut across by the main Roman roads running north-east from London to Chelmsford and Dunmow. He says the principal line, now marked by parish boundaries, follows the eastern watershed of the Roding for some 25 miles, and other sections of parish boundaries seem to mark roughly rectangular blocks between this line and the river. Drury suggests that probably in Essex estates with an average area of some five square miles, established in the pre-Roman period, retained their integrity through the Roman period and beyond, based on these ancient boundaries rather than on the later Roman roads. He sees similar divisions between the Colne and Stour valleys north-west of Colchester but without the dating evidence provided by Roman roads, and cites other possible examples at Little Waltham in the Chelmer valley and around Braintree. However, he suggests a different pattern, apparently of Roman origin, based on straight

19 Martin, E., *Wheare most Inclosures be* EAA 124 (2008) p.215 and Martin, E., "Suffolk in the Iron Age" in Davies, J. & Williamson, T., *Land of the Iceni*, UEA, Norwich, 1999 pp.52 ff.
20 Rackham, O., *The History of the Countryside*, London, 1986, p.156-8.
21 In *Archaeology in Essex to AD 1500*, CBA Research Report 34, 1980, ed. D G Buckley.
22 Rodwell, W., "Relict Landscapes in Essex" in *Early Land Allotment*, ed. H C Bowen & P J Fowler, BAR 48, 1978.

23 Bland, R., & Johns, C., *The Hoxne Treasure*, British Museum Press, 1993.

lines in the Dengie Peninsula and around Thurrock. This supports the evidence for local variations in landscape planning as we see them in Norfolk and Suffolk.

The rich farming area around Thornham and Eye, with direct access to the river, might well have been the source of wealth for the estate of Faustinus, identified in the official Roman guide, the Antonine Itinerary. The estate may have extended from Stoke Ash to the crossing of the River Waveney four miles up the road at Scole. Somebody wealthy certainly owned land near here, as a magnificent treasure of gold and silver from late Roman times was found in 1992 some three miles away at Hoxne,[23] near the confluence of the Rivers Dove and Waveney. This could have been within the estate, but no large Roman house has been found in this area so far. Perhaps we have not looked in the right place. We would expect the main house for a large estate to have mosaic floors and underfloor heating, which usually leave identifiable evidence even if the house itself were built of timber, as were so many of our sixteenth-century great houses.

This lack of substantial houses is typical of our region. It seems that in East Anglia very few people chose to invest in expensive country houses of the type recognised by archaeologists as Roman villas. Numerous examples have been identified in other parts of the country including the Cotswolds, which was a comparably rich agricultural area. Of course such Romanised buildings were clearly exceptions to the norm, the equivalent of the stately homes of the eighteenth and nineteenth centuries. Only a few examples of the largest type have been recognised in East Anglia, most notably Gayton

Part of an early Roman plate or shallow dish found during field walking at Thornham. It appears to have been copied from imported fine pottery known as "terra nigra" (black earthenware). Continental potters stamped their names in the centre, where this fragment has part of an unintelligible mark.

Thorpe in Norfolk and Castle Hill, Ipswich, and Stanton Chare near Ixworth in Suffolk. These might have been official residences rather than manor houses. We will examine them and some other large houses in chapter four.

Although some large buildings might have gone undetected, it seems unlikely that many had the large mosaic floors, under-floor heating systems and tiled roofs of the great villas. However, it is worth noting that a fine group of roof timbers, from at least two buildings, was found reused in a brewing complex at Scole.[24] They included part of an elaborate hipped roof. These timbers, which are displayed at Ipswich Museum, are a reminder that in this region the building of large timber frames has always been highly developed, although we only find evidence from the Roman period when the timbers are preserved in waterlogged conditions, as at Scole. Richard Darrah points out that these timbers show the woodworkers were skilled in using the axe, adze and saw.

Most of the timber used was oak. In some cases a tree of the correct size was felled and squared by hewing with an axe or adze. Larger trees were sawn into planks and beams. Some straight grained trees were split into planks,

24 Darrah, R., "Wood technology" in Ashwin & Tester, *Scole Report*, EAA forthcoming.

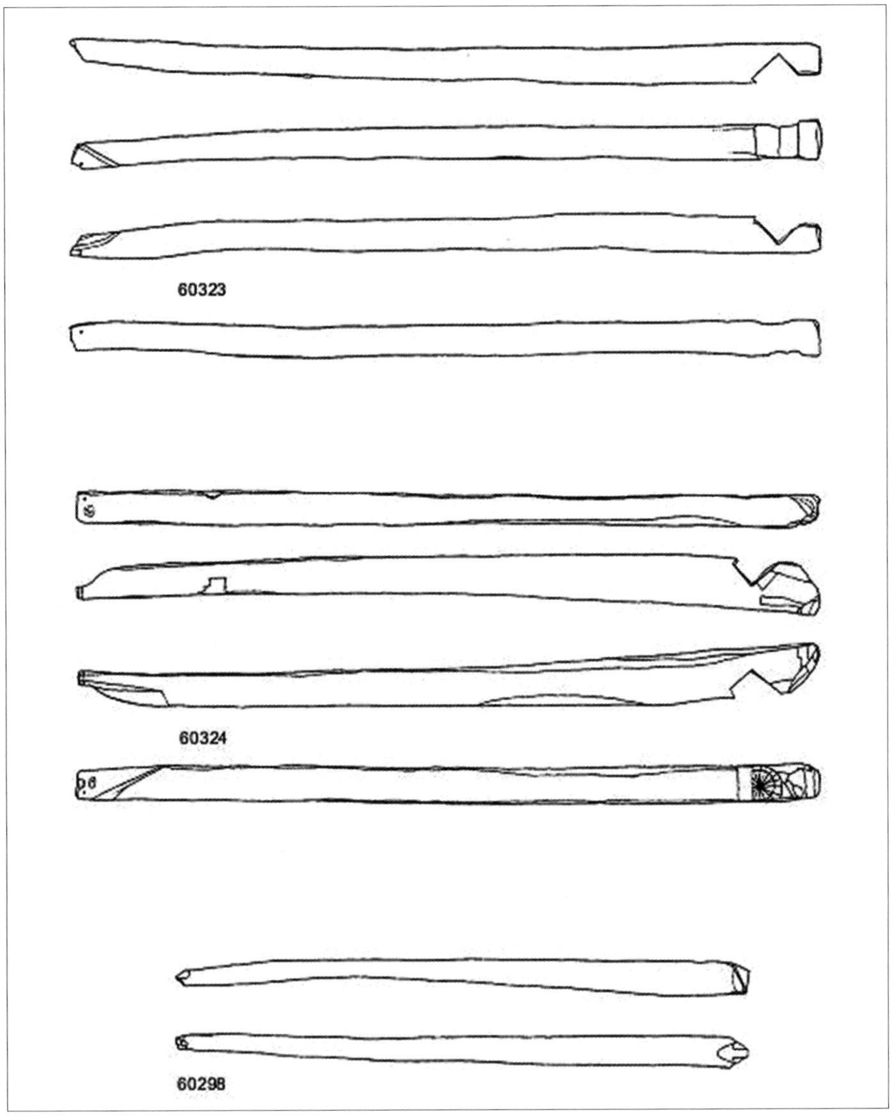

60323

60324

60298

The smaller rafters from the Scole house, showing cuts for joints to the larger timbers.
© Suffolk County Council
Archaeological Service

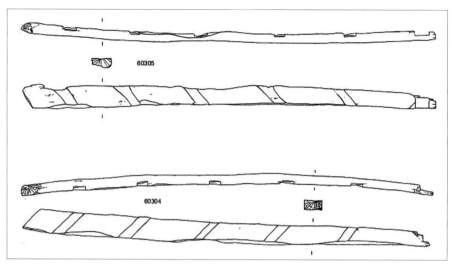

Two principal rafters from the roof of a Roman house preserved at Scole (but in Stuston parish), where they had been re-used to line a tank at the Roman maltings, show the cuts made for joints to construct a hipped roof. They are displayed at Ipswich Museum.
© Suffolk County Council Archaeological Service

probably by using wedges. This is a rare example of the survival of components of large timber-framed houses and commercial buildings that must have been common features of the Roman countryside in East Anglia. It is worth emphasising that we only need to look at examples in Suffolk that survive from the sixteenth century and earlier to see that such houses could be large and comfortable.

As long as the footings are kept dry and the roof is watertight these buildings can last for hundreds of years. If the roof was thatched and the floor made from beaten earth, they leave little for the archaeologist to find. Even so the very small number of mosaic floors found in Suffolk remains remarkable, although we know they are vulnerable to intensive agricultural activity which has been typical in the county up to the present day. We hear stories of possible examples being destroyed by the plough without any record being made.

There is evidence that skilled craftsmen did work here, as a house at Windmill Hill, Capel St Mary, is remarkable for having glass mosaic tesserae. These were probably used to pick out the details in a very high quality tile mosaic or for special wall decoration. Such a feature is uncommon, although others are known from stray finds at Martlesham and Whatfield, while three stray ones turned up in the aisled hall of the massive Fishbourne Palace in Sussex. However it is clear that a number of Roman houses in East Anglia did have colourful mosaics on the floors and paintwork on the walls, sometimes combining pictures with bright patterns

There is some evidence of possible smaller villa-type houses in northeast Suffolk. A mosaic floor was reportedly found in the mid-twentieth century on a site parallel to the Halesworth to Bungay road (Stone Street) but then buried, and crude red tesserae from a simple tessellated floor were found at South Elmham St Peter's. There was also a large rectangular structure with flint footings at Chediston.

A site on high ground beside Clay Street in Thornham Magna, on the north side of the presumed Roman road, has produced evidence of significant Roman occupation, including tiles that are likely to be part of an underfloor heating system or hypocaust. This was probably a substantial building occupied throughout the Roman period by prosperous farmers. Finds include several fourth-century coins, enamelled bronzes and pottery with first-century greyware and later mortaria manufactured in the Nene valley and others from Ditchingham in the Waveney valley.

Less than a mile south-west of this area, just inside the parish of Wickham Skeith, surface finds suggest the presence of a really substantial Roman building with a bath house. Quantities of roof and flue tile have been found high on a south-facing slope which is likely to be the site of a villa with an underfloor (hypocaust) heating system. At the bottom of the slope more tile was found, and in the sides of a stream which feeds into the River Dove there are substantial concrete footings with Roman floor tile embedded in the top. Perhaps this is the base of the latrine for the bathhouse, flushed directly by the stream. Several brooches and a cosmetic grinder have been found, as well as substantial quantities of pottery, including samian. A second site on the other side of the stream was originally found by a group fieldwalking with Stanley West. It may have had a long history as it has produced Bronze Age and Early Saxon material (Saxon finds include a brooch, a buckle and a sleeve clasp). These could have been the centres of profitable farms upstream from the settlement on the main road at Stoke Ash. At a site in Thrandeston, just to the north, there is evidence of another substantial building with tesserae, a tiled roof and heating system,

Other buildings such as a small bath house excavated at Stonham Aspal in the 1960s might have been part of farmsteads.[25] The-two roomed building was timber framed on stone footings with a tiled roof, glazed windows and brightly painted walls. It seems to have dated from the early third century, with some later alterations. No house was found, but animal bones suggested that the main animals were mature cattle, with some sheep and pigs. In 1871 Hamlet Watling reported finding many patterned Roman flue tiles at Stonham, but it is not clear whereabouts.[26]

At Farnham, near Stratford St Andrew, a small structure 17ft by 9ft with

25 Smedley, N., & Owles, E.J., "A Romano-British Bath-house at Stonham Aspal", PSIAH vol.30 (1966) p.222-251. Hamlet Watling reported many Roman finds in this area.
26 *Journal of the British Archaeological Association* 27 (1871), p. 385.

Did the typical East Anglian rural house in Roman style look something like this pair of cottages in the estate village of Euston? The thatched roof and the rendered walls coated with white are likely features. There is no evidence for Roman chimneys, so we are left wondering how they heated the rooms, as no small houses boasted elaborate underfloor hypocaust systems.

The results of a geophysical survey of the site of a group of Roman buildings at Wyverstone near Bacton, interpreted as showing the round houses within an enclosing ditch on the left. The area of concentrated blue towards the right can be resolved into a rectangular building that was probably a bath house. The straight red line might mark a channel bringing water to the bath house.
© Suffolk County Council Archaeological Service

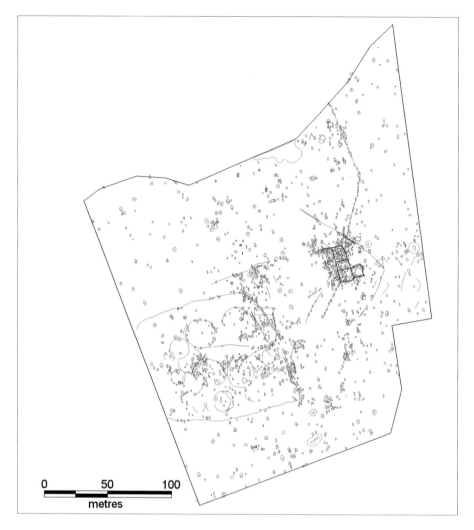

projecting bays to east and west, creating a roughly cruciform plan, was excavated in 1971. It had been built in stone using the local coralline crag and had plastered walls and glazed windows. It appears to be a bath house, and building debris nearby suggests there was also a house.[27] It may be that these bath houses were associated with houses that were not recorded because they had timber frames based on sleeper beams resting directly on the ground or because their footings were very slight, but we can never be sure.

A geophysical survey of a site in Wyverstone close to its boundary with Bacton has revealed a number of round houses in a ditched enclosure.[28] Outside this enclosure there appears to be a small rectangular bath house, and roof tiles, box flue tiles and tesserae were found in the area of the bath house. Metal detector finds indicate activity in the Iron Age and Roman periods into the fourth century. In the absence of excavation we cannot be sure, but this suggests that people were living in round houses in the Iron Age and continued doing so through the Roman period, adding a Roman-style bath house outside the enclosure. Perhaps this was not uncommon in East Anglia.

Outside Stowmarket at Cedars Park people were certainly living in round houses during the Roman period just as they had in the Iron Age, but there was also evidence for the flint footings of a small three-roomed rectangular corridor house and postholes for substantial timber uprights. The

27 PSIAH vol.32 (1971), p.208; Ipswich Museum 1971.135.
28 Woodhouse, H., *Bacton Archaeological Report*, Cambridge University and Suffolk County Council, 2007.

footings had been damaged by ploughing so that only a few courses survived, but they might have been the base for a timber superstructure. There was evidence of use in the second and third[29] centuries and signs of two possible bath houses. Presumably East Anglians adopted the idea of the Roman baths as the centre of social life, without necessarily changing the design of their living spaces. Occasional finds of oil flasks and strigils support the view that those who could afford it bought into the culture of using Roman baths, which were the direct ancestor of the modern Turkish bath. Rooms were heated to create a steamy atmosphere in which slaves rubbed down their masters, and mistresses, with olive oil before scraping off dirt, sweat and oil with a curved metal strigil. They could finish with a cold bath before being dried, and enjoy the company of their friends in one of the warm rooms, perhaps relaxing over a board game or being read to by a slave. If so, here as in Rome, the baths became the centre of social life.

At Burgh by Grundisburgh Edward Martin has interpreted the Roman buildings within the Iron Age enclosure as a villa complex at the centre of a large farming estate.[30] It stands on the edge of a small stream, one of several in the region called the Lark, which finds its way into the Fynn and so into the Deben at Martlesham. The indications of a large house include underfloor heating, tesselated floors, painted wall plaster, roof tiles, window glass and door locks. The presence of bones from sheep, cattle and a smaller number of pigs and horses suggest the economy of this valley was mainly pastoral, producing meat, milk, wool, hides and draught animals from well-watered grasslands.

Martin makes a strong case for considering that the group of parishes now known as Burgh, Grundisburgh, Clopton and Otley at the head of the Lark valley formed a single Saxon estate and that this originated from the villa's landholding. If the Iron Age enclosure really was the headquarters of an independent state in the territory that later became the Wicklaw, perhaps its "royal seat" or estate remained in the hands of the same family or their successors even beyond the end of Roman rule. However, by the time of the Domesday Book its land had been fragmented into fourteen manors. Perhaps St Botolph's bones were lodged here in the tenth century,[31] because there was still a belief in the prestige, sanctity and security of this special place, which more recent legends associated with a buried golden calf and visits by the supernatural dog known here as Galley Trot. The substantial Roman buildings were just one phase in its complex history and it is possible that it simply retained its special function through the Roman period. As well as being an administrative centre, it might always have had some religious status, marked today by the dedication of its church to St Botolph.

At Exning, near the edge of the Fens, a stone farmhouse with a bath house and one mosaic floor replaced an aisled timber-framed building, over 100ft long with posts 18ft apart, built in the early second century.[32] Other buildings are recorded further up the Fen edge at Thistley Green in Mildenhall, where a two-roomed building with a hypocaust was found in 1932.[33] Another extensive site in Mildenhall is noted in the Fenland Survey[34] with a reference to earlier finds, including tesserae and tiles, and spreads of pottery revealed by deep ploughing in the 1950s.[35]

As other finds of building materials are reported in Lakenheath and Eriswell there was certainly significant activity on the edge of the Fens.[36] This

29 PSIAH vol.40 (2003), p.367.
30 Martin, E., *Burgh: Iron Age and Roman Enclosure*, EAA 40, 1988.
31 Scarfe, N., *Suffolk in the Middle Ages*, Woodbridge, 1986, p.50.
32 Webster, C.J., *Cambridge Antiquarian Society Proceedings* vol.76 (1987) p.41
33 *Archaeology of Roman Suffolk*, p.51.
34 Hall & Coles, *Fenland Survey*, English Heritage, 1994, p. 110.
35 Briscoe in Proceedings of the Cambridge Antiquarian Society vol.55 (1961), p.66-7.
36 Hall & Coles, *Fenland Survey*, English Heritage, 1994, p.112, and Briscoe as above.

37 Jackson & Potter, *Excavations at Stonea, Cambridgeshire, 1980-85*, British Museum, 1996, p.687.
38 Malin, T., *Stonea and the Roman Fens*, Tempus, 2005.
39 Gurney, D., *Settlement, Religion and Industry on the Fen-edge*, EAA 31 (1986), p.137.
40 *A Roman Maltings at Beck Row, Mildenhall, Suffolk*, EAA Occasional Paper 20, 2004.

Plan showing the two rows of postholes for the Roman aisled barn excavated at Beck Row, near Mildenhall. The barn probably looked very similar to the typical great medieval barns of East Anglia, its main function presumably being to store corn after the harvest.
© Suffolk County Council Archaeological Service

might be linked to the Roman development of agriculture in the Fens, where it is argued that sheep became a key feature, in some parts for wool and in others for salted meat from lambs, as suggested for the important complex at Stonea Grange.[37] On the basis of such evidence Tim Malim suggests that large numbers of sheep were being raised on the rich pastures.[38] Many were killed young, presumably for meat, much of which could have been preserved with locally produced salt to supply the army. The presence of cheese presses and loom weights in the region suggests that dairy products and woollen cloth were also important.

Fenland itself was dominated by waterways, but much of the land could be farmed in the earlier part of the Roman period when there is evidence of systematic management, although it suffered from increased flooding in the third century. Many sites show evidence of freshwater flooding in the middle of the third century.[39] This might have been caused by a rise in sea level and heavy rainfall, but such factors are notoriously difficult to determine. Enclosures of Iron Age and Roman date appear to be fields used to manage grazing livestock taking advantage of rich grasslands. Sites on the higher dry land had the attraction of access to the rich soils and extensive waterways of the Fens without the risk of flooding. There is also evidence of corn growing on the edge of the Fens.

A building at Beck Row, Mildenhall, has been interpreted as a malting because charred sprouted cereal grains were found in association with a T-shaped flue.[40] This was inside a large aisled barn some 35m long by 10m wide. It seems that the flue was part of a kiln for drying and malting wheat and barley; the main fuel was the chaff from processing spelt wheat. The building

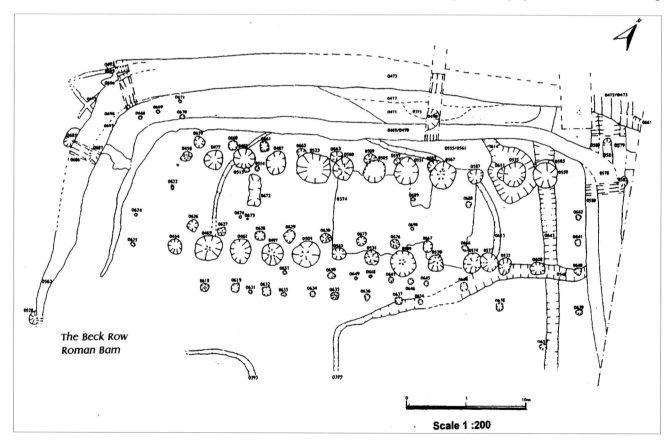

The Beck Row
Roman Barn

Scale 1 :200

had been destroyed in a catastrophic fire, perhaps not surprising when a high temperature kiln was operated in a timber building, and was rebuilt on the same site in a similar form before being burned down again in the middle of the third century. Fragments of millstones used in the construction of the second building suggest that the first barn at least might also have contained a mill for grinding malt for brewing or grain into flour. Comparable evidence for a grain processing complex, including milling and brewing, was found on the far side of the Fens at Orton Hall Farm near Peterborough.[41]

41 *Nene Valley: Orton Hall Farm*, EAA 76 (1996).

Closer to the Wash the wealth of the area along the edge of the chalk north of the River Wissey can be attributed to the profits from combining iron smelting and mixed farming to exploit the natural resources of the area. The key building complexes stand at the head of the valleys, but the valleys themselves while rich in finds indicative of activity during the Roman period do not contain substantial buildings. Occupation at Denver marks the start of the Fen Causeway linking Norfolk to middle England across the Fens. Settlement extended for about 2.5 kilometres along the Causeway to Nordelph and included salt making, which was a significant industry in the Fens. South of the Wissey the chalk edge abuts directly against the peat fenland.

Presumably this combination of different and complementary resources with successful farming was the basis of substantial communities along the Little Ouse at Feltwell, Hockwold and Brandon. It also explains the considerable wealth demonstrated by several groups of pewter tableware in the area, the great silver treasure from Mildenhall and the prosperous town and religious centre at Icklingham and Lackford straddling the River Lark (see chapter seven). Further south there is evidence for wealthy residents in the Iron Age and Roman periods at Freckenham and for a prosperous settlement at Exning near Newmarket. The Fens terminate short of Cambridge, where the crossing of the River Cam gave access to the main road route out of southern East Anglia to middle England, still in use as the A14 along the southern edge of the Fens to Huntingdon.

The Roman settlement at Cambridge was not enclosed by walls until the fourth century. This suggests the walls might have been built to protect a depot where supplies demanded as taxation were collected ready for shipment to the armies on the Rhine and in northern Britain. Possibly the authorities were anxious to guard against theft by local people who resented the taxes as much as any concern about foreign raiders penetrating this far from the sea.

David Gurney has drawn attention to the growing number of finds of aisled barns in East Anglia, identifiable by the pattern of postholes for the main timbers. One at Kilverstone near Thetford had five pairs of posts, and others are known at Brettenham, Norfolk, East Winch, and the Harford park and ride site at Norwich. At least seven of these large planned buildings set in spacious enclosures are visible on air photographs of an extensive field system at Hockwold-cum-Wilton. Whether they were simply farm barns or they incorporated living accommodation is unknown, but they have the same form as medieval and more recent corn barns. They might be standard Roman buildings used alongside traditional round houses.

Generally evidence for farm buildings is elusive, but sometimes we find evidence for the processing of crops. The footings of kiln structures for drying grain have been identified in a number of places, and a fourth-century example

These rows of postholes excavated at Flixton represent a rectangular building about fourteen metres by twelve. What was it? It might have been a granary, with the posts supporting a floor strong enough to carry a heavy weight of grain, or perhaps it was a temple with aisles. Pottery finds suggest a late Iron Age or early Roman date.
© Suffolk County Council Archaeological Service

was excavated on the line of the Hadleigh bypass in Suffolk. There has been some debate about whether these were used to make malt for brewing or were used for drying grain, as was done in relatively modern times in Scotland. In recent years kilns that could achieve the high temperatures needed to make malt have been used at a lower temperature to dry moist grain when needed outside the malting season. This might well have been done in Roman times, but the only clue in modern structures is where a kiln was used for malting the high temperature is likely to have made the tiles of the floor brittle. Modern kilns often use perforated tiles for flooring, but there is no evidence for tiles in the floor of these Roman kilns and Peter Reynolds built a reconstruction using a floor of wooden planks covered with a slurry of chalk and clay.[42] Because there was no flow of air through the floor it was not very efficient for drying grain, but it is said to have produced acceptable malt for brewing.

Other evidence for brewing includes the presence of the plant known as sweet gale or bog myrtle. A sample of malted grain for brewing at Colchester burned in the Boudican revolt was a mixture of spelt wheat and barley in the ratio of 10:1. It seems that most of the beer (cervisa) brewed in southern Britain was made from wheat (mostly spelt) rather than barley, which is generally used for modern beers.

We have already mentioned some limited evidence for watermills, but there are also signs that handmills were operated for small-scale grinding of corn into flour. These might be made from the same lava stone imported from the Rhine valley which was used for larger millstones, but some seem to continue the tradition of using quern stones made from puddingstone, a local conglomerate containing hard pebbles that provided suitable means of creating a grinding surface. Pairs of stones were cut to provide circular grinding surfaces between which grain was converted into flour. This seems to have been the standard method of producing flour in the Iron Age. Milling by hand was a slow and laborious process, but would have to be done on a regular basis because while grain lasts a long time if properly stored, flour only keeps for a short time.

We know that Britain exported hunting dogs before the conquest, but there is little evidence of game among the bones found in household rubbish.

42 Reynolds & Langley "Romano-British Corn Drying Ovens", *Archaeological Journal* 136 (1979), p.27-42.

Hilary Cool draws attention to the higher proportion of deer bones, particularly red deer, from the fort at Caister-on-Sea and suggests the garrison might have been exploiting a local abundance of game.[43] Apparently they were also eating badgers. Not many hare bones appear in kitchen rubbish, but the way Boudica used a hare for divination before her campaign against the Romans means the animal might have been under religious protection.[44] Indeed, Caesar tells us that Britons considered it wrong to eat hares, hens and geese.[45] Cool notes that chickens are common in food debris from large towns including Colchester, military sites and villas which we might consider Roman, but are rare on British rural sites. A rabbit is reported in a Roman-age pit at Lynford in Norfolk, although we await confirmation of dating by carbon 14. If it is confirmed we are left wondering if it was imported as a delicacy or kept as a pet.

We have suggested that East Anglia was of particular value to the Roman administration as a source of food for its armies. One clue which may simply confirm what had been happening for a long time is that in the fourth century the emperor Julian took steps to restore the protection for the transport of grain from Britain to the Rhine.[46] We are told that in AD359 while campaigning in Germany he built granaries to store the corn regularly brought from Britain, in place of those which had been burnt. The Roman sources also tell us that where the Rhine flows into the Atlantic Ocean at a point on the coast 900 stadia, about 103 miles, from Britain Julian had timber gathered from the forests around the river and 800 boats larger than galleys built which he sent to Britain to convey grain.

These sources say that before Julian's time corn was shipped from Britain over the sea and up the Rhine, but the barbarians had blocked transport up the Rhine, so ships unloaded in coastal ports. Transport from there by wagon instead of river was very expensive, so Julian provided more ships and reopened the Rhine navigation, which was seen as an important achievement. This is just one episode that happens to have been recorded, and we may be sure supply traffic across to the Rhine was a regular feature of life on the Orwell and Yare estuaries. No doubt our ships also supplied the needs of garrisons in north-eastern Britain that could be serviced by sea. We are not told about transport of the corn within Britain, but presumably every effort was made to get East Anglian corn to the sea by using the rivers.

The Waveney seems to have been a focus of commercial activity. The quantity of broken pottery suggests a considerable population in Flixton and the neighbouring parish of St Margaret's from the first century. Some "Belgic type" material has been found at Flixton quarry, as well as quantities of Samian. Occupation continuing through into the fourth century is shown by the finding of some Nene Valley and Oxford wares. There were substantial structures in Flixton where one early Roman building appears to be a large granary about twelve by fourteen metres, supported on timber posts in a location that produced evidence of a number of Iron Age four-post structures, probably earlier granaries.[47] This might have been a collection point for grain that was to be exported by boat. Fragments of cheese presses found beside the Waveney confirm the importance of dairy farming, no doubt making the most of grazing land along the valley.

We shall see that the Waveney valley was also a busy area for the pottery industry, no doubt taking advantage of water transport along the river and

43 Cool, H.E.M., *Eating and Drinking in Roman Britain*, Cambridge, 2006, p.113.
44 Dio Cassius 62.6.
45 Caesar *Gallic Wars* V.12.
46 Zosimus III,5,2 and Eunapius Fr.12, and Ammianus Marcellinus XVIII,2,3 cf. Libanius *Oration* 18,82.
47 PSIAH vol.40 (2001) p.95/6.

48 Cool, H.E.M., *Eating and Drinking in Roman Britain*, Cambridge, 2006, p.71.
49 Bowman, A., *Life and Letters on the Roman Frontier*, British Museum, 1994.

through the Great Estuary to northern East Anglia and to the sea. Local traders were also bringing goods into the region, as examples of Nene Valley types, different grey wares, imported samian and later Oxford ware were distributed throughout the Waveney Valley and its hinterland. We cannot tell how many pots arrived containing specialist products, perhaps distinctive foods from other areas, rather than as empty items for sale in their own right, but they certainly suggest a thriving economy.

The Rivers Gipping and Stour flowing into the Orwell estuary and the River Deben could be used to bring the produce of many inland farms to the coastal haven at Felixstowe, and it is reasonable to think there would have been a major port there throughout the Roman period. The army was campaigning in the north from the initial conquest of the Brigantes and creation of the legionary fortress at York in the early 70s, through the campaigns of Agricola in what we know as Scotland. We know that Agricola used the fleet in support of his legions, and he would need to receive food supplies by sea to feed his fighting army and to maintain stocks for the garrisons through winters in potentially hostile territory. Although the northern frontier of Britannia fluctuated over the years it always required garrisons that could be supplied up the east coast.

A decorated pottery beaker found at Felixstowe bearing decoration created with an applied clay slip. It was a practical drinking vessel.

No doubt some of the grain required for the garrison troops on Hadrian's Wall was transported by sea from the East Anglian ports to the supply base at South Shields on the River Tyne. The demands increased and the requirements were more elaborate when emperors themselves were on campaign in the north-east, including Hadrian (AD122), Severus (207-211) and Constantius (296/7 and 306). For produce from the north of East Anglia there was the Great Estuary through which the Waveney as well as the Yare entered the sea. Corn would have been transported as grain, because once ground flour will keep for only a limited time. One sample preserved in the supply base at South Shields by a fire in the late third or early fourth century consisted of equal amounts of spelt (triticum spelta) and bread wheat (triticum aestivum).[48] The evidence suggested the grain was cleaned near the entrance to the granary to remove weed seeds, particularly corncockle, which is poisonous and had to be picked out by hand. Presumably individual units then had to grind the grain as it was needed.

The writing tablets from the fort at Vindolanda, behind Hadrian's Wall at Chesterholm, include references to wheat (frumentum), barley (hordeum) and grain for malting (bracis, which might be spelt or emmer).[49] They mention a maltster (braciarius) and a brewer (cervesarius), so some of the grain was destined for beer (cervesa) rather than bread. To get some idea of the scale of demand consider Stuart Piggott's calculation that a single Roman legion would need about 500 bushels of corn every week, which he calculated as the crop off a little over seventy acres.[50] In experiments at Butser Farm in Hampshire Peter Reynolds established that Emmer wheat could achieve a yield of more than 2.5 tonnes per hectare, with an average of about two tonnes, using farming methods of the Late Iron Age or Roman periods.[51]

Along the coast areas of marshland had probably been used for sheep grazing on a large scale since the Bronze Age. David Buckley illustrates this for Essex with a 1940s photograph of men on horseback rounding up a large flock of sheep in the wide open spaces of Wallasea Island before the land was "reclaimed" for arable farming after the Second World War.[52] Was this true of the East Anglian coast generally through the Roman period? He also emphasises evidence for the importance of maritime traffic on the coast, from a Bronze Age paddle found in the Crouch estuary to the early twentieth century coasters. He refers to the numerous dock and wharf facilities with associated industries, including the Roman period activity at Elms Farm, Heybridge, on the River Blackwater. More work is needed to identify such sites elsewhere on our rivers.

A specific coastal industry was the manufacture of salt by heating seawater to evaporate the water, separating the salt from the brine. The process created quantities of conspicuous red debris including burnt clay and the remains of hearths, forming features we refer to as red hills. It is possible

50 "Native Economies ..." in *Roman and Native in North Britain*, ed. I.A. Richmond, 1961, p.23.
51 Reynolds, P., *Iron Age Farm*, British Museum, 1979, p.61.
52 Buckley, D., "Lost and Found: the Archaeology of the Essex Coast" in *The Rising Tide*, ed. A. Aberg & C. Lewis, Oxbow Books, 2000.

This reconstruction of the gatehouse of the fort and supply base at South Shields (Arbeia) at the mouth of the Tyne gives an idea of the scale of defences provided for the coastal forts.

53 for one on Trimley Marshes
(TM2536) see PSIAH vol.40
(2001), p.107.

that the bright red colour is increased by a biological organism that flourishes in salt and creates a bright red pigment. Many have been found in Essex, but fewer are known in Suffolk. Five have been recorded on the edge of the Orwell estuary in Trimley, on sites which are now ploughed on the edge of reclaimed saltmarsh,[53] but this presumably marked the limit of high tide at the time, and five on the Deben marshes. Red hills are known at Alderton and Hollesley, including some on the creeks behind Shingle Street, and there was at least one on the edge of the Butley River near Sudbourne.

At Sudbourne itself there were salt workings on the original coastal edge with a Roman settlement on higher ground just behind it. Tony Greenacre has been finding Roman and later saltworking sites on the landward side of the marshes. He has also found a Roman salting site in Oak Wood, Capel St Andrew at TM371487, which supports this being more of an estuary, with Burrow Hill as an island, before the growth of Orfordness. Thus salt workings can sometimes indicate changes in the pattern of tidal limits along the coast. There were at least eight on the Alde at Iken and Snape. The presence of a large amount of briquetage, the fired clay debris typical of salt

*Excavating the Roman site
beside the River Alde at
Barber's Point, Friston.
© Suffolk County Council
Archaeological Service*

working, along with ordinary Roman pottery on an island in the river at Barber's Point suggests this might have been a collecting and processing centre for the salt from works along the river. It was operating from the second to the middle of the third century, but was flooded by rising river levels early in the fourth century. There was also an extensive salt working site on the Blyth near Wolsey's Bridge at Blythburgh.

The nature of the coast further north might have been less suitable for salt works where there are cliffs. However, we have lost much of this coast to erosion and round the north coast of Norfolk David Gurney reckons the Roman coastline was about two kilometres further out, so any evidence disappeared long ago. Certainly salt was being produced in the Fens, particularly from the early second century to the end of the third. David Gurney has mapped the known sites and reckons saltmaking may have been important to the local economy.[54] Charles Green excavated a site at Denver in 1960 and found evidence which suggested saltmaking would have been a seasonal activity using the salt water and peat fuel. Did salt workers also cultivate oysters? Such an occupation could have provided alternative seasonal work for them.

British oysters were valued at Rome, where Juvenal claimed an expert could recognise one from Richborough in Kent at the first bite,[55] although Pliny the Elder was critical of their quality.[56] Tacitus mentions British pearls but says they were inferior to those from the Indian Ocean,[57] and Pliny confirms this but adds that Julius Caesar had used them proudly in a breastplate he dedicated in a temple of Venus at Rome.[58] He suggests that production was not highly developed in Britain, and we lack evidence, apart from the large quantities of oyster shells found among food debris, showing they were widely available as food. How were they transported?

A particularly rough type of pottery container might have been used to transport salt. A similar material referred to as VCP, "very coarse pottery", in the West Midlands and Welsh border area was apparently used in Iron Age and Roman times to transport salt from the inland production site at Droitwich. Was salt an export item? Was it used to preserve meat and fish? A quantity of very coarse pottery has been found at Stoke Ash, where it might have been used for salt to preserve meat.

What was the role of salt, fish and oysters in the local economy? It would help if we could date any of the rectangular oyster pits and the fish traps in our rivers and establish whether there were more salt works than we have found so far. Some timbers on the foreshore of the River Deben below Sutton Hoo have been interpreted as the possible remains of fish traps and radio carbon dated as Late Roman or Early Saxon.[59] Christopher Currie gives references from Roman authors, including Varro and Columella,[60] to the enthusiasm for creating ponds to keep both marine and freshwater fishes.[61] Apparently they were both expensive status symbols and sources of profit. Could this explain the strange tank beside the River Yare at Brundall, some 100 feet long and five feet deep?[62] It is much more likely to have been a fish tank that doubled as a swimming pool than the Roman dock claimed by some. However, Hilary Cool finds little evidence for the eating of fresh fish in Roman Britain.[63] This contrasts with the wealth of evidence for the consumption of shellfish, salted fish and fish sauce.

Individual pottery kilns of the Roman period have been found at a

54 Gurney, D., *Settlement, Religion and Industry on the Fen-edge*, EAA 31 (1986), p.143.
55 Pliny, *Natural History* ix, 169; Juvenal, *Satires*, iv, 141.
56 Pliny, *Natural History* xxxii, 62.
57 Tacitus, *Agricola* 12.
58 Pliny, *Natural History*, ix. 116.
59 Tom Williamson, *Sutton Hoo and its Landscape*, Windgather 2008, p.87.
60 Currie, C., "Sea Ponds, with reference to the Solent in Hampshire" in *The Rising Tide*, ed. A. Aberg & C. Lewis, Oxbow Books, 2000.
61 also Pliny, *Natural History*, ix, 170.
62 Malster, R., *The Norfolk and Suffolk Broads*, Phillimore, 2003, p.18.
63 Cool, H.E.M., *Eating and Drinking in Roman Britain*, Cambridge, 2006, pp. 175, 201, 237.

An exposed section of a red hill beside the river Alde shows the distinctive colour of the debris from making salt in the Roman period. Some might see it as an early example of industrial pollution in this rural setting.
© Suffolk County Council Archaeological Service

64 *Archaeology of Roman Suffolk*, p.61.

number of locations,[64] and it seems that plenty of pots to meet local needs were made within East Anglia. Only fine wares such as glossy red samian and colour-coated vessels had to be imported from elsewhere, although by the third century colour-coated wares were being made at Pakenham and near Thetford. Skilled potters set up their manufacturing enterprises at locations that provided suitable clays, used a fast wheel to turn the vessels and fired them in kilns built into a hole in the ground.

The kilns consisted of a pit from which the fire could be stoked through an arch or short tunnel leading to the round oven. Inside the oven pots were supported above the floor to keep them clear of the fire, generally by a mushroom-shaped clay pedestal in the centre of the floor on and round which pots were stacked. Some, including examples at Pakenham that produced drinking vessels and others at Stowmarket, had permanent raised floors pierced by holes to allow the hot air to rise round the pots. The clay structure of the kilns became heavily fired and, being partly buried in the ground, often survives along with "wasters", the broken pieces of rejected pots. These kilns must have consumed much wood for fuel, and local woodlands were no doubt coppiced to produce a regular supply.

Coppicing in the traditional manner at Bradfield Woods, where different panels of the wood are harvested in rotation while the rest grow again from the stools. This is a deliberate recreation of procedures that were common throughout the Middle Ages.

It is important to note that firewood is a totally renewable resource. It is well established that in the Middle Ages East Anglian woodlands were carefully managed to produce a steady supply of underwood for such uses as fencing poles and tool handles as well as logs and bundles of brushwood for

A jet pendant that was found at Colchester showing cupids making a pot. The two cupids appear to be working together to form the clay into a pot. Jet from Whitby on the Yorkshire coast was a popular material for jewellery.
© Trustees of the British Museum

A Samian bowl imported from Gaul and found at Castle Hill, Whitton. This type of high quality tableware with its glossy red slip finish was mass produced in factories in Gaul and traded across the empire.
© Colchester and Ipswich Museum Service

65 Darrah, R., "Wood technology" in Ashwin & Tester, *Scole Report*, EAA forthcoming.
66 PSIAH vol.41 (2006), p.242.
67 Plouviez, J. in Blagg et al, *Hacheston*, EAA 106 (2004), p.185.
68 *Roman Pottery Manufacture at Bourne Hill, Wherstead*, EAA Occasional Paper 9 (2001).
69 *Journal of British Archaeological Association* vol.37 (1881), p.152.
70 West, S.E., *West Stow: The Prehistoric and Romano-British Occupations*, EAA 48 (1990).
71 Frere & Clarke, "The Romano-British Village at Needham, Norfolk", *Norfolk Archaeology* 28 (1945), p.213, quoting Rev H. Tyrrell Green FSA.

fuel. Cropping areas of coppiced woods at intervals of twelve to fifteen years allowed the trees to grow back naturally from the stools, while a limited number of larger trees, including oaks, were left to grow for many years to provide structural timber. By Roman times such a system must already have been embraced, as without woodland management timber would have been in short supply. The woods were managed just as much as fields were. Evidence from the excavations at Scole showed that basketwork well linings were made from large numbers of straight rods of hazel, with some ash and birch.[65] Richard Darrah points out that these must have come from managed woodland that was coppiced or pollarded.

There were pottery kilns on the edge of the town at Combretovium, and others were found about two miles south-east, exposed in advance of gravel extraction 500 yards west of Barham church. It stands on high ground overlooking the Gipping valley at a point where metal objects have been found spanning the Iron Age and the whole Roman period. Excavation revealed a probable ten-post roundhouse and a six-post building which were erected in the Iron Age, and a massive fourteen-post rectangular barn with smaller timber buildings constructed in the Romano-British period. Apparently the potters had obtained clay for the kiln structure and the pots from a series of pits in the immediate area. They were producing grey wares in the late first and early second centuries.[66] Pottery was also produced at the market town at Hacheston between the first and third centuries, and some might have been made there in the fourth, although there is no evidence of kilns after those marking an intensification of activity in the third century. Some groups of drinking beakers were deliberately oxidised during firing to create an orange colour.[67] Kilns provide evidence of an early production site on Bourne Hill at Wherstead which was active in the middle of the first century.[68] Its products included bowls that were based on early Roman glass bowls that might have been brought to Colchester by the military. However the design of the kiln is different from any at Colchester and more like one at Martlesham. Perhaps local potters were trying to cash in on the military market, particularly if we are right in arguing that the nearby road was a direct military highway from the Stour estuary northwards through Ipswich.

Henry Prigg recorded two Roman pottery kilns on West Stow Heath in 1881[69] and later found others, all in the area between the River Lark and the modern road, just outside the town at Icklingham. Two more were located by Basil Brown in 1940 and another three were excavated by Stanley West during his exploration of the Anglo-Saxon settlement in 1965-72. Details of all these kilns together with eighty-four pits and two rectangular buildings related to them were published by Stanley West in 1990.[70] He suggests that they operated over about seventy years, ending in the middle of the second century (about AD80-140), although three kilns were operating in the third century nearby in Icklingham itself.[71]

The production of pottery in the valley of the River Waveney during the Roman period should be seen as a major enterprise, with a number of kilns producing pottery apparently in woodland clearings or on marginal land. This was not some rustic craft centre but a considerable manufacturing operation of the kind that one would expect to find sited in an urban location in today's environment. Perhaps we should compare it with the sequence of industrial sites along the Severn valley in the Ironbridge Gorge at the start of the

Opposite page: *A potter at work in the Ipswich Museum display. Perhaps this is the type of workshop to be found at Wattisfield and elsewhere along the Waveney valley.*
Ipswich Museum

Industrial Revolution. The largest complex of pottery making in Suffolk during the Roman period has been found in the Wattisfield area above the head of the Waveney. [72] It made use of a good local source of clay for potmaking which was still used through the Middle Ages and in more recent times. The clay contains a high proportion of mica, a mineral that gives the fabric of the pots a distinctive glint or sparkle. The Wattisfield products were sold over a wide area.

It is possible that the Roman industry grew from Iron Age production using pit-clamp firings, suggested at a poorly recorded site at Pear Tree Farm, Wattisfield.[73] This pottery industry spread into what are now the neighbouring parishes of Botesdale, Rickinghall and Hinderclay. It has been suggested that the owner of the large villa at Stanton Chare, which is not far from these potteries, might have derived his wealth from this industry,[74] although this can only be speculation as the villa could have had an administrative role linked to Peddars Way. This is one example of pottery production on a commercial scale by specialist potters which is found at a number of places in Roman Britain, many in similarly rural locations.

However, there was an industrial suburb outside the small town of Brampton on the River Bure where almost a hundred and fifty pottery kilns have been found, producing standard grey pots and pans as well as more specialist flagons and mixing bowls, many of which were doubtless shipped down the river. The dates of excavated kilns ranged from the late first to the early third century. Mortaria

A storage pot decorated with a face. Sometimes these were used in cremation burials, but they seem also to have been in general domestic use.
Ipswich Museum

(mixing bowls) from here stamped by "Aesuminus" have been found on an Antonine Wall fort near Edinburgh. To have operated on this scale they must have depended on the ordered society and reliable communication system under the auspices of the Roman Empire. The collapse of imperial government might have been the most significant factor in the loss of these industries and of the highly developed potting skills on which they relied. Certainly the whole tradition of fine pottery production that had developed in Britain during the Iron Age and Roman period disappeared at the start of the fifth century.

Returning to the Waveney valley, the local clay at Homersfield and Mendham was used to produce jugs with face masks made in special moulds,[75] as well as a wide variety of household wares. Some of the pots produced at Homersfield in the second and third centuries AD were decorated with distinctive stamped designs. The clay here also contained some mica, but not in as high a proportion as that found in the Wattisfield area where the pots have a definite twinkle. The Mendham site was particularly active in pottery manufacture during the second and third centuries. This is attested by the many thousands of pottery sherds recovered from the site, with many appearing to be pottery wasters, that is pots that went wrong when fired in the kiln. At Homersfield production on a commercial scale might have started before the Roman conquest, as pre-Roman Iron Age coins of both the Iceni and Trinovantes have been found in the area. Three Roman pottery kilns that were operating in the second century have been found at Needham,[76] where the settlement on the north bank of the River Waveney apparently had an Iron Age mint, judging from a find of coin moulds.

Nearby at Flixton they were producing tiles, including both tegula and imbrex types for roofing as well as the box flue tiles for hypocaust heating systems and thick tiles suitable for flooring or for use in the tile courses of buildings, from kilns spread over at least ten acres. Some fragments preserve the delicate fingerprints of women or children employed in the manufacture, and the distinctive signatures of the tilers were discovered on many of them, indicating continuous production over a long period of time. The tile works were located on higher ground up the valley side above a pottery production area. The tiles were being made in an area with a good supply of clay, marked by the naming of Heavy Land Wood, where there was extensive woodland for fuel and a beck providing plenty of water. This would have helped in preparing the clay but is not of sufficient size for the tiles to be transported by water, so they were presumably carried about two miles by pack animals or wagons downhill to the River Waveney where they could be loaded into barges.

One pottery at Ellingham near Bungay specialised in the production of mortaria, the strong mixing bowls with a heavily gritted inner surface. No Roman kitchen was complete without one of these bowls that could be used in pounding herbs and fining down any mixture before cooking. We might equate a slave using a mortarium and a pestle with the modern electric food mixer. At the Ellingham site the mortarium kiln included stamped mortarium fragments in its structure showing at least two and possibly four makers using the kiln, one of whom was called Regalis.[77] He is also known to have worked at Colchester, and some of his mortaria have been found at South Shields, so presumably he was supplying military units in the north by sea. This was in

72 Spread over the parishes of Wattisfield, Botesdale, Hepworth, Hinderclay, Market Weston, Rickinghall Inferior and Superior (Swan, V.G., *The Pottery Kilns of Roman Britain*, 1984, p.115).
73 Swan, V.G., *The Pottery Kilns of Roman Britain*, 1984, p.54.
74 *The Archaeology of Roman Suffolk*, p.62.
75 Smedley, N. & Owles, E.J., "A face-mould from the Romano-British kiln site at Homersfield", PSIAH vol.30 (1965), p.211.
76 PSIAH vol.23 (1939), p.236, and *Norfolk Archaeology* 28 (1945), p.187.
77 Hartley, K. & Gurney, D., *A mortarium kiln at Ellingham, Norfolk*, EAA Occasional Papers 2 (1997).

Above: *A typical roman roofing tile or tegula. These tegulae were laid in interlocking rows, then the join between rows was covered with curved imbrices to keep out the rain.*
© Trustees of the British Museum

Below: *The bronze mortar from a two piece cosmetic grinder. A solid bronze pestle was used in the groove to grind powder materials to prepare make-up. It might have been used particularly in preparing popular types of mascara and eye shadow. It was found in a Roman well at Lakenheath.*
© Suffolk County Council Archaeological Service

the period between the campaigns of the emperors Hadrian and Severus, as he was probably working at Ellingham from about AD170 to 190. A total of 837 sherds of mortaria were recovered during the excavation, of which some represented between thirty-seven and forty-nine individual types, stamped by Regalis. These kilns were also producing flagons. Regalis' mortaria have also been found at Scole.

Distinctive grey mortaria are common on Norfolk and Suffolk sites. Some were made at Brampton and in the Wattisfield area, but there might also have been kilns at Caister-on-Sea, where large numbers of mortaria fragments were found together in a pit.

Bronze and iron

The production of decorated bronze objects had a long history in East Anglia and continued throughout the Roman period. Many items have been found, including a wide variety of brooches which were clearly a popular form of decoration as well as a practical method of securing clothing. Although we have evidence of bronze working it is not possible to say which specific objects were made locally in the first century. However, clay moulds to make terret rings, to guide chariot reins, and strap-joining plates for horse harness were found at Waldringfield beside the Deben,[78] which is intriguing as most of the known bronzes have been found further north. Gilbert Burroughes has found clay moulds for making bronze brooches of early Roman type at Chediston.

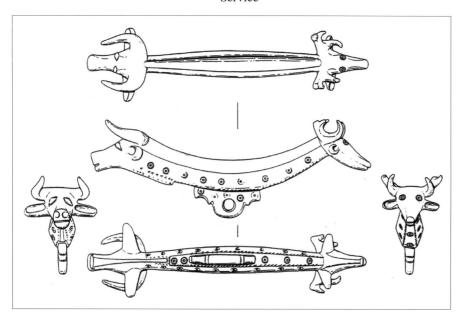

E.T. Leeds discusses some of the horse harness and brooches from Santon Downham, Westhall, Saham Toney and Lakenheath in *Celtic Ornament*,[79] in which he describes the "dragonesque fibula" from Lakenheath as a fusion of pre-Roman scrolls and Roman decoration early in the Roman period. He also discusses the origins of the enamelled escutcheons on "Celtic" hanging bowls from Anglo Saxon graves, seeing in them a resurgence of native British styles which had been present but restrained during the Roman period and flowered again after the end of Roman dominance so that they influenced later Irish designs.

Here we can see British craftsmanship adapting to the needs of different rulers while preserving the traditional skills. In terms of personal decoration, as seen in the metalwork on harness and chariot as well as the colourful textiles they wore, it is clear that the leading British warriors of East Anglia could put on a good show. They adapted the traditional skills to their civilian roles under the Romans in producing a wide variety of decorative brooches, including some with enamel inlays.

The basic purpose of Iron Age and Roman brooches was to secure clothing in the manner of a safety pin. The bow of the brooch could be decorated in many different ways. One distinctive type had a flat plate instead of a bow and often represented an animal picked out with bright enamel inlay. As we shall see, some types apparently indicated the wearer's rank, particularly so-called "crossbow" brooches, and others seem to be associated with temples so presumably had a religious significance.

Some ornamental bronzes have also been found. Particularly notable is a pair of bronze lions, probably mounts from a piece of furniture, which were found on the site of a Roman house at Capel St Mary (see chapter four). They were probably made locally as they have the lentoid eyes typical of "Celtic" work. A fine bronze figurine of a dog about 95mm long found at Charsfield might have come from a temple associated with healing outside the market town at Hacheston.[80] A figurine of a three-horned bull from Holbrook is portrayed standing with a band round the body, suggesting that it had been prepared for sacrifice.[81]

Various types of bronze jugs or bowls were made, but presumably at the end of their useful life they were generally recycled for the metal rather than being discarded like broken pottery containers. However, one distinctive type of bowl does occur in our region at the end of the Iron Age and the start of the Roman period which is thought to have been made locally. It has a pouring spout, which in an example from Ingoldisthorpe near Snettisham represents a fish identified as the common bream by Paul Sealey in his comments on a similar fish spout from Beck Row, Mildenhall.[82] The spout is protected by a perforated strainer plate inside the bowl, designed to remove solid material from the liquid.

Other examples are known from Brandon and Crownthorpe. A complete one was found in the "Doctor's Grave" at Stanway outside Colchester. Analysis by Patricia Wiltshire showed that the material held by the strainer was mostly mugwort or wormwood (artemisia).[83] This strongly suggests that the bowl had been used to prepare a herbal remedy against intestinal worms, while the pollen present suggested the bitter medicine had been sweetened with honey to make it more palatable. This establishes the use of the Stanway bowl, confirmed by medical instruments in the grave, but it is possible that

A brooch in the shape of a dragon that was found at Wetheringsett. When new the bronze shone brightly with a golden colour, set off by an inlay of coloured enamel. © Suffolk County Council Archaeological Service

78 PSIAH vol.36 (1986) "Archaeology in Suffolk 1985", p.155.
79 Leeds, E.T., *Celtic Ornament*, Oxford 1933, Dover reprint 2002.
80 PSIAH vol.38 (1994) p.200; the dog is now in Ipswich Museum.
81 PSIAH vol.41 (2006) p.237.
82 *A Roman Maltings at Beck Row*, EAA Occasional Paper 20 (2004).
83 Crummy, P. et al., *Stanway*, Britannia Monograph 24 (2007), p.394.

other such bowls were used to strain non-medical infusions or flavoured Celtic beer. Their use to strain wine is less likely as they are not generally associated with wine amphorae.

It might seem surprising that rural East Anglia was home to iron smelting as well as smithing. It seems that people had developed the skills needed to produce iron from the ore in nodules found in the ground in many areas. No doubt a great deal more could be collected from the surface in those days. This must have made iron a readily available local material. The smelters constructed furnaces in which they could achieve the heat of about 800 degrees Centigrade needed to drive off the slag and produce iron blooms that could be hammered to produce iron suitable for the making of tools and nails. The actual working of this iron into artefacts required the skills of the blacksmith. At John Fulcher's site at Coddenham village there was a furnace used to smelt iron from the rich ore found in sandstone nodules on the fields, while many large nails had been discarded around the site, suggesting that they were seen as expendable. Smithing of iron was widespread. Evidence for it was found during excavations at Hacheston[84] but these failed to produce certain evidence of iron smelting. Here as elsewhere bronze was being worked, including the casting of finger rings, and a sprue of tin-lead alloy suggests pewter objects were being cast.

Nowhere else in East Anglia had the quantity of natural iron ore available in north-west Norfolk, where there is plenty of evidence of iron smelting using ores from the Greensand Measures north of the River Nar. Tony Gregory pointed out[85] that the series of substantial Roman buildings, the majority of those that can properly be called villas in East Anglia, are sited along the Icknield Way at the edge of the chalk escarpment, notably Park Farm, Snettisham, West Newton, Appleton, Congham, Grimston, Well Hall, Gayton, and Gayton Thorpe. To the east this chalk is covered in the north by boulder clay and to the south by Breckland sands, but the Greensands to the west are dissected by watercourses draining into the Wash. At the head of each valley carved out by these watercourses is one of these villas, whose occupants no doubt exploited the various landscapes suited to mixed farming. Almost certainly they were also ironmasters, deriving significant wealth from the iron industry.

Tony Gregory noted evidence of iron working furnaces at Park Farm, Snettisham, which dominated the Ingol basin, and groups of shaft furnaces have been excavated at Ashwicken near Gayton.[86] John Smallwood identified at least eight shaft furnaces at North Wootton and estimated that evidence of both smelting and smithing iron extended over about five hectares near the church.[87] About fifteen other iron working sites are known in West Norfolk, including Shouldham and Wormegay.[88]

There seems to have been an extensive iron smelting industry in that part of Norfolk, and perhaps skills in using the new metal were perfected there early. An unusual burial at Shouldham from perhaps three centuries before the Roman conquest might be significant as it included a large iron sword with the hilt formed as a remarkable human figure. British swords were longer and heavier than the standard Roman army sword. Iron probably made a significant contribution to Icenian wealth, although John Smallwood thinks it was not large enough to displace agriculture as the main source of income.

David Gurney draws attention to metal moulds for making brooches,

Opposite page: *The "Doctor's Burial" is one of a group of elite burials at Stanway, near Colchester. The "doctor" was probably a Catuvellaunian druid living about the time of the Claudian invasion. In the corner stands a large pottery wine amphora, and to the right of this the "doctor's" surgical instruments are laid on a gaming board with the counters, thirteen blue and thirteen white glass, all in place. In front of this is a bronze saucepan for heating wine, and then the squashed remains of the bronze strainer bowl, perhaps used in preparing a medicinal drink.* © Colchester Archaeological Trust

84 Blagg et al, *Hacheston*, EAA 106 (2004), p.200.
85 Gregory, A., "Romano-British Settlement in West Norfolk and on the Norfolk Fen edge" in Miles, D., *Romano-British Countryside*, BAR103 (1982), pp.351-375.
86 Owles, E. & Tylecote, R.F. "A Second Century Iron Smelting Site at Ashwicken, Norfolk", *Norfolk Archaeology* 32 (1960).
87 at TF640243; J. Smallwood in *Britannia* 20 (1989), p.243.
88 Smallwood, J., "The Archaeology of West Norfolk" in NAHRG Annual 15 (2006), p.10, and see also the map on p.54 of Dymond, D., *The Norfolk Landscape,* London (1985).

——————oOo——————

IRON IN THE FAMILY

The blacksmith turned from his anvil. "We of the Iceni were the first to master the skills of working iron. We traded iron tools for gold and silver before anybody else in Britain. My ancestors became expert at finding the richest lumps of native iron and built furnaces producing mighty heat to separate iron from slag. They released the breath of the dragon when they tapped the furnace. Frightening is the power of the Icenian dragon. Now I heat the iron again on my hearth and hammer it into shape. Give me a hot fire, a tub of cold water, a solid lump of iron and my strong right arm will use this hammer to produce any tool you need. Just pay me in pure silver coin."

——————oOo——————

which were generally made in clay moulds. These two-piece metal moulds are unique to Norfolk. They were made from a distinctive metal and have very large mass to disperse the heat. At Felmingham in Norfolk this type of mould was being used to produce a distinctive type of brooch, known as "the Icenian rear hook" because of the distinctive, but inefficient, use of a hook to retain the spring. These might have been regarded as a particularly Icenian, some would even say Boudican, "badge". Perhaps the metal mould was itself a local invention, as the only other known examples are from Old Buckenham and Brancaster.

If so, we might be seeing the origin of the wealth of Iron Age and Roman West Norfolk in the skilled working of metal, continuing from the very large number of fine bronze objects made in the Bronze Age and the Early Iron Age in East Anglia. So far our only evidence for iron smelting in Icenian territory before the Roman conquest seems to be pieces of slag at Park Farm, Silfield, near Wymondham,[89] but this does not mean it was not happening elsewhere. Perhaps one day the proof will be found.

Beside a late Roman circular building near Thetford a collection of blacksmith's tools had been buried in a pit. This included the fittings for a pump for raising water. Only the iron parts survived, but they matched the wooden double action force pump found at Silchester.[90] These are sophisticated pieces of hydraulic engineering and show that these smiths could produce far more elaborate items than simple tools such as the farming equipment mentioned above.

Imports

The Roman pottery which constitutes an important part of our archaeological evidence includes many imports. There was the fine decorated red tableware of the type we know as Samian which was made in Gaul, modern France, as well as large jars (amphorae) in which wine, olive oil and fish sauce was brought from the continent. Much of the Samian pottery came from the factories in East and South Gaul, which suggests it probably came on ships trading from the Rhine estuary, perhaps forming a return cargo for the vessels that carried East Anglian grain to the Roman garrisons on the Rhine frontier. The continental site at Domburg near Walcheren on the south-west side of the Rhine estuary by the Scheldt was a trading centre with links to England in both the Roman and Anglo-Saxon periods.

Mark Hassall reports the finding of over 150 Roman altars at Domburg and at Colijnsplaat, 25km from Domburg itself,[91] from shrines to the goddess

89 Ashwin, T., "Iron Age Settlement in Norfolk" in Davies, J. & Williamson, T., *Land of the Iceni*, UEA, Norwich, 1999, p.116.
90 Boon, G.C., *Roman Silchester*, London, 1957, p.159-161.
91 Hassall, M., "Britain and the Rhine Provinces: epigraphic evidence for Roman Trade" in *Roman Shipping and Trade ...* CBA Research Report 24, 1978.

An enamelled bronze brooch in the form of a lion, found at Gedding. Many such brooches were worn, showing a variety of animals enhanced by brightly coloured enamel set into the bronze background.
© Suffolk County Council Archaeological Service

Nehalennia, some dedicated by merchants, including four declaring themselves as trading with Britain "negotiator Britannicianus", of whom two were in the pottery trade "cretarius". These altars were set up about AD200 beside the sheltered waters of the Rhine estuary to mark the successful conclusion of trading voyages across the sea. No doubt the traders had paused here on their outward voyage to pray for the protection of this goddess to guide and guard them, promising a new altar if they returned safely.

Millstones might also have been included in return cargoes, as from Roman times until the later Middle Ages the hard volcanic lava from quarries in the Rhine valley at Niedermendig was valued for grinding grain in mills turned by hand or driven by slave, donkey or waterpower. This stone is coloured from grey to black and with its distinctive honeycomb appearance is easily recognised when fragments turn up on fields or are seen incorporated in church walls. It is clear that many households were using these millstones to make flour.

Judith Plouviez points out that some of the enamelled brooches found at Hacheston are continental types, far less common in west Suffolk.[92] That might reflect the easier access for eastern markets to goods brought directly to East Anglia from the Rhine estuary, also seen in the quantity of East Gaulish Samian pottery. The finds made during excavations at Hacheston suggest there was a trading settlement there before the Roman conquest, but it is less clear whether it continued to function after about 370. It may just have received fewer coins and less of the latest style of pottery, as there is some evidence of an early Saxon presence in the area.

Imports of wine in large pottery wine jars or amphorae might have been a significant item as Diodorus Siculus tells us that the Gauls loved wine and drank it unmixed so that they got into a drunken stupor or went mad.[93] Ancient Greek and Roman drinkers always mixed their wine with water, and they disapproved of this northern intemperance. He says Italian traders made good profits transporting wine by river on boats and across level plains on wagons, then selling it at the incredible price of a slave for one jar of wine, so perhaps the British became equally popular customers. We do find that amphorae were imported to the Colchester area before the Roman conquest, and finds across our region show that this wine trade continued and expanded. Fewer amphorae seem to have been used in later years, and it might be that

92 Blagg et al, *Hacheston*, EAA 106 (2004), p.89.
93 Diodorus Siculus, 5. 26.3.

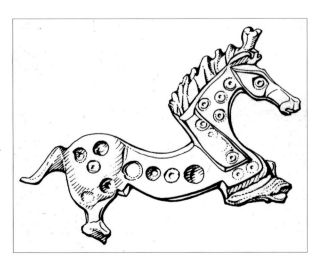

A bronze brooch in the shape of a horse found at Hacheston. It was decorated with inlays of coloured enamels, including some turquoise.
© Suffolk County Council Archaeological Service

Examples of the typical range of Roman coins, using three different metals: a gold aureus of Vespasian, a silver siliqua of Septimius Severus and a bronze sestertius of Domitian.
© Colchester and Ipswich Museum Service

more wine arrived in Britain in wooden barrels. Some of these survive in waterlogged condition because they were used to line wells. From London there is evidence of barrels for 400, 500 and 1,000 litres, so they would tower above men on the boats.

Coins

Coins were in circulation before the Romans arrived, as we saw in the first chapter. In the Roman period we find far more coins, presumably because they were more common and more widely used. In addition to a probable growth in trade we should remember that the Roman soldiers who maintained order were paid in coin sent from the imperial treasury, and many taxes had to be paid in coin. It seems that much of the gold and silver coin from the army pay chests was exchanged for low denomination bronze which could be used in ordinary shopping. Any surplus retained to meet the tax demands had to be changed back into silver and gold so that the precious metals returned to the treasury through the tax collectors, while the bronze stayed in local circulation.

Particularly in the last two centuries of Roman rule, many of these bronze coins were lost, no doubt because people would not search for them among the discarded cabbage leaves and general rubbish on the ground any more than we spend time over the odd penny coin. The fact that some silver, and a very few gold, coins do turn up as casual finds on Roman sites suggests significant local wealth, as people would be more careful to retrieve them and the losses are likely to be a very small proportion of the coins in circulation.

At all levels of society some people stored their reserve cash in a bag, pot or box that could be concealed under the floor or buried in a secret location. When for any reason the owner failed to retrieve his reserve it might stay until a modern archaeologist comes upon the hoard, be it a pot of small change or a box of solid gold coins. In the absence of any equivalent of modern banks this concealment of stored wealth would be normal practice, and we should not assume it was only done at times of perceived danger. We can only speculate in individual cases whether the owner simply died without telling his heir where to find the cash or the entire family was the victim of brigands or of a plague.

Coin finds give us some measure of economic activity. Jude Plouviez has pointed out that a study of all the coins found in Suffolk shows a general correspondence with the typical variations in numbers found in Britain at different periods established by Richard Reece.[94] However, in the second half of the fourth century there is a marked drop in numbers for the south and east of the county. This applies to finds from both town and rural areas, although town sites always produce more coins than any rural sites, and this is especially true of Wenhaston, Hacheston and Pakenham in the first and second centuries. It is particularly noticeable that Hacheston has a very high figure in the 330s when its area seems to expand, but falls remarkably low after that. Perhaps the east of the county was seriously affected by threats of attack from the sea in the later fourth century, or it might have become subordinated to the military authority at Walton Castle and Burgh Castle in a way that destroyed the market economy.

This coin evidence is important because in towns throughout Britain the end of Roman administration often seems to be marked archaeologically by "dark earth" deposits, averaging one to two metres deep, which obscure any structural evidence during the transition from Roman to Saxon periods. Brian Hobley notes that "many other European historic towns have similar deposits, e.g. the early trading centres of Birka and Sigtuna in eastern Sweden and Kaupang in Vestfold (Norway)."[95] In Britain does this result, partly at least, from the apparent later Roman practice of disposing of rubbish in heaps on the surface instead of burying it in pits?[96] Presumably the heaps of rubbish spread out and became mixed with the decaying remains of buildings made from timber, wattle and daub, clay lump and thatch.

Similar waste disposal methods might well have been used in Scandinavia quite independently. In Britain it might be linked to the declining power of the Roman administration. It also seems that the population of towns declined, so presumably there were deserted buildings gradually decaying and offering suitable places for the remaining inhabitants to dispose of their rubbish.

Coins help archaeologists to date sites, but the evidence needs to be handled with care. The one certain fact is that a coin can only have been lost after it was minted, so it offers a secure earliest date. While many coins were quickly returned to the treasury and melted down to produce the latest issues, some remained in circulation for long periods, certainly well over a century. A worn coin is a sign that it was in circulation for a long time, but if coins were put into the owner's reserve soon after they were minted they might return to circulation in good condition at a much later date. It is unwise to rely on any coin having been lost soon after it was minted.

At the end of the Roman period, when no more new coins entered Britain as the army had been withdrawn, we have no idea how long the existing stock of coins remained in active use. The later gold and silver coins generally had a high proportion of precious metal, so their value would be recognised without the need for backing by the imperial authority, and they would no longer be lost through taxation or recalled for conversion to the

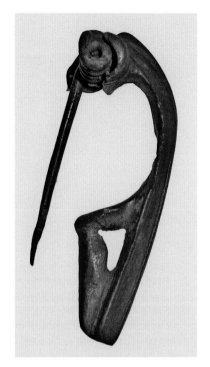

A bronze brooch from Colchester, not unlike a large safety pin as it was designed to fasten clothing. Some were developed with elaborate decoration, but many remained simply functional.
© Trustees of the British Museum

94 Plouviez, J., "A Hole in the Distribution Map" in *Roman Small Towns in Eastern England and Beyond*, ed. A E Brown, Oxbow, 1995.
95 Hobley, B., "The London Waterfront" in *Waterfront Archaeology: Britain and Northern Europe*, CBA Research Report 41, ed Milne & Hobley 1981, p.5.
96 Blagg et al, *Hacheston*, EAA 106 (2004), p.198.

latest issues. The large number of silver coins in the Hoxne hoard that had been clipped shows the continuing use of coins after the end of Roman government and suggests there was high-value economic activity in Suffolk at that time. We shall return to this in chapter seven.

The hoards of coins and valuable gold and silver treasures, as well as the number of individual coins and brooches lost during the Roman period, are evidence of significant wealth in the region. This implies a thriving economy derived, we must assume, mainly from farming, but with contributions from industrial activity including pottery production, salt manufacture and metal working. We lack evidence to tell us how significant were other commercial activities such as fishing, both in rivers and on the open sea, and overseas trade. Nor can we tell how much locally-produced wealth was taken out of the region through taxation.

The reign of the emperor Hadrian (117-138) marked the end of expansion for Rome. His consolidation of the empire within its existing boundaries brought substantial building programmes, but it was the end of the acquisition of new territories. Rome had relied on exploiting newly conquered people as a source of slaves and wealth. Now it had to start living within its resources and rely on the inhabitants of the provinces to pay for expenditure on the citizens at Rome and on the large professional army. The army was vital to defend the frontiers and to maintain order throughout the empire. It is unclear to what extent local produce might have been taken as tax in kind or how far tax payments returned to the region through the purchase of supplies for the army. Either way the demand to supply the military and pay for the

Some of the 117 engraved Roman gems found at Snettisham in Norfolk in 1985. They were all carnelians prepared for use in signet rings. Scrap silver and gold and other items showed they were part of a collection intended for making jewellery but probably buried in the second century.
© Trustees of the British Museum

No doubt local farmers were still transporting their produce, crops and animals along the traditional long-distance route throughout the period of Roman rule. Today this stretch of Cowpasture Lane between Mellis Great Green and the modern electrified railway line has become overgrown, leaving only the footpath. However, at this point the original road is about thirty feet wide between the ditches, and it should be recognised as a significant ancient monument of our transport system, older than the military roads created by the Roman army. Tax gatherers and other officials followed the new roads, but farmers kept the old tracks in use.

central administration of the empire at the behest of the imperial government must have contributed to economic activity.

How the local population regarded the requirement to produce sufficient surplus to meet the taxes is not recorded. References to unrest within the province at various times do not specify the causes, but it seems that not all military interventions were responses to outside invasion and a number of usurpers sought to become emperor with British support. It is notable that when Carausius set himself up as an emperor he did not declare Britain independent. He seems to have tried to set up a better administration in Britain within the Roman Empire but in defiance of the two official emperors.

Britain seems to have behaved differently from other provinces, and perhaps found common cause with those in the Rhine valley as the other western frontier area. East Anglia, being geographically close to the mouth of the Rhine, must have been a significant part of this.

Towns and country houses

4

TACITUS was keen to praise the achievements of his father-in-law Agricola, governor of Britain from AD78 to 84. He describes him encouraging the Britons to construct the buildings of Roman towns such as forums for the markets and administrative offices, temples and proper town houses that would encourage them to live together and develop the arts of peace.[1] The archaeological evidence shows little sign that he had any success in East Anglia. Even the large country houses that were a feature of other parts of southern Britain are lacking.

We might blame a slow start to development on the effects of the Boudican rebellion, but decades or even centuries later there is no sign of any attempt to catch up. Perhaps then, as in more recent times, East Anglia chose to do different. We have seen evidence of a flourishing agricultural and manufacturing economy, but it appears that profits were invested in portable wealth, hence the gold and silver treasures, the collections of coins, the widespread presence of fine pottery and metalwork, but a dearth of large stone buildings.

The towns of Roman Norfolk and Suffolk were not places that a Roman from Italy was likely to consider centres of civilisation. In the whole of East Anglia only Colchester, covering 108 acres (43 hectares) within its walls, shows evidence of being a truly urban centre. *Colonia Victricensis Camuloduni*, the Colony of the Victorious at Colchester, was established as a community of Roman citizens who had retired from the army, so from the start it had a planned grid of streets and a number of public buildings. These included the great Temple of Claudius and the adjoining theatre. Outside the substantial walls was the only circus known in Britain, providing a monumental setting for chariot races. In the second century there were magnificent courtyard houses, each with tessellated floors throughout, high quality mosaics in several rooms and elaborate underfloor heating systems. It remained a proper Roman town.

At some stage late in the second century a massive bank was built inside the town wall to improve the fighting space for soldiers. This might have been motivated by the civil war when the governor Clodius Albinus declared himself emperor in 193 before being defeated near Lyons in France by Septimius Severus. Order was restored by Severus, but the third century was an uneasy time on the continent, with the imperial frontier under frequent attack. Although Britain seems to have avoided the worst upheavals, it would have been sensible to provide strong defences for wealthy towns like Colchester. We cannot tell whether the main fear was of attack from over the sea or internal unrest within the province. The town does seem to have flourished during the third century, but there are signs of a decline in population during the fourth century, with wealth concentrated in a smaller number of large houses.

In the north at Caistor-by-Norwich *Venta Icenorum*, the Market of the Iceni, had a street plan and some public buildings, but it was always relatively small, covering perhaps 28 hectares. Its core was made even smaller when its

1 Tacitus, *Agricola* 21.

Opposite page: *In the Roman kitchen reconstructed at Ipswich Museum the slave is using real Roman pots and other genuine objects are included in the display.* © Colchester and Ipswich Museum Service

2 Myres, J.N.L. & Green, B., *The Anglo-Saxon Cemeteries of Caistor by Norwich and Markshall*, Society of Antiquaries Research Report 30, 1973.
3 The survey by Nottingham University is summarised in *Current Archaeology* 216 (March 2008).

massive walls, 4m thick and 7m tall, were built to enclose 35 acres (14 hectares), probably late in the third century. However, outside the walled town there was a very large walled enclosure of 6.3 acres (2.5 hectares), usually described as a "temple precinct". Its wall was only 2ft 6in (75 cm) thick, built of flint with some chalk blocks, but the report notes "Unusually for a temple site, the finds in no way betray its function", only a Romano-Celtic temple in a prominent but not central position. At some stage occupation extended well beyond the town wall south of this precinct, as the Anglo-Saxon graves of the "Caistor" cemetery were cut through remains of Roman occupation.[2] One of the cremations is in a cist of tiles, and four apparently Anglo-Saxon cremations were in reused second century Roman pots, possibly from a collapsed kiln.

We still know too little about activities outside the security of the walls. The small size of the area enclosed by the walls is comparable to Carmarthen and Caerwent in the west, and geophysical survey suggests that even then it was not densely occupied. Perhaps it was a base for control over the Iceni by the central administration rather than a truly Icenian place. It did have in a central position the standard forum and basilica complex, presumably providing market space and offices. There were temples, and a geophysical survey[3] appears to show a theatre opposite two temples. However, large areas

Peter Froste's painting of the circus at Colchester, based on a number of excavations on the site of the modern garrison buildings in Colchester. The Roman town is seen in the background.
© Colchester Archaeological Trust

of apparently open space may simply reflect a failure to locate timber buildings based on sleeper beams. Only excavation will tell us the answer. The survey showed up a number of circular structures that suggest there was a large Icenian settlement of round houses here before the Roman town was laid out. It also seems to show at least one post-Roman enclosure cutting across a street, suggesting there was continuous occupation related to the large Saxon cemeteries outside the town, although early Saxon enclosures are unusual.

From all we can see, the towns of Suffolk and the rest of Norfolk lacked formal planning and large public buildings. They appear to have grown up as market centres and their distribution is not very different from that of the area's more recent market towns. A farmer could walk or ride to market and back in the day with plenty of time to complete his business in the town. Presumably these towns also served as the focus for contact with the imperial government for administrative, legal and taxation purposes.

Most of those writing about the Roman administration of Britain base their accounts on what happened elsewhere in the empire or on what they would like to think happened here, but we have little specific evidence. We do know that Britain was under a very senior Roman politician who governed it on behalf of the emperor and in strict accordance with his instructions.

Later Britain was divided into two provinces, when East Anglia was

A pottery jar decorated with a racing chariot, found at Colchester. Perhaps it was purchased as a souvenir after watching races in the circus.
© Trustees of the British Museum

NO GREAT CITY

"Marcus, what is this place? Its walls are massive enough to protect a city, but inside there is only space for a few buildings. Its river is only just wide enough for our ship to reach the quay." "Venta Icenorum, my lord, market place of the Iceni. After that ungrateful people rebelled against our imperial authority, we allowed them to restore their farms and produce food for our soldiers. We laid out a small town for them, but then found we had to enclose it with these walls to guard our administrators and the stocks of food." "Does it have the proper public buildings?" "Do not be surprised that its market place and offices are small, but it does have adequate temples and a theatre so the gods are honoured. Most people live in the countryside on their farms. The nearest true town is the Colony of Victory at Camulodunum, but it is many miles by road and a rough voyage round the coast by water." "Find me a carriage and we will ride directly to the great house on the estate known as Villa Faustini. It is the next place in our guidebook."

almost certainly in "Upper Britain" based on London. After AD312 Britannia became a Diocese of four, later five, provinces in which East Anglia was probably part of the province of Maxima Caesariensis under a provincial, and above him a diocesan, governor, both presumably based in London. It has been suggested that the Icenian territory might have been placed in Flavia Caesariensis, administered from Lincoln, based on the unproven assumption that all former Icenian lands were kept as a unit based on Venta Icenorum. There must be a possibility that lands around the Wash west of Peddars Way were part of a separate unit centred perhaps on Stonea in the Fens or on Water Newton near Peterborough, which might logically belong to Lincoln, while the eastern unit remained attached to London.

The truth is that we have no evidence about the organisation of these communities. Certainly some local administration was delegated to local councils based in larger towns. The members were probably chosen from the wealthiest local citizens, who would be mostly, if not exclusively, great landowners. This was standard Roman practice, and we should note that these councils only had powers delegated by the governor. It should in no way be seen as some sort of local democracy, a concept as alien to Roman imperial authority as it is to its nearest modern successor, the Roman Catholic Church. Obedience to the authority of Rome was paramount.

The local council responsible for the southern part of Suffolk was presumably the colonial council of Colchester, where we know the citizen body was regulated by a formal census, as we have the tombstone of the Italian politician Gnaeus Bassus, who was one of its census officers.[4] In the early days of the empire the status of its senior inhabitants as retired soldiers with full citizen rights would have given them greater rights than neighbouring communities, but this distinction became less important as time passed, although the title of *colonia* always carried prestige. Most likely a significant number of its residents and landowners were always either descendants of the original colonists or later retired soldiers, who were not British by birth. It will clearly have had a distinctive Roman feel, in contrast to the native British communities in the region.

Northern Suffolk and Norfolk were presumably part of the community of the Iceni centred on Venta Icenorum, although we have no records about its administrative history or its boundaries, and even its integrity as a unit is uncertain. It is particularly frustrating that when the Notitia Dignitatum lists officials in fourth-century Britain and includes the manager of a woollen mill (procurator gynaeci) in Britain at Venta it fails to say whether this was our Venta Icenorum or Winchester (Venta Belgarum). Positive evidence for such an imperial official in our region would be extremely interesting in view of the importance of our cloth trade in the Middle Ages.

A Roman speaking Latin would not have thought any town in Suffolk or in Norfolk apart from Caistor merited the title of *oppidum*, town, but would almost certainly have used the humbler name *vicus*. Archaeologists have attached this term to the civil settlements beside forts, but in Latin it just refers to a small community, perhaps nearest in meaning to the modern use of village as being larger than a farmstead or hamlet. As the *v* in Latin was pronounced like English *w*, this term is presumably preserved in the Wickham place names which are generally found in parishes neighbouring these towns, meaning the Anglo-Saxon *ham* beside the Romano-British *vicus*. For

Taken in very dry weather, this air photograph of Caistor-by-Norwich (Venta Icenorum) shows up the street grid of the Roman town as white lines. The church of St Edmund stands in the bottom left-hand corner of the walled enclosure (near the light strip), and the river Tas is visible near the top of the photo.
© Cambridge University

convenience we will refer to them as market towns.

The evidence suggests a series of small towns, without formal plans or public buildings, providing market centres and manufacturing enterprises to support members of the rural communities, of whom the vast majority lived on scattered farms. Access to rivers, seaways and roads made the towns valuable links between the farmers, manufacturers, fishermen and other producers and the wider world. No doubt they also served the local tax collectors as bases of operation and were points of contact with the Roman officials supervising taxation and legal procedures, as well as for the soldiers who maintained order in the name of the emperor. We do not have enough evidence to be confident about the size of these market towns, but it might be reasonable to suggest an average area in the region of 50 acres and a population of between 2,000 and 4,000.

So far we do not know how many of these Roman market towns grew from existing pre-Roman market centres, or even how far market trading had developed in our region before the conquest. At Hacheston Judith Plouviez detected signs of a pre-Roman settlement with small ditches and palisades enclosing circular buildings,[5] while finds included twenty-two Iron Age coins and a number of early brooches, with early local and imported pottery. She sees signs of similar activity at Long Melford and Coddenham, so it is likely that some at least of our towns existed before the conquest. By contrast the

4 CIL XIV, 3955 from Nomentum in Italy, his home town.
5 Blagg et al, *Hacheston*, EAA 106 (2004).

6 see Norman Scarfe in *Historical Atlas of Suffolk*, 3rd ed. Suffolk County Council, 1999, p.77.

town at Pakenham developed over the site of an early Roman fort, although we do not know whether that was placed near an existing settlement.

It remains to be determined whether in the early years of occupation the Romans placed their garrisons in open countryside on "green field" sites or close to existing settlements that could supply their local needs. At present we cannot tell how far this pattern of market towns was a creation of the Roman period or an existing feature of our topography. If we accept the view that the population of Roman Britain at its height was near six million, it comes close to the estimate for the high Middle Ages before the devastating effect of the Black Death. It is notable that the number of market centres is much fewer than the medieval ones.[6] Were there really fewer of them, or have we more to find?

The remains of the Roman stone walls enclosing the site of the town of Venta Icenorum can be seen in this view looking over the site from the south-west. The medieval church of St Edmund stands in one corner.

We can only recognise the market towns from the spread of finds identified during field walking and metal detecting. Small concentrations of finds can be assumed to mark farmsteads, while dense finds of pottery and metalwork over an extensive area of intensive occupation suggest a commercial centre, particularly when supported by the presence of significant numbers of coins. These tend to be much less common on farm sites and even

in villas, except where groups of coins have been deliberately concealed for safe keeping.

The towns are generally placed on the main roads, so probably somewhere beside the road there would be a mansio or guest house complex. The purpose of this was to provide facilities for weary travellers, and in particular for officials using the Imperial Post, which provided the link for the military and administrative bodies controlling the outlying areas of the Empire. Tired horses were changed for fresh mounts at the mansio and the traveller, whether soldier or civilian, might have enjoyed a visit to the existing local market centre. They had many similarities to the present-day system of Travel Lodges that are linked with modern motorways, as they made it possible to wine, dine and relax in the bath house. Here the latest gossip from Rome could be discussed, and after an overnight stay the refreshed travellers could continue their journey. However, in the absence of specific archaeological evidence so far this can only be a matter of speculation. It has been suggested that some of the small towns, including Cambridge, started as mansios. Initial construction of roads was carried out by the army and the finds of equipment, such as a military entrenching tool found at Stoke Ash, are likely to have been items lost by soldiers engaged in this work or who were marching along the roads.

The largest of the towns in Suffolk was probably the one that developed across the site of two forts at Coddenham. The name of this site can be misleading, as it is some distance from the modern village which is tucked away in a side valley. The Roman forts are on the extreme edge of the parish beside Baylham House and close to Baylham Mill. The core of the town seems to overlie two early forts revealed on air photographs. They are on a terrace just above the flood plain of the River Gipping. This was once known as the River Orwell all the way from Rattlesden to the sea. The river is substantial at this point and would certainly have been navigable for moderate-sized boats, as it was turned into a navigation for barges from Stowmarket to Ipswich in the eighteenth century.

The main roads heading north from Colchester and east from Long Melford crossed the river here, and most of the south to north road is known as it headed towards Caistor-by-Norwich. This was a major road junction, with other roads radiating to the east towards Hacheston, past the ditched enclosure at Burgh by Grundisburgh, and directly towards Kelsale, as well as that running west. There might also have been a road north-west up the valley to Pakenham, but no trace has yet been found (see chapter two). This convergence of routes by road and river presumably justified its Roman name of Combretovium, the Confluence, which appears on the Antonine Itinerary and the Peutinger Table.

There is evidence of a pre-Conquest settlement here before the forts were built, as first-century hut circles and numerous first-century coins and brooches have been found well away from the actual forts. The sixty-eight Iron Age coins are almost equally divided between Icenian and Trinovantian issues. This is not surprising if Combretovium was already a trading centre on the river fairly close to the boundary between these two major groups, and perhaps other lesser groups, if Burgh by Grundisburgh was the focus for one. The Romans probably sited their fort here to keep an eye on this meeting point for traders at the river crossing, which would itself be a matter of concern for the military planners. It must have been a focal point for the region throughout the Roman period.

At Combretovium a flint wall foundation was recorded in the 1820s and a sketch seems to show two small rectangular rooms with a hypocaust.[7] Some cremation burials were also found, including one accompanied by a bronze mirror showing Nero addressing his troops (see chapter one), perhaps associated with the garrison of one of the forts. The fine "Barking" statuette of Nero was found nearby and might also have come from the fort.

Stanley West carried out a small excavation across the road north of the forts in the 1950s.[8] Excavation in 1973 in advance of the building of a new main road some distance to the east of the forts revealed features ranging from circular buildings of the late Iron Age to rectangular timber buildings of the second to third centuries, as well as pottery kilns, cremation burials and an early well. More recent metal detector finds show that occupation spread a considerable distance on the east into the grounds of Shrubland Park. Finds suggest there was less activity in the fourth century, but there are significant pottery and metal objects from the Early Saxon period. There was an Early Saxon hall building associated with some fine gold items tucked back in the valley below Coddenham village beside the original road leading directly to the church,[9] with a cemetery on top of the hill overlooking it. Presumably this focal point retained its significance until it was overtaken by the expansion of Ipswich further down the river. Surprisingly little is known about what was probably the largest Roman town in Suffolk. On the other hand there is increasing evidence of activity down the river in the area of modern Ipswich, and we will return to that.

Further up the A140 at the Stonhams Hamlet Watling, who became the schoolmaster at Earl Stonham in 1855, reported finding large amounts of Roman material in the valley between Little Stonham Hall and Earl Stonham Rectory, but this has yet to be confirmed by modern investigators. However, it led to his interest in the Roman road and other likely sites on it.[10] J. Raven records one early find of Roman material: "My friend and correspondent, Mr. H. Watling, of Ipswich, thus writes to me about Stoke Ash, after treating of Baylham, Coddenham, Crowfield, and Stonham, all abounding in fictile and other remains: 'Stoke Ash is decidedly the most important place, and the finest description of pottery is found here…just below the White Horse Inn on the same side…It is a curious fact that the opposite side was devoted to burial purposes. Some vessels containing calcined bones were inverted on a square tile'.[11]

The Rev C.E. Searle, who was curate of Earl Stonham from 1864 to 1870 before becoming Master of Pembroke College at Cambridge, wrote to the editor of the Quarterly Journal of the Suffolk Institute of Archaeology:[12] "I venture to send you notice of a small 'find' of Roman remains at Stoke Ash, in this county, which I acquired in October last. The Stonham postman observing some labourers digging gravel in a field by the side of the high road leading from Ipswich to Norwich, saw them toss out several fragments of strange-looking pottery, which he brought to me. They consisted of the ordinary kinds of pottery usually found in Roman sites – brown, blue and grey: the most interesting were the samian, of which there were portions of several vessels – one, a hunting scene, with potter's mark (Albuci), is very

7 Plouviez, J., "A Hole in the Distribution Map" in Brown, A.E., *Roman Small Towns*, 1995, p.78.
8 West, S.E., "A Roman road at Baylham, Coddenham", *Antiquaries Journal* vol.35 (1956), pp.73-5.
9 map SROI: HD1467/1 (Pennington 1773).
10 For more information see Plunkett, S.J., "Hamlet Watling, Artist and Schoolmaster 1818-1908", PSIAH vol.39 (1997), p.48.
11 Raven, J., *History of Suffolk*, 1895, p.25.
12 published June 1869, p.43.

spirited. The rim of the light brown vessel, too, is singularly elegant, and the handle of the amphora is interesting for the name Ennius Julianus (abbreviated). I went myself to identify the spot, but unfortunately the pit was filled; but, from numerous fragments scattered over the surface, I judged that the men were right when they said that they had buried a considerable quantity. From them I obtained five 'old halfpennies', which were found with the pottery; these were second brass coins of Domitian, Hadrian, Antoninus in bad preservation, and third brass coins of Tetricus the Younger and Salonina – very good and legible. I picked up a flint arrow head, and have another curious chipping from the same place, which was probably a knife. The whole field looked very inviting for excavation, and I heard that old pots were frequently turned up in an adjacent field."

Both modern and nineteenth-century finds of large pieces of Roman pottery with no signs of later abrasion in the area near the River Dove crossing at Stoke Ash reinforce the view that this was the site of a substantial settlement that we can call a market town. The presence of a considerable amount of Iron Age material not far away in Thornham suggests the commercial centre may have had a predecessor in this area before the Roman

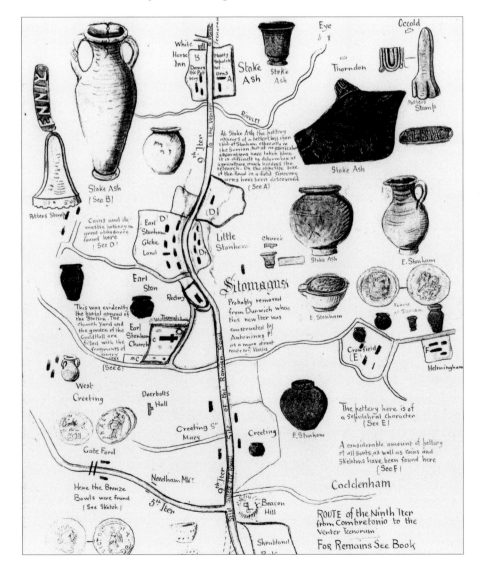

Hamlet Watling's map of the Roman road between Coddenham and Stoke Ash, treating Stonham as Sitomagus.

13 Gurney, D., *Settlement, Religion and Industry on the Roman Fen-edge, Norfolk*, EAA 31, p.64ff.

conquest. More recently at Stoke Ash fine pottery, metalwork and coins have been found in the area of the settlement. Systematic field walking reveals a concentration of evidence that shows this was a small town extending for about a mile north to south along the road. It stretched from north of the White Horse crossroads to south of Stoke Ash church, where finds in the 1960s led to the naming of a road as Roman Way. More surprisingly it covered at least three quarters of a mile east to west, in the area between the Dove and the road west from the White Horse crossroads, probably the original route to Pakenham. This area is large enough to suggest that in the Roman period the town was a major market centre for the surrounding farms. Finds include two brooches of a distinctive type based on a coin of Hadrian showing cavalry soldiers and three infantrymen above an eagle, sometimes called the "adlocutio" type. Seven brooches of this type found at Hockwold have been claimed as evidence for a religious site, so perhaps there was a temple near the river.[13]

A small excavation by Mike Hardy near the point where the main road crossed the river in Stoke Ash has revealed two distinct periods of activity separated by a level surface of clay that might be the floor of a building or a flood deposit. The first period belongs to the early phase of Roman activity as it contains large pieces of pots that were made before the middle of the

second century, early brooches and first-century coins, including one of the emperor Vespasian.

The upper level showed continuing activity late into the Roman period, which is confirmed by the presence of a late coin. Evidence of meat preparation was provided by many animal bones, including cow, pig, horse and sheep as well as dog and a small bird. A significant number of bones showed cut marks typical of butchering, and some had been split open to extract the marrow. The presence of many fragments of very rough pottery of the type probably used to hold salt suggest that meat was being salted to preserve it.

One unusual find from the area of the town is a complete enamelled seal box. Complete boxes are quite a rarity but their significance is unclear. Judith Plouviez has recorded forty-nine seal boxes from twenty-four sites in Suffolk, but cannot identify any common feature of these sites. Presumably this shows that formal documents were being handled in this area. Seal boxes were used to protect the wax seal bearing the impression of the seal ring worn by the sender of a message, which covered the knot fastening together the two leaves of a writing tablet in which the message was written in wax panels inside the wooden frame. They were used to preserve the privacy of commercial or official messages while in transit and remind us of the importance and ubiquity of written documents throughout the Roman world. Finds from Vindolanda on Hadrian's Wall have revealed that ordinary messages were often written in ink on thin wooden tablets which might contain routine daily ration returns for soldiers or a communication between mother and son about new socks and undergarments. These are an unusual survival preserved by waterlogged conditions; such ephemera usually disappeared as completely as the average modern memo or personal letter. In East Anglia only the metal seal boxes survive.

Jean Bagnell Smith, in her study of votive finds from Great Walsingham,[14] suggests that the presence of over twenty seal boxes among the finds from this presumed shrine is evidence of their use to keep communications between a suppliant and the god private. If suppliants making requests to the god wrote their pleas, together with the vows to

14 Bagnall Smith, J., *Britannia* 30 (1999) p.21.

Left: *The enamelled lid of a seal box found at Stoke Ash. The bronze box protected the wax seal that prevented anybody tampering with the message on the inside faces of a set of writing tablets bound together.*

Right: *The back of the seal box, showing the holes through which the securing string was threaded.*

15 Rogerson, A., "Excavations at Scole 1973", *Norfolk*, EAA 5, 1977, and *Current Archaeology* 140.
16 these timbers have been preserved and put on display at Ipswich Museum.
17 Frere, S., "A Claudian site at Needham, Norfolk", *Antiquaries Journal* vol.21 (1941), pp.40-55.
18 *A mortarium kiln at Ellingham*, EAA Occasional Paper 2 (1997), p.1.
19 David Gurney in *Roman Small Towns*, ed. Brown, A.E., Oxbow, 1995, p.56.

Above; *Lifting part of a large millstone found next to a Roman wooden structure at Stuston near Scole.*
© Suffolk County Council Archaeological Service

Below: *The wattle lining of a Roman well at Scole.*
© Suffolk County Council Archaeological Service

perform a service to the god if their requests were granted (*nuncupatio*), on pairs of wax tablets these could be secured with a seal protected in a seal box. The contents would be known only to the god and need not be revealed until the god granted the favour and the suppliant performed the promised vow (*solutio*). This additional use of seal boxes might explain their presence at some other locations.

At Stoke Ash the quantity of pottery, the scatter of metalwork and the complex series of apparently early tracks that focus on this one location suggest that it was a marketing and administrative centre. It probably lay at or near the southern boundary of the Icenian territory on the fringe of Trinovantian lands. Lack of alternative evidence suggests that the buildings of this extensive settlement all had roofs of thatch or other organic material, rather than the tiled roofs of tegula and imbrex type that we associate with really Romanised structures.

The settlement at Stoke Ash appears to have been larger than that at Scole and extended significantly further along the edge of the river. At Scole itself, where the road crossed the River Waveney, several sites have been excavated and the evidence suggests commercial and industrial occupation directly beside the roads. Scole was certainly the site of a small commercial settlement with industrial premises located near the point where the main road crossed the river and side roads ran east to west both north and south of the river.[15] A probable wharf for small barges has been identified to the west of the town and the river must have contributed to its role as a market centre. There was an area of iron working and smithing and evidence of furniture manufacture, including fragments of legs, perhaps those of a couch, that had been turned on a lathe. There was also a tannery, and large quantities of worked leather, well preserved because of the waterlogged conditions, were found in one of seven wells neatly lined with planks. These leather fragments included parts of shoes of different sizes; the soles of some were heavily studded, showing the standard Roman practice of protecting the leather soles of outdoor footwear by inserting rows of metal studs.

An artificial water channel led to timber structures which incorporated large reused roof timbers from an earlier Roman building,[16] apparently part of a malting and brewing complex. Wooden tanks had been used to steep the grain and a large oven was presumably the malt kiln. A temple on the east side of the town was notable for having a tiled roof, while other buildings were presumably thatched as no evidence of roofing survived.

Further down the Waveney there is evidence of towns on the north bank at Needham, near Harleston, and Ditchingham, near Bungay, both approached by Roman roads from the south. Needham appears to have had a mint before the conquest, but its later status is unclear.[17] In Ditchingham the crossing at Wainford is marked by a substantial settlement, involving pottery making, not far from the mortarium kiln at Ellingham.[18] From Ditchingham a road led north directly to Brampton, near Aylsham.[19]

Brampton had a defensive ditch, but no wall, enclosing six hectares of a settlement area of perhaps 75 acres (30 hectares). It is at a crossroads where the major road to the Fen Causeway and Peterborough crosses the River Bure and also crosses a road going north. We have already mentioned its industrial suburb producing pottery. Inside the defences only one masonry building, a bath house, has been found so far, but timber workshops contained evidence of bronze and iron working. The discovery of a number of figurines makes it likely there was at least one temple, which is not surprising. Out of more than eleven hundred coins there is a peak in AD259-75. Brampton church is remote from the present village and known Roman site, but it has Roman-looking tiles and stones in the north-west corner of the nave which might have been recycled from the town.

Presumably Brampton was the market centre for north-east Norfolk, an area of rich arable farming land. The Bure is still a substantial river at this point and was probably navigable in the Roman period. The main Roman road can be traced eastwards to Smallburgh and may have headed for the coast or turned south to the Saxon Shore fort at Caister-on-Sea. The road going westward crossed the River Wensum at Billingford, close to the spot in Worthing where a Roman parade helmet was found in the river in 1947. Whether it was dropped accidentally or deliberately deposited in the water we shall never know. There was an early Roman fort slightly downstream at Swanton Morley, presumably to monitor the river crossing. The settlement at Billingford extended east of the river on both sides of the road, judging from finds from metal detecting and field walking, which include about fifteen hundred coins. In surprising contrast to the find at Brampton only a tiny proportion belong to the period AD259-275, which suggests the Billingford

Excavating the waterlogged Roman timbers of an industrial structure at Stuston, near Scole. Some of the timbers proved to have been recycled from the frame of a hipped roof. The wood survived because it had never dried out.
© Suffolk County Council Archaeological Service

20 "Antiquities of Suffolk" in *Suffolk Chronicle* of 1888 or before.
21 Newman, J., PSIAH vol.37 (1992), p.389.

settlement might have been less urban at that time, although one is left to wonder why this difference. As the other finds are mostly personal items rather than household utensils, perhaps the permanent population was relatively small, being swelled by those attending markets or fairs.

Going south from Ditchingham the straight Stone Street section (Margary 36) of the Bungay to Halesworth road leads to Holton, where the Roman route must have changed direction to use the crossing over the River Blyth at Mells. Then it picked up Wenhaston Street on the way to the Roman site on the Blackheath side of the village. The Blyford Bridge crossing could be part of an older "linear" north-to-south long-distance route.

At Wenhaston a large area of settlement overlooking the River Blyth from Blackheath has been identified by field walking and metal detecting. However, there has not been any excavation and there is no evidence for the layout of buildings or of a road system. The finds range from late Iron Age through Roman to Early Saxon, so the town might have had a long life. The size of site and the quantity and range of finds are very different from any other known Roman site in the north-east quadrant of Suffolk and are comparable to Hacheston, so perhaps it was another market centre. The core of the medieval village overlaps the Roman site, which extends beyond it south-east along the river. To the north Hamlet Watling recorded the finding of a bronze statue of Venus near Blyford Bridge.[20] He described it as a nude figure about six inches high, holding a dove. Perhaps there was a shrine beside the traditional river crossing. Gilbert Burroughes has noted on an air photograph features immediately north-east of the point where the modern road from Blythburgh to Wenhaston crosses a tributary stream close to the river Blyth itself which might be quays or docks for small river craft. This might provide evidence of the Roman use of this waterway, which operated as a navigation to Halesworth in more recent times.

Crossing this tributary, the Roman road southwards was adopted as the old line of the A12, which has been diverted to create Thorington Park. John Newman found Iron Age and Roman pottery, with a possible second or third-century pottery kiln, in modern quarry workings adjacent to the line of this old east coast main road.[21] John notes a dog leg in the old road which might be avoiding existing Iron Age activity. The next section of the road, probably the route to Kelsale East Green and Hacheston, survives as the Darsham Straight of the current A12.

In that area there has been much debate about the location of the place named as Sitomagus in the Antonine Itinerary or Sinomagus in the Peutinger Table. Dunwich has been suggested, but it appears to be too far from Combretovium. If it was a coastal site it would have been destroyed by the sea long ago, and there is no convincing evidence of a town in the surviving area. Neither Wenhaston nor Hacheston fits the distances in the documents. The distances in the Peutinger Table can be brought close to those of the Antonine Itinerary if we accept the argument that Peutinger's *Ad Taum* results from the edge of the map being torn so as to leave only Ad Taum from *Ad Venta Icenorum*. If we add an X to the start of both figures we get XXXII from Venta (same as Antonine) and XXV to Combretovium (Antonine XXII), which suggests a location near Saxmundham. A site at Knodishall has been suggested because it has produced a great deal of Roman building material, but this seems more typical of a large villa complex than a town. Recently

The "Darsham Straight" on the A12 north of the railway crossing at Darsham station is part of the Roman road from Hacheston to Wenhaston. The Roman route preserved this alignment through Thorington Park direct to Wenhaston.

Rob Steerwood has found significant spreads of material at Kelsale East Green, which would suit the distances and could be on the line of the possible road from Hacheston to Wenhaston and on the extended line of Margary 35 projected beyond Peasenhall.[22]

The site at East Green needs further exploration to determine whether the settlement really is extensive enough to merit inclusion in the Itinerary and the Peutinger Table and to locate the missing road links. It lacks a good waterway, but it would not have needed a long journey to reach the river Fromus at Kelsale or the Hundred River flowing into the sea at Thorpeness. Neither is a large river, but they might then have accommodated small boats capable of moving cargoes to and from the coast. Rob Steerwood has noted a number of trackways in the area that might well be of pre-Roman origin.

There was probably a route on the line of the modern road through Saxmundham and Friday Street to Stratford St Andrew, where it crossed the River Alde. The modern A12 has been diverted around Glemham Park, but retains the likely line at Little Glemham through Marlesford to Hacheston Five Ways. Here on the edge of Wickham Market the Roman town lies beside the river Deben, which was probably navigable by small vessels to this point, giving access from the sea at Felixstowe after a journey of some eighteen miles. It was also only a mile from the river Ore, which takes a more northerly course to Snape and Aldeburgh. Much of the direct road from Coddenham (Margary 340) remains in use, passing close to the Iron Age enclosure at Burgh by Grundisburgh.

At Hacheston excavation revealed some circular buildings and sufficient early coins, brooches and pottery to suggest pre-Conquest occupation.[23] There were twenty-two Iron Age coins equally divided between Icenian and Trinovantian issues, as was the case at Coddenham. In the Roman period there

22 Steerwood, R., "A Context for Sitomagus" PSIAH vol.40 (2003) 253-61.
23 Blagg et al., *Excavations at a large Romano-British Settlement at Hacheston, Suffolk, 1973-74*, EAA 106 (2004).

were rectangular timber buildings, probably based on sill beams, with thatched or wooden shingle roofs as there was little brick or tile, although the presence of some suggests they must have been in use somewhere in the town. In the excavated area there was one substantial timber building about 6m by 8m which stood from the mid second century to the early fourth, and a number of smaller buildings, probably shops without solid frames. There was no evidence of a planned layout, although some buildings fronted on a metalled road.

Trading is confirmed by the number and variety of objects found, and particularly by the large numbers of coins. More than 3,000 coins were recovered, mostly from metal detecting rather than excavation, and 2,372 could be identified and dated. They showed flourishing activity from the second until the middle of the fourth century. There were very high numbers for the period 330-348, remarkable even for what was the most prolific time for Roman coins. However, there is only a tiny number for the years after 364, which is also true of Wenhaston and of many rural sites in south-east Suffolk. There was a dramatic decline in the loss of the later coins, in marked contrast to the evidence from the west of Suffolk. Either this area did not receive new supplies of small change and went on using the many older coins (after all a number of our Victorian pennies were in circulation for over a hundred years) or trading declined dramatically.

Other evidence for what was really happening may have been obscured by a change in methods of waste disposal. In the early days most rubbish was buried in pits, but in the later third or early fourth century people apparently started making heaps of rubbish on the surface which were carted away to form manure heaps to be spread on ground that was then ploughed. Some of this seems to have involved cultivating areas that were previously used for housing or were extremely close to standing buildings. After repeated ploughing the archaeologist is left with an area of dark earth, rich in decayed vegetable matter, containing a mixture of objects from different periods without any recognisable features.

During the Roman period there was a local pottery industry at Hacheston, as eight kilns have been identified, showing production from the first to the third century, although apparently not in the fourth. They were making fairly basic grey cooking and storage pots, mixing bowls (mortaria) and drinking beakers. There was a significant amount of iron working, showing that blacksmiths were producing the large numbers of iron tools needed for farming and for manufacturing activities as well as quantities of iron nails. An iron spearhead found among the charcoal waste from a hearth was probably intended for hunting deer. There was also some bronze working, as waste from casting was found, as well as the pattern for making finger rings. One piece of waste looks like material from casting pewter, perhaps for spoons.

It seems to have been a small but busy working town. There was some Early Saxon activity there, as one sunken-featured building was found in the town and another two were excavated close to a Roman cremation cemetery on the edge of the town at Gallows Hill. A distinct Anglo-Saxon settlement on the edge of the town might mean that British people were still living in the town before the communities merged and in due course developed the present site of Wickham Market. Perhaps they were in a similar relationship to that between early Saxon West Stow and Roman Icklingham. Roman pottery in the sunken-featured buildings suggests the new residents were happy to use Roman pottery, of which there must still have been plenty about, as well as their own distinctive pots.

Turning to the south-western part of Suffolk, at Long Melford the Roman town was on the east side of the River Stour. Presumably the river was navigable to that point, as it is not far upstream from Sudbury which was reached in the eighteenth and nineteenth centuries by barges carrying thirteen tons each on the Navigation. It has been suggested that earthworks in Cutter's Field down Liston Lane are the remains of Roman docks. The town seems to have spread along the northbound road from Chelmsford to Pakenham (Margary 33a) and seems to have been the destination of the westbound road from Coddenham (Margary 34a). The number of finds of Iron Age material suggests there was a settlement before the Roman conquest. Because the early Roman material includes imported Lyon Ware and a large iron sword of the *spatha* type carried by cavalrymen there might have been a fort there, but none has been located. The Roman town extended under the southern part of the medieval settlement, and some idea of its extent was revealed during the laying of sewers in the 1950s.[24] In one substantial building on Liston Lane, west of the modern village, a black and white tessellated floor round a red tile was interpreted as a bath. North of this there appears to have been a cemetery. Another group of burials, including one in a coffin of Northamptonshire limestone within which the body was encased in a plaster-like material, were probably of fourth century date.[25] They had been cut through pits and ditches containing earlier Roman domestic rubbish, including painted plaster, roof

24 Smedley, N., "Roman Long Melford", PSIAH vol.28 (1961), pp.272-89.
25 Boulter, S., in "Archaeology in Suffolk 1997", PSIAH vol.39 (1998), pp.236-9.

This fine blue glass bowl, found in a burial at Long Melford, is indicative of the fine quality of some Roman glass.
© Colchester and Ipswich Museum Service

tiles and fine pottery, suggesting wealthy residents. Presumably they had abandoned this area before the burials were made, so after being occupied from the middle of the first century this particular part of the town went out of use and became available for burials. More recently isolated inhumation burials, dated to the late second and early third centuries, have been found both east and west of Little St Mary's.

Perhaps the town was shrinking by the fourth century, but we cannot be sure what was happening in other parts. At least somebody could afford a coffin of Barnack stone so, as we find further north on the edge of the Fens, there was wealth in the area. Excavation south-east of the village in Chapel Field revealed a substantial Roman road which might be a branch from the main Chelmsford to Pakenham road, if that ran on the present line of the main street.[26] There was evidence of settlement in this area including a fine blue glass bowl, now in Ipswich Museum.

Further up the Stour valley finds suggest that there was a town at Wixoe, but this site needs further investigation. Air photographs have shown foundations in one corner of the settlement for a building with at least five or six rooms. This was confirmed by finds of flint and mortar foundations as well as wall plaster and tesserae collected from the surface.[27] Writing in Archaeologia in 1803, Walford reports finds in a ditched enclosure near Watsoe Bridge on the boundary between Steeple Bumpstead and Birdbrook, on the Essex side of the Stour, with a cemetery in a field called Stulps.[28] He also records the finding of many coins on the Suffolk side in Ensford Field, Wixoe (the modern OS map marks an Ains Ford), and a coin hoard, including a gold issue of Honorius, in Ford Meadow, Sturmer. Two inhumation cemeteries and part of a large building were reported in the 1950s.[29] Finds in the area included roof and flue tiles, tesserae, wall plaster, glass, oyster shells, samian pottery and coins of the first and second centuries. Iron waste and slag suggested some industrial activity.

Pakenham is on the south side of the river Black Bourn facing Ixworth, at the point where the Roman road from Long Melford crossed the river. There does not seem to have been a settlement before the Roman conquest, and the market town developed across the site of a Roman fort that seems to have been occupied for only a short time.[30] During excavation in 1985 Judith Plouviez found evidence of rapid development of the new town, divided into regular plots and provided with a number of roads on solid aggers, which suggests official planning of the layout (a feature lacking at Hacheston in the east).[31] In the later first and second centuries much rubbish was being buried in pits associated with timber-framed buildings. In one area pottery kilns were operating in the later second and third centuries, producing fine wares including decorated drinking vessels. There was debris from bronze and iron working. Coin finds show continuous occupation to the end of the fourth century, but there was no sign of Anglo-Saxon activity in the excavated area.

This seems to have been an exclusively Roman town. It is notable that the large villa complex at Stanton Chare is only three miles to the north, the Ixworth villa is only just across the river and Redcastle Farm is only a mile and a half to the west. All of these have shown evidence of Early Anglo-Saxon activity, as has Grimstone End at the south-east edge of the site, which was used for burials and pottery kilns in Roman times but was

26 Avent, A. & Howlett, T., "Excavations in Roman Long Melford 1970-1972", PSIAH vol.34 (1980), pp.229-49.
27 St. Joseph, "Air Reconnaissance in Roman Britain 1973-76", *Journal of Roman Studies*, vol.67 (1977), p.159.
28 *Archaeologia* 14 (1803), pp.61-74.
29 PSIAH vol.27, "Archaeology in Suffolk 1954/5".
30 Plouviez , J., "A Hole in the Distribution Map" in Brown, A.E., *"Roman Small Towns"*, 1995, p.79.
31 PSIAH vol.36 (1986), "Archaeology in Suffolk 1985", pp.153-4, also EAA 106, p.198.

used for the manufacture of textiles in the sixth century.[32] It looks as if only the town centre might have been abandoned with the end of Roman government.

At Icklingham the town extends along a Roman road on the north side of the river Lark south-east of the modern village across the route of the Icknield Way, which crossed the Lark here on its way north to Thetford and the Wash. The road was found to be 24ft wide when sectioned[33] and apparently ran from Pakenham in the east towards the Roman sites on the edge of the Fens around Mildenhall. Small boats could have carried bulk goods to and from Icklingham along the River Lark, and we have already seen that pottery from dredging suggests the straight channel of the Lark from Mildenhall Fen to Prickwillow was a Roman creation.[34] It provided a link to the Fenland waterways and to the Wash. A collection of pewter items found with a large number of indented beakers in the bed of the Old Slade at Isleham Fen might have been the cargo of a Roman barge engaged in this trade.[35]

A geophysical survey by English Heritage in the area of the Roman town at Icklingham showed an extensive settlement focused on the road along the

32 Plunkett, S.J., "The Anglo-Saxon Loom from Pakenham, Suffolk", PSIAH vol.39 (1999), pp.277-98.
33 *Britannia* 1978, p.448.
34 Colin Pendleton, personal comment.
35 Phillips, C.W., *The Fenland in Roman Times*, (1970).

This leopardess, probably bronze inlaid with silver spots, is one of the items stolen from the probable site of a Roman temple at Icklingham in the 1980s.

valley and on the presumed line of the Icknield Way. It suggests the Icknield Way itself ran through the centre of the town and close to the temple site in Lackford across the river, and not along the modern footpath at its eastern edge. Beyond the dense activity of the settlement there are signs of an organised field system, and further out into the forest area a scatter of abraded Roman pottery suggests the land was manured to support arable farming on this marginal Breckland.

The valley itself was very different before the draining of the Fens. Henry Bunbury writing in the *Proceedings of the Suffolk Institute of Archaeology* in 1851 recalled as a boy hearing bitterns booming in the deep fen between Barton Mills, Tuddenham and Icklingham. He noted that before the drainage there were marshes both above and below Icklingham, extending upwards to Culford and Timworth and downwards nearly as far as Mildenhall. Icklingham had good river access by the Lark to the Fens and the Wash. It is likely that it was Camboricum, perhaps "the ford at the bend" or "crooked ford", of Route 5 of the Antonine Itinerary. This makes it one of the few places in East Anglia to which we can attach a Roman name, although some would place Camboricum at Hockwold on the Norfolk bank of the Little Ouse.

One group of pewter vessels found at Icklingham. They could be polished to look like silver when displayed for serving dinner.
© Trustees of the British Museum

The possible Christian church and the lead tanks associated with it are discussed in chapter six. This was clearly an important feature of the town, suggesting it might have had regional significance for Christians. Finds of coins and brooches were recorded as early as 1720, and five coin hoards have been found as well as many scattered coins. Two hoards included coins of Honorius, so they cannot have been concealed before the end of the fourth century. In 1981/2 an important group of bronze masks and figures was stolen by illicit metal detectorists and sold in America. They included an ornate leopard,[36] described by Martin Henig as a masterpiece of a lithe and dangerous leopard with a spotted coat, evidently inlaid with silver.[37] Another appears to be a head of Atys with his Phrygian cap, although Henig identifies it as Vulcan.

A substantial building referred to as "the villa" was excavated by Henry Prigg in 1877. It had a large room 25ft by 17ft with the lower part of the walls, of flint with red tile course, standing up to 2ft 6in high and a hypocaust below the floor with pilae 18in high.[38] There were also other smaller rooms, and he considered this to be "the western termination of a range of buildings of some size and character".[39]

Several hoards of pewter vessels have been found in the parish, including a group of nine pewter vessels found on Berners Heath (GR 799754), about two miles north-east of the known settlement, by an RAF bomb disposal team in 1956.[40] There were also an iron key, a saw blade and two pieces of Roman pottery, one being samian. The pewter vessels had been turned on a lathe to create a decoration of concentric grooves. There were three shallow circular pewter bowls between 5in and 6in diameter and about 1in deep, a shallow flat-bottomed bowl about 6½in diameter, and a circular tray just over 12in diameter. There was also a cup 5½in diameter and 2½in deep, a conical cup of similar size, and a fragment from the neck of a jug.

An oval dish was broken, but had probably been about 9in long, decorated with an incised or stamped image of a fish. Some claim this fish as a Christian image (see chapter six) but others see it as simply showing that the dish was intended for serving fish. It might be a coincidence that a large group of pewter from Appleshaw near Andover in Hampshire included a similar dish with an incised fish and a bowl marked with a chi-rho.[41]

Another group was found in 1960 by a bomb disposal team in the west of the parish (GR 737738) at a depth of over 10ft.[42] The items were inside a thin bronze bowl or cauldron over 12in diameter and 9in deep. Joan Liversidge suggested it had been spun on a lathe in the late third or fourth century, and noted that it had been patched at least five times, so it had presumably been in use for a long time. Inside, resting on a packing of hay or straw, was a pewter dish 6in diameter on a 1in high foot or stand, with a pottery bowl inside it. The British Museum has many other pewter vessels from Icklingham and Mildenhall, forty of them said by Joan Liversidge[43] to be from the Icklingham "villa", including a cup with a beaded rim marked ISARNINVS.[44] This might be an error, as Stanley West lists a total of 41 items, but none from the "villa".[45] He refers to two hoards found in the nineteenth century at unrecorded locations from which 27 items are in the British Museum and four in Ipswich Museum,[46] in addition to the 1956 and 1960 finds. Whatever the precise details, presumably some prosperous local

36 illustrated on back cover of *Archaeology of Roman Suffolk*: the group was published in *The Independent* newspaper 28/9/1989.
37 Henig, M., *The Art of Roman Britain*, London, 1995, p.39-40.
38 illustrated in *Archaeology of Roman Suffolk*, p.42.
39 Prigg, H., "Icklingham Papers 1901"; *Journal of the British Archaeological Association* vol.34 (1878), p.12-15.
40 Liversidge, J., *Proceedings of the Cambridge Antiquarian Society* vol. 52 (1959), p.6.
41 British Museum, *Guide to the Antiquities of Roman Britain*, 1964, p.43.
42 Liversidge,J., *Proceedings of the Cambridge Antiquarian Society* vol. 55 (1961), p.6.
43 Liversidge, J., *Britain in the Roman Empire*, London, 1968, p.207.
44 British Museum *Guide to the Antiquities of Roman Britain* 1922, p.85: A. Birley, *People of Roman Britain* records five names on a dish "Ixarninus, Florenti(us), Licinius, Curati(us), Martinus" and two who might have been successive slaves looking after it on another dish "Flaetio, Fidelis".
45 West, S.E.& Plouviez, J., "The Roman Site at Icklingham", *Suffolk*, EAA 3 p.63.
46 British Museum registration 1844.2-23, 1 to 9 and 1853.4-11, 1 to 18; Ipswich Museum 1936.244, 14, 15, 16, 18.

Three bronzes which, like the leopardess on page 123, were stolen from Icklingham in the 1980s. The two high-quality bearded heads on the left might represent gods or family ancestors. Unusually the eye of the youth below has survived.

residents chose polished pewter dinner services in place of the more expensive silver of the Mildenhall Treasure.

A number of burials have been found. A group excavated by Henry Prigg in 1871 included two in stone coffins, which are now in Moyses Hall Museum, and in one of these the body had been covered with lime. Another was in a lead coffin enclosed within a wooden coffin from which the nails survived. Pottery kilns were excavated in 1937 in Kiln Field, and there were more pottery kilns about a mile away at West Stow. A spread of pottery marks occupation on the opposite bank of the Lark in Lackford parish, so it is likely the town extended across the river. Tom Lethbridge excavated two small buildings in Lackford on the site of the Anglo-Saxon cemetery which he interpreted as mausolea, although no burials were found in them, and it must be significant that this was the place where the "Cavenham crowns" were found (see chapter six). Nina Layard described the findspot as on a slight elevation overlooking the River Lark opposite Icklingham "about midway between the Icknield Way and the Black Ditches", and Lethbridge confirms this.[47]

If we accept that the main route of the Icknield Way was further west than they believed, this site would be close beside it, which would make its location very significant. Miss Layard found there a variety of Roman pottery and a bronze feather which had presumably belonged to the "regalia". There were significant religious centres on both sides of the Lark. Lethbridge pointed to a number of Roman objects turning up in the Anglo-Saxon cremation cemetery and to some of the pots being "debased Romano-British shapes", suggesting a British component among the people buried at Lackford in the fifth century. The evidence is far from conclusive, but is consistent with the idea that some at least of the local population gradually merged with the newcomers rather than being wiped out or expelled.

Stanley West sees the presence of spelt wheat and stinking mayweed (anthemis cotula) in the fifth century settlement at West Stow as evidence of interaction between the Romano-British population farming the heavier soils round Icklingham and the incoming Anglo-Saxons.[48] Perhaps West Stow began as the home of a group of immigrant soldiers and their families employed to protect the local British population before they started to dominate them, as Gildas reported. Certainly there seems to have been a substantial Roman town at Icklingham active up to the end of the Roman period and possibly beyond, whose inhabitants might have been prepared to pay the Anglo-Saxon soldiers with food rations. As we noted in the last chapter, there was considerable activity along the edge of the Fens in the area of Mildenhall, Eriswell and Lakenheath. The inhabitants of this prosperous area probably looked to the market centre at Icklingham or northwards to Hockwold on the north side of the Little Ouse.

At Hockwold an extensive series of settlements apparently covered more ground than any others in the area, being about ten kilometres long and reaching into Weeting and into Brandon parish (Fenhouse Farm), south of the river. Here again it makes sense to look at a community centred on the river rather than to view the water as a barrier. There were certainly two and possibly three temples, of which we will say more in chapter six. Aerial photographs have revealed groups of enclosures, while field walking and limited excavation have shown signs that houses spread along the valley,

47 Nina Layard, *Antiquaries Journal* vol.5 (1925), p.258; Tom Lethbridge in *Cambridge Antiquarian Society Quarto Publications* NS VI (1951), pp.7-8.
48 West, S.E., *A Corpus of Anglo-Saxon Material from Suffolk*, EAA 84, (1998), p.261.

although few specific buildings have been identified so far. The largest amount of domestic occupation debris seems to come from the second and third centuries, but activity continued later at the temples. This was presumably a significant trading area for the Fen edge.

We have already noted the number of Wickham place names that are adjacent to known sites of Roman market towns in the county, confirming the view that they were derived from the Roman word "vicus", the likely term for a small market town. Wickham is a name which it seems was used in many parts of England for a settlement next to a Roman town, as recognised by Margaret Gelling.[49] Examples in Suffolk are Wickham Skeith, next to Stoke Ash, and Wickham Market, next to Hacheston. Norman Scarfe adds Wicken or Wyken Hall in Bardwell,[50] next to Pakenham, another Wickham, as it is *Wicam* in Domesday Book.[51] Wickhambrook should be another example, and is near to the Roman villa at Lidgate, but so far we lack evidence of a town there.

The derivation of neighbouring "camp" villages from the Roman *campus* seems equally sensible. The word can be found in the Roman Campus Martius, the large open area beside the River Tiber close to the city of Rome used originally for public assemblies, exercise and games. Did the Roman towns in Suffolk each have an open campus, which in some cases retained its Roman name in use by the local population even after they became subject to Anglo-Saxon rule?

Perhaps the death of King Anna of East Anglia and his son Jerminus in 654 at the hands of King Penda of Mercia at Bulcamp, on the River Blyth opposite Blythburgh, was the result of a violent conflict staged on the ancient campus attached to Roman Wenhaston. Sam Newton refers to a Norse saga recording a battle fought on a specially prepared ground, so perhaps it was more of a personal combat.

It may be that use of the campus was the origin of the game of camping, a local ball game referred to by Thomas Tusser in his *Five Hundred Points of Good Husbandry*, published in its final form in 1580, a game that could have been played on these open spaces. For December he instructs his readers "Get campers a ball, to campe therewithall" and expands this by saying "In medow or pasture (to growe the more fine)/ let campers be camping in any of thine:/ whiche if ye doe suffer when lowe is the spring,/ you gaine to yourselfe a commodious thing." Spring here refers to shoots or young growth. However, it seems that generally a special place was designated for camping and Norman Smedley identifies an earlier reference to a "camping pightel" in a deed of 1486.[52] Camping was a violent and potentially dangerous team game involving keeping possession of a ball and passing it within the team.[53] It may be that this game developed in the Middle Ages to be played on the open campus outside Roman settlements, and later other open areas were designated as Camping Closes or Camping Lands.[54]

The game's origin is unknown, and it is just possible that it was directly descended from one of the ball games enjoyed by Roman players on the original campus. In addition to Bulcamp there is Campsey Ash, adjoining the Roman settlement at Hacheston. One place name might provide evidence that later landowners translated the word derived from the sports centre of the previous Roman settlement when naming their villages: the Wickham in Wickham Skeith confirms the recognised status of the Roman presence at

49 Gelling, M., *Signposts to the Past*, 1978, p.72.
50 Scarfe, N. *Suffolk in the Middle Ages*, Woodbridge, 1986, p.6.
51 *Domesday Book*, folio 421 and 439b.
52 Smedley, N., *Life and Tradition in Suffolk and North East Essex*, Dent, 1976, p.141.
53 Detailed description in E. Moor, *Suffolk Words and Phrases*, 1823, and in A.O.D. Claxton *The Suffolk Dialect of the Twentieth Century*, 1968.
54 See map 70 in *Historical Atlas Of Suffolk*, Suffolk County Council, 1999 edition, and the accompanying article by David Dymond.

Stoke Ash, but Skeith is an uncommon Scandinavian word for a racecourse, which looks like a direct translation of campus. The name of the adjoining village of Thwaite is Danish for a clearing, so these names demonstrate a Danish or Viking influence in naming places presumably during the time when this was part of the Danelaw from AD870 to 917.

It is possible that the Roman campus recognised by the Scandinavian settlers as a skeith some time before the Domesday Book was compiled remained an open space. The location of this campus at Wickham Skeith might still be marked by a number of landscape features as the church stands immediately at the east end of an enclosure marked by a substantial ditch curving away from the north-west corner of the churchyard. The north side of this large enclosure is marked by a track, in places a solid causeway that reaches the north side of the church directly from the south end of the Roman town at Stoke Ash, passing south of Wood Hall.

Finds suggest that there was activity in the Roman period along this route between Stoke Ash church and Wood Hall. The track continues westward directly to the site of the Roman villa noted above. The south-east corner of the campus has been destroyed by the landscaped grounds of Wickham Hall, but its southern side is marked by a pronounced bank and ditch along the minor road west from the Hall gates. Its south-west corner is marked by a rounded 90-degree bend in this road at Daisy Green, where the west side is a field boundary that appears to be the original line of a diverted footpath. There is a substantial moat outside this south-west corner. It seems most likely that the northern side of the campus is the south side of the present Green with its pond which lies between the "campus" and the most likely line of the track to the villa site. The modern road running north from the Green

Wickham Skeith fits Margaret Gelling's criterion as the next parish to the east (right) is Stoke Ash with its Roman town. The outline of the racecourse (skeith or campus) might be defined by the straight lane in the foreground as its southern boundary, the lane below the pond as the northern limit. Its suggested western limit is just off the left side of the photo and its eastern limit is in line with the church some way beyond the right side of the photograph.

(and from the north-west corner of the campus) leads straight to the river crossing at Wickham Street, which might take its name from this Roman road, if such it is, and the track beyond the crossing leads straight up the hill to join Clay Street, which appears to be a significant Roman route. The enclosure lies on an extensive, fairly level, plateau.

Towards the south of the county the road system suggests a town near Hitcham or Brettenham, where the name of the latter, meaning "settlement of the Britons," might be significant. The evidence for an important Roman port and military presence at Felixstowe is discussed at length in chapter five, but it presumably also functioned as a local market centre. The distribution of known market towns provides a pattern that would give an adequate number of market centres to serve the many individual farmsteads, as all would have a centre within a possible single day's return journey to market and shops.[55] However, there may be more to be found, as the scale of settlement at Stoke Ash has only recently been recognised, and the full extent of settlements at Sicklesmere and at Lattinford in Capel St Mary parish is uncertain. The size of the site at Kelsale East Green also remains to be proved.

The story of Roman Ipswich has yet to be uncovered, and it remains unclear whether various finds represent an extensive settlement or unrelated buildings. We shall discuss the villa complex at Castle Hill below. At one time there was thought to be no other significant settlement, but recent discoveries reveal signs of developments both under the medieval quay on the Orwell and on the town side of Handford Bridge. The latter could have been reached by the direct road down Crane Hill, continuing the alignment of the Roman road from Colchester through Ardleigh and Copdock. On this edge of the modern town centre there is evidence of a Roman settlement between the River Gipping, now represented by the Alderman Canal, and Handford Road. This

55 *Archaeology of Roman Suffolk*, p.57.

site has not yet been thoroughly explored but building materials, pottery and coins indicate substantial occupation throughout the Roman period.[56] Roof tiles and hypocaust tiles for underfloor heating indicate that there were substantial buildings in the area, and the presence of high-quality imported pottery suggests residents of fairly high status.

One corner of the area was excavated in 2003 to reveal a planned field system in the first and second centuries, altered by the creation of a large enclosure made from substantial timber posts[57]. This has been dated to some time between AD150 and 250, although it is not clear how long it lasted. A ballista bolt and military mount indicate a Roman army presence in the second to third century, so perhaps the enclosure was a stores compound for military supplies and taxes in kind at a place beside the river where there was no walled town to provide security. There was a kiln producing a large amount of pottery. Activity there seems to have stopped in the third century before the construction of a high-status building which lay outside the excavated area but contributed roof and hypocaust tiles and fragments of marble facing found in pits there. Fine marble from Carrara in Italy and from Turkey was also found. About a quarter of the tile fragments were burned, so they might have been used to create later hearths, almost certainly by the early Anglo-Saxons.

The 231 Roman coins from the site suggest an interesting story. Until the mid-third century the pattern of coin recovery is typical of the area, then falls low in the late third century (c.AD260-290), but is high in the fourth century and continues into the fifth, which is unusual in south-east Suffolk apart from the Castle Hill villa at Whitton and at Felixstowe. Very interestingly limited fifth century evidence leads up to a sixth-century settlement with at least ten buildings, including Anglo-Saxon halls and sunken-featured buildings, which respect the Roman alignment of the site.

This looks as if it might indicate continuous use of the site from late Roman to Anglo-Saxon times, with the introduction of early Anglo-Saxon-style buildings. Are new people keeping the existing layout, or is the resident population adopting imported building methods? In view of the burials of Anglo-Saxon warriors with spears and shields across the river on Hadleigh Road in the later sixth and early seventh centuries, was this the home of an Anglo-Saxon military unit guarding access to the upper reaches of the Orwell/Gipping river system? The section of the River Gipping beside the site is almost certainly an artificial cut created before the tenth century. Perhaps it was a Roman creation to provide a canal or to act as the leat for a Roman watermill on the site of Handford Mill. It could have received additional power from the water flowing downhill past the present site of St Matthew's Church.

Burials in the area might be related to this settlement, as a large cinerary urn containing fragments of bone and ashes was found at the corner of Burlington Road and Burlington Road South (now Dalton Road) early in 1863. Others were found at the same time, all broken except for one of grey fabric, ornamented with black dots,[58] and a pottery lamp has also been found in Burlington Road.[59]

Excavation on the Magistrates' Court site in Elm Street in 1975 revealed a first-century ditch and "a possible grave containing the upper part of a human skull".[60] Tom Plunkett reports that a digger driver found a Roman

56 PSIAH vol. 39 (1998) p.234.
57 Boulter, S., in *Ipswich Archaeological Trust Newsletter* 64, April 2005.
58 *Suffolk Chronicle* 21 November 1863; PSIAH vol. 21 (1933) p.260: Ipswich Museum 1920.50.21.
59 Ipswich Museum 1949.148.
60 Dunmore, S. et al. "Ipswich Archaeological Survey", *Suffolk*, EAA 3 (1976), p.135.

61 Fox, G.E., "Roman Suffolk", *Archaeological Journal* vol. 57 (1900), p.150, but he does not refer to a bronze lamp. He says pots illustrated in *Suffolk Illustrations, Fitch Collection* vol III.
62 PSIAH vol.34, p.295 and vol. 35, p.234.

shale bracelet in "black material" at some depth in Elm Street. This extends the evidence for Roman activity on the line of Handford Road on to the higher ground near the modern town centre, possibly as a roadside cemetery.

There is evidence of Romano-British activity in the area of the later quays along the waterfront between Stoke Bridge and the Old Custom House. This includes a bronze vessel, apparently a wine jug that has lost its handle, from the site of Wolsey's College near Stoke Bridge, which was purchased by the British Museum in 1857. A bronze lamp and other items are said to have come from Paul's malting on Albion Wharf.[61] A few coins and pieces of pottery were found during excavations in 1979 and 1982 north of St Mary Quay church,[62] and a Roman ditch was noted a little further north.

Excavation on the waterfront in 2005/6 revealed evidence of Roman activity on the foreshore of the Orwell securely stratified below the remains of a Saxon jetty beside the stream that formerly ran down Brook Street. This brook then continued as a fast-flowing stream straight into the Orwell, but was later diverted eastward by a Saxon waterfront revetment that allowed peat to build up as the sea level rose in the post-Roman period. Finds here included several shoes, at least one of which is said to be in a Roman style. This area awaits full exploration in advance of redevelopment.

Looking north from the end of Great Whip Street we see the direct link from Wherstead Road down to the ford. Despite slight local variations, the general alignment is remarkably straight between the summits of Bourne Hill and Christchurch Park.

However, the ford across the Orwell, which remained in use for wheeled vehicles long after Stoke Bridge was built for foot travellers and light traffic, was probably already being used in the Roman period. It is likely that the straight line of Wherstead Road marks a Roman road approaching the ford, crossing from Great Whip Street to Foundry Lane and continuing up Brook Street, then as the Avenue through Christchurch Park. Perhaps it went on to join the eastbound road at Henley. The timber roadway recorded in Norwich Road and also in Westgate Street and across Cornhill might be Roman in origin or have been in use in Roman times, but unfortunately it remains undated. This corduroy road of logs was exposed during the laying of sewers in Westgate Street some 1.5m below the Victorian street in 1881. Dr. Taylor, then Curator of Ipswich Museum, reported that the logs were piled on each other in alternate fashion as if to bridge the marshy places, and were secured together with wooden pegs.[63] Associated with this road were a bone comb and evidence of antler working. Dr. Taylor seems to have considered the road Saxon, but it is possible that even if the comb were Saxon the road itself might have been older. At the south-east corner of the town defences excavation of the Blackfriars revealed that the original line of Fore Street was cut by the first town ditch in about 917. Possibly the original Roman road ran diagonally from Cornhill to Fore Street, crossing Brook Street. This would enable it to avoid the deep valleys on that side of Ipswich by climbing Bishops Hill on its way to Felixstowe.

At present we can only say that the comprehensive excavation of the site for the Buttermarket Centre showed no Roman activity in that area on the rising ground behind the river. Perhaps this was simply a gap that the early Anglo-Saxon settlers could use for their cemetery before the later Saxon town extended across it. Roman settlement might have concentrated along the edge of the river near the brook. We might see a series of sites of activity along the river at the ford downstream from Stoke Bridge, at Handford Road and at Boss Hall below the Castle Hill villa complex, as all three were later crossing points. There might have been another substantial Roman building at the junction of Norwich Road and Valley Road, where John Newman discovered large fragments of Roman tegula and imbrex tiles that had been reused, apparently in the medieval Brooks Hall. [64]

Further up the hill near the junction of Valley Road and Dale Hall Road Reid Moir recorded that first-century pottery was found in 1926 during construction of Valley Road,[65] not far from early Roman pottery recorded by John Corder in 1902 in "Mr Fonnereau's sand-pit" near Dale Hall Lane.[66] A settlement at the Albany, off Tuddenham Road, has been interpreted as a moderately prosperous farmstead (see chapter three).[67] It might be related to an inhumation cemetery of over 70 burials, including part of a decorated lead coffin, nearby on Tuddenham Road reported by Frank Woolnough.[68] Further out John Corder recorded burial urns in a meadow at Westerfield Station, close to the possible line of the Roman road projected through Christchurch Park.[69]

It would, however, be helpful if possible to check the pottery found during construction of the "New Gas Offices" in Carr Street at the end of the nineteenth century. These were displayed by J.S. Corder in 1891 and recorded as Roman,[70] as were some from High Street, but later they were assumed to be

63 PSIAH vol. 6, p.341.
64 Newman, J., PSIAH vol. 39 (1999), p.376.
65 PSIAH vol. 21 (1933) p.259: finds are Ipswich Museum 1926.115 and 116.
66 PSIAH vol. 11, p.337: Ipswich Museum 1920.50.13 and 14.
67 PSIAH vol. 37 (1992) p.387 at TM1746.
68 SMR: IPS046, believed to be at TM172457: Ipswich Museum 1921.52.65.
69 PSIAH vol.11, p.337.
70 PSIA vol. 7 (1891), p.369.

71 *Ipswich, the Archaeological Implications of Development*, Scole Committee, 1973, p.7.

This coloured print of the mosaic floor from the Castle Hill villa at Ipswich, published by Henry Davy in 1855, is the best record of the mosaic as it was first uncovered. By courtesy of Steven Plunkett

"almost certainly…Late Saxon".[71] It is noted that the so-called "tetina" or "guttus" found when building "the Bank" in 1892 is a medieval jug. Presumably this is the "tetina" said by Hamlet Watling in a paper to the Ipswich Scientific Society in 1892 to have been found with a "gutturnium" near the Town Hall. As early as 1871 the guide to Ipswich Museum, then still in Museum Street, informs us that while the upper shelf of wall-case 79 displayed "a series of Roman urns found at Colchester in the year 1862" a lower shelf held "the Roman urns found in Ipswich and the neighbourhood". Were some of these really Roman? Of course they might all have been complete Thetford Ware pots in the museum collection, but perhaps it is too sweeping to assume that all reports of "Roman" finds in Ipswich were misidentification of Saxon or medieval material.

We might note that although Professor Henslow, the guiding figure of the early museum, was primarily interested in natural history, his personal intervention ensured that the Roman mosaic floor from Castle Hill was preserved and displayed in the museum by 1857. Sadly more recent curatorial mistakes have resulted in its deplorable fragmentation. Henslow usually

Drawn, Coloured and Published by H. Davy, Globe Street, Ipswich, May, 1855.

THE ROMAN TESSELATED PAVEMENT,

Discovered December, 1854, in the Castle Field, St. Matthew's, Ipswich, Suffolk, the Property of John Orford, Esq., and by him presented to the Ipswich Museum, and Deposited there March 16, 1855, under the Superintendence of Mr. R. M. Phipson, Architect, and Mr. F. Ransome.   Weight of the whole about 5 Tons.   Sketched on the original site, about 1 Mile N.W. of the Town.

seems to have recorded his finds meticulously; it would be interesting to know if he secured any other Roman finds from Ipswich for his museum. After all, he had excavated the Roman burial mounds at Rougham and recorded Roman finds at Felixstowe.

A photograph taken by Miss Elsie Cobbold in 1899 is captioned "Mr. Brown's timber-yard wall formerly the wall of the Grey Friars' orchard with Roman tiles built in". This was presumably along Friars Road north of its junction with Wolsey Street and opposite the churchyard of St Nicholas. Stephen Daniels told Bob Malster of reputed Roman finds in the Lady Lane area at the back of Smith and Daniels' shop in Westgate Street. A very uncommon Greek coin, an Alexandrian tetradrachma of the emperor Probus (276-281), was found here.[72] According to the *Evening Star* of 25th July, 1979, a wooden road outside Debenhams in Westgate Street and Cornhill had been sampled for dating. We are left wishing we knew more about these finds and wondering if others remain to be unearthed in Ipswich. Of course it is possible, as Judith Plouviez maintains, that all the Roman tile used by Saxons and others in Ipswich was collected from Castle Hill.

72 IM 1930.104

For a short time in the 1970s the mosaic floor from Castle Hill was displayed in the courtyard of Ipswich Museum, after being taken down from the wall of the entrance hall.

A tessellated floor from Castle Hill, Whitton, excavated in the 1930s and placed in the courtyard of Ipswich Museum. The tile cubes are larger and coarser than those used in the mosaic and would suit a passage or small room that was expected to be much used.

If wealth was not spent on impressive towns with expensive public buildings we might reasonably expect wealthy landowners to be building elaborate country houses like those of their contemporaries in the Cotswolds. Yet Norfolk only has a small group of large houses in its north-west corner, notably that at Gayton Thorpe, while in Suffolk just a handful have been located that appear to have the qualities of the really large country houses. It would be surprising if there were not more to be found, and at least we can presume there must have been a large house near Eye or Hoxne on the estate known as Villa Faustini, and one at Rougham to match the large burial mounds there. In fact some evidence of Roman buildings has been discovered about 250 yards east of the Rougham mounds, including a probable floor of opus signinum,[73] confirmed by surface finds of tile, tesserae and painted wall plaster.[74] The Mildenhall silver (see chapter seven) also implies a large mansion in which to display this elaborate dinner service.

Even though no house has been found at Hoxne to claim title as the focus of Villa Faustini, the treasures found there[75] by a metal detector user searching for a lost hammer give some idea of the quality of life in a wealthy household. The solid silver tigress handle from a large two-handled vase gives a hint that there was an elaborate silver table service comparable to the Mildenhall Treasure so guests could be entertained with a show of silver used to serve the food and drink. The four elaborate gilded silver statuette pepper pots are showpieces, part of an elaborate table presentation. They are even more remarkable for the neat working mechanism in the base that allowed a wide opening to pour in the pepper, small holes to sprinkle it or complete closure to keep the contents safe. The pepper itself was an expensive luxury imported from beyond the eastern limits of the empire, so it is apparent that no effort was spared when it came to flavouring the food.

There is an impressive array of solid silver cutlery, with seventy-eight spoons and twenty ladles, mostly in matching sets, as well as four silver wine strainers. The serving of wine involved straining it to remove any sediment and then mixing the clear wine with water, as throughout the classical world it

73 Fox, G.E., "Roman Suffolk", *Archaeological Journal* vol. 57 (1900), p.157, refers *Gentleman's Magazine* 1843, part 2, pp.190 and 528.
74 *Archaeology of Roman Suffolk*, p.51.
75 details in chapter seven.

was deemed barbaric to drink neat wine. At Hoxne this was presumably a public ritual using silver strainers, and one has the added refinement that the strainer is incorporated in a funnel and can be hinged back, perhaps when the funnel was used to add the water. One silver spoon does carry the name Faustinus, although a whole set of ten are inscribed Ursicinus, both common Roman names.

As no trace of a large Roman house has been found within this area, perhaps there never was one and the whole estate was run by a bailiff on behalf of an absentee landlord who lived in another part of the empire. Alternatively even a very large complex of buildings might have been timber framed throughout and so have disappeared, leaving minimal evidence. Of course there might be a palatial country house waiting to be found, but this would be exceptional in East Anglia.

The villa at Castle Hill, Whitton, now part of the north-western suburbs of Ipswich, is the most outstanding so far found in East Anglia in terms of size and the wealth of finds. Only Stanton Chare near Ixworth and Stanstead near Long Melford are comparable. We can safely assume that it was

The complex of buildings at Castle Hill, Whitton, Ipswich. The main block was excavated by Basil Brown in the 1950s and the bath house and aisled building were excavated by Suffolk County Council Archaeological Service in 1989.
© Suffolk County Council Archaeological Service

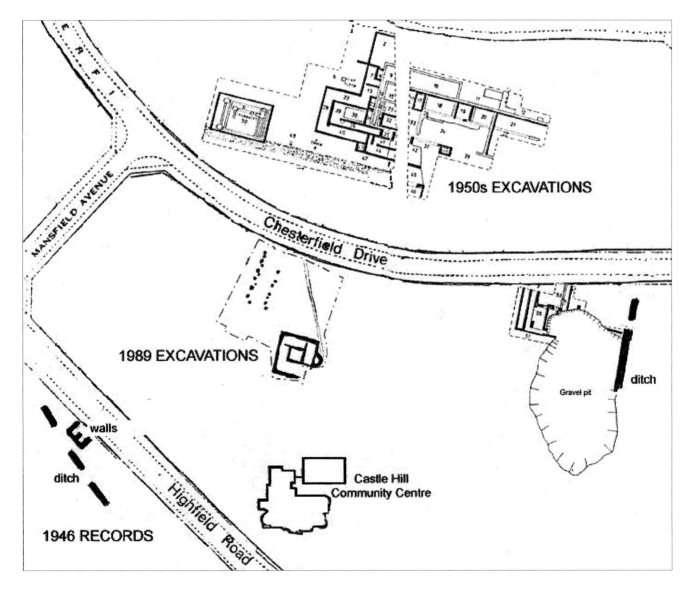

occupied by a man of some rank, perhaps one who played a key role in the administration of the area. Whether this means a wealthy local landowner or an official of the imperial administration we cannot tell. The villa stood on high ground, now between Highfield Road and Tranmere Grove, looking south across the Gipping valley. Such a south-facing site was often chosen in the Roman period, and there must have been extensive views over the river before the area was covered with modern houses. Just across the valley, and probably visible from the villa, was the main road from Colchester to Combretovium.

As a ridge slopes down to the river at Boss Hall it is possible the villa had direct access there not only to the route by water on the Gipping and Orwell but also to a ford. This point was Pottaford in 970.[76] If the name derived from finding many pots there, they might have been Roman ones eroded from the river bank as early Roman material was found near the river in 1988,[77] although it was also the site of Anglo-Saxon cremation burials. This remained a significant crossing point, known as Bordshaw Bridge, into the sixteenth century, so it might have been both a ford and a quay in Roman times. A road 6m wide running north to south up the west side of the villa might have been part of a route that left Ipswich on the line of the modern Norwich Road, possibly forming part of a road that started from Felixstowe. If so it kept to the higher ground at Castle Hill on its way to Combretovium.

A stone-surfaced road 3.8m wide ran at right angles into the villa complex. The buildings, perhaps grouped around a courtyard, seem to have extended over an area at least 120m by 130m. Some rooms had underfloor heating, mosaic floors and painted walls, and there was a bath house.

The first Roman building was timber framed, with glazed windows and concrete (*opus signinum*) floors, and possibly with walls of unfired clay blocks. Certainly when it was demolished a thick layer of clay was spread across the area as a base for the new building. This sealed pottery and coins of the Hadrianic and Antonine period, so the new building was probably started towards the end of the second century. Channels which were regarded by Basil Brown as part of a heating system were partly taken up by the walls of the new building. They might have been dug to define its original plan and to form foundation trenches. Perhaps only some were used because the plan was modified during construction leaving the empty channels noted by Brown. Alternatively they might be the work of later generations removing material from the footings to recycle in new buildings. The building, which created more extensive and luxurious accommodation for what appears to be part of the main house, featured at least one coloured mosaic floor heated from below by a hypocaust and other tessellated floors in red and white. Some rooms had underfloor heating with flues concealed in the walls, which were then plastered and painted in bright colours.

The quantity and quality of the finds indicate a high-status owner. They include a bronze lamp, fine pottery, carved bone pins and a surprising number of metal styli for writing as well as a samian ink pot and the base of a seal box. There was also a jet plaque showing an eastern god, probably Atys (see chapter six), which is now in Ipswich Museum, and a bronze figure of a dog. Reid Moir illustrated the dog as figure 50 in his report without further comment, but according to Basil Brown it had been found

76 Fairclough, J., "The Bounds of Stoke", PSIAH vol. 40 (2003), p.265.

77 Newman J. "The Anglo-Saxon Cemetery at Boss Hall", *Bulletin 8 of the Sutton Hoo Research Committee*, 1993, p.33 and fig.16.

by an allotment holder who gave it to the landowner, Mr. Percy Turner. Window bars, door fittings and lock components indicate concern about security.

There appear to have been some alterations to parts of the house over the years, but the details are unclear. A quantity of burned tile is probably the result of a fire in the middle of the Roman period that created the layer of burned material found by Time Team in 2003.

Coins show occupation throughout the fourth century and include issues of Theodosius towards the end of that century. There were also several bracelets of a late period and pottery from Much Hadham in Hertfordshire, which was produced in the fourth century. Some time in the fourth or fifth centuries, but possibly after the end of Roman government, the standard of living apparently declined, as crude hearths were created on some of the tessellated floors.

The site first attracted attention in 1854 when a large part of a decorated mosaic floor was discovered while building a farmhouse and was moved to Ipswich Museum. Unfortunately repeated moves in the museum in the 1970s mean that only a small portion of it can now be displayed. Previously almost half of it survived, so that it was possible to see the whole series of geometric patterns that enclosed the central panel, although the central panel itself which might have featured a small picture had been destroyed before it was recovered. The *Illustrated London News* reported that it had been found while "erecting a fence round a newly built farmhouse" and added that "quantities of Roman bricks have recently been dug out, most of which were used in the foundations of the premises just built".[78] This explains some at least of the removal of Roman building material that has been observed by archaeologists. In 1894 a large globular amphora was found in a gravel pit along with "a flower-pot shaped vase" and a black cinerary urn. The amphora was said to contain a large number of coins that were stolen by the workmen, so perhaps it had held somebody's savings.[79] In 1897 a further tessellated floor formed from pieces of red brick or tile and of white stone about an inch square in alternate rows was discovered when Mr. Henry Orford was extending the orchards, and although it was examined by Hamlet Watling it was not excavated.

In 1931 several trial trenches were dug on behalf of Ipswich Museum under the direction of J. Reid Moir. The work was funded "on condition that all specimens found should find a permanent home in the Ipswich Museum" by Mr. Crane of Chicago, head of an international engineering company which had a large factory in Ipswich and whose founder came from the Ipswich family that gave its name to Crane Hall and Crane Hill on the London Road. Unfortunately work had to stop when Mr. Crane died and the funding came to an abrupt end. A red and white tessellated floor was discovered, which is now displayed outside the museum. The base of the walls of flint rubble were said to be very solid, and in one case decorated plaster still adhered to the wall. Coin finds ranged from AD199 to 378.

Between 1948 and 1950 major excavations were carried out by Basil Brown, who had uncovered the Sutton Hoo ship while excavating there in 1939. At Castle Hill he had to dig to a considerable depth, resulting in a dispute between the Borough Housing and Museum Committees as to which

78 *Illustrated London News*, 10 February, 1855.
79 the amphora was on display at Ipswich Museum (ref. IM 1914.35).

80 Reid Moir, J. & Maynard, G., "The Roman Villa at Castle Hill, Whitton, Ipswich", PSIAH vol. 21 (1933), p.240-262.
81 Smedley, N. & Owles, E.J., "A Romano-British Bath-Hose at Stonham Aspal", PSIAH vol. 30 (1966), p.234.

The main block at Castle Hill with the numbers allocated by Jonathan Drake, based on the original plan by Basil Brown. Room 19 had underfloor heating and painted plaster on the walls, showing flowers and green marbling. Room 18 had a tiled floor and painted walls. Room 17 had the red and white tessellated floor lifted in 1931. Room 26 had a narrow tessellated floor uncovered in 1931. Room 32 was probably the site of the mosaic floor lifted in 1854; it had underfloor heating and glazed windows. Room 50 had a roof of stone slabs.
© Suffolk County Council
Archaeological Service

would pay the costs. Unfortunately pressure from the builders to develop the site and the threat of compensation claims because of the cost of filling up the deep excavations meant work was abandoned too soon. He did produce a plan of a substantial building about 15m by 33m in which at least two rooms had underfloor heating, but it has proved impossible to distinguish completely the different phases of construction or to tell how much larger the complete house might have been. Many finds from this excavation are displayed in Ipswich Museum.

In 1951 the main site was developed for housing, and more finds were made during building operations and subsequently in the local gardens. The 1930s excavation report refers to "certain very massive blocks of dressed stone" in the farmyard.[80] If this is correct the report would indicate a substantial stone structure somewhere on the site. Basil Brown refers to finding near a hedge what were "apparently bases where columns have stood".

We might note the surprising presence of stone roofing slabs in the remains of a separate building to the west of the main block that could have had an industrial use, perhaps for corn drying or malting. The stone, cut into diamond-shaped pieces with nail holes, must have been imported from either Belgium or south-western England, perhaps because they wanted to create a specially fireproof roof; the floor showed evidence of much intensive burning. Another part of the house had "small stone roofing slates". One fragment of a similar stone roofing tile is recorded at Stonham Aspal.[81]

Fragments of Mediterranean marble have also been found, perhaps from a high-quality *opus sectile* decoration. There were also ten coloured glass

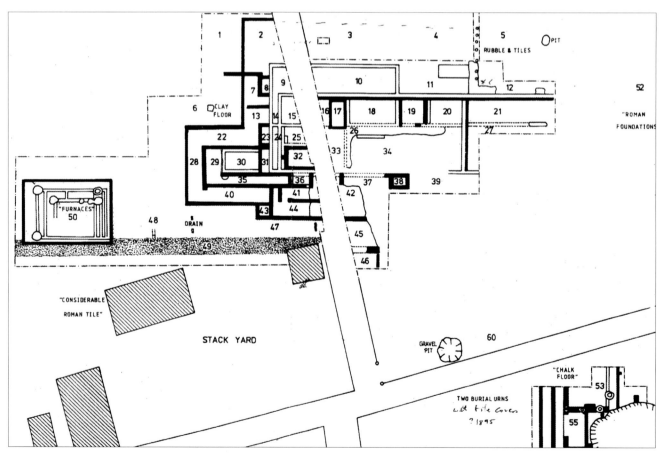

tesserae which are relatively rare on British sites, although they are also recorded in Suffolk at Stanton Chare, Capel St Mary, Whatfield and Martlesham. They were probably used to embellish fine details in high-quality mosaic floors in which the main design was completed with tesserae of tile and coloured stone. The finest example in Britain is the Bacchus mosaic from Leadenhall Street in London, now in the British Museum. Chris Catling[82] has suggested that because use of glass in mosaics is common in Trier and Cologne this London example might be the work of a continental craftsman. Perhaps the Suffolk examples were also the work of designers coming across the short sea crossing from the Rhine. Judith Plouviez notes the parallel evidence that the Roman period custom of barrow burial might have come across from the area that is now Belgium.

Debris uncovered during building work in Highfield Road, nearly 70m away from the main house, in 1946 included decorated plaster, roof tiles and box flue tiles from the heating system.[83] There were pottery and coins from the fourth century, and this appears to have been a separate high-status building. In 1989 Suffolk Archaeological Service excavated two buildings south of the main block, one of them being a timber-framed aisled building 19m by 13m with at least three clay ovens.[84] It probably had a tiled roof and most of the floors were earth, although one section had been altered by inserting flint wall foundations and a mortar floor. This building was probably used for agricultural or industrial purposes and could be described as a large barn. The other building confirmed the status of the complex as it was a bath house which had been altered at least once, probably after 360. The flint wall foundations had been robbed out but it was possible to see that the building was a thirteen metre square with one room extending further to the south-east and a semi-circular cold plunge bath projecting from the east side. There were three or four heated rooms with floors supported on piles of square tiles, red tessellated floors and painted walls. Three unheated rooms had floors of *opus signinum*, a pink waterproof concrete with crushed tile mixed in the mortar. The cold plunge bath was fed with water from the north through a wooden pipe with iron collars joining the sections. Finds from the 1930s excavation included a fine bronze oil flask, almost certainly used when bathing.

A visit by Time Team in 2003 explored a number of private gardens. Their geophysical survey helped to locate some features of Basil Brown's plan and revealed a previously unknown episode of burning in the middle of the Roman period. It confirmed that some features remain deeply buried. Sadly the programme concentrated on an ill-informed denigration of the work of Basil Brown.

All the excavations confirm that stone and tile, including much of that used in the foundations, was removed for use elsewhere, and finds of Anglo-Saxon pottery suggest that use of the building by Anglo-Saxons started soon after the end of Roman occupation. It has been suggested that "a significant quantity of residual Roman roof tile" found in a Saxon pit behind the former Crown and Anchor Hotel in Westgate Street[85] might be one example of the removal of building material from Castle Hill to the new Saxon town, although I wonder if the source might have been closer to hand. Roman tile has been found on a number of sites in the later Saxon town, but there is no evidence of how it was used or why quantities appear in rubbish pits, although much might have been used to create hearths.

82 Current Archaeology no.233 (August 2009) p.41.
83 near nos. 69 and 71 Highfield Road.
84 Plouviez, J. in "Archaeology in Suffolk 1989", in PSIAH vol. 37 (1990), p.160, and Ipswich Archaeological Trust Newsletter 59 (2003).
85 PSIAH vol. 38 (1993), p.216.

Certainly enough must have survived at Whitton to justify calling the remains Castle Hill, which implies substantial standing masonry, viewed presumably in the manner of the Anglo-Saxon poet's description of *The Ruin* where he speaks of a decayed Roman city, possibly Bath. He describes one building where the woodwork of the roof was stripped of tiles, the strong walls fell and the building sank into ruin, reduced to overgrown hills where formerly many men enjoyed life, wearing gold and rejoicing in their rich furnishings.[86] We know that much survived at Castle Hill to be incorporated in the foundations of the nineteenth-century farm buildings. One piece of masonry might still have been visible on the surface in the early twentieth century.

Unfortunately the ground plan recovered by Basil Brown's limited and incomplete excavation of the site clearly represents only part of the Roman complex.[87] It is likely, but not certain, that the block of rooms he excavated is part of the main unit. One is left wondering if it is only a west wing and wanting to add a group of large reception rooms in the uncertain area on the north side. Here the record does not tell us what lay behind a single strip of rooms including one with a hypocaust and painted walls and another with tiled floor and painted walls (Drake 18 and 19). They apparently opened on to a tessellated passage at the back of a courtyard where a fragment from a marble statue was found.

Another block on the east, balancing that known on the west, might have extended further south to include the rooms (Drake 53 – 57) found on the edge of a later gravel pit. Time Team did establish that there were definite gaps between some of the buildings. If we knew more of the access road (Drake 49) we could say whether the "asymmetrical" room noted by Reid Moir (his 7, Drake's 38) might be the entrance to the courtyard. This would still leave as completely separate buildings the substantial structure partially recorded to the south-west (Drake 61) and the aisled building and substantial bath house excavated in 1989. Reid Moir also

86 complete translation in Gordon, R.K., *Anglo-Saxon Poetry*, Dent, 1954, p.84.
87 The best published plan is in *Ipswich Archaeological Trust Newsletter* 59, 2003.

Excavation of the bath house at Stanton Chair (Chare) Farm, Stanton. The piles of tiles supported the floor above the space where hot air circulated in the hypocaust underfloor heating system.
© Suffolk Institute of Archaeology and History

88 PSIAH vol. 11 (1933), p.257.

reported rubbish pits "chiefly to the north and north-east of the villa" but failed to mark them on his plan. It is reasonable to see them as located behind the main complex.

The excavation in 1931 also revealed immediately south of the villa two cremation burials in black pots, each covered by a single tile. Less than half a mile to the south-east, between the railway and Dales Road, an extensive Roman inhumation cemetery was exposed during extension of the Bolton and Co. brickfield on the side of a small valley.[88] Burials were recorded over several years and the pots found with them were given to Ipswich Museum. The grave goods suggested these were more likely servants than the family who owned the villa, although there were two glass vessels, one of which was associated with traces of a lead box. Nails were found near many of the burials, but Reid Moir thought they belonged to wooden caskets for grave goods rather than to coffins, although that would be unusual. The bodies were placed more or less in rows, with the feet towards the west. Six female skeletons were remarkable for having their heads removed and placed between their legs. This practice, which is known in other parts of the country, remains unexplained and is not known elsewhere in the Roman world. The cemetery site had links with pre-Roman traditions, as finds of pottery from the Beaker period and from the Iron Age have been reported. In the 1930s Reid

Only the north range of the Stanton Chair villa, over 300 feet long, was excavated in the 1930s. Basil Brown and Guy Maynard based their reconstruction of a courtyard layout on the distribution of finds and on some test pits.
© Suffolk Institute of Archaeology and History

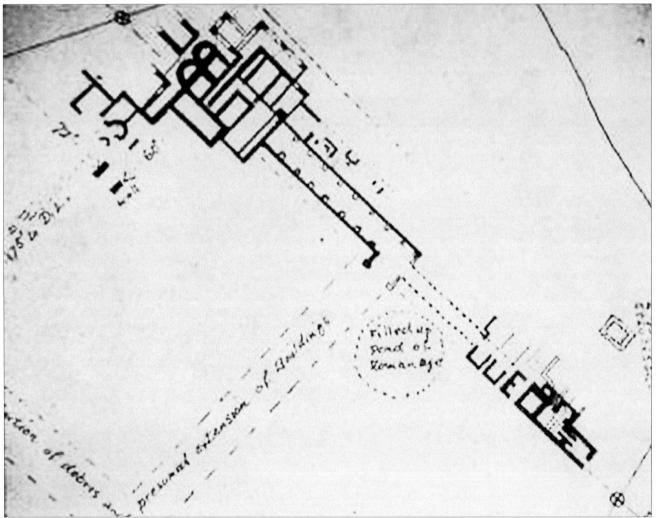

Moir found three "ritual" shafts, one more than 66ft deep, of a type recognised elsewhere in both pre-Roman and early Roman contexts (see chapter six).[89]

At Stanton Chare (or Chair), north of Ixworth, the group of rooms excavated by Basil Brown and Guy Maynard of Ipswich Museum between 1935 and 1939 appear to be the west wing, about 380ft long, of a very large courtyard villa.[90] The best plan is on page 120 of Rainbird Clarke's *East Anglia*. The true scale of this complex will only be revealed by further excavation. Its position is notable because it is not only near the town at Pakenham but stands at the start of the main stretch of Peddars Way which runs directly from here to the north coast of Norfolk at Holme. If the road was indeed an official boundary line, perhaps the villa had some official function in this strategic location and was the base for a local administrator rather than the centre of an agricultural estate.

The site overlooks a tributary of the Black Bourne which flows north-west into the Little Ouse in an area between the Breckland to the west and the chalky boulder clay of High Suffolk to the east. The excavated wing seems to have started as a timber-framed aisled hall, probably built before AD130 beside a pond. At least nine pairs of posts formed a nave 100ft long, with an entrance in the northern gable. About AD150 the pond was filled in, the southern end of the hall was given a projecting wing and a separate bath house was built beyond this. Towards the end of the century the baths were extended and linked to the main building. Some rooms had brightly painted walls.

In a separate building, in line with the other to the north and connected by a path, was another bath house. It is not clear when this was built, but a number of small bronze and silver coins ranging from Constantine I to Eugenius (AD392-394) found in the drains and furnace show the building was in use throughout the fourth century. These coins show people were living here until at least the end of the fourth century, and there is some evidence of Early Saxon activity related to ironworking hearths which left an extensive layer of iron slag. It would be interesting to know if occupation really did continue here well after the end of Roman government while power in the region gradually transferred to the newcomers.

It is still hard to believe that there were ever many great country houses in Roman East Anglia when so few have been discovered and we are finding increasing evidence of basic farms and smaller houses which should be much more difficult to detect. Some of the smaller houses do fall within the accepted archaeological title of villa, but they are not on the grand scale. One at Lidgate, never excavated but known from an outstanding air photograph and from surface finds, is a classic example of the medium-sized house generally called a winged corridor villa. The appearance of a large barn, about twenty-four metres long with substantial buttresses, within the enclosure around the villa invites comparison with a seventeenth-century manor house complex.

The many changes that could be made to a villa were revealed by excavations in 1959 in Exning parish but close to Landwade village. Timber structures of the Flavian period were replaced early in the second century by a timber-framed aisled building thirty-one metres long with painted plaster on some of the walls. Some of the walls were rebuilt in stone late in the third century, when a small bath house was added. Later the rest of the building was

A body buried at Dales Road, Ipswich, close to Castle Hill. The head had been placed carefully between the legs.
© Colchester and Ipswich Museum Service

89 PSIAH vol. 22 (1935), pp.141-9.
90 Journal of Roman Studies vol.30, p.171.

rebuilt in stone to include a semi-circular mosaic floor surrounded by red tesserae and new painted wall plaster. Part of the mosaic is now displayed in the Cambridge Museum of Archaeology and Ethnography. An extra room with a hypocaust was added shortly before the building was destroyed by fire towards the middle of the fourth century.[91] In its final form this is one of our more elaborate known villas, and one we can associate with the wealth of those living near the edge of the Fens in an area later reputed to have had a

residence of the Anglo-Saxon royal family, the Wuffings. A hoard of pewter, including a jug, was found in the bed of a former stream between Landwade and Exning about 1870.[92]

Two Roman houses near the town at Pakenham are only partially recorded.[93] One of them, at Redcastle Farm, Pakenham, had a decorated mosaic floor that was said to be "very handsome" when it was discovered in 1776. It was left open to visitors, until it was broken up by cows getting on to it. An excavation in 1953 exposed half of the building, revealing the short wing of a small winged corridor villa and a central reception room with an apse. This room had a tessellated floor, and some painted wall plaster and window glass was recovered. The pottery shows occupation between the middle of the second century and the fourth century.

This house had started as a simple rectangular structure on the site of the central room, but it has proved impossible to date this or the construction of the larger building. The site seems to have stayed in use as there is

These bronze lions, found fixed together by an iron rod, were probably used to decorate a piece of furniture in the villa at Capel St Mary.
Ipswich Museum

evidence of Saxon activity after the footings of the walls had been robbed out, and there was a new Saxon settlement within a few hundred yards of the house.

Another house half a mile east of Ixworth on the road to Stowlangtoft had an apsidal room with a hypocaust for underfloor heating, perhaps part of a bath house, that was uncovered in 1849.[94] The pillars were 14in high, made from flat tiles 7¾in square, 1½in thick, and about 14in apart. There was some painted plaster and red tesserae. A range of rooms with another hypocaust was excavated in 1948, and one of these rooms contained much painted wall plaster. There seems to have been another apse and signs that it was rebuilt more than once. A geophysical survey suggests there was a group of separate buildings here. This is supported by the finding of building materials on the field but has not been verified by excavation. A pipeclay figurine was found in a well. Again there was evidence of Early Saxon occupation nearby.

I will conclude this chapter with a few examples of sites that await further exploration. Remains investigated at Windmill Hill, Capel St Mary, in 1928 were once interpreted as a small town but are clearly those of a substantial house. Confusingly there is good evidence for a small town in the parish but it is some distance away at Lattinford Bridge, where the modern

91 Webster, C.J., *Cambridge Antiquarian Society Proceedings* vol.76 (1987) p.41; Greenfield, E., *Journal of Roman Studies* vol. 50 (1960); p.228, Hughes et al. *Cambridge Antiquarian Society Proceedings* vol.11 (1906), p.210.
92 *Cambridge Antiquarian Society Proceedings* vol.33, p.165.
93 Warren, J., "Antiquities found at Ixworth", PSIAH vol.1 (1849), pp.74-8, and see *Archaeology of Roman Suffolk*, pp.50-1.
94 PSIA vol.1 (1853) p.74: *Archaeology of Roman Suffolk*, ill. 29.

Judith Plouviez explaining the excavation of a Roman building at Hitcham in 2006. The main house was about 15 by 25 metres and was probably timber framed resting on flint footings. A separate bath house had painted plaster on the walls.

A12 cuts through it. Evidence of settlement here includes rubbish pits and a number of cremation burials.

The house site at Windmill Hill has produced many finds included tiles, nails and window glass, and a pair of bronze crouching lions about 6in long and joined by two iron bars, which appear to be mounts from a piece of furniture. Additional finds in 1946/7 of painted wall plaster and glass tesserae add to the picture of a high-status building. There are later reports of more glass tesserae, one with gold foil. Pottery and coin evidence confirm occupation at least in the first two centuries AD.[95] There was a Roman tile kiln just to the south. In 2002 Stuart Boulter found a large quantity of Roman roof tiles, flue tiles and hypocaust/floor tiles reused in the nave and south aisle walls of Capel St Mary church, which is within 100m of the site. A number of Roman cremations have been noted near the church, and the site overlooks the valley containing the presumed town site at Lattinford Bridge on the A12.[96] A third-century burial of a male skeleton in a lead coffin from Priory Farm, Great Wenham, with two folded pottery beakers and a glass bottle,[97] is close enough to be likely to belong to this villa.

At Stanstead, about two miles north of Long Melford, a geophysical survey and surface finds suggest the presence of a large complex of substantial buildings, including an aisled barn and a bath house, arranged around a central courtyard or garden. A small excavation confirmed the presence of flint walls and a white mortar floor laid over a tile base. At Rodbridge near Long Melford a courtyard building has been observed on an air photograph.

At The Plains Farm in Hitcham surface finds of Roman tile, of which more than 175kg was collected in one weekend, pottery, coins and brooches suggested a possible villa occupied from the first to the fourth centuries. A geophysical survey and excavation in 2006 established the presence of a bath house and a building with flint footings inside a rectilinear ditched enclosure.

95 Moore, I., "Roman Suffolk", PSIAH vol.24 (1948); Maynard, G., "Recent Archaeological Fieldwork in Suffolk", PSIAH vol. 25 (1950), p.209; Ipswich Museum 1928.229.
96 Ipswich Museum, 1927-33.1-12 and 1952-163, 164, 165.
97 found in 1952, now on display at Ipswich Museum.

A spread of Roman building material and surface finds at Knodishall, near Leiston, has been interpreted as a small town, but it seems more likely to be the remains of a substantial villa.

It is possible that the largest villa complexes had a military or administrative function, or alternatively they could have been built by retired military officers or by politicians in exile. It is intriguing that a Roman tile found close to the large villa at Gayton Thorpe in north-west Norfolk has the stamp of Legion VI ([L]EG VI VICT P [F]), apparently identical to one found in their legionary base at York.[98] It seems more probable that it was part of a building project under legionary supervision than that it travelled from York as ballast. The villa appears to be two houses, of the "winged corridor" type seen at Lidgate, joined together to create an impressive frontage almost 200ft long. It had at least two high-quality coloured mosaic floors and a recent geophysical survey suggests there was a detached bathhouse. We await reports of further excavations at Gayton Thorpe.[99]

To the west in the Fens a monumental stone administrative building and temple were constructed at Stonea in the time of Hadrian, perhaps as part of an imperial initiative to develop this land to provide food supplies for the army. They are certainly a testimony to Hadrian's investment in public works and confidence in the future of Roman power. These buildings remained in use for about a hundred years before Stonea apparently became simply a typical market town.

In general the second century was a time of secure prosperity for the Roman Empire after Hadrian stopped its expansion and consolidated the existing frontiers. However, Britain started to see problems at the end of the century, and the third century saw a significant decline in the security and prosperity of the empire, so perhaps it was unable to sustain ambitious schemes and elaborate public buildings.

If the height of Roman culture in Britain was represented by the buildings of Colchester, St Albans or Bath, then it seems that East Anglia never aspired to it. The occasional mosaic floor and bit of marble facing hardly suggests widespread adoption of the high life. Yet the quantities of material objects, fine pottery, expensive metalwork and coins show a prosperous countryside with busy markets. The massive structural timbers from Scole reveal an ability to construct large and sophisticated buildings on the scale of sixteenth-century manor houses without importing stone. But even the lords of small medieval villages could achieve stone churches, so we must see choice rather than necessity in the rejection of stone architecture and urban centres. The people of East Anglia generally remained in the country and built in timber. Many did adopt rectangular house plans, often with subdivisions into separate rooms, but we see no great aspiration to adopt ambitious Roman building schemes, so presumably Agricola would have been disappointed.

98 Journal of Roman Studies vol. 47 (1957) p.233, found in 1956 and in Norwich Castle Museum, a "brick" 4 x 3½ inches, compare CIL VII 1223r in Yorkshire Museum.
99 Current Archaeology 211, September 2007.

The coast under threat

5

THE SEA was always important to the Roman control of Britain. The invasion army had to come by sea; all trade and official communication between Britain and the rest of the empire involved sea voyages. Parts of the continental coast were within the empire but the coast north of the Rhine mouth was beyond imperial control and was occupied by people potentially hostile to the Romans who might raid the British coast or disrupt shipping. The whole coast of the province, including East Anglia, was a frontier of the empire.

We know surprisingly little about the fleet and the land forces that protected this frontier. Vegetius, who wrote about military matters in the later years of the Roman Empire, gives a glimpse of Roman naval patrols.[1] He speaks of scouting vessels which had around twenty oars on each side, giving them the same oar power as the Anglo-Saxon ship found at Sutton Hoo. They were used to locate and intercept hostile ships and observe their movements, for which they were camouflaged by having their sails and rigging dyed sea-green; the pitch daubed on them was also coloured, and the sailors and marines wore sea-green clothing. The Britons called them *Picati* and they clearly formed an important part of the protection of the coast and of merchant shipping. Vegetius says they operated in support of the large warships, which he says had between one and five ranks of oars on each side, but he does not say how many oars there were per rank. It remains unclear how many oarsmen crewed a large warship or where the ships were based.

The British fleet, the Classis Britannica, would control piracy which threatened shipping and coastal properties. This military task was a primary function of the Roman fleets, and two fleets were deployed in the Mediterranean to keep secure the sea they called *mare nostrum*, our sea. That required two fleets, even though all the shores of the sea were under Roman imperial control and earlier fleets had worked hard to eliminate pirates from the islands. In contrast the North Sea and Atlantic were open to the coastal inhabitants of Ireland and Scotland and all the nations on the continent north of the Rhine, any of whom could approach the coast of Britain without obvious hindrance. The idea that ancient sailing in northern waters was only along the coasts has probably been exaggerated, and it is likely there were enough adventurous characters prepared to risk the open sea and skilled at navigating across the ocean. We noticed in the first chapter that Julius Caesar had cause to respect northern seamanship.

The presence of the Classis Britannica, with its warships and scouting vessels, was essential to protect the coast and river valleys of East Anglia as much as any other part of Britain. The military, including the fleets, were responsible for policing and frontier protection as well as for the more obvious military demands of warfare and defence. They had to protect the communities of East Anglia from pirates who might land on the coast or bring their boats up the rivers. They maintained free passage for civilian traders as well as guarding military supply routes.

----------oOo----------

ALL AT SEA

Titus gripped the steering oar as the massive ship ploughed through the waves of the Saxon Sea. Wind filled the square sail high above him as he watched the angle of the rising sun. All seemed calm until the commander ordered the crew to their rowing stations on all three decks. Then he saw the smaller vessel ahead of them. No doubt the lookout had drawn attention to it. As they drew nearer he saw the green hull and uniforms of a scouting ship. Forty men would be pulling at their oars as they approached the massive trireme. Down came the sail and the mighty flagship slowed while the oarsmen took the strain. Titus looked down as the steersman of the scouting ship guided it into the lee of the warship. Did they bring fresh orders from Rome, or news of pirates on the high seas?

----------oOo----------

Opposite page: *Roman walls at Burgh Castle near Great Yarmouth still enclose three sides of the fort. The west wall beside the river collapsed through erosion.*
Mike Page

Obviously there were times when specific threats were greater, but throughout the period of Roman government there was a need for coastal protection. They also had to police the collection of any taxes due on goods imported or exported to and from this coast for trade with areas outside the empire.

The known market towns that were the main trading settlements were generally well upstream, perhaps for greater security as well as for access to inland routes, including the main roads. So far we cannot tell whether these sites were chosen by Roman administrators, perhaps with an eye to regulating trade, or arose from existing British settlements occupied in the Iron Age. This still leaves the question of whether there were final ports of export and import for goods subject to taxation or regulation on the estuaries later presided over by the shore forts as we shall see at Felixstowe.

For a start it is difficult to determine the line of the coast in the Roman period. Ptolemy, who wrote his *Geography* in Greek in the second century AD, refers to a promontory which might have been on the Suffolk coast. He calls this the coast of the "Germanic Ocean". Moving south along the east coast of Britain he proceeds from the mouth of the river Gariennus, which is generally accepted as the River Yare, to a promontory or headland (Greek *exoche*) followed by the mouth of the river Eidumanis, which Rivet and Smith suggest may be the River Blackwater.[2] Unfortunately this identification of the Blackwater is not certain, but if it is accepted there seems a strong case for the *exoche* being the West Rocks off Felixstowe, if this was part of a long extension of the Naze on the Essex side of the Stour and Orwell estuary.

Of course it is possible that a very long promontory at or near Dunwich or Easton Bavents has been lost to erosion, in which case one might wonder if Eidumanis could be the Orwell. Strang suggests the promontory was Orford Ness,[3] but this seems likely to be a more recent creation. Speed in the seventeenth century shows a significant eastward projection further north at Easton Bavents, but Bob Malster is convinced this is an error copied from Saxton's map. If any headland south of Lowestoft did project further east in the Roman period to create a conspicuous navigation point, the Eidumanis might well be the Orwell estuary, which is likely to have been much used by Roman shipping. Rivet and Smith give the positions in Ptolemy as: mouth of river Gariennus 55 degrees, 20 minutes north, 20 degrees 50 minutes east; the *exoche* 55 degrees 5 minutes north, 21 degrees 15 minutes east; mouth of river Eidumanis 55 degrees north, 20 degrees 10 minutes east; estuary of the Thames 54 degrees 30 minutes north, 20 degrees 30 minutes east. Ptolemy counted a degree of a great circle as 500 stades, reckoning 8 stades to one Roman mile, so one degree was 62½ miles (in fact one degree should be 600 stades = 75 Roman miles). Ptolemy had reckoned the circumference of the earth as 180,000 stades. Regarding the identification of Eidumanis, Ekwall suggests it could be Witham, but his identification of this with the River Witham in Lincolnshire puts Ptolemy's list out of order as he places it south of the Yare and the exoche. Rivet and Smith suggest the River Blackwater might have had the same name as the town Witham, which was recorded in AD913, but Bede names the river on which Bradwell stands as the Penta,[4] and the Anglo-Saxon poem on the Battle of Maldon seems to call the Blackwater the Panta, so there is no easy answer.

1 Vegetius, *Epitome* IV. 37.
2 Rivet, A.L.F. & Smith, C., *The Place-names of Roman Britain*, London, 1979.
3 *Britannia* vol. 28 (1997).
4 Bede, *History* III.22.

Andrew Breeze has put forward a good case for deriving Gariennus from the same root as the Welsh "garan", meaning a crane or heron.[5] He points out that the crane or heron was regarded as sacred by Celts. There are references to "the bull with three cranes", *Tarvus Trigaranus*, recorded in a dedication by sailors (nautae) in Paris and another in Trier on the Rhine. It is identified by Martin Henig with a silver figure from Maiden Castle showing the cranes as fearsome Greek harpies. In local dialect it makes the estuary of the Yare and Waveney "the river of the harnser". Sam Newton has identified the medieval name Goseford for the Deben estuary as "goose fjord", so perhaps we have two bird rivers on our coast.

There is general agreement that the mouth of the Yare, Waveney and Bure rivers formed a Great Estuary which flooded much of the low lands that are now drained and farmed. Flegg was an island. This meant there was a large sheltered haven with convenient navigation up the Yare to Caistor-by-Norwich and up the Waveney to Scole. It remains uncertain whether there was in Roman times a sand bar across the mouth of the estuary where Great Yarmouth now stands. In any case much of the estuary is likely to have been shallow and similar to Breydon Water today. We can assume deep navigable channels of the rivers Waveney and Yare to the south, passing close to Burgh Castle, and of the Bure to the north, closer to Caister-on-Sea and perhaps entering the sea north of a sandbank. There were probably extensive mud flats exposed at low tide and vessels of any size would have to keep strictly to the deep channels to avoid running aground.

On the north side of the Great Estuary at Caister-on-Sea finds of anchors, "probably of Roman date" from "the marsh which would have been open sea in the Roman period", are suggestive of vessels standing out in the deep water channel served by tenders. These might have been large warships rather than cargo ships.[6] The original reference is in the *Gentleman's Magazine* for 1837[7] in a report by the Rev. Thomas Clowes to Dawson Turner mostly about a brick-lined pit at Caister-by-Yarmouth which was at bottom 11ft. x 7ft. and at top 12ft. x 8ft. made from tegulae mortared together. The tegulae were 14in. x 12in. x 1 in. thick with turned up edges, giving 2in. thickness which held 1in. thick mortar filling the space, and each wall was 22 to 24 courses high, so the pit was about 4ft. deep. Could this be a fish tank? Clowes also reports skeletons, coins of the house of Constantine, one Commodus, one Domitian, and Roman pottery.

The site was a "few hundred yards to north west of Caister church by the side of the Norwich road." There are reports of Roman urns about a quarter of a mile to the east. Also "about 16 years ago" as he puts it some Roman urns had been discovered in another part of the parish south-west of the above pit and bordering on the marsh. Sinking a well beside the Yarmouth road "at a depth of 20ft. below present surface of the marsh a piece of plank was discovered which appeared to be a plank of a ship and the common rumour among the more inquisitive of the working people is that anchors have been found in the marshes at different times indicating that ships rode at anchor where now solid land is found." In reference to this Charles Green adds "Another [anchor] found close to the edge of the marsh about 1855 was reported to Charles Green by the grandson of the finder. He had often heard his grandfather describe the discovery but could not locate precisely the find spot".[8]

5 PSIAH vol. 41 (2006) p.227.
6 Darling & Gurney, *Caister on Sea Excavations*, EAA 60, 1993, p.3.
7 *Gentleman's Magazine*, new series 8 (2), p.521.
8 Lambert & Jennings, *The Making of the Broads*, 1960, p.116.

There is some evidence for a harbour south of the fort reached by a creek that later silted up, and there might have been a deeper water anchorage in the Pickerill Holme, which later served Fastolf's Caister Castle.

It is difficult to know what was happening on the Blyth estuary, although there is evidence of salt working near Wolsey Bridge and navigation was presumably possible at least as far as Wenhaston. Dunwich remains an imponderable, with the possibility of a promontory here in Roman times going out even further east than the lost medieval town. Further down the coast the Minsmere River is now a relatively small stream through the bird reserve, but its valley has been the subject of a great deal of drainage work. If the low lands there were flooded it would create a substantial area of water, and one of its feeder streams brings us close to the possible market town at East Green, Kelsale. Part of a direct route from the site to the Minsmere River is now called Wash Lane and the Wash. The original site of Leiston Abbey is close to the mouth of this river, and it has been suggested that it was one of the early Christian foundations of Anglo-Saxon times on significant coastal sites comparable to Walton Castle (Felixstowe), Burrow Hill (Butley), Icanhoe (Iken church) and Burgh Castle. Access to the Alde, Ore and Butley River systems requires more attention. We have no idea what was the origin and date of the "old borough" that gave its name to Aldeburgh, as any likely site was destroyed by coastal erosion long ago.

The market centre at Hacheston is close to the Ore, which flows through Marlesford, but probably had better access by river up the Deben. The entrance to the Deben was on the north side of Walton Castle, while the entry to the Orwell and Stour estuary was on its south side. Perhaps the combined estuary of the Orwell and Stour was protected by a longer promontory on its northern edge, extending beyond Walton Castle, which was itself destroyed by erosion. If there really was a very long promontory on its south side, extending from the modern Naze to the West Rocks, this would have been a fine sheltered haven giving access to the river systems of south Suffolk and north Essex.

As well as access to Colchester from the Orwell haven by the road from Mistley on the Stour, there was probably a supply base linked to Colchester at Fingringhoe on the estuary of the river Colne where it widens. Philip Crummy says finds there included military equipment, pottery and coins, including Claudian finds suggesting a military store base of the invasion period which would be accessible to large ships.[9] Smaller vessels, perhaps barges, might have navigated upriver to Colchester, as there is a report of a possible landing place in St Peter's Street where North Hill reaches the river.[10]

We should not forget that the west of the region had access to the sea through the Wash by way of the rivers that flow through the Fens. Although some of this land was farmed in the Roman period it was essentially dominated by large areas of water and by extensive tidal waterways. The appearance of dense settlement along the Suffolk and Norfolk edge of the Fens suggests that this was a busy and wealthy area, marked in north-west Norfolk by the group of large villas, truly exceptional for East Anglia, that overlook the edge of the Wash. These suggest wealth linked somehow to the waterway, perhaps through exporting the products of farmers and metalworkers. Higher up the system we have seen the extensive town beside

9 Crummy, P., *City of Victory*, Colchester, p.49.
10 *Colchester Archaeologist* issue 12, 1999.

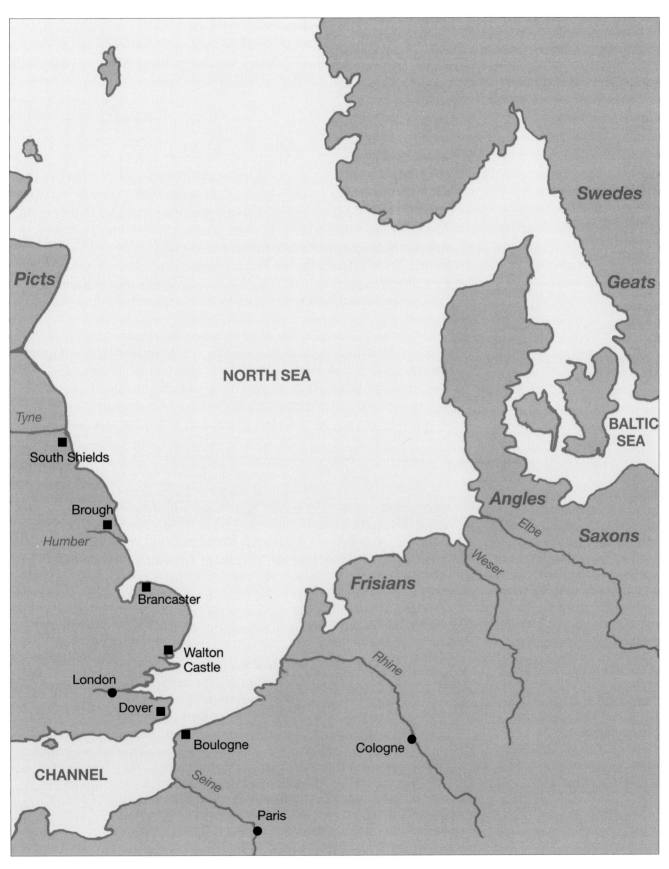

the River Little Ouse at Hockwold and the evidence of wealth in the valley of the Lark at Mildenhall and Icklingham. The convenience of this access for trading was offset by the easy access for hostile raiders able to sail directly up the rivers if they were not intercepted by the fleet which patrolled the coasts of Norfolk and Suffolk.

The security of the whole East Anglian coast depended on an effective Roman fleet being in control of the sea. This "British" fleet, the Classis Britannica, presumably originated from the Claudian invasion fleet of AD43. The older Classis Germanica had been raised by Drusus about 12BC for his German campaign, and continued to operate later in the Rhine area, presumably including the coast as well as the River Rhine. In AD70 Petillius Cerialis was putting down a rebellion in the Rhine area led by Civilis, the chief of the Batavians, who occupied the area of modern Holland. According to Tacitus Civilis feared that Legion XIV supported by the fleet from Britain (Classis Britannica) might attack the Batavians along their line of coast which was directly across the sea from Suffolk, but the Canninefates attacked the fleet and sank or captured the majority of the ships.[11]

Despite this Cerialis managed to defeat the rebels and was appointed governor of Britain in the following year. He brought with him Legion II Adiutrix, which had been formed as a new unit from members of the Mediterranean fleets. As it was based at Lincoln, this might have been a deliberate move to strengthen the possibilities of the army and fleet working closely together up the east coast as the area of Roman rule was extended northward. Certainly Agricola, governor AD78-84, used the fleet in support of his northern campaign.[12] Tacitus credits him with being the first commander to treat infantry, cavalry and navy as a single force working together.

One of his auxiliary units, a cohort of Usipi from Germany, mutinied while serving on the west coast of Britain and seized three Roman warships in which they sailed round the north of Britain. They landed at Roman "camps" on the east side before crossing the North Sea to land among the Suebi of Denmark and Frisii of Holland. We cannot say whether these rebels, whose story became notorious at Rome, visited East Anglia. It is likely there was one or more naval bases on our coast, but erosion has destroyed the most likely sites. Both Felixstowe and Brancaster have evidence of extensive activity from some time in the first century, well before any known fort was constructed.

There were lighthouses and major forts at Dover and Boulogne, the latter apparently being the headquarters for the fleet with a fort occupying twelve hectares. Although the prefects of the fleet were buried in Italy, navarchs, who commanded individual ships, and other officers are recorded at Boulogne. A trireme of Classis Britannica called Radians (*Resplendent*) is shown on a relief at Boulogne,[13] and there is reference to another called Pacatrix (*Peacemaker*). The name of a ship is given on the bronze model prow of a warship found in London as "AMMILLA AVG(usta) FELIX", the noble Ammilla fortunate lady.[14] There is no doubt that such ships operated off the East Anglian coast and in our estuaries throughout the Roman period.

Brian Philp suggests the Dover fort housed a squadron of at least ten warships with a garrison of 600 to 700 men in an area of about one hectare.

11 Tacitus, *Histories* IV. 79.
12 Tacitus, *Agricola* 25.
13 CIL XIII 3564, ill. in Desjardins, E., *Geographie historique et administrative de la Gaule ancienne,* 1876, I, 367; Boon, G.C., *Monographs and Collections I – Roman Sites,* 1978, refers a "*Pacatrix*" to Sutherland, C.H.V., *Numismatic Chronicle* ser 5, 17 (1937), pp.306-9.
14 RIB II 2432.1; ill. in Mason, D., *Roman Britain and the Roman Navy,* Tempus, 2003, p.113.

Probably it was the terminal for a regular ferry service operated by the fleet to Boulogne to service the Imperial Post. Tiles stamped CL(assis) BR(itannica) have been found at fort locations at Dover, Boulogne (*Gesoriacum*), Pevensey, Lympne and Richborough. Philp says there are 1,400 CL BR tiles from Dover and three or four are known from London. CL BR tiles were also found at the villa on the cliffs at Folkestone, which might perhaps have been the residence of the commander of the fleet.

Stamped tiles at ironworking sites in the Weald (Beauport Park, Bardown, Bodiam, Cranbrook and Hastings) show that the fleet was involved there, perhaps providing iron for military weapons and equipment. Being heavy, iron would be transported by ship, perhaps as part of the fleet's duties. The fleet was certainly involved in building work on Hadrian's Wall, as noted by inscriptions at Benwell granaries (RIB 1340) under Platorius Nepos (AD122–126). Building stones on the wall itself, apparently near Birdoswald (RIB 1944, 1945), record work by PED CLA BRI, which might mean "a landing party from the British Fleet". We have no direct evidence, but it would be surprising if this fleet did not have bases along the east coast so Felixstowe, Caister-on-Sea and Brancaster have to be good candidates. All three had forts later.

The total fleet was probably the size of a legion, about 5,000 men or more, with the Dover squadron equivalent to a cohort. Most of the ships in the two Mediterranean fleets, based in Italy at Misenum and Ravenna, were triremes, but most in provincial fleets may have been Liburnians which were fast ships, probably biremes with two rows of oars. The difference in size of

South Shields supply base: foundations of granaries with reconstructed Roman buildings beyond.

barrack blocks at Dover and Boulogne may be because they held the crews of different-sized ships. The crew of each warship, whatever its size, formed one centuria (century) with its own centurion, under a trierarch or navarch (ship's captain) with the gubernator (helmsman) as second in command at the stern and a proreta at the prow, a beneficiarius (administrator) and a medicus (doctor). All on board were milites (soldiers), as they do not refer to themselves as nautae (sailors). There is no evidence of use of slaves in war galleys at any time. The crew numbers are uncertain but a trireme might have had 150 oarsmen on three levels. On this basis a hexareme should have 300 men but presumably not six tiers of oars, so more likely there were two men to an oar on each of three levels.

Command of the British fleet was a very senior post in the hierarchy of appointments open to Romans of equestrian status, that is men of wealthy but not senatorial families. We know from the recorded careers of a few individuals that it could follow a number of commands of auxiliary units on land and lead to the post of procurator of the province, who was second only to the senatorial governor and able to report independently to the emperor himself.

The ranks of equestrian prefects depended on annual salary thus:

Sexagenarii = 60,000 sesterces per year – the lesser fleets

Centenarii = 100,000 sesterces per year – British, German and Black Sea fleets, lesser provincial procurators

Ducenarii = 200,000 sesterces per year – Italian fleets at Ravenna and Misenum, higher provincial Procurators, including Britain

Trecenarii = 300,000 sesterces per year – prefect of the corn supply, prefect of Egypt, prefect of the guard, Praetorian Prefect

Surprisingly little is known about the Roman fleets, but Pliny the Elder, a very well connected equestrian, was commander of one fleet in the Mediterranean. At the age of fifty-five, based at Misenum, he died in action supervising the evacuation of survivors from the eruption of Vesuvius in AD79. The Prefect of Classis Britannica was equestrian centenarius with the title procurator Augusti (imperial procurator), and may have reported directly to the emperor, unless he came directly under the governor of Britain, but there would have been a reporting problem if his base was in Boulogne, in a different province. Evidence of diplomas suggests fleets were treated differently, because their commander sent his return of veterans direct to the emperor while legions did so through their provincial governor, so presumably a fleet was not dedicated to any individual province.

One example is Marcus Maenius Agrippa[15] who, when Antoninus Pius was emperor (AD138-161), was procurator of Britain after being commander of its fleet. He came from Camerinum in Umbria and is recorded as a friend of the emperor Hadrian. He became prefect of the 2nd Flavian mounted cohort of Britons, and was later chosen by Hadrian to go on his British expedition in AD117. He became tribune of the first mounted cohort of Spaniards based at Maryport on the Cumbrian coast, then prefect of the heavily armoured cavalry wing of Gauls and Pannonians. After that he was appointed centenarial

15 CIL xi, 5632, Burn, A.R., *The Romans in Britain*, Oxford, 1932, no. 82.

procurator Augusti prefect of Classis Britannica, and finally he became ducenarial procurator of the province of Britain. His son became a senator, so the family was climbing in the Roman hierarchy.

Another prefect of Classis Britannica, Q. Baeienus Blassianus, from Trieste, had been Procurator in Armenia and Cappadocia before commanding the British fleet and went on to command the Ravenna fleet and then in AD168 became Prefect of Egypt, the highest equestrian post in the empire.[16] His earlier posts had included prefect of cohors II Asturum, prefect of Ala II Gallorum, procurator of a gladiatorial school in Rome and procurator of the census in Cappadocia.[17] Sextus Flavius Quietus[18] was primus pilus (Senior centurion) of Legion XX VV in Britain before becoming prefect of Classis Britannica. As chief centurion he led an expeditionary force to Mauretania for the emperor Antoninus in AD145.[19] He was buried at Rome.

The Roman Empire was at its most secure and prosperous height in the second century, but things began to fall apart in the third century, when it faced pressures from Germans, and later from Saxons, Goths and Alamanni, beyond the Rhine and Danube frontiers in the west and from the Parthians, and later the Persians, in the east. The Persians under their Sassanid king Sapor even captured the emperor Valerian in AD259 and humiliated him in public. Military domination of imperial government was very clear as different army units proclaimed their own candidates for emperor, leading to a series of destructive internal conflicts that endangered the rule of law within the empire and reduced the security of its frontiers. Britain was affected as early as the end of the second century when the governor Clodius Albinus made a bid for the purple, taking his troops into Gaul where they were defeated by Septimius Severus near Lyons in AD197.

As a result Roman historians record one major campaign in the early years of the third century that almost certainly created activity along our coast and involved Felixstowe, which was presumably then in use as a port for civilian traders and for military supply vessels. The successful emperor Septimius Severus needed to assert his power over Britain after the Caledonians and Maeatae invaded the north of the province in the aftermath of the defeat of Albinus, while Severus was regaining control in the east. At the age of sixty-three Severus campaigned in Scotland from AD208 to 211 in a large-scale operation using the fleet and the army. He campaigned into northern Scotland and restored Hadrian's Wall, including building a new granary at Corbridge.[20] He probably extended the granaries at the South Shields supply base, which was certainly in use at this time, as shown by imperial lead sealings,[21] and built coastal supply bases in Scotland. His son Caracalla consolidated military garrison posts in the north.

Felixstowe makes sense as one of points from which supplies were shipped north at this time. In support of this role of Felixstowe as a military supply base there is a peak of seventy-nine coins in the period AD192-222. This represents 20% of all the coins recorded up to AD296, when it is surpassed for the first time by a total of ninety-eight for the typically productive period AD296-317. It suggests activity in the early third century not seen on other local sites. Richard Reece notes that few coins of this period reached civilian sites, but they were used to pay the army.[22]

The coin records for Felixstowe, Caister-on-Sea and Brancaster all suggest activity at this date. Perhaps these key sites on the East Anglian

16 CIL XIV. 5341, cf. CIL VI.1643, XI. 5632.
17 Birley, A.R., *The Fasti of Roman Britain*, Oxford, 1981.
18 AE 1960,28 from Rome.
19 Birley, A.R., *The Fasti of Roman Britain*, Oxford, 1981.
20 RIB. 1151.
21 P. Bidwell, ed., *Hadrian's Wall 1989-1999*, Carlisle, 1999, p.76.
22 Reece, R. *Coinage in Roman Britain,* 1987, pp. 17 and 55.

estuaries, which later featured Saxon Shore Forts, were already operating as supply bases for the armies in northern Britain and on the Rhine by the time of the campaigns of Septimius Severus.

The operations would be supervised and defended by Classis Britannica, with possible support from the fleets of Germany, Moesia and Pannonia.[23] An inscription seems to show one individual, whose name is lost, holding command of all these fleets at the same time for this campaign. He had previously been tribune of Legion XVI Flavia in Syria, combined with the command of a cavalry wing, as its praepositus, then been sub-prefect of one of the Italian fleets, then procurator of an Alpine province.[24] He was buried at Rome.

The sea provided a means of transporting large quantities of heavy goods to any point on the coast. There is evidence of coastal forts that might have been naval bases and supply depots in the north communicating by sea with East Anglia. At Brough on Humber (*Petuaria*) about AD70 there was a fort of four and a half acres. A larger area was enclosed with a turf wall about AD200, and this was replaced about AD270 with a stone wall enclosing 13 acres. This has been seen as a town, but was almost certainly a substantial fort. In any case it is a likely location for a supply depot and naval base.[25]

Upstream from Brough, York (*Eboracum*) was an inland port with some evidence of substantial quay walls beside the River Ouse. At York a helmsman or ship's pilot (*gubernator*) of the sixth legion dedicated an altar[26] to the mother goddesses of Africa, Italy and Gaul, perhaps reflecting his travels: he declares himself a soldier (*miles*) of the legion, so a legion could have its own sailors.

South Shields (*Arbeia*) on the Tyne was a supply base for Hadrian's Wall. Recent excavation evidence has shown that the site had a long life. There is evidence of timber buildings before the first stone fort, which is mid-Antonine. The supply base associated with Septimius Severus continued into the late third or early fourth century, and at one stage it had twenty-three granaries able to hold 3,200 tonnes. It was replaced by a new fort, which again included a supply base, presumably the base of *numerus barcariorum Tigrisiensium*, with evidence of occupation into the fifth century "and perhaps beyond". This garrison was a unit of bargemen from the Tigris, no doubt chosen to transport supplies up the Tyne.

Possible supply ports further north include Newstead by Melrose on the Tweed (*Trimontium*), Inveresk, Cramond and Carriden on the Forth, and Carpow on the Tay. All of these were part of the east coast seafaring community within easy reach of vessels following the coast north from East Anglia.

One specific example of this link is the presence of mortaria made in Colchester, and one from Ellingham on the Waveney, found at South Shields and at sites along both Hadrian's Wall and the Antonine Wall.[27] They are also found in the Thames valley and on the Kent coast, showing coastal distribution southwards as well. There is likely to have been significant trade with London. We do have solid evidence that the waterfront along the Thames in London was advanced into the river by quays, with a final substantial quay inserted early in the third century. It is likely that trade with the Rhine valley was handled in the Orwell estuary and the Great Estuary of the Yare. The Orwell haven could have been a major port for grain transport to the Rhine,

23 CIL vi, 1643 (which CBA Research Report 18 p.18 gives as CIL vi, 1634).
24 Birley, A.R., *The Fasti of Roman Britain*, Oxford, 1981.
25 Wacher, J.S., *Excavations at Brough on Humber*, Society of Antiquaries, 1969.
26 RIB 653.
27 map in Ward-Perkins, B., *The Fall Of Rome*, 2005 p.186.

which was clearly not unique to Julian's campaign. We can compare Chaucer's merchant's concern about keeping open the seas between Orwell and Middelburg.

There might well have been activity elsewhere on our coast, undiscovered or destroyed by later activity or by coastal erosion. It is impossible to tell how many sites have been lost to erosion or to determine the precise location of the coastline in the Roman period. To understand more about changes of sea level in the past we need details from individual localities. Francis Pryor, the excavator of Flag Fen, has established that periods of deposition and erosion vary on a local basis within the Fen area, so even there it is not possible to establish a general pattern. Martin Carver's use of the 10ft. contour[28] looks too generous but could be a useful guide. Overall trends are affected by a gradual sinking of the land, while absolute height of sea level varies gradually over time. It is difficult to be sure how this affected the coast and the depth of water in the rivers at any specific time.

It is likely that as part of the consolidation of coastal defences after AD211, or at least within the period from AD200 to 230, the first forts of what became known as the Saxon Shore system were built. Forts of early design, the so called "playing card" shape with rounded corners, are known at Brancaster and Caister-on-Sea and at Reculver in Kent. Brian Philp argues strongly that construction of Reculver started late in the second century and was interrupted by the governor of Britain, Albinus, moving troops to the continent in AD197 for his civil war against Severus.[29] He suggests building of Reculver might not have been resumed until completion of the Severan campaign in north Britain, about 212-215. He argues this dating could also fit Caister and Brancaster, as well as a possible additional fort in this early series at Felixstowe (perhaps the West Rocks fort).

Brancaster was a 2.56 hectare playing-card-type fort, so it was probably built early in the third century.[30] The wall has rounded corners with square internal turrets, external ditch, internal rampart and four gates. The principia, the headquarters building, and four or five other buildings are known, having rough sandstone walls, chalk floors and one tiled floor. The cropmark of the largest building known, apart from the principia, is aligned with the civilian settlement rather than the fort, so it may belong to an earlier second-century fort. This building is similar to the principia at Brough on Noe which had been garrisoned by Cohors I Aquitanorum (RIB 283). Its presence at Brancaster is proved by stamped tiles, although by the time of the Notitia the garrison was Equites Dalmatae.

There appears to be a new ditch and some rebuilding in the mid to late third century. The earthworks of the civilian settlement, which have been identified by cropmarks on aerial photographs, extend over at least 23 hectares, in which the land is divided up by a series of ditches which also mark trackways. The plots may be house sites laid out in a regular manner. Pottery from this vicus indicates occupation starting before the end of the second century, continuing through the third century with some fourth-century material. No major road leads to Brancaster, although major roads do reach the coast a little distance either side near Hunstanton and near Holkham.

The fort was demolished long ago, as William Wilkins of Norwich recorded: "When I was there in 1788 the walls were all erased, but on the

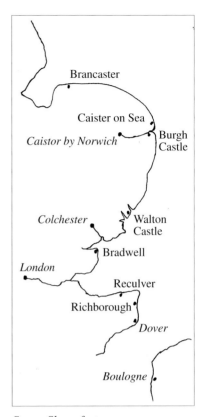

Saxon Shore forts

28 CBA 71, p.123.
29 Philp, B., *The Excavation of the Roman Fort at Reculver, Kent*, Dover, 2005.
30 Hinchliffe, J. & Green, J.S., *Brancaster Excavations*, EAA 23, 1985.

31 *Archaeologia* XII (1795), 134.
32 Morris, R., *Churches in the Landscape,* London, 1997, p.120.
33 Todd, M., *The Coritani*, Alan Sutton, 1991, p.44 quoting Leland, *Itineraria* iv, 181.
34 Darling & Gurney, *Caister on Sea Excavations*, EAA 60, 1993.
35 Darling & Gurney, *Caister on Sea Excavations*, EAA 60, 1993, pp.133-4.

Only the base of this building in the fort at Caister-on-Sea survives. It was built of mortared flints but supported a timber structure with a tiled roof. Part of this building burnt down and during the fire a soldier's savings, concealed some time after 340, fell from their hiding place in the roof space; the coins were found by modern excavators.

summit of the fosse are strewed numberless pieces of Roman tiles and urns."[31] Stone blocks from the fort walls are used in the church, particularly in the south wall of the chancel, and in a barn behind Staithe House and a barn at Brancaster Staithe. They are a distinctive stone probably quarried near Castle Rising, beside the Wash. Given the importance of the Wash it is likely there was a Shore Fort on the north side. It has been proposed that although Sidnacester, site of the see of Lindsey in the eighth century, might be part of Lincoln, or be Caistor or Horncastle, it could well be the missing fort.[32] Perhaps it was near Skegness, as in 1540 Leland said that Skegness formerly had a "castelle" but it had already been destroyed by the sea.[33]

Returning to Norfolk, Caister-on-Sea is a 3.54 hectare fort on the north side of the Great Estuary of the Yare.[34] It had walls with rounded corners which appear to have been built very late in the second century or early in the third century. Coins have been found with relatively high values from AD192 to 259, and unusually high numbers for AD192 to 222. Central Gaulish samian pottery and North Gaulish coarse wares suggest that Caister may have been supplied early in the third century by Classis Britannica from its depot at Boulogne.

The construction and design of the fort suggests similarities with Reculver and Brancaster. Coal found in Roman deposits at Caister could have formed a return cargo for supply ships taking grain to the north.[35] Caister also had what might have been a cattle processing area preparing meat for shipment, although the evidence is not conclusive. At least by the later years of the third century occupation apparently included women and children,

perhaps families of the garrison, and rubbish between the back of the rampart and the wall of a back alley suggests Roman forts were scruffier places than we sometimes think.[36]

Caister went on being occupied after the construction of Burgh Castle and activity does not end until at least AD370-390. It is possible that Caister, being constructed earlier than Burgh Castle, is the place named as Gariannonum. The assemblage of Middle Saxon material including two cemeteries, one inside and the other outside the walled fort, support the idea of a monastic site comparable to Butley and Brandon, so perhaps this was Fursa's Cnobheresburg.[37] The street visible today in the displayed area is not a Roman surface but overlies Anglo-Saxon debris with a fine Roman surface preserved below.[38]

Burgh Castle on the south of the Great Estuary was a 2.2 hectare near-rectangular fort, enclosed by a flint wall with tile courses. It had ten external bastions and was probably built late in the third century or early in the fourth,[39] since there is no evidence of significant activity on the site before the late Roman period. The external bastions are not bonded to the bottom courses of the wall, only at a higher point, which suggests they may have been added as a change of design after the building started. This suggests the fort was transitional in design from the early playing card shape forts with internal towers and rounded corners, as seen at Caister-on-Sea, Reculver and Brancaster, to the less rigid shape with projecting bastions apparently introduced at the end of the third century. There are records of finds of 2,500 Roman coins starting in the 320s with peaks in Constantinian and Valentinian

36 personal comment: David Gurney.
37 Darling & Gurney, *Caister on Sea Excavations*, EAA 60, 1993, p.255.
38 David Gurney, personal comment.
39 Morris, A.J., PSIAH vol. 24 (1949), pp.100-120, and Johnson, S. *Burgh Castle*, EAA 20, 1983.

The surviving footings of the guard chamber at the gate into the Roman fort at Caister-on-Sea, from where sentries could check on those entering and leaving the fort. Part of a red tile course survives, although most of the walling is made from mortared flints.

The projecting bastions, which enabled archers and artillery to fire on anybody attacking the wall of the fort, seem to have been added to the design after work started. The strips of red tiles between the courses of flint are typical of much Roman walling.

periods. Aerial photography suggests an area of 40 hectares of Roman agricultural landscape around it.

An unusual group of glass vessels, now in the British Museum, was deliberately buried in a bronze bowl with a bronze bell inside an iron-bound wooden bucket. These were dated by Harden to the first quarter of the fifth century as they include a mixture of Roman-style handled flasks and bowls and Germanic cone beakers and stemmed beakers.[40] It has been suggested more recently that this group may be mid to late fourth century in date.[41] Also found in the fort was a Roman helmet, now in the Time and Tide Museum at Great Yarmouth. It has been compared to a more elaborate example from Holland which is inscribed as belonging to a Stablesian horseman.

In the south-west quarter of the fort, under part of the later Norman motte, was an Anglo-Saxon cemetery with burials dated by radiocarbon to the seventh to tenth centuries. A quantity of Ipswich Ware pottery could not be associated with any structures, so it remains uncertain as to whether this was the Cnobheresburg where St Fursa established his monastery in the 630s. A harbour below the site of the west wall might be marked by enigmatic layers of foundations, including stonework and decayed oak piles, extending over a width of 11ft. and apparently a length of 200ft. excavated by Harrod.[42] He interpreted his finds as the missing west wall of the fort, but observations in 1961[43] located the position of the collapsed west wall at the top of the cliff. Harrod's finds at the foot of the cliff which might well have been the edge of deep water in the estuary are likely to be the remains of a quay.

Excavations in 1994 close to the church dedicated to SS Peter and Paul some 250m north-east of the fort revealed no significant activity before the late Roman period,[44] but showed ditches of late third or fourth century date indicating a changing landscape. There was an apparent shift from larger enclosure to smaller plots, which were probably agricultural, although there was a small amount of Roman building material in some features: much of it came from a late Saxon feature and may be re-used.

In 1994 an evaluation by Trevor Ashwin for the Norfolk Archaeological

40 Johnson, S. *Burgh Castle,* EAA 20, 1983, p.88.
41 Darling & Gurney, *Caister on Sea Excavations*, EAA 60, 1993, p.251.
42 *Norfolk Archaeology* 1859, 5, pp. 146-160, Johnson, S. *Burgh Castle,* EAA 20, 1983, fig.4.
43 Johnson, S. *Burgh Castle,* EAA 20, 1983, p.11.
44 Wallis, H. *Norfolk Archaeology* vol. 43 (1998), p.62.

Unit on a holiday camp site at Burgh Castle found a single piece of Iron Age briquetage for salt in a north-south ditch. So far there is no evidence of Roman saltworking in the Great Estuary, but it may be worth noting that in addition to the shoreline there were islands in the estuary which have not been examined.

Reedham church occupies a prominent site on a peninsula of high ground projecting into the Great Estuary near the junction of the rivers Yare, Chet and Waveney, within sight of Burgh Castle. It is a very likely place for a lighthouse designed to enable navigators to take bearings while finding their way through the open waters of the estuary. David Gurney says there were a number of islands in the estuary, so navigation may have been tricky. In fact it is likely that much of the estuary was very shallow, with only limited channels suitable for ships.

A nineteenth-century report of foundations "in a field near the church" may refer to the site of a Roman pharos, that is, a lighthouse with a circular base. In the church is a great deal of re-used Roman tile, and the tower is built with the same distinctive stone quarried near Castle Rising that was used at Brancaster, so perhaps the lighthouse was built at the same time as that fort. There is a tradition that St Felix founded a church at Reedham,[45] as well as nearby at Loddon and at Babingley near the Wash. Reedham would be easily accessible by water from Fursa's Cnobheresburgh, whether Burgh Castle or Caister-on-Sea, and it is likely that the two saints did work together. The next parish to Reedham is Wickhampton, which might be another of Margaret Gelling's Wickham names, suggesting a significant Roman settlement at Reedham. This may explain the existence of two separate reports, one linking St Felix to Reedham and the other linking it to King Edmund, which seem at first sight surprising.

45 Williamson, T., *The Origins of Norfolk*, Manchester, 1993, p.144.

At Burgh Castle the wall on the left was protected by the earth mound of a Norman castle motte, so the facing flints and tiles are well preserved. Where the wall was accessible the good flints were robbed out of the facing to be recycled in later buildings.

46 Milne, G., "Maritime Traffic between the Rhine and Roman Britain" in CBA Research Report 71 *Maritime Celts ...*, 1990.
47 CIL. XII 686.
48 RIC Postumus 30, 76, 214.
49 in Maxfield, V.A. & Dobson, M.J., eds., *Roman Frontier Studies 1989,* Exeter, 1991.

There is a debate about the function of the forts of the Saxon Shore. It seems likely that they met several needs, as they could house the soldiers garrisoned there to police the area as well as those manning the naval ships, and at the same time provide secure storage for goods collected to supply the army. Gustav Milne[46] correctly dismisses Cleere's distinction between military and civil ports, although I prefer to describe the Saxon Shore forts, and other coastal forts, as garrison posts guarding principal ports (or perhaps better havens as in the Orwell haven) than as either fortifed ports or naval police stations. This allows for the fact that some appear to be sited high above any possible wharf but are well placed to dominate a harbour area. I would compare the relation between the medieval castle and harbour at Orford. Walton Castle at Felixstowe would certainly fit this category and be well placed in relation to traffic between East Anglia and the Rhine.

In fact the shore forts around the British coasts were visible symbols of Roman imperial authority. Whichever major British river you entered to find a port, you could not miss seeing one of these massive forts with their solid stone walls. Equally those leaving the province were reminded that the Empire kept watch over the sea as well as the land.

A dedication at Arles by an officer of *Classis Britannica Philippiana* shows this fleet still existed under emperor Philippus (AD245-7).[47] In the chaos that followed the disgraceful capture of the emperor Valerian by the Persians in 260 a breakaway Gallic Empire (Imperium Galliarum) of the German provinces, Gaul, Britain and parts of Spain, was set up by Postumus.

He issued many coins that showed warships, some of them inscribed to the god of the sea *Neptuno Comiti* (to my ally Neptune) and *Neptuno Reduci* (to Neptune who guides me back),[48] so presumably there was successful naval activity in the North Sea. In 274 the emperor Aurelian defeated Tetricus, the last ruler of the breakaway Gallic Empire.

Even then things were not always peaceful on land, as under Probus (AD276-282) a rebellion was led by a governor of Britain and in about 277 Probus settled in Britain some Burgundians and Vandals, perhaps also some Franks, taken as prisoners of war, and used them against future rebellions. We do not know if these events affected East Anglia, but they might have led to a change in the organisation of the British fleet. N. Hodgson suggests a likely reorganisation after the recovery of the Gallic Empire by Aurelian in AD274 and before the appointment of Carausius in AD286.[49]

Perhaps it was at this time that at South Shields the fort was entirely replanned for replacement of Cohors V Gallorum by Numerus Barcariorum which remained the plan of the fort until the end. We might link this with the building of new forts on the Saxon Shore as part of its reorganisation, and Walton Castle with the external bastions that are clearly shown on a seventeenth-century drawing might belong to this period.

The tower of the medieval church at Reedham is built of recycled stone from a Roman tower or lighthouse. The grey stone was probably originally quarried near Sandringham and brought here by water.

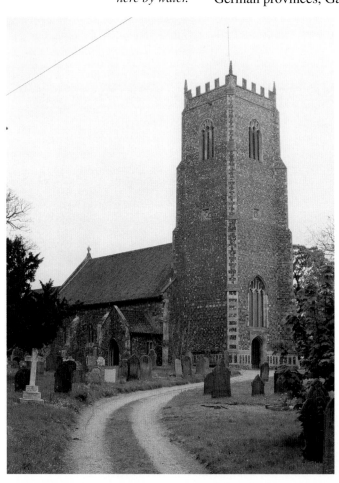

This might also have been the occasion for big changes at Caistor-by-Norwich, if we accept Sheppard Frere's interpretation of the excavation by Donald Atkinson in the 1930s.[50] The forum and probably the public baths, both apparently built in the second century, were totally destroyed in the 260s or early 270s. At that time the massive new walls were built, enclosing only fourteen hectares, although aerial photographs show clearly that the original grid plan of the streets of Venta Icenorum had extended over thirty hectares. The destruction might have been caused by raiders from the North Sea coming up the river or by a local rebellion against central Roman authority, represented by the administrative and tax collecting offices attached to the forum.

Thus the defences could have been part of the response to attacks from the continent where the imperial provinces were certainly facing incursions over the Rhine. Alternatively they were designed to protect the administration responsible for collecting taxes and sending vital food supplies to troops protecting the frontiers, which might have seemed threatened as much by local dissent as by attack from the sea. Both considerations might have affected decisions as the archaeological record is unclear, but it seems that the forum was replaced on a smaller scale and it is not certain that the basilica, the main assembly hall attached to it, was ever rebuilt. The construction effort was clearly devoted to the stone walls which were over 9ft. thick at the base, reducing by offsets to 5ft. at the top, and about 17ft. high. They were backed by substantial earth banks, had some external towers and an impressive south gate.

According to William Camden (1551-1623) the faces of all four gates were still visible in his time, and a century later John Kirkpatrick noted "ringbolts in the walls, whereto ships were fastened" which suggests there was a substantial wharf on the river frontage. However this could only have been used by relatively small boats, as a borehole survey shows the river has moved west over time but was never a really big waterway. The defences were a massive and expensive undertaking, and the way they ignored existing properties and street lines means that they must have been imposed by a strong central authority. The uncertain dating leaves it unknown whether this was the breakaway Gallic Empire (260-273), the emperor at Rome or even the rebellious Carausius (after 286).

Whatever the situation had been before, the new defences must have needed a substantial garrison of troops from the end of the third century and through the fourth. One is tempted to see the small fortified town as an integral part of the so-called Saxon Shore system. If so, who were its defenders? As many of the troops deployed by the empire on garrison duty were Germanic in origin, this might explain the apparently early start to burials in the two Anglo-Saxon cemeteries.[51] One of these was sited in part of the

50 Frere, S.S., "The Forum and Baths at Caistor by Norwich", *Britannia* vol. 2 (1971), pp. 1-26, and "The South Gate and Defences of Venta Icenorum", *Britannia* vol. 36 (2005) pp. 311-327.
51 Myres, J.N.L. & Green, B., *The Anglo-Saxon Cemeteries of Caistor by Norwich and Markshall*, London, 1973.

The walls of Reedham church include large amounts of recycled Roman tile incorporated in the medieval structure. They are evident here to the left of the window opening.

52 Faulkner, N., *The Decline and Fall of Roman Britain*, Tempus, 2000, p.128.
53 Crummy, P., *City of Victory*, Colchester, p.115.

original town east of the new walls, and the other was a little to the west at Markshall. There is much argument about the precise dating of the burials, which certainly continued into the sixth century.

So far we cannot see exactly how the events of this disturbed period affected people in Suffolk, but they cannot have been impervious to any threats from across the sea. However we have seen that evidence from coin finds at Wenhaston and Hacheston suggests that both these market towns, which are not far from the coast, flourished until about AD360; their trade seems to have declined rapidly in the 360s and 370s.

It is likely that walled towns were used to protect essential supplies for government use from interference by foreign pirates or disaffected Britons. This is supported by evidence from Colchester where Neil Faulkner interprets a large rectangular masonry aisled building (Building 127) as a possible government store to hold taxes paid in kind and military supplies.[52] The building, constructed between 275 and 325 on the Culver Street site, was at least 45m long and 17m wide.[53] It had no decorative finishes, so seems to have been a massive store building.

We have no idea what was happening at Combretovium at this time, but moving to the west it is likely that the walled towns at Cambridge and Great Chesterford provided similar strong points on the River Cam, which was navigable from the Wash. They might also have been placed to secure a line of defence for the rest of the province if East Anglia was abandoned to invaders. There had been a fort at Great Chesterford after the Boudican rebellion, and

Surviving evidence of the strong stone walls that surrounded the town of Venta Icenorum (Caistor-by-Norwich). Most of the stone has been removed for recycling in more recent times, but parts of the rubble core of the wall survive.

the construction of a wall around the town in the fourth century suggests renewed interest in its strategic position.

Writing about Roman tactics Vegetius refers to garrisoning towns or forts at suitable points to protect convoys on the roads.[54] This might explain second and third century military material at towns including Scole, though some might have belonged to military beneficiarii from the governor's staff outposted to the towns as administrators.

In 286 the emperors were keen to deal with pirates who were attacking Britain. They appointed Carausius (Marcus Aurelius Mausaeus Carausius) to take command of the Channel area and its approaches with a special fleet. Had the Classis Britannica ceased to exist, or was it incorporated in this special force? His task was to deal with the Franks and Saxons from Germany north of the Rhine who were attacking the coast of Gaul.[55] With his headquarters at Boulogne he was in effect commander of the Classis Britannica, whether or not the post was given a new title. J.C. Mann suggests Carausius may have had a total of 9,000 infantry with detachments from legions added to his fleet command. He had troops on the continent and in Britain where Legion II might have come under his command. He originated from the coast of Belgium or Holland, then known as Menapia, so presumably he knew the North Sea well.

It seems that he waited for the pirates to attack a neighbourhood and then destroyed them on their way home, recovering the booty but apparently failing to return it to its true owners. By keeping the goods he built a strong treasury, but his behaviour was reported to the emperors. When he was charged with keeping loot he declared himself emperor in 286, in opposition to the official emperors Diocletian and Maximian, although some of his coins were issued in the name of all three of them as joint Augusti, but clearly without their agreement. He seized control of Britain and of additional forces, including legionary troops as well as Franks, and controlled the Channel. He seems to have relied on his naval ability, in contrast to Maximian. He issued an improved coinage of better silver which was probably calculated to improve his standing with merchants, as giving a more secure basis for trade, and with troops, who thus received payment with the security of higher silver content.

He may have been taking advantage of the availability of silver from British mines to demonstrate the economic power of an independent British and north Gallic state. Some of the new coins carried messages of a fresh start, including *Pax Britanniae*, Peace in Britain, *Victoria Germanica*, Victory in Germany, *Restitutor Britanniae*, The restorer of Britain, and *Renovatio Romanorum*, Renewal of the Romans. Two designs used abbreviations RSR, identified as *Redeunt Saturnia Regna*, The Golden Age returns, and INPCDA, for *Iam Nova Progenies Caelo Demittitur Alto*, Now a new generation comes down from heaven above.[56] Both come from Virgil's Fourth Eclogue celebrating the birth of a child as the start of a Golden Age after civil wars. Another inscription, *Exspectate veni*, Come, long awaited one, refers to Virgil's Aeneid.[57] We might compare the quotation from Virgil in a mosaic floor at Lullingstone in Kent.

He may be proclaiming a new independent state, but it is clearly a classical Roman state. Presumably he would have claimed to be creating a state more truly Roman than that ruled from Rome. An intaglio showing a warship cut into a cornelian that was found on the Thames foreshore at

54 Vegetius, *Epitome*, 3.8.
55 Eutropius, 9.21.
56 *Current Archaeology* 153.
57 Virgil, *Aeneid* II. 282.

Southwark is probably third century. The style has been compared to ships on the coins of Carausius and Allectus.[58] There are three figures in the ship and the figurehead is a goose or swan. There is a similar intaglio of a merchant ship from Caistor-by-Norwich.

Cunliffe argues that the forts of Portchester, Lympne and Richborough were built by Carausius.[59] He also refers to the fort at Oudenberg on the Belgian coast 16km from Bruges.[60] The walls of Burgh Castle as we see them today and the fort of Walton Castle at Felixstowe, which survived until it fell victim to coastal erosion in the eighteenth century, might have been constructed at that time, judging by the use of external bastions.

In 293 Constantius, as Caesar the junior colleague of the emperor Maximian, took Boulogne by building a mole across the harbour entrance. Then Carausius was assassinated by Allectus, his finance officer and chief of staff, who took his place. Constantius had to take time to build ships before he could cross the Channel to defeat Allectus in Britain and save London in 296. He marked the occasion by issuing the large gold "Arras" medallions illustrating his arrival by ship to save London. In all it had taken Constantius some six years to recover Britain for the empire. Allectus might have been responsible for a large complex of massive buildings in south-west London intended as his palatial administrative headquarters. The timbers have a tree ring date of 294, and the design of chalk and timber-framed foundations is the same as that used in the later series of Saxon Shore forts, so we may be seeing the work of the same engineers who worked on the forts under Carausius. In 297 Constantius sent British stone masons to work at Autun, so perhaps they had developed their skills working for Carausius and Allectus.[61]

At least one individual in north-west Suffolk took the precaution of burying his savings in a pot and marking the spot with a pile of large flints.[62]

58 Acquired by the Museum of London in 1999 (*The Times* 26.8.99).
59 Cunliffe, B., *Richborough* vol V p.262.
60 cf. Mertens in CBA Research Report 18 *The Saxon Shore*, 1977.
61 Panegyric Lat. viii (v) 21.
62 Faye Minter in Newsletter of Suffolk Institute of Archaeology and History 64 (2007), p.11.

There were 258 coins of Carausius and 347 of Allectus. Perhaps it is a mark of those disturbed times that he never recovered his cash.

A late Roman list of officials and military commanders known as the Notitia Dignitatum, which some authorities think was probably compiled in about AD395, includes the *comes litoris Saxonici per Britannias*, the Count of the Saxon Shore in the Britains. The title of Count in the later empire marks out a senior commander, so the Saxon Shore was seen as a serious responsibility. There is no agreement as to the meaning of the Saxon Shore; it has been suggested that it was a coast defended against the Saxons or an area occupied by Saxons. The most likely explanation is that it was the coast of the Saxon Sea, because the Saxons lived on its shore. Before the First World War it was known to us as the German Ocean, but since then has been the North Sea. It is plausible to suggest that while the Romans called the Mediterranean *mare nostrum* – our sea – sometimes they called the area in which the Saxons operated *mare Saxonicum*.

It is possible that the system of forts of the Saxon Shore was created by Carausius, either as part of his campaign against the Saxon raiders or as defence against the central empire. It clearly included features of an earlier system and was used and modified later, right through to the end of Roman Britain. We do not know when the title Count of the Saxon Shore was created, but it might have been in the Constantinian period when *comes* titles were first used. We cannot tell whether Nectaridus, Count of the coastal district, who was killed in the "barbarian conspiracy" of AD367, held this title, but it is quite likely. Nectaridus is said to have faced a combined attack by Saxons, Franks, Picts, Attacotti and Scots.[63]

Although the Romans reported this as a combined assault by terrorists threatening the empire, it might have been a number of independent attacks by unconnected groups who saw the weakness of imperial control. A weak central government felt the world was turning against it and believed that this disparate collection of their north-western neighbours had formed some sort of alliance. This looks like imperial paranoia, but we need not doubt that all these people were attacking the frontiers of the empire. Under these circumstances our coast would certainly have been vulnerable, even though it was less than a decade since Julian confidently restored the grain convoys to the Rhine.

There were almost certainly signal stations along the coast to communicate with ships at sea. On the Yorkshire coast a series of square stone towers possibly 75ft. high, of which five are known including those at Scarborough and Filey, were probably built in the fourth century. On the north-west coast an extensive series of towers was built in the second century from the end of Hadrian's Wall at Bowness on the Solway to Maryport. Unfortunately coastal erosion has destroyed many of the most likely sites on the coast of East Anglia. Possible surviving candidates include Warborough Hill at Stiffkey, which has a stone-built Roman platform on a mound. Gramborough Hill at Salthouse is sited on a mound similar to Stiffkey; G.E. Fox calls it Greenborough Hill, and says a tumulus excavated in 1855 had produced Roman pottery and bricks.[64] Muckleburgh Hill at Kelling is higher, but may just be a natural formation as it is close to Gramborough. Beeston Hump at Sheringham has produced no known Roman evidence, but it is a good natural position. The report of a station at Corton is not reliable, but A.J. Morris says that in 1814 cliff falls revealed foundations of a Roman building of "great

Some of the collection of over 600 coins of Carausius and Allectus that had been buried in a pottery jar on the edge of a Roman ditch in Suffolk, at a spot marked with a pile of flints. They originally had a silver wash and were minted in London.
© Suffolk County Council Archaeological Service

63 Ammianus XXVII, 8.
64 Fox, G.E., "Roman Norfolk", in *Archaeological Journal* vol. 46 (1889).

65 PSIAH vol.24, 1948, pp.100-120 (quotes *Eastern Daily Press* 12.4.1933).

trees hewn and squared" placed crossways and with "rubble and flint built upon them" in a square twenty-five yards each way.[65] He also refers to Dinah's Gap, a little to the north of Caister-on-Sea, where remains of Roman walling 2ft. thick with Roman coins and kitchen rubbish were reported on the cliff edge in 1917.

In the Notitia the Count's command included a list of garrison commanders who have been located at the Roman forts on the coast of south-eastern England between the Wash (Brancaster in north Norfolk) and Portsmouth Harbour (Portchester). The most plausible allocation is:

The outline of parts of a double arch formed with Roman bricks suggests that the chapel of St Peter's-on-the-Wall at Bradwell in Essex was probably converted from the gatehouse of the Roman Saxon Shore fort of Othona. The central pillar would have stood in the middle of the access to St Cedd's eastern apse, which looks more like a compromise based on the original structure than a new Saxon building. The square windows might be survivals from the Roman design.

Brancaster	Branodunum	equites Dalmatarum
Burgh Castle (or Caister-by-Yarmouth)	Gariannonum	equites Stablesiani
Bradwell	Othona	numerus Fortensium
Dover	Dubris	milites Tungrecani
Reculver	Regulbium	cohors prima Baetasiorum
Richborough	Rutupis*	legio secunda
Lympne	Lemannis	numerus Turnacensium
Portchester	Portus Adurni	numerus exploratorum
Pevensey	Anderita*	numerus Abulcorum

*Rutupis and Anderita (Anderidos) do not appear in the text of the manuscript but are named on the insignia. There is a facsimile of the text of the Bodleian ms in Mothersole *The Saxon Shore*.

The unit commanders are listed as praepositi, apart from the praefectus of Legion II at Richborough and the tribunus of the cohort at Reculver. It is notable that the Count's forces based at these nine forts included Legion II. The Duke of the Britains commanded the army in the north, including Legion VI. There was probably a third senior commander in Britain who is missing from the surviving copy of the Notitia. The continental commands in the Notitia of *Dux Tractus Armoricani* and *Dux Belgicae Secundae* both have a fort (Marcis and Grannona – no location has been identified for either of these) listed as *in litore Saxonico*, and *Litus Saxonicum* appears on both insignia. Neither has been positively identified on the continental coast, and there must be a possibility that these were on the British coast but under continental command. It seems more likely that they were in France or Belgium, on the continental coast of the Saxon Sea, and perhaps at one time there had been a unified command covering both sides of the sea.

St Cedd's chapel of St. Peter at Bradwell on the estuary of the Blackwater stands in the correct position on the line of the wall where the gateway of the fort would have stood. Long after its consecration as a Christian church by St Cedd in the seventh century it was used as a barn, but it has been restored to Christian use.

The official list of officers in Notitia Dignitatum gives only the headquarters of each unit, and many of its troops might be elsewhere. Thus in about AD90 to 100 the Vindolanda tablets show that of the 761 men of Cohors I Tungrorum at least 336 were at another fort, probably Corbridge. A commander based in one fort might command troops posted to one or more other forts, or be directly responsible for other forts. The Notitia only gives his "office address", not his area of responsibility.

The garrisons of Branodunum and Gariannonum are both cavalry units, presumably suited to cover large areas of open country in East Anglia. Walton Castle does not appear in the list, so either it was omitted, possibly through damage to the original manuscript from which our versions are derived, or it was subordinate to another fort in the system. Clearly there were forts on most, if not all, the estuaries of the east and south coasts. Many were early foundations that were garrisoned through most, if not all, of the Roman occupation. We might note Brough (*Petuaria*) on the Humber estuary, while round on the west coast known forts include Cardiff, Caernarvon, Ribchester, Lancaster and Ravenglass.

The Count of the Saxon Shore apparently had no ships under his direct command, but on the continent the Duke of Belgica II, *dux belgicae secundae*, did have a fleet. He commanded the Prefect of the Sambrican Fleet "at the place called Quartensis or Hortensis", which might have been Etaples on the River Somme, where CL SAM tiles have been found. We should consider the fact that *Praefectus Classis Anderetianorum*, the Prefect of the Anderetian Fleet, was based at Paris. The name of this fleet must mean that it had been based at Pevensey (*Anderita*), supporting the idea that at an earlier stage some British forts included naval bases. It may be that a later emperor was worried about a powerful commander in Britain setting up an independent power as Carausius had done, and moved control of the fleet to the continent, where the prefect was accessible to central authority in the person of the emperor in Italy or the Prefect of the Gauls in Trier.

Ships based at Paris would enter the Channel by the River Seine and could be posted for operational purposes to any of the ports on the British coast, regardless of the commander's office. It is interesting that *milites Anderitiani* are based at Mainz in the Notitia, and an interesting group of Roman ships has been recovered from the Rhine there.[66] Four of these ships, found in 1981-2, are described as a light galley type of warship, carvel built, with thirty oarsmen and a mast step, about 60ft. long and with a shallow draught of 18in. that would make them suitable for use on the Rhine. The ships had been built in the late fourth century and were apparently abandoned at the end of their serviceable life at a small harbour on the river. They might be the ships called *lusoria*, fast scouting warships perhaps similar to Vegetius' camouflaged scouting vessels. They are also comparable to the Nydam ship. It is worth noting that they are found so far up the Rhine and at a river port associated with the Anderitiani.

Walton Castle at Felixstowe was clearly one of the Roman forts of the Saxon Shore type. A drawing attributed to John Sheppard and dated 1623 provides the most important evidence for the form and indeed the existence of Walton Castle as a Roman fort. Supporting evidence for its existence comes from two eighteenth-century observers.[67] In 1722 Dr. Knight wrote to the Society of Antiquaries of London that some distance east of Walton "are

66 Haywood, J., *Dark Age Naval Power,* Anglo-Saxon Books, 1999, p. 71.
67 Fairclough, J. & Plunkett, S. "Drawings of Walton Castle ..." PSIAH vol. 39 (2000), p. 419.

This nineteenth-century engraving shows remnants of Roman masonry from Walton Castle on the shore at Felixstowe before it was engulfed by the sea.

the ruins of a Roman Wall situate on the Ridg of a Cliff next the Sea between Landguard ffort and Woodbridge River, or Bawdsey Haven. tis 100 Yards long, five foot high above ground, 12 broad at each end turnd with an Angle. its Composd of Pepple and Roman bricks in three courses. all around footsteps of buildings, & severall larg pieces of Wall cast down upon the strand by the seas undermining ye Cliff, all which have the Roman brick. At low water mark very much of the like is visible at some distance in the sea. There are two Entire Pillars with Balls, the Cliff is 100 foot high."

A more detailed account is given by John Kirby in his *Suffolk Traveller* of 1754: "Part of the Foundation of the west side of it is still to be seen; being now one hundred and eighty seven yards in length, and nine feet thick; it is called by the country people Stone-Works. How much longer it was we cannot judge, part of the south end being washed away; and the sea, which is daily gaining upon this coast, having swallowed up the ruins. Such was the condition of it about the year 1740: but since then the sea hath washed away the remainder of the foundation. There can be no doubt but Walton Castle was a Roman fortification as appears from the great variety of Roman urns, rings, coins etc. that have been found there ... The coins that have been lately taken up here are of the Vespasian & Antonine families, of Severus & his successors to Gordian the Third and from Gallienus down to Arcadius and Honorius. It is certain that the castle had the privilege of coining money, for several dies have been found for that purpose."

The discrepancy in the length of the standing wall suggests that Dr. Knight simply noted a significant length of wall which he called in round figures 100 yards, but Kirby was making a survey for his map so actually measured the precise length. Similarly, Knight's estimate of a hundred feet for the height of the cliff means that he was impressed by its height but not that he measured it.

The map of Felixstowe and Walton produced by Kirby in 1740 shows Walton Castle as a ruin on the cliff edge and shore. Grose[68] shows the remains on the beach and says "Its remains in 1766 when this view was drawn were only visible at near low water, the sea having gained so considerably on this

68 Grose, F., *Antiquities of England and Wales*, Supplementary Volumes, London, 1783-87.

Elizabeth Owles, Keeper of Archaeology at Ipswich Museum, holding a Roman tile recovered by divers from the site of Walton Castle. Today the sea conceals large amounts of Roman masonry.

coast as to wash away the cliff on which it stood. A gentleman now living remembers the ruin of the castle to have stood at least fifty yards within the extremity of the cliff." A view by Isaac Johnson, *Remains of Felixtow Castle 1780*, shows exposed in the water below the cliff what appear to be footings of a wall turning a corner at right angles.

Isaac Johnson himself wrote in *Excursions on the Sea Coast of Suffolk* that the castle had been "on the Top of the Cliffs about sixty Feet above the Beach, and it was of a Quadrangular Form, the remains of it or Foundation Stones appeared in 1780 as represented herein about 100 yards from the shore, the sea having undermined the Cliffs and let down the Foundations left them as a monument of its irresistible Power. The Castle had the Privilege of coining Money, Dies for that Purpose having been found here, Urns, Rings, and many coins have been found here also, about the year 1780 I was with a Gentleman at Felixstow Lodge the then Residence of Mr. Fludyer where we were favoured with a Sight of many curious Articles which had been picked up on the Beach at different times. I noticed several Coins amongst them, particularly several of the Roman Emperors, which were of Gold, and the Impressions remarkably well executed, they seemed to be about the Size of our present Currency of Sovereigns [probably solidi of the later years of the Roman Empire]. Most of the remains of the Stone Works are fished up, and now form Part of the Fortifications lately erected at Ha[rwich]".

However, much does still remain under the water, as was discovered in 1969 when "a great deal of rubble and natural rock formation was found, then divers came across what appeared to be a long wall about 9ft. thick and 4ft. to 5ft. high ... red brick forms a levelling course on the walls. Several points were found where the brick was in three layers and approximately twenty inches above a further three layers were found. The wall consisted of pieces of flint-like stone joined together with septaria. At one point where three large pieces of masonry are visible at low water … These pieces contained many red brick layers, and after further dives came to the conclusion that these had once formed part of a large circular column which had fallen over. From this point the largest piece of wall runs for approximately 90 yards almost parallel with the shore, the other wall runs about forty yards out to sea. Covering the whole area lie many pieces of fallen masonry containing quantities of red brick. These were far too numerous to plot and extend a great distance out to sea and to the North of the main ruins. Many parts of the masonry were covered with marine growth, this had to be removed to find the red brick ...".[69]

Remains of the Roman fort can still be observed at low tides. Some of the stones visible at low water are septaria in their natural position, but the divers' report confirms the presence of masonry, including typical Roman tile courses and what sounds like a collapsed corner bastion. All of this is consistent with the remains of Walton Castle being completely removed by coastal erosion of the cliff in the first half of the eighteenth century. Before this, the headland on which it stood was presumably the most easterly point of Felixstowe bay and commanded the access to both Orwell and Deben estuaries, making it a very suitable site for a Roman fort of the Saxon Shore.

The fort appears to have been rectangular, as were the early forts, but with projecting bastions that are a feature of the forts built apparently towards the end of the third century. Perhaps, like Burgh Castle, it was built when the

69 Errington, J., manuscript report in Ipswich Museum files, 1969.

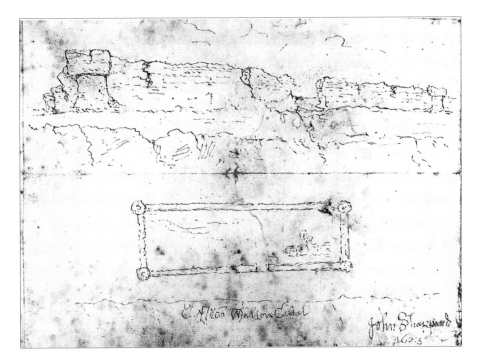

Left: *This copy of a seventeenth-century drawing is the only visual record of the Roman fort of Walton Castle at Felixstowe before its loss to coastal erosion in the eighteenth century.*
Courtesy of Mr A. T. Copsey

Below: *Clearly visible in the front of this window opening at Walton Old Hall are blocks of tufa, almost certainly recycled from Walton Castle.*

new design was being introduced. The presence of tufa in the walls of Walton Old Hall at Felixstowe suggests that some of the building material was brought from Kent, probably from the valley behind Dover where it occurs naturally so that it was used extensively in Roman work at Dover. We know that in the thirteenth century stone was being taken from Walton Castle to the Old Hall, which strengthens the case for believing the tufa came from Roman structures.

Brian Philp has argued that the similarities between Brancaster, Caister-on-Sea and Reculver suggest they were part of an early system of forts and sees a gap that would be filled by a fort at Felixstowe.[70] There is a possibility that the tufa was brought from Kent by Classis Britannica for a fort that preceded Walton Castle, in which some of the earlier stone was reused. It would be surprising if the Orwell estuary were left without a fort when the first series was created.

Almost certainly the castle was later occupied by the Priory of St. Felix, which was founded or re-founded before 1100 and moved to a site close to Walton church in the fourteenth century. Accordingly it is very likely that when Aaron Rathborne surveyed the area in 1613 the land he referred to as Old Abbey Close was the walled enclosure of Walton Castle.[71] He describes "A close of arrable called the greate longe dole wherein Richard Pettyward hath a small peece, this close lieth between the ould Abbye and the cliffe east, Pettywarde plott. pightle and an ould ... lane there west, and the same lane north and the ende of the high streete and the cliffe south containing twenty two acres. A close of arrable or pasture grounde called the ould Abbye lienge between the cliff east and south and the close last mentioned west containing six acres and one roude. A small close of meadowe pasture or ferme grounde called his ould abbye ponde open to that last mentioned south and to John Stannarde grounde northe and abutting on the cliffe east, containing two acres."

A volume of maps produced in 1784 by Isaac Johnson[72] "drawn from the

70 Philp, B., *The Excavation of the Roman Fort at Reculver, Kent*, Dover, 2005.
71 Rathborne, A., *A survaye of the Mannor or Mannors of Walton cu. Trymley & Felixstowe Priorie in ye Countie of Suff ...*, 1613, ms in SROI, HB8/1/201.
72 Johnson, I., *The Estate of Hon George Nassau in Felixstowe ...*, 1784, SROI HA 119/3/2/1/1.

Actual Survey of John Kirby made in Years 1740 & 41" shows Great Long Dole next to the cliff, with "stone castle" in the sea. If we accept that Rathborne's Old Abbey Close was Walton Castle and assume that the west wall was not seriously eroded when measured by Kirby we have some evidence of the dimensions of Walton Castle: one acre is 4,840 square yards and one rood is a quarter of an acre, so six acres and one rood equals 30,250 square yards. Kirby gives one side of Walton Castle as 187 yards (561ft.) long, so the other side should have been 162 yards (486ft.). This is the best estimate we are likely to achieve and is consistent with the dimensions of other Saxon Shore forts.

There are early records of coin finds, including the 420 Roman coins collected by the Rev. William Myers in the years 1742-44 from Walton Castle and its neighbourhood. Presumably he selected the best quality coins but they do indicate the chronological spread of those recovered. They ranged from Pompey the Great (66BC) to Honorius (AD417), including twenty-three of the first century, fifty-five of the second, ninety-nine of the third and two hundred and forty of the fourth. In 1753 Philip Thicknesse, the Lieutenant Governor of Landguard Fort, bought a fisherman's cottage at the location later known as Cobbold's Point. He extended it and in front erected a stone arch salvaged from the remains of Walton Castle, and this features in an engraving supposedly copied from an early work by Gainsborough, who was friendly with Thicknesse. His wife's description of the cottage includes this arch: "The entrance to the cottage was through a very large arch, built with stones taken from among the rocks at low water, many of which were of such a size, that it required no less than ten men to lift one of them ... the South entrance into the cottage ... led into a room called the Roman parlour, from its being entirely paved with Roman brick, taken from an old ruinous castle half a mile distant from the cottage, built by the Romans ... the top and sides were entirely covered with shingles, shells, talc, small pieces of looking-glass, and spar, besides a great number of small copper coin, dug out of the ruins of the castle."[73] This had become Felixstowe Lodge, the home of Sir Samuel Brudenell Fludyer, by the time of Isaac Johnson's visit about 1780.

Walton Castle is missing from the list in the Notitia. C.E. Stevens suggested removing Portchester as unoccupied at the time and making Walton *Portus Adurni*,[74] but M.W.C. Hassall rejects this,[75] as Cunliffe has found later coins at Portchester, which seems the best candidate. He proposes that Walton was paired with Bradwell at the start of the list and had been lost from the top of the manuscript, and may be missed from the stylised map used as insignia because that was derived from the list. Unfortunately the copy of the Notitia, thought to have been made in the tenth century, from which our four surviving manuscripts were made in the fifteenth and sixteenth centuries has been lost, so it is difficult to reconstruct the original document on which our theories are based. One aspect of this is the very different portrayal of the forts in the copies of the insignia.[76] There is the additional problem that there might well have been other forts on the coast of East Anglia, as excavation evidence suggests that the fort at Caister-by-Yarmouth continued in use after the construction of Burgh Castle rather than being replaced by it.[77] Other sites may well have been lost to coastal erosion long ago, leaving no remains, and some of the forts might have been subordinated to others.

The Rev. William Myers, an eighteenth-century vicar of Walton-cum-Felixstowe, recorded evidence of Roman activity at the West Rocks which suggests there might have been a second fort protecting the Orwell estuary some two miles out to sea. We have already seen that the Essex promontory of Walton Naze might have extended far out, enclosing a huge haven,[78] and the West Rocks may have been the end of the promontory listed by Ptolemy. Ships leaving Felixstowe and Harwich today have to take a long sweep to the north to avoid the very shallow water where the promontory would have been.

Myers, in a letter written in 1762, but not published until after his death, describes the evidence for Roman masonry "at the place which is now called The West Rocks, where large ruins are now to be perceived at low water. This information I have had from several at Harwich; and our fishermen, who go thither to catch lobsters, assure me, they have seen several ruins of brick-work, square stones, etc. like the ruins of old buildings; the place, they say, is large, and full of deep holes, and from thence to Walton in Essex the sand lies like a ridge, and there is not above five or six feet water, or scarce so much at low water. The captains of the custom-house sloops on the Harwich station assure me they have often seen broken tiles and bricks there at low water. I suppose they took bits of Roman bricks for broken tiles, several of them being

73 *Gentleman's Magazine* 1809, pp.1012-16.
74 Stevens, C.E., *Archaeological Journal* vol. 97 (1941).
75 Hassall, M.W.C., in CBA Research Report 18 – *The Saxon Shore*, 1977.
76 Mothersole, J., *The Saxon Shore*, Bodley Head, 1924, p.18 and Alexander, J.J.G., in *Aspects of the Notitia Dignitatum* ed. Goodburn & Bartholomew 1976, BAR S15.
77 *Caister on Sea Excavations by Charles Green* – EAA 60, 1993.
78 Fairclough, J., & Plunkett, S., "Drawings of Walton Castle and Other Monuments in Walton and Felixstowe", PSIAH, vol. 39 (2000), p.448.

now worn very thin; and, but the other day, I examined a fisherman of Manningtree, one Philip Long, who uses the West Rocks, and he says, he has often found broken bricks there with mortar on them."[79]

As Myers had seen the last remains of Walton Castle fall into the sea he was well qualified to recognise evidence of Roman masonry. The West Rocks was the source of much septaria for the Roman cement manufacturers and many smacks were dredging there between about 1845 and the 1870s. This doubtless reduced the height of the rocks, removing some of the septaria in the Roman masonry and simply discarding any bricks. They did not remove it all, as there is a report that in the early part of the twentieth century a "hard hat" diver who was working on the seabed near the West Rocks reported seeing what he thought were Roman columns amongst white seaweed.[80] These might be the ruins of some monumental Roman structure or the cargo of a wrecked Roman ship. Certainly a fort on a long promontory ending at the West Rocks would have guarded the access to a secure haven at the mouth of the estuary.

The main port has been completely destroyed by the sea, leaving only a small fragment of its settlement on the edge of today's coastline. The evidence for the remaining part of Roman Felixstowe and Walton is extensive, but, owing to the rapid building expansion of the town since the middle of the nineteenth century and the uneven record of random discoveries, it has always been difficult to marshal the evidence into a coherent picture. Numerous discoveries over the past two hundred years, including coins, pottery, jewellery and burials, indicate that there was a large settlement at Felixstowe from the early Roman period, well before the construction of Walton Castle, continuing into the late fourth century at least.

Our impression of the Roman town is distorted because, while some finds were made as the fort itself was eroded by the sea, many objects were uncovered by diggers seeking coprolites for the fertiliser industry in the nineteenth century. They were digging on the land known as The Park which was Johnson's Great Long Dole. Other finds were retrieved from the foundation trenches during housebuilding, so that much evidence was poorly recorded or lost altogether. The available evidence reveals that, although no buildings have been identified, finds of building material, including tiles and painted plaster, indicate substantial houses. The exceptional number of bronzes of religious significance also reflects a town of some size, with one or more temples.[81]

Roman burials are usually found just outside a town, and those on the north side of the valley known as The Dip presumably mark the limit of occupation in that direction. Professor John Henslow found two skeletons here after a cliff fall in 1853, each with bronze armlets in pairs, one larger and one smaller.[82] The seaward extent is unknown because coastal erosion has removed all evidence of how far the land reached in Roman times.

Major E. St.F. Moore gave a detailed report of some nineteenth-century finds made by coprolite diggers in The Park not far from Old Felixstowe church.[83] He noted that many interesting Roman items had been found but a lot had been bought by visitors who took them out of the county. His own collection included brick flue-tiles, samian pottery, amphorae, flagons, a small glass perfume bottle, bronze pins, small tweezers, a mirror, several brooches, rings of gold and silver, some set with stones, a gold chain formed of twisted

79 *Archaeologia* X (1792), 350-9.
80 Bacon, S., *The Suffolk Shoreline and the Sea*, Colchester, 1984.
81 *The Archaeology of Roman Suffolk*, p.70.
82 Henslow, J.S., in PSIAH vol.1 (1853), 218.
83 in *EA Notes and Queries 1885* (NS vol.I, p.11), see also *Proceedings of the Society of Antiquaries of London 1885-87*, 2nd series vol.XI, p.12.

wire and a bronze armlet. He also reported numerous coins both of silver and bronze including among others issues of Severus, Gordian, Gallienus, Victorinus, Constantine and Arcadius. Many cremation urns were unearthed, some containing bones and ashes and either closed with a cover or in some cases a stone. Presumably the Roman inhabitants benefited from the oyster beds in the rivers Orwell and Deben, judging by the quantity of oyster shells turned up, with those of the mussel, periwinkle, cockle and edible snail (*helix aspersa*). There were also two brooches, one a round brooch of lead covered with a layer of silver embossed with flowers and foliage, and the other a circular bronze brooch 1½in. in diameter decorated with stars in yellow and blue enamel.[84] Also reported were a bronze thimble, a bronze brooch with blue enamel, a small bronze bell 1½in. across, and a circular bronze plate 2¼in. across, and a bronze object shaped like the spout of a vessel. The British Museum has on display an extremely fine globular vase of Samian ware from Felixstowe with decoration showing a dog following a hind and a stag among vine branches.[85]

84 probably Ipswich Museum R.1940-79.
85 BM 81.6-26.9, presented by A.W. Franks in 1881.

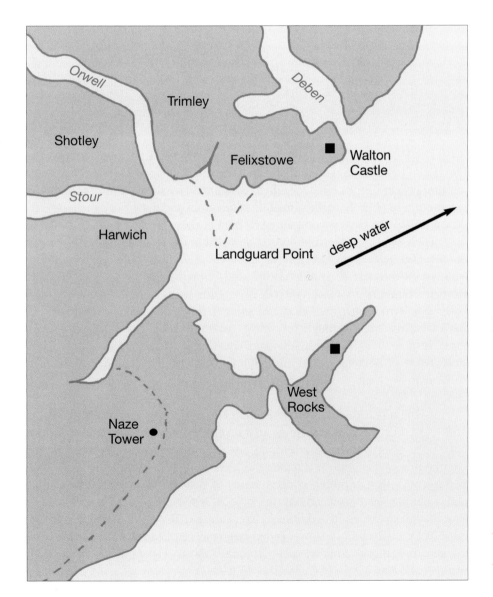

It is impossible to reconstruct the Roman coast line with any certainty. However it is probable that a long promontory extended beyond the Naze out as far as the West Rocks. Certainly much land has been lost to coastal erosion where Walton Castle stood beside the Deben estuary. As a result the greater Orwell Estuary would have been well protected from the storms of the open sea. No doubt much of the estuary, including the area of the later Landguard promontory, was shallow but there would have been deep channels providing access to the rivers and the port.

The Park apparently extended from Felixstowe High Road, across The Dip (Reed Pond Valley) towards Ferry Road and probably included the south-western corner of the cemetery which contained Henslow's 1853 skeletons. It is tempting to place here the complete samian pot and glass perfume bottle, as they are likely to have accompanied Roman burials.

There is also a record of finds in a pocket in the loam about 3ft. 6in. deep on the cliff edge near the fort in 1920 by H.C.E. Hopegood,[86] including a crossbow brooch of about AD300 and coins of Postumus and Tetricus, Roman emperors in Gaul AD260–273, with many animal jawbones and some ash. Two bronze crossbow brooches from Felixstowe are on display in Ipswich Museum. Although the finest crossbow brooches were gold, even these bronze ones probably indicate somebody with official status. They were worn prominently, pinning a man's cloak at the shoulder as seen in some paintings and mosaics. They tend to be found in burials of the fourth century.

In the nineteenth century two small excavations were carried out on the cliff edge, probably somewhere near Brackenbury, where the precise locations have been destroyed by later coastal erosion. In 1843 Henslow and his son George found "a sort of kitchen midden in the London clay cliff near Felixstowe". Rough pottery, bones, cores of deer horns, a skull, rusty nails, and a Samian vase were among the objects discovered in it. In 1897 Frank Woolnough and Gerald Arbuthnot, excavating a Roman rubbish pit on the edge of the cliffs at Felixstowe, found large pieces of samian and Castor ware vessels and black cooking pots among "about a couple of bushels of fragments", also a coin of Caracalla (AD198-217).

86 note by Hopegood with drawing in Ipswich Museum files (I.E. Moore in "Roman Suffolk" PSIA vol.24 (1948), p.172, wrongly calls him "Hopwood").

Three evaluation studies were carried out in the vicinity of Brackenbury and Foxgrove in the 1990s by the Archaeological Service of Suffolk County Council. It should be emphasised that all three were very limited exercises involving a few small trenches, designed only to identify the presence or absence of archaeological deposits rather than explore them. In other places this type of evaluation has failed to detect Anglo-Saxon cemeteries which were revealed only by full excavation, but I am assured that they very rarely miss Roman evidence completely. In fact the most productive of the Felixstowe evaluations, at the site of the Brackenbury Battery near the edge of the cliff, did produce clear evidence of significant activity in the Roman period.[87]

There was sufficient Early Bronze Age material to suggest a possible settlement, but only two sherds of Iron Age pottery were found, so we can at least say there was a prehistoric presence here and relate this to the scattered indications from chance finds elsewhere in Felixstowe. The bulk of the Roman pottery belonged to the second and third centuries, with at least two sherds from the fourth century. The second-century finds confirm that Roman occupation here started before the introduction of Saxon Shore forts. Substantial ditches were found, and the large quantities of domestic refuse in these included a "fairly high percentage of fine wares including imported Samian and Rhenish wares", suggesting that this Roman occupation was of relatively high status.

Structural evidence was confined to a single large posthole, of which the post-pipe (decayed remains of the actual bottom section of the post) was clearly identified. The packing of Roman tile (including fragments of tegula and imbrex and one partially burnt piece of box tile), septaria and fragments of German lava quern suggest a Roman date. However the stratigraphy is difficult because much of the Roman material was found, as frequently happens in Felixstowe, in a layer of brickearth in which it is usually impossible to distinguish archaeological features. This concealed any evidence for the period in which the post pit was dug, so it could possibly be later.

It might be significant that one piece of tile in the packing had been burnt, so it could have come from a building destroyed by fire, but this could as easily have happened at some time during the Roman period as at its end. It is possible that the tiles came from an oven of the type sometimes interpreted as a corn drier, now thought more likely to be a malting kiln and so evidence of brewing,[88] but they are more likely to come from a domestic building with a tiled roof. If we can rely on a single fragment of box tile, it also had a heating system. The excavator suggested that this post "may indicate the presence of a substantial aisled building on the site" but we are left to speculate whether the remains come from a private residence or perhaps a commercial warehouse related to the port, hence the imported fine wares and pieces of quern. Alternatively, perhaps it was a religious complex, if the reported finds of objects with religious significance, coins and a possible ritual shaft[89] could be firmly related to this location, but most seem only to be noted as from the edge of the cliff or just "from Felixstowe".

At present this is the highest point on the cliffs, and if this position stood out as much before the considerable coastal erosion it would be a suitably imposing site for a temple within a ditched rectangular enclosure, but such use remains a matter of speculation.

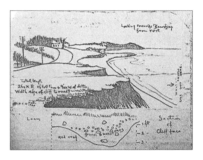

H.C.E. Hopegood's record of his excavation at Felixstowe in 1920. The finds suggest that he was recovering the remains of Roman burials exposed by coastal erosion on the edge of the cliff.

87 Suffolk Archaeological Unit, report 95/7 on FEX 088.
88 Hinchliffe with Green, *Excavations at Brancaster 1974 and 1977*, EAA 23 (1985).
89 See chapter six.

90 Felixstowe Archaeological Movement, *Bulletins,* September 1961 and March 1962; SROI qS Felixstowe 913.
91 Plouviez, J., "A hole in the distribution map" in "*Roman Small Towns in Eastern England and Beyond*", ed. A.E. Brown, Oxbow, 1995, p.71.

The presence of a large ditch dated by pottery finds to the Early Saxon period of such size as "more commonly enclosed areas of activity while the pottery and mussel shells…suggest occupation in the vicinity" indicates continuity beyond the end of Roman government. If we accept the argument for post-Roman activity then this could be linked to the Early Saxon pottery and the reports of skeletons found during the digging of military trenches at Brackenbury in 1939. With them were rings and Roman pottery, but these are not necessarily associated with the burials, which might well be later insertions. The easiest option seems to be that there was a domestic residence of relatively high status here during the Roman period, but the preservation of the archaeological deposits leaves the possibility that one day positive evidence about its true nature might come from a proper excavation.

As set out in Appendix 5 the main Roman road was almost certainly the line now taken by the High Road, continuing directly over the cliff at Brackenbury before descending to the shore. The original Roman port was presumably some distance south of the later shore fort.

One site in Felixstowe, at Foxgrove Gardens, might have been the centre of an estate on the edge of town or a self-contained house on a limited site within a town-type development. It has produced evidence of a substantial building including septaria footings of two walls 18in. wide, tesserae from a mosaic floor, window glass, painted wallplaster, roof tiles (tegulae and imbrices) and box flue tiles suggesting a hypocaust heating system. This is sufficient for Judith Plouviez (personal comment) to describe it as indisputable evidence that here once stood a Roman building of substance and status. It is ironic that the best evidence for a substantial Roman structure was not produced during a professional excavation. Its discovery is noted in the papers of a short-lived amateur group, the Felixstowe Archaeological Movement, in 1961 and 1962.[90]

The first mention of finds in this vicinity appears rather earlier in an article by Samuel Wall in the *Felixstowe Times* of 26th February 1938 in which he noted that many fragments of Roman pottery were dug out during the construction of the Foxgrove Gardens road in 1925. Subsequent finds in the garden of 11 Foxgrove Gardens by the owner's son resulted in a more thorough excavation undertaken by the FAM. They found building material, including decorated wall plaster, together with walls and at least one hearth, a couple of pits containing building debris, and a great deal of pottery, mostly of the second and third centuries. A first-century bronze "dolphin" brooch and a few fragments of first-century Samian and Belgic ware pottery suggest occupation started earlier. A coin of Carausius was found nearby. This was a major site of domestic occupation – a building of status.

Many finds have come from the southern part of Cliff Road, that is the section that is a direct continuation of High Road East beyond Church Road and along the cliff to number 61, just past the site of Brackenbury Barracks. These and numerous finds at various points scattered along Golf Road, added to the records of earlier finds from The Park, suggest occupation on a significant scale in an area extending over half a mile north to south and about half a mile inland from the known site of the Shore Fort. Even if limited to this area, the settlement would extend over far more than the 18 hectares (45 acres) suggested by Judith Plouviez.[91] It would rival the size of Combretovium, at an estimated 40 hectares (100 acres) the largest Roman town in Suffolk. At Brancaster the evidence from air photographs offers an interesting comparison regarding the extent and nature of occupation outside a Saxon Shore fort, particularly when we note that it reveals only part of the extent.

Inland at Exeter Road, near the crossing of Garrison Lane and High Road, a group of finds might be evidence of a separate small settlement. A number of cremation urns and other pots from Fairfield Avenue and Glenfield Avenue, found in 1936-8, mark its cemetery, beside the Roman road believed to have run through Walton to Trimley (note the name of Micklegata or Great Street Farm) and Stratton Hall. Not far away and immediately west of the Grove is the Roman site on Cow Pasture Farm which can be approached by a raised causeway suggestive of Roman construction.

Regarding the status of the port, two Roman lead seals found at Felixstowe are engraved in Roach Smith's *Collectanea Antiqua*.[92] They show a bull which might represent Legion VI based at York and the letters PBI which could be for Provincia Britannia Inferior, indicating the northern province of Lower Britain as the origin of a consignment. Similar finds are recorded from Burgh Castle, Richborough and Brough-under-Stainmore. They may be taken as supporting evidence for goods being shipped through Roman Felixstowe under official supervision.

In any case it is most likely that the significant amount of activity at

92 Henig. M., "A Roman Lead Sealing from Burgh Castle", PSIAH vol. 36 (1985), p.36.

Walton Old Hall at Felixstowe, the remains of the Bigods' substantial manorial centre, contains not only flints and freshly imported Caen limestone but also septaria and tufa, some of which were brought from the ruins of the Roman fort known as Walton Castle.

Felixstowe in the Roman period related to a port exploiting the estuaries of the Orwell and Deben. Agricultural produce destined to feed the army or for sale would be brought down the rivers in small boats or barges for transfer to larger seagoing ships which had brought other goods along the coast or across from the continent.

It has been calculated that it was as quick to travel from Felixstowe by sea to the Rhine valley as to go by road to Bury St. Edmunds. Martin Carver compares progress by walking at fifteen miles per day, rowing forty-one miles per day and sailing eighty-two miles per day. From Felixstowe it would have been easiest to reach Colchester by boat up the River Stour beyond Wrabness, then taking the direct road to the Roman colonia, although it would also have been possible to take the open sea route by sailing round the Naze and up the Colne.

It is likely that the port at Felixstowe came directly under the administration of the colonia, as we have noted that the veterans and their descendants probably had total control of the northern part of the territory of the Trinovantes. Perhaps the name of the Colneis Hundred, applied to the whole peninsula between the Orwell and Deben estuaries, originated as the Ness of the colonia of Colchester. We have seen that south Suffolk is likely to have become part of the colony's territory. If this was the situation, it suggests that Felixstowe, including Walton Castle, would have been the local market centre for an area of rich farming land and valuable deepwater havens for seagoing ships, dependant on the colonia to which it had easy access by water.

It seems that Roman ports at Felixstowe protected by Walton Castle and possibly a fort on the West Rocks, on the Great Estuary protected by Burgh Castle and Caister-on-Sea, and behind the Wash guarded by Brancaster were important economically and strategically. They were threatened from the late third century onwards by people the Romans generally called Saxons. This seems to have been a name used by the Romans to describe Germanic peoples who were outside, and sometimes hostile to, the Roman Empire, while they called Germans those living within the empire in the provinces of Germania or serving with the Roman army in auxiliary regiments.

At the same time many Germanic troops served in Britain as part of the regular Roman army throughout the Roman occupation. Some German troops were part of the original invasion army of AD43, which may have included Batavians who are certainly named as being in Britain in AD84. Many more were to follow. One of the obvious trading partnerships for our ports was the Rhine valley, so merchants must have crossed the sea regularly. When we see evidence of Germanic influence in East Anglia either side of the end of Roman government it is not always clear whether these are visiting traders, peaceful immigrants or hostile pirates seizing property and land. Perhaps we should see them as signs that the people of the North Sea were starting to challenge the dominance of Rome.

Religion changes 6

THERE HAS been much debate about the significance of the conversion of the Roman emperors to Christianity in the fourth century. Long before the conquest of Britain, Romans had absorbed the Greek pantheon and combined their own Italian deities with those of Greece, giving their poets scope to expound their myths in Latin. As long as all citizens honoured the chief gods of the Roman state, individuals were free to worship the gods they chose and to develop their own codes of morality.

The emperor Constantine I (AD306-337) chose Christianity as his own religion in 314, having been victorious while fighting under a Christian banner. He made it legal for Roman citizens to be Christians under the Edict of Toleration, but there was no compulsion to abandon the old gods. Constantine was determined to fashion an official version of Christianity, so he personally presided over the church council at Nicaea that adopted the Nicene Creed. The pressure to convert to Christianity, and particularly the official version enshrined in the Nicene Creed, became much greater under the joint rule of the emperors Theodosius I (379-395) and Gratian (375-383), who finally removed the altar of Victory from the Senate House at Rome.

Thus was ended the resistance of traditionalist senators, and things changed under pressure from strict Christians. All pagan worship was banned and even those Christians who did not conform to the Nicene Creed could be condemned as heretics, a new concept in Roman religious attitudes. A specific version of Christianity was now imposed by Imperial Edict.

It is difficult to gauge how far this affected East Anglia, particularly as Britain was already becoming detached from the central administration. We have no idea how many people became Christian, or if they retained some affiliations with other, older beliefs. What we do know is that a significant number of Christian objects have been found in our region, so clearly the new religion made an impact.

We know little about religion in Britain before the Roman conquest. Most of that has to be derived from what we can learn of religion after the conquest. We know the Britons worshipped gods who could be identified with those of their conquerors. Thus the only inscription from Suffolk in the first volume of *The Roman Inscriptions of Britain* is the bronze base of an equestrian statuette dedicated to Mars Corotiacus found at Martlesham.[1] Mars was well known as the Roman god of war, already identified in the Roman world with his Greek equivalent Ares. Presumably there was a local god whose name could be rendered in Latin as Corotiacus, and we might assume that he had something to do with warfare. Most of the figure is missing, but there is the stump of a horse's hoof and the mark for a second hoof, while a foe lies on his back with raised knees. It suggests the type of portrayal of a soldier riding down an enemy seen on the tombstone of the Thracian cavalry soldier Longinus Sdapeze, now displayed in Colchester Museum.

Presumably this local god of war was portrayed as a victorious mounted soldier riding over his conquered opponent. The inscription on the

1 RIB 213.

Martlesham statuette tells us that it was set up by a lady called Simplicia who "set up the offering for herself willingly and deservedly" and that it was made by a man called Glaucus, which is a Greek name, suggesting a Greek craftsman was making bronze statues in East Anglia. Probably in accordance with ancient practice Simplicia prayed to the god, being careful to use both his British and Roman names to be sure of getting his attention, asking some favour in return for which she would dedicate a statue. When her wish was granted she set up the figure of the victorious god, noting that she did it of her own volition unaffected by any pressure, but adding that the god had earned it.

Glaucus was careful to include his name as maker, perhaps in the hope of future favour from the god, if not also in the hope of more commissions. Can it be accidental that this one inscription recorded from Suffolk comes from the parish later called Martlesham? Ekwall prefers to derive the name from martens (pine martens) but is notoriously reluctant to accept Latin or native British derivations.[2] Even though Mars is the second commonest Roman deity represented in Britain, one feels this has to originate from a recollection that there had been a shrine to Mars there, because Martis is the correct Latin possessive meaning "of Mars".

Can we see significance in a "Priest's holding", Prestetun in the Domesday Book, located here by W.G. Arnott?[3] Perhaps it really would be pushing the case too far to see the neighbouring parish of Woodbridge as derived not from Ekwall's prosaic "wooden bridge" but from "Woden's bridge", thus attaching to it the name of the northern god with the military attributes of Mars. The possible coincidence has to be interesting if we note that authorities on placenames happily accept the use of Grim in Grimston and Grim's Ditch as referring to an alternative name of Odin, the Norse equivalent of Woden. Could we trace a connection from the British Corotiacus through the Roman Mars to Woden, who was claimed as the ancestor of the Anglo-Saxon kings buried across the river at Sutton Hoo? Too fanciful, or the product of a long local tradition?

In contrast to positive prayers to the gods there were also times when people wanted the gods to harm their personal enemies, particularly if they had stolen property. This could be done by scratching the message on a thin piece of lead, folding this and dedicating it to a god at a temple or sacred site. One such curse tablet or *defixio* was found at Brandon, where it had apparently been thrown into the River Little Ouse. Parts of the message are unclear, but it apparently targets the thief who has stolen an iron pan. The thief, whether male or female, slave, freedman or freedwoman, is sacrificed to the god Neptune, apparently to be killed with hazel.[4] The list of possible suspects is a standard formula used to cover all possibilities.

The reference to hazel is unique and might refer to ritual killing by strangulation with a hazel withy or by drowning under a hazel hurdle. A similar lead curse was found across the river at Weeting. Both places adjoin the Roman town at Hockwold, where a temple and several religious objects have been found. It is notable for including in the formula about the thief "*si paganus, si miles*" meaning "whether civilian or soldier".[5] This reminds us that the standard Roman meaning of pagan was a civilian as opposed to a soldier, rather than our more usual interpretation as either "countryman" or "non-Christian".

2 Ekwall, E., *Oxford Dictionary of English Place-names*, 4th ed., Oxford, 1960.
3 Scarfe, N., *Suffolk in the Middle Ages*, Woodbridge, 1986, p.20.
4 *Britannia* vol. 25 (1994) p.293; *Archaeology of Roman Suffolk*, p.68, with illustration.
5 *Britannia* vol. 25 (1994), p.296.

The British kept their traditional gods but identified them with Roman equivalents, just as the Romans had adopted the Greek pantheon. They also worshipped the official gods of the Roman state, because the Roman authorities insisted that all within their empire should honour Jupiter as chief god because he was chief protector of the state. Just as individuals made bargains with the gods to achieve their wishes and protect their safety, so the state's security and prosperity depended on all its subjects making offerings to Jupiter. This became an issue in dealing with Christians, who believed there was only one true god and refused to worship any other.

Figurines of deities found in Suffolk include representations of Mercury, Hercules, Venus, Mars and Apollo, all recognisable throughout the empire by their traditional attributes. Presumably when identified with local deities they were worshipped in the same shrines and woodland groves that had been regarded as their sanctuaries before the conquest.

Public worship of the classical Graeco-Roman gods required the sacrifice of animals at altars in the open air in front of temples which housed the cult statue and treasures. Many local people must have visited the great classical temple of Claudius at Colchester, but such grand structures were unusual in Britain. More often we find a simpler style known as Romano-Celtic; a square central building, which presumably formed the sanctuary, surrounded by a covered passage that might have sheltered worshippers. So far none has been identified in Suffolk, and only a few in Norfolk. However two examples of the standard design stood side by side in the town of Venta Icenorum (Caistor St Edmund) and opposite them seems to have been a theatre, which fits the pattern at Colchester and St Albans

A bronze figure of a dog found at Charsfield. The number of finds from this location suggests it was the site of a temple or shrine.
© Suffolk County Council Archaeological Service

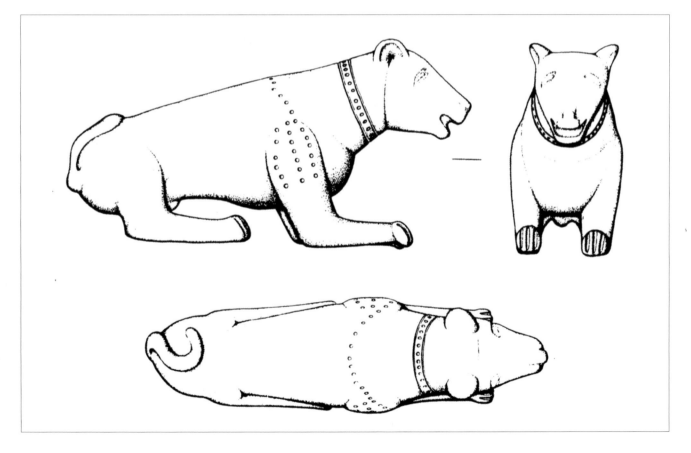

Two figures wearing the distinctive pointed Phrygian caps typical of portrayals of Atys or Mithras, taken from a colour-coated pot found on the possible temple site at Lackford in 1982.
© Suffolk County Council Archaeological Service

where theatres stood next to temples. Presumably, as in classical Greece, serious plays had a religious element and were dedicated to gods. Perhaps also religious ceremonies could be seen here by large audiences that were never allowed inside Roman temple buildings. Another such temple stood in its own enclosure outside the town wall of Venta Icenorum (see chapter four).

The lack of evidence is less surprising if, in common with most other buildings in the region, temples were generally built in timber, so not leaving the rectangular stone footings by which they are identified elsewhere. It is possible that fragments of stonework, tesserae and several metal objects found close to the Waveney at Oakley mark a temple site on the outskirts of Scole. Certainly a timber temple has been excavated on the other side of the Waveney on the edge of Scole.[6] A group of figurines and other metalwork from Charsfield are likely to be votive offerings at a shrine or temple. A fine bronze dog, on which the incised decoration includes a collar, is on display in Ipswich Museum.

It has been suggested that two types of brooch are generally found on temple sites, the "adlocutio" type and the "horse and rider".[7] The former has a round plate showing two rearing horses and their riders facing a file of three soldiers with shields and an eagle, while the latter simply shows a man on horseback. Some people link the mounted figures with Mars, and we do have the evidence above for a dedication to an equestrian Mars in Suffolk. Groups of adlocutio and horse-and-rider brooches have been recorded at possible temple sites at Lackford (Mill Heath) and Hockwold (Leylands Farm). The latter has produced eight horse and rider and possibly seven adlocutio, while there is also evidence here suggesting worship of Cybele and Atis (see below). Horse-and-rider brooches are recorded at other sites including Ipswich, Coddenham and Undley as well as from five sites in Norfolk, and two adlocutio ones have been found at Stoke Ash.

6 Judith Plouviez, personal comment.
7 Gurney, D., *Settlement, Religion and Industry on the Fen Edge*, EAA 31, 1986, p.89.

Traditional religions sometimes required the sacrifice of animals, which was familiar in Greek and Roman religion, but the most important religion in pre-Roman Britain required human sacrifice supervised by the Druid priesthood, which led the Romans to prohibit Druid activity. We have no evidence for Druid activity in East Anglia, but during the Boudican revolt Dio accused the British of ritual sacrifice of captives in all their sacred places and especially in the grove of Andate, their goddess of Victory. It could be significant that the revolt occurred when Suetonius was defeating Druid resistance on Anglesey.

Dio's accusation certainly implies the presence of sacred groves in the woodland of East Anglia. Perhaps this explains the presence of six gold torcs found in the Chantry estate area of Ipswich beside a spring that became a holy well used as a boundary marker in the tenth century.[8] Most probably they were buried for safe keeping within a sanctuary in a grove of trees beside the spring. This would be a place under the protection of a god in whose care they could be left, but they might be retrieved and borrowed from the god if circumstances demanded it and the priests agreed.

Worship of some eastern gods spread throughout the empire, and one of these was Atys, who was represented as a youth wearing a pointed Phrygian cap. The heads of figurines of Atys have been found at Eriswell and Mildenhall, the one from Mildenhall being a small bronze head wearing a soft pointed *pileus* or Phrygian cap.[9] Another from Felixstowe appears to be a mount from a bowl.[10] One of the stolen bronzes from Icklingham also appears to be an Atys, although Martin Henig thinks it is not youthful, so suggests Vulcan.

Atys is portrayed on a fine jet plaque from Castle Hill, Ipswich. Solinus in the second century described jet as a British speciality, black and like a jewel which when rubbed attracts things as amber does. Found on the Yorkshire coast and worked in York, it was used for various ornaments including fine pendants of Medusa. The lover of Cybele, the great mother goddess from Phrygia in Asia Minor, Atys castrated himself beneath a pine tree, according to the story told in one of the finest of the poems of Catullus. The priests of Cybele demonstrated loyalty by castrating themselves as Atys had done. As the great mother goddess who brought fertility through the story of a cycle of castration and death followed by rebirth, Cybele was celebrated in a period of mourning followed by ecstatic celebration, with noisy parades with drums and cymbals leading to sacrifices of bulls and self-flagellation by her priests.

These representations suggest that such ceremonies might very well have been performed in East Anglia. They were an example of the rituals performed by followers of various ancient "mystery" religions that promised salvation from suffering in this life and in some form of life after death, following the example of a deity that experienced death and resurrection. As pine trees feature in celebrations for Atys it has been suggested that the hand of a statuette holding a pine branch found on the Sawbench temple site at Hockwold on the Norfolk side of the Little Ouse shows that Atys and Cybele were worshipped there.[11] There was also a bronze jug with the head of Atys depicted on the handle.[12]

At a different location in Hockwold, Leyland's Farm, was a circular structure of timber and chalk about 30ft. across with a floor of rammed chalk

A jet plaque showing a figure wearing an eastern hat, so probably representing Atys. Found at the Castle Hill villa in Ipswich. Jet was obtained from Whitby in Yorkshire and widely used for Roman jewellery; a tradition revived by the Victorians. © Colchester and Ipswich Museum Service

8 Fairclough, J., "The Bounds of Stoke and Ipswich", PSIAH vol. 40 (2003), p.265.
9 in the Ashmolean Museum, 6.5 cm high; Green, M., *The Gods of Roman Britain*, Shire, 2003, fig.7.
10 Ipswich Museum 1962.163.
11 Henig, M., *Religion in Roman Britain*, 1984, p.113.
12 Green, M., *The Gods of Roman Britain,* Shire, 2003, p.23.

One of the bronze crowns found on Cavenham Heath. The decorative features had been removed before it was buried.
© Colchester and Ipswich Museum Service

The three crowns found on Cavenham Heath, but in Lackford parish, where a temple might have stood across the river Lark from Icklingham. They are now in Ipswich Museum.

13 Henig, M., *Religion in Roman Britain*, 1984, p.137; see also EAA 31 (1986).
14 see Nina Layard in *Antiquaries Journal* vol. 5 (1925), pp.258-265.
15 Lethbridge, T., *Cambridge Antiquarian Society Quarto Publications* NS VI (1951), pp.7-8.
16 illustrated on cover of SIAH Newsletter 23, Autumn 1986.

and painted plaster on the walls, possibly a temple or an associated religious building. Here were found the ceremonial headdresses or crowns known as the Wilton Crowns, which might have been worn by priests of Cybele,[13] as might the three headdresses known as the Cavenham Crowns, two of them sheet bronze and the third a chain cap, which can be seen at Ipswich Museum.[14] Miss Nina Layard obtained them from the landlord of the Crown Inn at Mundford in 1918.

She described the findspot as on a slight elevation overlooking the River Lark opposite Icklingham, about midway between the Icknield Way and the Black Ditches, on Cavenham Heath but in Lackford, and Tom Lethbridge confirmed this.[15] The regalia, which had been decorated with silver plaques and gems or glass imitations which had been removed, had been found at a depth of about eighteen inches. Over an area about thirty yards either side of the spot Miss Layard found a variety of Roman pottery, said to range in date from first to fourth century, two roofing tiles, animal bones, oyster shells and a bronze feather which had presumably belonged to the regalia. The two sheet bronze crowns have adjustable fastenings to adapt them for different sized heads, and the chain headdress might have been worn over a leather cap. A similar chain headdress, now in the British Museum, was found at Stony Stratford in 1789 with three out of five silver ornaments still in place.

The probable site on Mill Heath at Lackford has produced two figurines, as well as many brooches and coins which might have been votive offerings at a square timber-and-clay building decorated with painted wall plaster. Judith Plouviez comments on two figures in a hunting scene shown on a colour-coated pot found in 1982 on the possible temple site at Lackford who wear the distinctive pointed Phrygian caps typical of figures of Atys or Mithras.[16]

In the Saxon cemetery which he excavated there Lethbridge found that many of the cremation urns were covered by Roman tiles. He excavated two small rectangular Roman buildings which he interpreted as burial vaults, as

17 Dio Cassius 62.7.
18 Dio Cassius 62.6.

one had a few human bones in it, but both appeared to have been looted, perhaps in Saxon times. He also noted numerous fragments of Roman pottery between the cemetery and the river, in the area directly opposite the Roman town at Icklingham, which apparently spread across the river.

Some authorities think that in Gaul Cybele as the Great Mother (*Magna Mater*) was identified with Andarte. If so, she might be the British goddess Andarte whom Dio Cassius records as being a goddess of victory worshipped by the Iceni in her grove with human sacrifices during the Boudican revolt.[17] Could she be the Andraste in whose name Boudica released a hare at the beginning of her campaign?[18] If she were, that might explain the later enthusiasm for the cult of Cybele among the Iceni.

Perhaps when Christianity was introduced to East Anglia the local population saw an affinity between Cybele, mother of Atys, and Mary the mother of Jesus, as we have a notable number of later pilgrimage sites linked to Mary. These include Our Lady of Grace at Gracechurch in Lady Lane at Ipswich, Our Lady in her Holy House at Walsingham in Norfolk, the great Lady Chapel attached to the Priory of St Mary at Thetford, and the image of Mary and Lady's Well at Woolpit.

According to one version of the story Atys was resurrected after three

A silver and bronze ritual head-dress found at Stony Stratford. A more elaborate version of the type found on Cavenham Heath. © Trustees of the British Museum

19 SIAH Newsletter 61 (Autumn 2005).
20 Bagnall Smith, J. *Britannia* 30 (1999) p.21.

days on 25th March; immersion in blood from a slaughtered bull was compared to baptism, and there were links to "The Unconquered Sun" as with Mithraism, which was much concerned with the triumph of light over darkness. Worship of Mithras, whose birth was celebrated on 25th December, and his association with the Unconquered Sun as a supreme god were popular with the Roman army. Then Constantine declared his victory in battle came through Christ, who is hailed as light of light in the Nicene Creed, suggesting a direct link to the sun. Constantine's concept of Christ owed much to the Mithraic tradition.

While figures of Priapus, bringer of good luck and particularly of fertility, are rare in Britain two have been found in Suffolk, one at Pakenham which is 8cm tall with a prominent phallus and another near Bury St Edmunds.[19] The latter has the large phallus which distinguished Priapus but wears a pointed hat reminiscent of the Phrygian cap of Atys, although this Priapus has a long pointed beard whereas Atys is shown as a clean-faced youth. Could there have been a local cult of Priapus, perhaps linked to the castrated Atys? It might be significant that two phallic pendants, one showing a figure riding a prodigious phallus, were found at Icklingham.

Both Cybele (and so Atys) and Priapus were linked to Dionysus/ Bacchus who features on the Mildenhall silver. The wild figures of Bacchic revellers in the outer ring of the great Mildenhall dish include Pan with his pipes. We can identify this god of the untamed countryside with Faunus, who is celebrated in a collection of fourth-century treasures, presumably from a shrine in his honour at Thetford. Although Faunus was an Italian rural god he is linked here by inscriptions on silver spoons with a number of Celtic gods who are otherwise unknown. Two woodpeckers on a gold ring are presumably reminders that Faunus was the son of a woodpecker, and a fine gold buckle portrays a satyr.

A significant collection of votive finds from Great Walsingham[20]

The fourth-century Thetford Treasure included 22 gold rings (one inscribed in Greek for Iao Abrasax) and several silver spoons inscribed to Faunus, whose woodpeckers feature on one of the rings.

suggests the presence of a shrine close to the River Stiffkey not far from the medieval Christian shrine of Our Lady at Little Walsingham. Masks of Cupids and representations of Satyrs do suggest a link with Dionysus/Bacchus, although the largest group including three statuettes as well as two goats and three cocks relate to Mercury. The presence of over 6,000 coins and huge quantities of pottery from the second to fourth centuries as well as over twenty seal boxes discussed in chapter four show much activity here.

More mysterious are the so-called ritual shafts that have been found in East Anglia, and elsewhere in Britain. One was recorded somewhere along the cliff at Felixstowe: "On 28 May 1873 Mr. Gervas Holmes discovered, on the cliff top, about a mile north of Felixstowe, a hearth with burnt and broken bones about 4ft. below the surface. Beneath the hearth was a floor of red crag about 18in. thick below which was a well 30in. square and about 8ft. deep, with sides of well preserved wood. At the bottom of the well was a Roman vase of Castor ware, containing earth and acorns, but there was no sign of calcined bones. The vase is 7½in. high, of brownish red ware with concave sides, most likely a drinking vessel."[21]

James Reid Moir excavated two shafts at Ipswich in the Dales Road brickfield close to the Castle Hill villa and a Roman cemetery.[22]

21 Manning, C.R., *Archaeological Journal*, vol. 31 (1874), p.303; Ross, A., "Shafts, pits, wells – sanctuaries of the Belgic Britons?" in Coles, J.M. & Simpson, D.D.A. eds., *Studies in Ancient Europe – essays presented to Stuart Piggott*, Leicester, 1968, p.264.
22 Reid Moir, J., PSIAH vol. 22 (1936), p. 141.

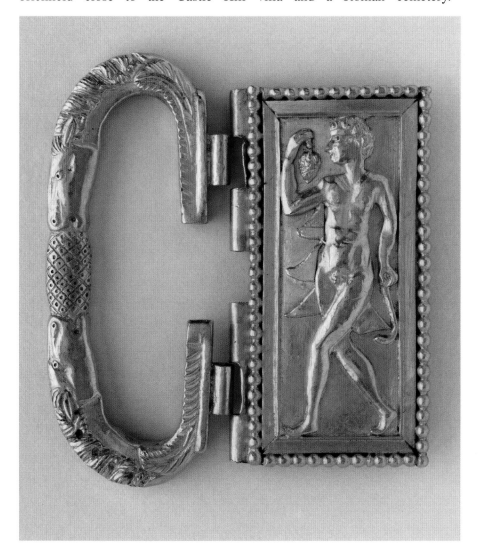

Gold belt buckle from the Thetford Treasure. The young satyr holding a bunch of grapes might be linked to the woodland god Faunus, who features on other items in the treasure. The loop is formed by two horses' heads facing each other.
© Trustees of the British Museum

A bronze version of a wild boar which was a popular image in Iron Age and Roman Britain. This one was found at Colchester.
© Trustees of the British Museum

Unfortunately he did not reach the bottom of either, and a third was left untouched. He abandoned the first shaft at a depth of 29ft. when the sand threatened to collapse; it had only revealed one piece of pottery that might have been Roman and some animal hair, but it was an artificial shaft lined with timber and clay. In the second he reached a depth of 66ft. before the inflow of water defeated his pumps. This had been dug through clay and sand and then cut into the chalk from about 40ft. below the surface. The contents included two pieces of silver sheeting, interpreted as mountings from a casket, and a small cylinder of polished marble with pieces of brick below them. Anne Ross[23] links the finding of animal fur that might be from a hare at a depth of 20ft. in both pits to the report by Dio Cassius that Boudica released a hare in honour of her goddess Andraste.[24]

At Calke Wood, Rickinghall, a shaft 30ft. deep was recorded which contained fragments of Beaker pottery, but "in the sides of the pit were to be seen occupation sites of Roman and earlier date".[25] Men digging clay there reported some two dozen shafts about 15ft. deep, some containing Romano-British pottery and others Iron Age material. However, these shafts might well be natural chalk solution holes, although they could still have been used for ritual purposes; Judith Plouviez notes there is nothing distinctive in the Calke Wood ones. Anne Ross points out that a small bronze boar now in Ipswich Museum was ploughed up in a field next to this wood in Wattisfield.[26] Clay was being dug there in the Roman period for pottery making. Three shafts were excavated in Shrubland Park Quarry, Coddenham, in 1999 to a depth of 4.5m but were not bottomed. Iron Age pottery was found in them, but they might still be natural holes.

Tony Gregory published a detailed account of a shaft between 40 and 49ft. deep excavated in 1874 at Ashill in Norfolk, within a 12-acre enclosure.[27] The filling of the lower part of the shaft included many Romano-British pots, including at least fifty complete vessels, while the packing of layers of hazel twigs with nuts suggested the lower fill was deposited at intervals of several weeks. These were marked by the different

23 Ross, A., "Shafts, pits, wells – sanctuaries of the Belgic Britons?" in Coles, J.M. & Simpson, D.D.A. eds., *Studies in Ancient Europe – essays presented to Stuart Piggott*, Leicester, 1968.
24 Dio Cassius 62.2.
25 Wacher, J.S., PSIAH vol. 28 (1958).
26 Moore, I.E., "Roman Suffolk" PSIAH vol.24 (1948), p.168 and fig 5.
27 Gregory, T., "The Enclosure at Ashill", *Norfolk*, EAA 5 (1977); Robinson, B. & Gregory, T., *Celtic Fire and Roman Rule*, Poppyland, 1987, p.77.

stages of growth of the nuts, between late spring and autumn. With all these shafts it is impossible to say whether they were dug as wells or for religious purposes, but there can be no doubt that the filling of the lower part of the Ashill shaft was part of a formal ritual. It probably started in the later years of the first century AD, while the upper part remained open into the second century.

More recently Rosalind Niblett has published evidence of a number of votive pits of the second and third centuries AD at Folly Lane, Verulamium.[28] These pits were used in some religious ceremonies, involving the deliberate burial of objects at a considerable depth. Although the East Anglian evidence is less clear it does seem that these might be votive or ritual pits. Perhaps they were seen as some form of communication with a spiritual underworld.

Alison Taylor reports a subterranean shrine two metres deep at Cambridge.[29] Under its gravel floor were a dog and a cow's skull. The wood lined cellar was filled with wood ash holding over two thousand nails as well as iron hinges and brackets. On top was a horse with its head split open surrounded by six complete pots, three small dogs with iron collars formed a triangle round a bowl, and a cow had a sheep between its legs. All this was covered by large numbers of broken pots and glass vessels, oyster shells and meat bones, suggesting debris from a great feast. The intaglio of a seal ring showing Bacchus might link this to Bacchanalian rites. Other pits in Cambridge with pots placed beside animals might have ritual significance.

We can be sure that the people living throughout East Anglia visited the great Temple of Claudius at Colchester with its adjoining theatre, which was almost certainly used for religious ceremonies. The classical temple itself held a large statue of Claudius, who was declared to be a god after his death, and there or in the surrounding enclosure would be statues, altars and inscriptions in honour of later emperors, as most were declared gods when they died. A great altar in front of the temple would be the focus of elaborate ceremonies and sacrifices invoking the favour of the deified emperors from the past and honouring the divine powers that protected the current emperor. These were seen as a means of uniting the province and emphasising its place in the empire as a whole.

However, we know from the accounts of the Boudican revolt that many Britons saw it as a symbol of Roman oppression and an excuse to exact taxes to pay for the priests, the ceremonies and the sacrifices. We have noticed that the bronze head of Claudius found in the River Alde might have been looted from the temple complex, and we do not know how the statuette of Nero from Barking was used, but both are high quality portrayals of early emperors. Presumably the divided view continued when the temple and its functions were restored after the suppression of the revolt. This very Roman function apparently remained at Colchester even though London became the provincial capital. The Colchester temple must have been the Roman equivalent of Canterbury Cathedral, at least until the emperor Constantine declared Christianity an official religion for the whole empire.

Until then the followers of Christ had been in an uncertain position. At times they seem to have been tolerated as supporters of yet another mystic religion from the east, like Cybele and Atys from Asia Minor, Mithras and the Unconquered Sun from Persia, or Serapis and Osiris from Egypt, all of whom had their followers in Britain, as throughout the empire. Some emperors were

28 Niblett, R., *The excavation of a ceremonial site at Folly Lane, Verulamium*, Britannia Monograph 14 (1999).
29 Taylor, A., *Cambridge, the hidden history*, Tempus 1999, p.33.

The remains of a Roman Christian church excavated at Icklingham. The apse (Building C) was probably a font and Building B might have been a church, although it might have been a hall for novitiates awaiting baptism while the main church was further east beyond the area excavated. One of the lead tanks was found just north of the apse (at A on the plan). © Suffolk County Council Archaeological Service

less tolerant because they regarded Christ as a criminal properly executed in Judaea, while his followers, claiming there was only one true god, caused offence by refusing to worship the gods of the Roman state, an act of treason in Roman terms, punishable by death. Sometimes they were largely ignored as long as they did not stir up trouble, but on occasion they were sought out and executed, giving us stories of Christian martyrs. A few are known in Britain, but none in East Anglia.

Adopting Christianity, whether as a personal choice or to conform with imperial edicts, meant accepting significant changes of attitude. Christians were obliged to worship only one omnipotent god and to accept certain rules of behaviour. Their religion required observation of a moral code based on the

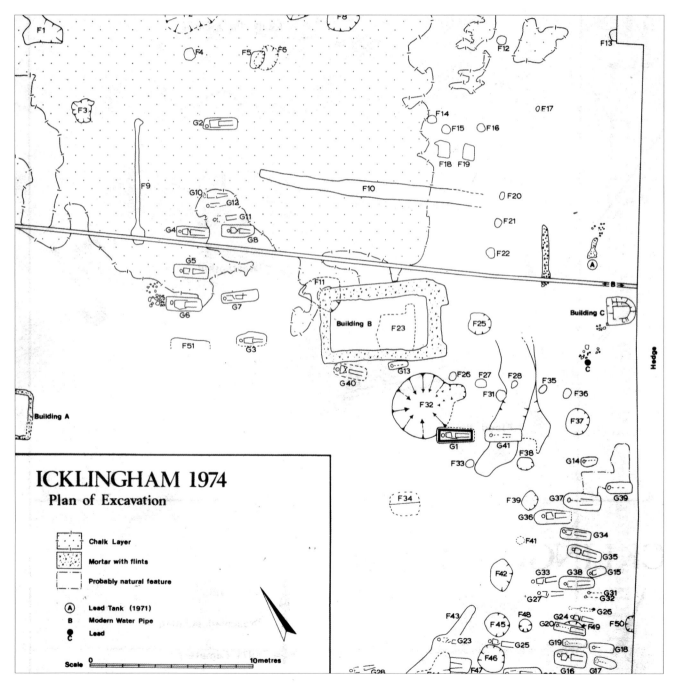

teachings of Jesus: this had been no part of traditional Roman religion, although it was a feature of some of the eastern "mystery" religions. The Bible told the story of Jesus in the New Testament and brought with it the ancient theology of the Jews in the Old Testament.

How far could the ancient stories of classical Greek and Roman mythology be interpreted as providing moral lessons acceptable to Christians? After all, these stories had long been the inspiration for literature and art. Because the story is presented on mosaic floors in houses which also have Christian decorations, it has been suggested that Bellerophon killing the Chimaera could be interpreted as good triumphing over evil, later portrayed in similar style as St Michael or St George killing the dragon. Classical stories of the ultimate return of a lost Golden Age could be interpreted as foretelling the Second Coming of Christ to save the world.

It seems to have taken time for the Christian and Jewish stories to enter the repertoire of artists. We need not assume that the presence of classical mythology in paintings, mosaics, silverware or other works of art meant the owner or commissioner of the work was hostile to Christianity, but it is likely that many still worshipped the old gods in private, as later emperors found it necessary to legislate against this. There are no simple answers. It seems as if, while the traditional role of "the spirit of the place" (*genius loci*) had been usurped by an omnipresent Christ, there was still room for stories of local miracles to be attached to local saints. They could be revered as closer to god but were not actual deities, although when medieval clerics paraded figures of saints through the fields we recall stories of statues of ancient fertility deities carried around on carts.

What impact did the declaration that Christianity was the official religion of the empire have on the people of East Anglia? There was a focus of Christian activity at Icklingham, where the presumed church is represented by the outline of a rectangular building and a plaster-lined apse inside an inhumation cemetery.[30] This looks like a baptistery where new converts were admitted to membership of the church by baptism with water. A large lead tank was found near the building, and two more have been discovered nearby.

One of these was found in 1726 and poorly recorded, but the other two had clear Christian symbols. On opposing sides of both were Chi-Rho symbols which look like X across a P; the X is the Greek letter for CH and P is the Greek letter R. Thus they are the start of the name of Christ in Greek, the language widely used by Christians in early times. We should remember that Greek was the language of early Christianity and many Christian terms that occur in Latin, such as *ecclesia* for a church community, are simply transliterations of Greek words. One tank, found in 1939 and now in the British Museum, had the addition of A and W on either side of the Chi-Rho.[31] These are Alpha and Omega, the first and last letters of the Greek alphabet, symbolising God's statement in Revelations 21 "I am the Alpha and the Omega, the beginning and the end". The other tank, found in 1971 and holding a collection of iron objects, is now in Ipswich Museum.[32] The 1939 tank has a diameter of 81cm and stands 33cm high. The 1971 tank is 77cm x 34cm.

The discovery of the 1726 tank was described soon afterwards. "About three years ago a Leaden Cistern was found here by a Ploughman, the Share

30 West, S.E. & Plouviez, J., "The Roman Site at Icklingham", *Suffolk*, EAA 3 (1976).
31 BM, PRB 1946.2-4.1.
32 Ipswich Museum, R. 1972.43.

This lead tank from Icklingham, below, with its Christian inscription, left, was probably used as a font.
© Trustees of the British Museum

striking against the Edge of it. The Treasure it had conceal'd was gone. The Cistern is in being: it contains about 16 Gallons, perforated on each Side for Rings to lift it by. There is ornamental Work on the Outside of it, imitating Hoops of Iron, but cast with the Thing it self. On one Side is a Mark [inverted V], perhaps intending the Measure or Use of it." It was illustrated in Gough's 1789 edition of William Camden's *Britannia*.[33] The tank was thought to have disappeared, but Frances Mawer[34] points to a tank in the Cambridge Museum of Archaeology and Anthropology[35] which has the distinctive inverted V motif, which is not an A and so remains mysterious. The decoration on the Cambridge tank, which measures 67cm x 31cm, is similar to that on the other two.

It has been suggested that these tanks might have been used for baptism or for some kind of ritual washing, perhaps the formal washing of feet, although there is nothing distinctively Christian about the 1726 tank.

The appearance of a fish on a pewter dish[36] from another part of Icklingham might be another Christian symbol, since the early church used this symbol because the Greek word for fish, *ichthus*, represented the Greek phrase: "*Iesos CHristos THeou Uios Soter*", meaning "Jesus Christ, son of God, saviour". A word of caution is needed here, though, because it could just have marked this as a dish for serving fish. This dish was included in one of three hoards of pewter vessels found in Icklingham: nine vessels were found in 1839, at least twenty-two vessels in 1853, and a further nine vessels, together with a saw blade, in 1956.[37] Pewter vessels are believed to have been made in Britain in the fourth century. Another pewter platter was found in 1962 together with a bronze bowl and a pottery bowl.[38] It has been suggested that these might be some sort of ritual deposition.

The centre of Christian activity at Icklingham probably had an earlier

33 Petts, D., *Christianity in Roman Britain*, Tempus, 2003, fig. 3.
34 *Britannia* vol. 25 (1994), p.232.
35 Accession Z.46783.
36 in the Elveden Estate collection.
37 Liversidge, J., "A New Hoard of Romano-British Pewter at Icklingham", *Proceedings of the Cambridge Antiquarian Society* vol. 52 (1959), pp.6-10.
38 Liversidge, J., "A Bronze Bowl and other Vessels from Icklingham", *Proceedings of the Cambridge Antiquarian Society* vol. 55 (1962), pp.6-7.

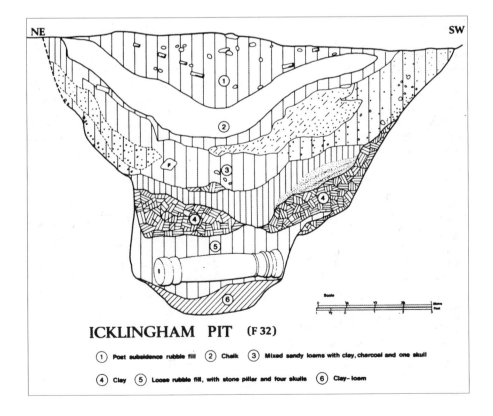

ICKLINGHAM PIT (F 32)

① Post subsidence rubble fill   ② Chalk   ③ Mixed sandy loams with clay, charcoal and one skull

④ Clay   ⑤ Loose rubble fill, with stone pillar and four skulls   ⑥ Clay-loam

A cross section of the pit (feature F32 on the plan on page 198) showing how the stone pillar was covered by layers of material. The layer of chalk extended over much of the site and might have been intended to cleanse the area before its conversion to Christian use.
© Suffolk County Council Archaeological Service

Roman gold ring found in Suffolk, showing the Chi-rho symbol in reverse so that it would appear the correct way round when used to authenticate a seal. It also shows a bird and a tree.
© Trustees of the British Museum

religious use, as a large sealed pit contained six human skulls, a small stone pillar and some fragments of unusual decorated tiles. The pillar was just over 1m high, and weathering on one face suggested it might have formed part of the portico of a building, perhaps a temple. Taken together, the evidence points to remnants of an earlier pre-Christian temple being buried and deliberately sealed under a layer of chalk before the site was used for Christian worship. This replacement of temple with church was the approach used in Gaul by Martin, Bishop of Tours from 371 to 397.

Of the burials in the cemetery, including those excavated in an adjoining area in 1871, three were in stone coffins and one in a lead coffin, which suggests these were individuals of some wealth. The stone coffin excavated in 1974 was actually buried in the edge of the pit. We might compare the existence of a Christian church with its own cemetery at Butt Road, Colchester, where a number of burials were in wooden coffins lined with lead.

This silver plaque from the Water Newton church plate shows a very clear Chi-Rho symbol for Christ with the Alpha and Omega for the beginning and the end. Similar feather-shaped plaques were dedicated elsewhere to other gods.
© Trustees of the British Museum

At Icklingham the lead tank excavated near the "baptistery" contained a collection of ironwork, including hinges and nails. Stanley West sees this as evidence that the church was deliberately dismantled and the wooden doors burnt, after which the metal fittings were buried in the tank. When and why was this done? Elsewhere in Icklingham two groups of coins buried in pots included issues of Honorius, indicating that individuals were hiding their savings as late as AD400, if not later. If occupation continued, did Icklingham remain an important Christian centre after the end of Roman rule?

The three lead tanks, the church itself, and the use of stone coffins suggest that this might have had the status we would later describe as a minster, serving the needs of a wide area with several priests presided over by a senior cleric. Did Christian worship survive here alongside the incoming Anglo-Saxon settlement at West Stow? At Ivy Chimneys, Witham, in Essex an octagonal structure has been interpreted as a Christian baptistery beside a Romano-British temple on a site that seems to have had religious significance in the Iron Age and throughout the Roman period, although it did not continue in use after the Roman occupation.

We know nothing about the interior of the presumed church at Icklingham, but a notable hoard of silver found in 1975 at Water Newton (*Durobrivae*), near Peterborough, appears to be some of the equipment for a Christian church. Bowls and ornamental silver leaves have Christian inscriptions. One very delicate item which had to be heavily restored is interpreted by the British Museum as a hanging lamp. Could this be an early version of the bronze hanging bowls found in Anglo-Saxon burials which are seen as Celtic products? Those hanging bowls might have been lamps, or they and that from Water Newton might have contained holy water for ritual use.

It seems the Durobrivae church had been presented with silver vessels for the communion service and silver leaves, some gilded, comparable to those used in earlier regalia such as the Cavenham Crowns. A gold seal ring now in the British Museum but found in Suffolk shows a bird pecking a bush above a reversed chi-rho that would appear the correct way round on a seal impression.[39] It seems impossible to say whether this was a purely personal seal design or one with a religious or administrative function, but its symbolism is clearly Christian.

Three of the silver spoons in the Mildenhall treasure had inscriptions within the bowl showing the chi-rho between alpha and omega. These are unequivocally Christian. The decoration on the Great Dish is clearly derived from classical mythology. At its centre is the head of Oceanus, god of the deep and wild sea that surrounded the world, rather than Neptune, god of the Mediterranean. Its appearance is strikingly similar to the head on the great stone pediment of the temple of Sul Minerva at Bath.

Could this magnificent piece of silver plate have been manufactured in Britain? This is above all an island in the Ocean. Round the head Nereids, sea spirits, swim among seahorses and other marine creatures, while the outer circle is full of Bacchic revellers dancing and making music with Bacchus himself, Silenus, Pan and a drunken Hercules. Elsewhere in Britain the presence of mythological scenes on mosaic floors of buildings with Christian decoration at Frampton, Lullingstone and Hinton St Mary suggests they were not seen as conflicting. Indeed, the portrayal of Bellerophon killing the

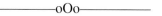

A New Start

The bishop stood ready to pray before the altar in his new church. Christian paintings decorated the walls. A few months ago he had watched as men took down the old temple. In the bottom of a deep pit they put the central pillar of the portico and the skulls that had hung beside it. They covered the whole site with a thick layer of white chalk to symbolise the fresh start. Now there was a proper house inside which to celebrate Christ and share the holy meal. There was a lined pool in which he would baptise new members of the community of Christ. He consecrated the lead tanks for holy water. Their decoration symbolised in eternal form and in the Greek letters of his church the holy name of Christ as Chi and Rho, while Alpha and Omega honoured him as the beginning and the end. He prayed his church would stand until the Day of Judgement and that soon even the nearby temple of the mother goddess, home of wicked idolatry, would be demolished.

—————oOo—————

39 British Museum P&E 1983,1003.1.

Chimaera at all three locations might have been interpreted as the triumph of good over evil, as acceptable to a Christian as to a non-Christian.

So in the Great Dish some message of eternal happiness in the isles of the blessed might have been presented as a version of Christian paradise for true believers, based on generations of acceptance of the myths of Greece and Rome. It is not difficult to see the Mildenhall head with dolphins poking out of his hair as Oceanus, but the Bath head is less simple to identify. The temple at Bath was apparently dedicated to a local deity called Sul or Sulis who is identified with the Roman Minerva, the Greek Athena whose symbolic owl is featured on the pediment. However, the head has a clearly masculine moustache, but also the snakes associated in legend with the fearsome Gorgon, who was traditionally female. There is much we do not understand about the iconography of religion in Roman Britain. The Hoxne Treasure has chi-rhos on two spoons, a monogram cross on two sets of tableware (spoons and ladles) and on a necklace, while a spoon is inscribed *VIVAS IN DEO*, "may you live in God". There will be more about the Mildenhall and Hoxne treasures in the next chapter.

Burial practices might be affected by views about an after-life, although it is impossible to know exactly what people had in mind when they organised a funeral and in particular how they decided what to place in the grave. Comparatively few burials survive in East Anglia from the Roman period, and most seem to represent single individuals or small groups rather than large communal cemeteries. The inhumation cemetery at Icklingham, which is probably Christian, is the exception. During the first two centuries the usual practice was cremation, but after that we more often find inhumations. The change seems to have been a gradual one during the third century, and there is no obvious explanation. We cannot tell how many bodies were disposed of in

This group of fine late-Roman silver found at Water Newton, the Roman town of Durobrivae near Peterborough, was probably an early set of Christian church plate. Several items show the Chi-Rho symbol and there are other Christian inscriptions.
© Trustees of the British Museum

The great silver dish from Mildenhall with the head of Oceanus, god of the deep sea, in the centre, then a ring of nereids, sea spirits, riding on sea monsters. The outer ring of revellers includes Bacchus, god of wine, with Silenus, Hercules with his lion skin and Pan with the horns and feet of a goat. They are accompanied by dancing satyrs and maenads, the attendants of Bacchus/Dionysus.
© Trustees of the British Museum

ways that leave no trace, particularly if no grave goods were included, as it is these that draw attention and make it possible to date a burial.

It is believed that during the Iron Age the practice of excarnation was widespread in Britain. This involved exposing bodies, perhaps on elevated platforms, to allow natural decomposition aided by birds and insects eating the flesh. It is possible that this local practice continued in the Roman period and might explain the occasional appearance of stray human bones in some deposits. It is also possible that the ashes from cremations were thrown to the wind or cast into rivers in ceremonies similar to those performed beside the Ganges in India.

Two Iron Age burials are worth noting because they are rare in our region, although they have similarities to practices more common elsewhere in Britain. At Mildenhall, an extended body was flanked by two horses, and laid beside the body were a long iron sword, an axe and a gold torc, showing a character of some importance. The burial might have been covered by a mound, but its discovery in 1812 was poorly recorded.[40] Another inhumation further north at Shouldham was buried with a remarkable iron sword on which the hilt was formed as a human figure. Found in 1944, this is now in Norwich Castle Museum.[41]

Most conspicuous are elaborate burials in barrows which followed a long tradition from early prehistoric times in Britain, a tradition seen at its grandest in the late Iron Age, presumably royal, burial in the Lexden tumulus at

40 *Archaeologia* vol.25 (1834), appendix.
41 reference 1949.4:A.

Colchester. At Rougham four Roman barrows were excavated in 1843-4 by Professor J.S. Henslow from Cambridge, who was vicar of Hitcham but is better known as Charles Darwin's tutor. Henslow published a detailed account of his finds and an edited version was produced by Professor Churchill Babington.[42] The largest, and latest, mound, known as Eastlow Hill, was said then to be about 17ft. high; it still survives, but is overgrown. It contained a rectangular flint and tile chamber on a concrete floor based on the original ground surface. A male skeleton was found in a lead coffin that had been enclosed in a wooden casket, of which the nails survived.[43] The body had apparently been wrapped in a fur coat or animal skin, as hair was found among the bones, but there were no grave goods.

The second barrow covered a chamber about 2ft. cubed built from Roman tiles, containing a large iron lamp and a large square glass urn 16in. high holding a

Above: *The stone head from the pediment of the temple of Sul at Bath.*

Right: *The central face of Oceanus on the great silver dish from the Mildenhall Treasure.*
© Trustees of the British Museum

cremation. As the finds were kept at Rougham Hall this was probably the lamp displayed at a meeting of the Suffolk Institute of Archaeology in 1849.[44]

The third mound was 54ft. diameter covering another small brick chamber below ground level. Inside the chamber was a glass urn which had been 11in. high but was broken into many pieces. As well as the cremated bones it held a small glass perfume flask and a very corroded coin of Trajan. There were several pottery vessels including a samian dish with the potter's mark ALBVCI, and what was possibly a bone knife handle. An iron lamp with remains of a burned wick in the spout hung from a twisted iron rod driven into the side of the chamber.[45] Handles suggested a small wooden chest and bones might have come from an offering of food. There might also have been rich fabrics, as Henslow recorded traces of gold leaf. This was certainly a well-furnished burial. Another mound was badly damaged, but it had contained two cremations in pottery urns, along with some other vessels.

There was evidence of a villa, including roof tiles, a few hundred yards south of the barrows, so presumably these were the graves of generations of its owners, who maintained the tradition of marking the burials with substantial mounds. The same tradition can be seen in the Bartlow Hills, just across the Cambridgeshire border near Haverhill, although at Bartlow all six burials were cremations. Such mounds are said to be found in the Roman period also in the Rhineland and northern Gaul, so perhaps we have property owners with continental connections. In Britain they are confined to the south-east, which was most open to continental influence, but there is also the possibility of a local fashion as seen at Lexden, so we might be looking at families linked to Colchester.

42 PSIAH vol.4 (1874), p. 257.
43 said to have gone to the Fitzwilliam Museum.
44 PSIAH vol.1 (1853), p. 150.
45 some of these finds are in Moyses Hall Museum.

Silver spoons from the Mildenhall treasure, some showing Christian inscriptions.
© Trustees of the British Museum

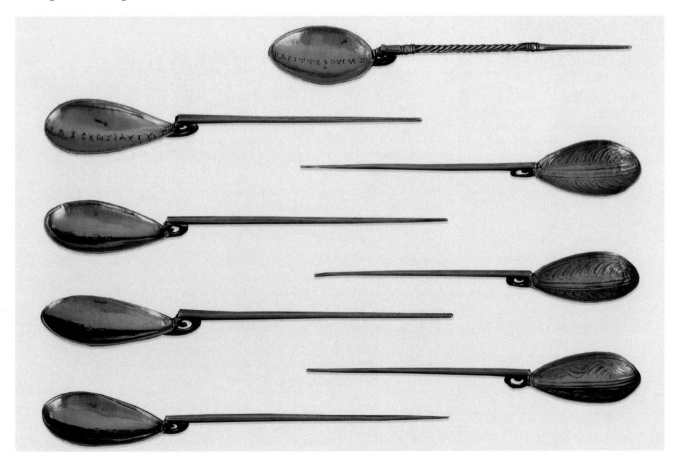

46 Smedley, N. & Owles, E.J.,
PSIAH vol.28 (1960), p.203, and
vol.29 (1961), p.67.
47 Brown, B., et al., "Excavations
at Grimstone End, Pakenham",
PSIAH vol.26 (1954), pp. 189-207.
48 Plunkett, S.J., "The Anglo-
Saxon Loom from Pakenham,
Suffolk", PSIAH vol.39 (1999),
pp. 277-98; West, S.E., *A Corpus
of Anglo-Saxon Material from
Suffolk*", EAA 84, 1998, p.87.

*One of the Bartlow Hills burial
mounds, constructed to mark the
burial place of an important
individual, perhaps a member of
one of the local landowning
families.*

One conspicuous Roman barrow stands impressively beside the causeway leading to Mersea Island from Colchester. The barrows at Rougham were clearly placed to attract the attention of all those using the road between Long Melford and Pakenham/Ixworth, as they are close beside it. Was the inhumation without grave goods a Christian owner of the estate who was given a proper chamber for his tomb, perhaps seen as comparable to the tomb of Jesus himself, and an even larger mound than his predecessors?

An apparent case of repeated use of a significant site was found at Grimstone End, Pakenham, not far from the Roman market town and the Ixworth villa and close to Roman pottery kilns.[46] A Bronze Age barrow had second century Roman cremations in pots, including one in a flagon, placed in the edge of the ditch and three inhumations in the mound were thought likely to be Anglo-Saxon.[47] Understanding of the use of the site was complicated by the presence of two sets of Anglo-Saxon loom weights in huts built across the ditch of the barrow, representing a centre for the manufacture of large textiles, and Basil Brown later found further evidence of Anglo-Saxon activity there.[48] It looks as if the barrow retained its role as a place for burial, and the excavation report suggests other evidence of activity in the area had been destroyed before it could be investigated.

It is possible that the area was named Grimstone because the ancient mound of the barrow was linked by tradition to a great god of the past

identified by Anglo-Saxons as Woden, for whom we have seen that Grim was an alternative name based on his use of disguises. Given its continuing use as a burial place, this seems more likely than it being derived from a Scandinavian personal name.

A possible later use of a Roman coffin might explain the stone coffin built into the south wall of the nave of Pakenham church. This section of wall appears to be part of the Norman structure marked by surviving Norman doorways in the nave, so it is unlikely to be a medieval coffin. We know that in the eighth century the monks of Ely sought a stone coffin for St Etheldreda in the ruins of Roman Cambridge, so perhaps the later builders of this church incorporated this relic from a cemetery near the Roman town down by the river. We cannot tell whether the coffin is occupied but it might contain a body treated as a relic. A Roman stone coffin was reused in the Early Anglo-Saxon cemetery at West Stow. Looking at stone slabs used in the early fabric of Gosbeck church, Bob Carr has suggested that here, and elsewhere in Suffolk, we might be looking at pieces cut from stone coffins. As Gosbeck is close to the Roman road out of Combretovium they might have been Roman coffins and this could explain the lack of evidence for burials comparable to those outside the Roman town at Cambridge. In Suffolk good building stone was at a premium in the early Middle Ages.

The burials associated with the villa complex at Castle Hill, Ipswich, were described in chapter four.

Much effort has been spent trying to determine whether specific burials were pagan or Christian. I doubt whether ancient religions had the total control of burial rites demanded by the medieval church. It is worth noting that there was no structured "pagan religion". Pagan was simply used by the Christian church to describe all those who did not recognise Christ. In earlier days it had simply meant somebody who was not a soldier, and only later was it used for those who refused to become soldiers of Christ. As we have seen,

Above: *Eastlow Hill at Rougham. The Roman barrow as it was in 1987.*
© Suffolk County Council Archaeological Service

Left: *This Roman barrow stands beside the road on to Mersea Island in Essex. It must have been a very conspicuous monument to a member of a wealthy family.*

49 Filmer-Sankey, W., *Snape*, EAA 95, 2001, p.265.

people worshipped different gods in different ways. Religious belief might influence burial practice, but there was no invariable connection and no reason to believe all early Christians insisted on burial in a churchyard with feet to the east without any grave goods. Pretty certainly personal preference, local tradition and family wealth were the main factors in determining the treatment of the dead.

Even the single cemetery at Snape which was in use for a comparatively short time in the Early Saxon period shows a great range of rites. William Filmer-Sankey attributes this to the richness and variety of pagan Anglo-Saxon religious belief,[49] and we might wonder whether there could also have been British and Christian elements involved. "Furnished" burials were not exclusively non-Christian, as can be seen in a number of rich burials of French royalty under the church of St Denis. St Cuthbert retained some "grave goods" at Durham. How the body is dressed for burial and what else might be placed in the coffin is determined by the wishes of relatives. Present-day practices vary as much as at any time in the past.

Is this a Roman coffin in the wall of Pakenham church? The entire coffin appears to have been built into the fabric of the wall.

The East Anglian Kingdom

AFTER the "Barbarian Conspiracy" of AD367 Rome recovered control over Britain, the general Theodosius, on behalf of the emperor Valentinian, restoring military discipline after the failure of the army to protect the province. However in 383 a victorious general in Britain, Magnus Maximus, led his army from Britain into Gaul and replaced Gratian, the son of Valentinian, as ruler of the western part of the empire, making his base at Trier. Four years later Maximus moved to take Milan and this provoked the emperor in the east, Theodosius the Great, the son of the general who had recovered Britain in 367, to oppose and kill him in northern Italy.

Apparently Theodosius had to send a new army to control Britain in the last years of the fourth century, but we cannot be sure what impact these events had on East Anglia. The main focus of military activity might have been on the northern frontier, with a restoration of Hadrian's Wall as a barrier against the Picts. Claudian, the court poet at Rome, praised the general Stilicho in 398 for making the sea more peaceful by subjugating the Saxons as well as the Picts, Franks and Suebi. He portrayed Britannia wearing the skin of a Caledonian beast but draped with a sea-blue gown "sweeping over her footsteps like the waves of Ocean" and no longer needing to watch for Saxons to arrive with every change of wind.[1] At least our coast shared the relief, if only for a while. No doubt the forts of the Saxon Shore played a part in this security operation, but we do not know whether military intervention was needed in our small towns as the extent of disruption within the region is still unknown.

Nor can we be sure how ubiquitous the presence of Roman soldiers might have been in East Anglia. The same distinctive late Roman buckles and belt fittings were apparently worn by military officers and senior officials, so they simply reveal an official presence. Tom Plunkett notes their wide distribution in Suffolk, mainly on the basis of metal detector finds.[2] This suggests that most areas accessible by waterways or by main roads had some official presence, assuming these items were lost there by men entitled to wear them. We have no idea of the status of those who buried hoards of coins, perhaps their personal savings, early in the fifth century, although those who buried gold coins at Eye and Hoxne were very wealthy, while somebody collected low-value bronze coins in a pot at Little Bealings. Other collections have been found at Tuddenham St Martin near Ipswich, at Sutton near the Deben (although this one could be mid-fourth century), and near the edge of the Fens at Brandon, Freckenham, Icklingham and Mildenhall. We are finding the savings that their depositors failed to recover.

One remarkable find gives us some idea of the lifestyle of the wealthiest families in the region at this time. The Mildenhall Treasure[3] was found at West Row on the edge of the Fens near Mildenhall in 1942, at the height of the Second World War. Gordon Butcher was ploughing a field when he unearthed the silver treasure. His employer, Sidney Ford, collected thirty-four Roman silver objects which he took home, cleaned and placed on his

1 Claudian 18, *Against Eutropius* I 392; and 22, *On the Consulship of Stilicho* II 247.
2 Plunkett, S.J., *Suffolk in Anglo-Saxon Times*, Tempus, 2005, p.27.
3 Painter. K.S., *The Mildenhall Treasure*, British Museum, 1977; Hobbs, R., *Treasure, Finding our past*, British Museum, 2003, pp.71-8.

sideboard. It was not until 1946 that he was persuaded he must declare his find to the authorities, claiming he had believed them to be pewter and so did not have to be reported.

The delay leaves us ignorant of how the treasure was buried. When Gordon Fowler and Tom Lethbridge searched for the find spot in 1947 they had no success, either because all trace had been destroyed by later cultivation or perhaps because Sidney Ford remained unhelpful. It was even suggested the items were not found there, because some experts believed they could not belong in so remote a corner of a distant province. The other finds described in this chapter make it clear that there was in fact a remarkable amount of portable wealth in Roman Suffolk. However an implausible story did circulate that the treasure had been brought to Suffolk from North Africa, seen as a more likely source of such Mediterranean treasure, by American airmen, despite the fact that the Americans did not take over the Mildenhall air base until after the war.

Nonetheless, it is a remarkable collection of fine silver plate that was probably intended for display as well as for serving food. Any owner might use the finest plate on special occasions, but at other times put it on show to impress visitors. The element of use can be illustrated by a contemporary picture in the fourth-century manuscript *Vergilius Romanus*, now kept in the

The silver treasure found at Mildenhall was presumably the elaborate dinner service of a wealthy local family.
© Trustees of the British Museum

Vatican Library.[4] It has been suggested that this copy of the poems of Virgil, perhaps the greatest Roman poet, was made in the provinces, and either the Rhine valley or even Britain itself have been proposed. In support of this it is contrasted with the more "painterly" version of the *Vergilius Vaticanus* which was probably produced at Rome. If it is a British work then the paintings are particularly significant, and one scene shows a dinner party. The main characters, although shown as fourth-century diners, are taken from Virgil's epic *The Aeneid* about the foundation of Rome by refugees from Troy. In this scene Dido, queen of Carthage, entertains Aeneas, the Trojan who will found Rome, and a second guest who might be his son Ascanius. A large fish is placed before the diners on a dish with a beaded rim that looks similar to the

In this scene from the manuscript of Virgil's Aeneid known as Vergilius Romanus Dido, queen of Carthage, entertains Aeneas, the Trojan who will found Rome. A large fish is placed before the diners on a dish with a beaded rim that looks similar to the large niello plate from Mildenhall. Vatican Library ms. Vat. Lat.3867 f.100v. © Biblioteca Apostolica Vaticana

large niello plate from Mildenhall. In front of each guest is a smaller bowl that resembles the flanged bowls from Mildenhall. The guests are drinking from vessels that look like the conical glass beakers found at Burgh Castle[5] and the drink, presumably wine mixed with water in classical fashion, is poured from ewers with single handles that might match the tigress handle from the Hoxne hoard. As well as a ewer an attendant carries a handled serving dish or patera (a fine bronze one was found at Prickwillow in the Fens, and there was a silver one in the Backworth treasure from Northumberland). Thus we can visualise this table service in use, but we cannot be sure where it was made. The Great Dish is a remarkable piece of work for which more than eight kilograms of silver was beaten into shape with hammers, creating a circle over 60cm in diameter. The decoration was probably then chased on to the front using a series of small hammers and punches, before adding details with engraving tools.

The decoration on the Great Dish is clearly derived from classical mythology. At its centre is the head of Oceanus, the wild god of the deep sea, which we have compared to the magnificent head on the great stone pediment of the temple of Sul Minerva at Bath. The wild hair, flowing moustache and oval eyes look remarkably similar. Could this magnificent piece of silver plate have been manufactured in Britain? Some have argued that imperial control of the silver coinage implies that such silver plate would be produced at the imperial mints.

5 see chapter 5.

However, there does not seem to be any evidence that individuals were prevented from creating their own silverware, if the material was legitimately in private hands. We know that the wealthiest in late Roman times had great quantities of gold and silver, and the great casket in the Esquiline Treasure was clearly designed and inscribed for a private owner. It is suggested that items of gold jewellery in the Thetford and Hoxne treasures were made to order in Britain, so we should not reject the possibility of local manufacture. Britain is an island in the Ocean, so the portrayal of sea spirits swimming among seahorses and other marine creatures is especially appropriate.

We can imagine educated British diners appreciating the mythological stories associated with Bacchus, god of wine, Silenus, Pan and a drunken Hercules without necessarily seeing any religious or philosophical messages, Christian or otherwise. Beyond question three of the silver spoons in the Mildenhall treasure are Christian, with chi-rho inscribed in the bowl between alpha and omega. These were certainly designed for a Christian market, and their users could not avoid seeing the religious message and remembering that Christ's final instructions to his followers were given during a meal, "Do this in remembrance of me".

Inscriptions on two other spoons might have led them to drink toasts in honour of Pascentia and Pappitedo, who could have been their hosts. The two smaller platters with Bacchic scenes have Greek letters scratched on the back, giving the possessive (genitive) form of the name Eutherios. One important individual with this name was an Armenian eunuch who served as a senior official under the emperor Julian in Gaul from AD355 to 361, so it is just possible that these items at least had once belonged to him. This would place them in the fourth century, while it is suggested by K.S. Painter that the covered bowl was probably made in the third century and might be the earliest

One of the Mildenhall spoons which is inscribed "Long life to Papittedo" was possibly given as a christening present. The inscription on another spoon reads "Long life to Pascentia".
© Trustees of the British Museum

6 Martial *On Spectacles* 7, but note
the Loeb edition prints the correct
Latin "ursus" for bear, but
misprints the translation as "boar".
7 Martial *Epigrams* X 44, Tethys
was the goddess of the ocean.
8 *Pappitedo vivas* and *Pascentia
vivas*.
9 Toynbee, J., "Silver Picture
Plates of Late Antiquity",
Archaeologia 108 (1986), p.15.

item in the set, perhaps a family heirloom.

Three flanged bowls have a variety of animals round the rim, but one shows a central figure of a hunter attacking a bear, perhaps collecting a beast for the arena. Martial describes an execution in the amphitheatre where the condemned man "hanging on a real cross gave his naked flesh to a Caledonian bear", while he was eaten alive like Prometheus.[6] Elsewhere Martial refers to Caledonia, modern northern Scotland, as a remote location out in the Ocean when he addresses Quintus Ovidius "going to visit the Caledonian Britons and green Tethys and Father Oceanus".[7] Two single bones from bears have been found in Roman contexts at Colchester, so perhaps they were used in public displays in the colonia.

The complete set of items from Mildenhall are: the great Oceanus dish and two small plates with Bacchic decoration, the large niello dish, a fluted bowl with handles, a flanged bowl with a domed cover, six flanged bowls, two goblets which could be used as plates on stands, five ladles with cast dolphin handles, one without its handle, and eight spoons (two with chi-rho, one inscribed "long live Papittedo" and another "long live Pascentia").[8]

The set had been brought together from different sources, and we cannot tell what other items belonged with it. However it does present an image of formal dining on a grand scale. Jocelyn Toynbee argued that the great Oceanus dish would never have been used, but only put on display mounted on a shelf on the wall or resting on a cupboard.[9] Surely it is possible to see this dish, although normally displayed as an ornament, being used on very special occasions, heaped with fruit rather than greasy sauces, which I agree would seem undesirable. Perhaps it is not too fanciful to see guests comparing the head of Oceanus to their bearded host, and then comparing ladies of the company to the dancing Bacchants or Maenads in the outer ring. As the drink flowed perhaps there was a guest who would play the pipes of Pan while younger men took the roles of Satyrs and invited the ladies to dance, recalling

The inscription on this spoon from the Mildenhall Treasure is clearly Christian as it shows the Chi-rho between alpha and omega. It is one of three with this inscription.
© Trustees of the British Museum

the wild dance of the followers of Bacchus/Dionysus in Euripides' play *The Bacchae*. Did one drunken old soldier in the group need supporting like Hercules on the dish?

We have no idea when the treasure was buried, but as with the Hoxne treasure it might have been decades after the end of official Roman government.

Some local residents of more modest wealth chose to use pewter dinner services. Pewter is an alloy of lead and tin which, because of the tin, can be polished to give a shine similar to silver, but at less cost. We have noted that over forty pewter vessels have been recovered from different locations in Icklingham. Nine items from West Row, Mildenhall, including a tray 15in. in diameter[10] and other finds from the Cambridgeshire Fens suggest this fashion was particularly prevalent in the Fenland area.

At the death of the emperor Theodosius in 395 Britain appears to have been a stable part of the Roman Empire, and by 398 the coast was secure. Within a few years the peace was shattered, because Alaric was leading his Goths into Italy and Stilicho, on behalf of the emperor Honorius, was unable to support the western provinces. According to Claudian he drew to his support at least one legion that had been posted to guard the "remote Britons" where it had restrained the fierce Scots and seen the designs tattooed on the faces of dead Picts, so presumably it was removed from the northern frontier.[11]

In response the army that remained in Britain created three rival emperors, first in 407 a soldier called Marcus, then a senior British civilian, Gratian, and finally a soldier called Constantine. The first two had little impact but the last, proclaiming himself Constantine the Third, led an army into Gaul. Initially he had success against German and other invaders, but in the end he was defeated and killed by the official Roman government. Meanwhile, with the main defence force removed from the island, Britain seems to have suffered attack by Saxons, which might well have affected the East Anglian coast.[12] We have no information about the activities of the empire's naval forces at that time, but ships based in Britain might have moved to continental bases in Gaul.

The British communities apparently ejected Constantine's officials, and this can be taken as the end of Britain's membership of the Roman Empire. Zosimus claims that the Britons took up weapons and freed their towns from the foreigners attacking them. Later, writing about Italy, Zosimus refers to a rescript of the emperor Honorius telling the towns in "Britain" to look after their own defences. However, the reading of the text is disputed, and Honorius might have been writing to the towns of Bruttium in Italy. If the rescript referred to Britain it would be a formal declaration that the imperial army could no longer protect the British provinces and that the Britons were no longer bound by the law forbidding civilians to carry weapons.

There seems little doubt this was the end of a Roman army in Britain funded from the imperial treasury. Presumably, if the officials in charge of the provinces had been expelled, there was no authority at Diocesan or Provincial level, so individual communities had to look to their own administration and defence. We can guess that British leaders, the leading landowners of the area, would have used the walled towns of Colchester and Caistor-by-Norwich as power bases, but might the commanders of the forts at Walton Castle, Burgh

10 J. Liversidge, *Proceedings of the Cambridge Antiquarian Society* vol.52 (1959), p.7.
11 Claudian 26 (*The Gothic War*) 416.
12 Gallic Chronicle iv. 62 and Zosimus VI.5.2-3.

13 Ward-Perkins, B., *The Fall of Rome*, 2005 p.19 and 135, quoting Eugippius' *Life of St Severinus*.
14 collected by Robert Fitch of Norwich in the nineteenth century and transferred to Ipswich Museum in 1962.
15 West, S.E., *A Corpus of Anglo-Saxon Material from Suffolk*, EAA 84, 1998, p.37 and fig. 45.
16 Gildas, *De Excidio Britonum*, 20.

A bronze belt slide from Felixstowe in Ipswich Museum. This type of fitting was part of the uniform worn by Germanic troops in the army of the later Roman Empire.

Castle and Brancaster have carved out territories for themselves? Presumably they had to induce the local population to pay, or at least feed, their garrisons if they were to stay as part of the local protection network.

When things reached a comparable state on the Danube frontier some fifty years later we have a record in the *Life of St Severinus* by Eugippius, who tells us that under the Roman Empire the soldiers in many towns had been maintained at public expense to defend the frontier but the system broke down. In his time the imperial garrison of only one town, Batavis (modern Passau in Bavaria), was still operational and they only survived by sending a detachment of their own troops every year across the Alps to collect pay from Ravenna in Italy. Even this failed in the end when the detachment was killed by barbarians and their bodies were found washed up on the bank of the river. In future the soldiers had to obtain pay from the inhabitants of the town. The Danube was much closer to Rome, so it was even easier to ignore the British towns.[13] Those soldiers and officers who stayed had to find local paymasters.

Stanley West has drawn attention to a distinctive bronze belt slide from Felixstowe in the Fitch Collection[14] which "suggests that the shore fort was occupied in the late Roman period by troops including detachments of Germanic origin from Northern Gaul".[15] A number of other objects typical of the fifth to sixth centuries are recorded from Felixstowe and Walton. Perhaps a Germanic garrison remained in occupation of Walton Castle after the end of Roman administration. Presumably a local British population caused the later Anglo-Saxon rulers to call the town Walton, if its name can be derived from "weala-tun" for "settlement of the British", as in the origin of the name Wales. But some prefer "wealh-tun" for "settlement at the wall", which could refer to the stone fort.

It seems the British made one last appeal in 446 to the Roman military commander in western Europe, Aetius, who had been consul three times, but he could offer them no help.[16] They had paid their taxes to fund the Roman army, so now they had to pay the troops who remained, bring in new troops whom they would pay, or take up arms themselves. We should not under-estimate the significance of this change. Ever since the incorporation of the original province of Britannia in AD43 administration had been controlled from the centre. Even administrations that broke with Rome such as the "Gallic Empire" and the rule of Carausius kept the format of imperial control. There was no serious local independent government within the province. It was very much control from the centre and military enforcement, with uncomfortable problems when rival emperors competed. Hence the walled forts and towns as strong points of authority against internal dissidents as well as overseas raiders. The official road system with its Imperial Post existed so that administrators could move rapidly between key points and serious military units could be deployed without delay to deal with any threat.

The loss of control in 410 left a vacuum which was probably filled quite quickly in East Anglia by Anglo-Saxon warlords and further west by British "tyrants". Strong men, and perhaps women too, as in days of Boudica and Cartimandua, took power by whatever means they could and defended their territories, but we have no clear evidence. They saw, and projected, them-selves as the true heirs to Roman imperial authority. In any case it would not be surprising if a significant proportion of the regular Roman troops who had maintained the imperial peace in East Anglia and protected it from external attack were ethnically Germanic. It is possible that they were now more conscious of their German origins than of their Roman citizenship and might feel as close to their relatives across the North Sea as to their British neighbours. The ordinary folks no doubt went on farming and grumbling.

Gradually Anglo-Saxon power extended westward, but certainly started early in East Anglia. Even so the Hoxne treasure and other evidence suggest some wealthy Romans or British did survive for some time on our patch. This fits later reports.

There is evidence of considerable contact between the Roman Empire and those north Europeans who remained outside its frontiers. As East Anglia is close to Germany within the North Sea Zone, we should not be surprised that we find archaeological evidence for a mixture of Roman and Germanic objects before and after the end of Roman government. The presence in East Anglia of "tutulus" and "supporting arm" brooches, associated with Germanic people north of the Rhine, makes sense.

The difficulty of drawing any sharp lines in terms of date or fashion is emphasised by a woman's body found buried at Scole. She had not been buried in a formal grave; her body was found placed in a large pit. She was wearing a string of beads held in place by two brooches, one a late fourth or early fifth-century Germanic "supporting arm" brooch, the other a first or early second century Romano-British "Colchester derivative" type.[17] Thus she is displaying objects at least two hundred and fifty years apart in age and from apparently different cultures. Here at least is positive evidence for a Briton, proud of her Roman heritage, combining it with the immigrant Anglo-Saxon style. This might have been the most common response. Perhaps some of the brooches we see as Anglo-Saxon were made by British craftsmen applying their traditional skills to continental designs.

Although Roman government in Britain came to an end by 410, the survival of the main roads and some elements of the field systems show that people did not stop farming here in East Anglia. Environmental evidence, particularly analysis of pollen from excavations, confirms this continuity of farming. Some things did change. There might have been a decline in population and some Anglo-Saxon immigrants did arrive from Germanic lands beyond the North Sea, nobody made pottery to the standard achieved by previous generations or brought in new coins. Some people adopted Germanic designs for fashion accessories and the decoration on pottery, and used different burial customs. Even before 410 there would have been a considerable Germanic presence in the region, including the many regular troops in the Roman army who were of Germanic origin, and there were doubtless extensive trade contacts with the Rhine valley which would lead to social contact and probably some intermarriage. These people might have come from either side of the Rhine, that is from either inside or outside the empire.

It is worth remembering that the Roman Empire was cosmopolitan and non-racist. There is no evidence of racial prejudice as such; the key distinction was between those living inside the boundaries of the empire who all counted as "civilised Romans" and those outside who were "uncivilised barbarians". All civilised Romans were expected to be capable of using Latin in everyday life, but the educated were literate in Greek as well as Latin, and other

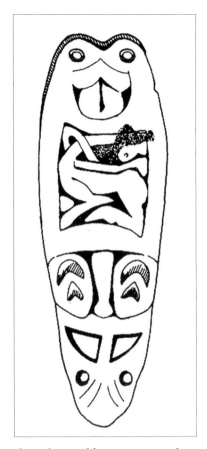

One of several bronze strap ends from Felixstowe in Ipswich Museum. Such fashionable dress ornaments provide evidence that activity at Felixstowe continued into the ninth century.

17 Dark, K., *Britain and the end of the Roman Empire*, Tempus, 2000, p.20.

18 RIB, 1965.
19 Norwich Castle Museum,
NWHCM : 2005.297,
unfortunately found in dumped
topsoil from an unknown source.
20 Thomas, C., *Christian Celts*
ed.2, Tempus, 2003.

A Roman magical gem inscribed at the bottom with the name of Abrasax in Greek letters. This was not found in East Anglia, but one of the Roman gold rings in the Thetford Treasure was inscribed with the name of Abrasax in Greek letters.

© Trustees of the British Museum

languages were tolerated.

A number of Greek inscriptions have been found in Romano-British contexts, and some in eastern languages, including Palmyrene on a memorial at South Shields.[18] A gold talisman from Billingford in Norfolk has an inscription in Greek, as well as Latin and a number of magical symbols, on behalf of Tiberius Claudius Similis.[19] It calls upon the god Iao, named Abrasax whose letters as Greek numerals add up to 365, the number of days in a year (A=1, B=2, R=100, S=200, X=60). This gave his name mystical significance, and he was adopted by Gnostic Christians and portrayed with a cockerel's head and legs like snakes. The interest in him reflects a sophisticated use of Greek letters and of mathematics. Charles Thomas has documented the continued awareness of the application of numeric values to Latin letters in Christian western and northern Britain long after the end of Roman government.[20] In those areas messages survive because they were inscribed on stone, but we lack any such evidence for our region. He shows the elaborate thinking behind such compositions, and we can only wonder whether any of it survived in East Anglia. One of the rings in the Thetford Treasure (see chapter six) shows Abrasax and has a Greek inscription to Iao on the front with Abrasax in Greek on the back. If people lived inside the Roman Empire they were required to accept Roman law and frequently chose to adopt Roman names which concealed their ethnic origin. From another part of the empire we might note the typically Egyptian mummy head in the Ipswich Museum collection which has the full tripartite Roman name of the person, Titus Flavius Demetrius, inscribed in perfect Greek lettering, a fusion of three great cultures. The attitude seems to have been truly multicultural, and there is no way of telling the ethnic origin of a person by the country of origin of their possessions. After all, owning a Japanese video recorder and car does not make a modern Englishman Japanese. However the combination of archaeological evidence and the limited historical record do suggest that the population of Romano-British eastern Britain contained a significant number of people of German origin. It is sometimes said that the Roman army in our region contained only what are described as "Germanic mercenaries" towards the end of the Roman period, but there are specific references to regular troops of Germanic origin serving as part of the regular army much earlier. They surprised the British by swimming across wide rivers during the initial conquest of Britain. Batavians from the Rhine valley formed an important part of the regular army from the campaigns of Agricola in the first century to the late garrisons on Hadrian's Wall. As the wooden writing tablets from Vindolanda have revealed, troops from different units were regularly posted to forts other than the headquarters of their units. We might expect troops from the coastal territories of Batavia and Frisia, in modern Holland and Belgium, to be serving with the fleet along our coast. Regular Roman soldiers who were ethnic Germans were probably a common sight throughout East Anglia and may have felt sufficiently at home to settle here when they retired. It would be easy for them to keep in touch with their ancestral homelands across the sea.

We have already suggested that Britain probably saw itself as different from other provinces of the Roman Empire and had most in common with the people of the Rhine area. As Britain became detached from the empire it would be natural for the eastern side of the country to see itself belonging to the North Sea Zone and to forge closer links by sea with northern Europe. The inhabitants did not have to reject all the legacy of Roman culture, but they adopted much that we classify as Anglo-Saxon.

One area can demonstrate the difficulty of deciding exactly what was happening in the closing years of Roman rule. In north Suffolk finds from field walking reveal a difference, so far unexplained, between sites in the Thornham area and those along the valley of the Waveney. In the Thornham area the pottery we find for the later Roman period includes significant amounts of Hadham-type wares for which production sites are known in Hertfordshire and Essex, but not much Oxfordshire ware, while the Waveney valley sites have much Oxfordshire ware and little Hadham-type ware. This may reflect some feature of the supply routes, but there may be some other factor which also led to the apparent scarcity of roofing and heating tiles in the Thornham area.

The Hadham-type wares are sometimes called Romano-Saxon pottery because some of them are decorated with designs also found on early Anglo-Saxon pottery, particularly bosses or dimples. Some have argued that they were being made for an immigrant Saxon population, but this is not now generally accepted. It is not clear whether these designs did originate outside the Roman Empire or were copied by Anglo-Saxon potters from the Romano-British designs after they became fashionable in the Roman Empire, as part of the two-way links between eastern England and the Rhine valley. Apparently Hadham wares were in circulation in the third century and reached the height of their popularity in the fourth century.[21]

The typical Hadham pots are coated with a red slip: they were produced at Little and Much Hadham, near Bishop's Stortford, in Hertfordshire, from about AD250 to 400 and appear along the east coast mainly during the later fourth century. It is possible that these wares were also produced at Essex potteries, including that at Inworth, near Tiptree, which would be better suited to heavy loads of pottery being transported by water to markets in Suffolk.

In the post-Roman period occupation along the Waveney seems to be concentrated in the valley itself, as fieldwalking has revealed Early Anglo-Saxon wares in Bungay, Flixton and South Elmham St Margaret. There is a concentration of Middle Saxon Ipswich-type pottery in St Margaret. At Scole late Roman activity is followed by Early Anglo-Saxon evidence and Middle Saxon features without any evidence that there was a break in farming this land. Environmental evidence suggests many crops were being grown in Middle Saxon times.

Just south of Scole bridge in Oakley there is evidence of high status activity in the sixth to seventh centuries, marked by the bronze bridge and tuning peg of a lyre and three gold coins including a Merovingian tremissis of 605.[22] All three parishes of Thornham Parva, Thornham Magna and Stoke Ash have produced significant amounts of Ipswich-type wares (so has one site at

21 Roberts, W.I., *Romano-Saxon Pottery,* BAR 106 (1982).
22 West, S.E., *A Corpus of Anglo-Saxon Material from Suffolk*, EAA 84, 1998, p.86.

Mendlesham[23]) and both the Thornhams have produced Early Anglo-Saxon wares. It may be that we are seeing evidence for significant foci of activity in these areas continuing into the post-Roman period. St Margaret and Flixton are associated with the early days of the bishopric of the East Angles, and it may be that the town site at Stoke Ash/Thornham became the centre of an early Anglo-Saxon royal estate.[24]

We have seen evidence for a Christian presence in Roman East Anglia but have no idea how it fared in the face of newcomers. We do know of Christian activity among the leading Britons around St Albans in later years as Bishop, later Saint, Germanus of Auxerre visited the martyr's shrine in 429 during his campaign against the Pelagians. They were promoting a British heresy, or at least the authorities of the church in Rome called it heresy, that had been propounded by a late-fourth-century British preacher and philosopher who studied at Rome and then travelled and preached in Africa and Palestine. Pelagius claimed that man had free will and was responsible for his own destiny, while the official view, set out by St Augustine of Hippo, was that man's destiny was determined by God and man could only pray to receive the grace of God to save him. Whether East Anglian Christians joined the debate we can only speculate, but it is interesting that Britain was seen as the origin of a significant variation of Christian belief.

One fifth-century continental bishop, Faustus of Riez, who had been abbot of Lerins, was probably born in Britain but opposed the Arian creed and so was removed from his bishopric about AD460 by Euric, King of the Visigoths, who was an Arian Christian. Sidonius Apollinaris read and praised a book that Faustus wrote, using his knowledge of classical philosophy to support Christianity. Sidonius entertained a priest and monk called Riochatus who was taking the book to people Sidonius calls Faustus' Britanni.[25] These might be exiles in Brittany, but some identify the messenger with St Riochatus of Wales and see Britanni at this date as the inhabitants of Britain itself.

Gildas, writing his book *De Excidio Britonum,* "The Ruin of Britain", in western Britain about AD540, refers to events immediately after the departure of the Romans, about a century earlier. Some historians reject Gildas because of the extravagant language in which he condemned the rulers of his day, but this was common practice among Roman authors trained in the confrontational language of Roman law courts. Gildas wrote good Latin, and, although he telescoped the early history of Britain and confused some events in the process, there is no reason to doubt the veracity of his account of events nearer to his own time. He tells us that Scots and Picts attacked northern Britain but that after a famine they went home. Later at a time of plague these enemies returned, so the ruling council and the proud tyrant (perhaps the Vortigern of other accounts) invited Saxons to help. The first Saxons arrived in three keels which Gildas says was their name for warships, they gripped the eastern side of the island, and were followed by more Saxons in ships.

The Saxons, as fighting soldiers, claimed from the British *annonae*, that is provisions from annual produce as a tax payment, so they were settling as soldiers but clearly not as farmers. Later they complained their monthly allowance (*epimenia*) was not sufficient, so broke their treaty (*foedere rupto*) and plundered the whole island. The reference to them receiving payment suggests we should see them as setting up, initially at least, military communities where they and their families got their food from the British and

23 West, S.E., *A Corpus of Anglo-Saxon Material from Suffolk*, EAA 84, 1998, fig. 158.
24 Fairclough, J. & Hardy, M., *Thornham and the Waveney Valley*, Heritage Publications, 2004.
25 Sidonius Apollinaris *letters* ix 3 and ix 9.6.

A group of Ipswich ware pots, made in Ipswich in Middle Saxon times and traded over a wide area. The pot at back left went wrong while being fired in the kiln and was thrown away nearby.
© Suffolk County Council Archaeological Service

did not farm the land themselves. Their task was to fight, just like the Roman army but not like the British civilian population who had been forbidden to carry weapons under Roman law. When the British refused to provide as much as the Saxons demanded the latter turned aggressive and raided all the way across Britain before returning to the eastern side of the island, which matches our experience of finding early evidence of an Anglo-Saxon presence dominating Suffolk.

Tom Lethbridge suggested that perhaps many of the Anglo-Saxon immigrants came from Angeln by way of Frisia as individual families, rather than as tribal units. Then new units were formed in Britain based on the most powerful families who emerged as rulers of the Angles, Saxons and Britons living in their areas, while the different races gradually amalgamated. In due course one family dominated the others and the dynasty of the Wuffings claimed to govern all of East Anglia on the basis of their descent from both the Germanic god Woden and the Roman Caesar ("Cassar"). Perhaps their name, suggesting an affinity with the wolf, encouraged them to favour the legend of the wolf that suckled Romulus and Remus in Rome's foundation myth. Certainly an important Anglian wore a late-fifth-century gold pendant found at Undley near Lakenheath. It shows the wolf suckling Romulus and Remus below a Roman imperial bust and surrounded by a text in runes. The wolf appears again in the eighth century on a coin of King Aethelbert on which he uses the Roman title REX as king, while the moneyer Lul shows his own name in runic letters.

The earliest Anglo-Saxon settlements, in the fifth century, were established in eastern England by groups who can be seen as these soldiers drawing food taxes from the local British people as the latter continued with the farming. We have noted that Stanley West[26] sees the presence of spelt wheat and stinking mayweed (*anthemis cotula*) in the fifth-century settlement at West Stow as evidence of interaction between the Romano-British

26 West, S.E., *A Corpus of Anglo-Saxon Material from Suffolk*, EAA 84, 1998, p.261.

population farming round Icklingham and the incoming Anglo-Saxons. Were these items coming in as part of the local British annona payment to the Anglo-Saxon soldiers who claimed to protect them and depended on them growing the food? Presumably increasing demands for payment greater than just the food requirements of the annona enabled the leaders of the East Angles to build up the wealth shown in their burials, above all at Sutton Hoo. The presence of so many weapons in the burials must reflect the military culture of these people.

At West Stow Stanley West interpreted the presence of Roman coins and pottery as evidence of scavenging, but perhaps these items were still being used by the British population at Icklingham, who were using up existing stocks in the absence of new supplies. Some of these items, including samian pottery that must have acquired heirloom or antique status, found their way to the new settlers. Certainly they were using large numbers of Roman tiles as the bases for their hearths.

We cannot say whether such immigrant communities of warriors with their families, if indeed West Stow was initially a military foundation, might have settled here by agreement with the authorities even before the end of Roman government. Perhaps they came only after the British found themselves without any official defenders. In either case they might well have expected the local Britons to carry on farming and produce their food while they concentrated on developing their fighting skills. The local inhabitants knew from long experience how to farm their land productively, and it would have been foolish for incomers to ignore such indigenous knowledge.

Tom Lethbridge noted Roman shapes among the early cremation urns in the extensive Anglo-Saxon cemetery at Lackford, directly opposite Icklingham across the River Lark, and found a Roman bronze spoon and silver ring inside an urn of the type he called Frisian-Angle.[27] This encouraged him to believe the native population survived here and blended with incoming Angles and Saxons. Henry Prigg had noted similar circumstances among those he excavated near Icklingham, saying "I have obtained cremated remains enclosed in urns of undoubted Roman fabric".[28] He says two urns in a "mixed Romano-British and Saxon cemetery in Icklingham" were "of precisely similar make" to those from Roman kilns he had excavated at West Stow, but of course those were of first/second-century date, so his identification is not reliable. In fact neither Lethbridge nor Prigg offers conclusive evidence.

It is notable that Anglo-Saxon sunken-featured buildings have been found within the area of Roman settlement at Lakenheath. At Stonea in the Fens early Anglo-Saxon buildings were constructed on a road surface within the town in a position of dominance, but perhaps deliberately respecting the property boundaries of the existing Romano-British population.[29] Further west at Orton Hall Farm, near Peterborough, Don Mackreth sees an Anglo-Saxon group taking over a working Romano-British farm and keeping the existing layout.

Because Gildas was writing in western Britain when it was still under British rulers rather than Anglo-Saxon control, his knowledge of events over a hundred years earlier in the east of the country would have been very limited, so they do not feature in his story.

27 *Cambridge Antiquarian Society Quarto Publications* NS VI (1951).
28 *Journal of the British Archaeological Association* vol. 37 (1881), p.152 ff.
29 Malim, T., *Stonea and the Roman Fens*, Tempus, 2005, p.228.

The reconstructed buildings of part of the Anglo-Saxon village at West Stow. They are based on the original remains of the village excavated here by Stanley West.

Presumably Anglo-Saxon warrior leaders or warlords who claimed rations for their troops gradually became landlords of estates which their British tenants farmed, paying rent in goods and services. Some of these military communities do not seem to have established themselves until the sixth century. Was there a real break, or did an archaeologically invisible occupation fill the gap?

A distinct group of warriors were so proud of their military status that many were buried with spears and shields in a cemetery in the Handford or Hadleigh Road area of Ipswich. Tom Plunkett has called them "Guardians of the Gipping". They were buried with their womenfolk, so presumably their home was at this point where the river valley becomes narrow enough for them to control access inland by that route. If they lived in the halls and sunken-featured buildings excavated by Stuart Boulter immediately across the river beside Handford Road it might even be that they took over a Roman military supply base with its massive timber fence. It is a suitable strategic position where a presumed Roman road crossed the Orwell and the river provided quick access to Walton Castle and the open sea.

The archaeological record shows that early in the fifth century the supply of new coins to Britain stopped and the pottery production industry came to an end. The coins had reached Britain as the pay for military garrisons and imperial officials, and once these payments came to an end there was no reason for coins to enter Britain. We have no record of the last payment to a garrison in East Anglia. As the currency disappeared from the frontier regions of the empire, so presumably did the complex economic structure that had grown up.

Pottery is the material that gives us the clearest evidence for this. Pots of different shapes, many of them decorated, all produced to a high standard by skilled potters, were traded within the empire. Some, particularly the fine samian wares which were produced in vast quantities in the earlier part of the Roman period on a truly industrial scale, had been sold throughout the empire. Others had a more local distribution but can still be found traded far from their place of manufacture. The archaeological importance of pottery is that pots are relatively easily broken but the broken pieces, particularly of high quality Roman products, are remarkably robust, so survive in the ground.

New designs and fabrics were frequently introduced, and so can be dated, until suddenly early in the fifth century the whole industry in Britain came to an end. The collapse was so absolute that we do not even see a return to pre-Roman Iron Age standards, as the quality of design and manufacture is much inferior, without the use of potter's wheel or proper kilns. Presumably the industrial potteries depended on the Roman organisation for distributing their wares to a wide commercial market so that they reached not only the rich owners of great houses but also the owners of the most ordinary farms. It was not until perhaps the eighteenth century that anything similar was achieved. Broken pottery provides us with evidence of this distribution system, and we can only assume that such perishables as clothing and footwear or furniture were distributed in the same way where we lack the proof. The loss of the payments to the army destroyed the basis for the industries of the province which had been built on the foundations of earlier Iron Age production. Perhaps people had become complacent about their standard of living and

*Spear heads and shield bosses from the Anglo-Saxon
cemetery at Hadleigh Road (Handford), Ipswich, the remains
of the long spears and circular shields that were buried with
their warrior owners. The metal bosses formed the centre of
the wood and leather shields and protected the handgrips.*
© Colchester and Ipswich Museum Service

*Below are examples of the jewellery found in Anglo-Saxon
burials at Hadleigh Road (Handford), Ipswich, presumably
the prized possessions of the warriors' wives.*
© Colchester and Ipswich Museum Service

failed to see that it depended not only on Roman military protection but also on contact with the Roman finance system.

It is impossible to say how long the pottery and coins typical of the Roman period remained in use, but large numbers of silver coins in the Hoxne hoard had been clipped. This misuse of stamped coin was unlikely to take place before the end of Roman government, so they were almost certainly in use for some time after 410. The hoard was discovered in 1992 by Eric Lawes, using a metal detector. Fortunately he reported his discovery after extracting the first few finds, so most of the hoard was excavated systematically by a team from Suffolk Archaeological Service.

Much of it was removed in blocks so that these could be taken apart slowly in the Conservation Laboratory at the British Museum. As a result very small fragments of the more fragile items have been preserved. It was possible to see exactly how groups of objects had been packed carefully in a wooden box 370 by 510mm and over 150 mm deep (the precise depth of the box is unknown as it was compressed in the ground). Even though none of the wood survived, traces on the iron show that it was oak. Some items had been placed in smaller boxes, two of them secured by silver padlocks, and others seem to have been wrapped in cloths and straw or hay, all within the large box. In addition to some 14,865 coins there was a spectacular collection of gold jewellery and silver tableware.

The workmanship of the gold jewellery is very fine and the gold is remarkably pure, being of a higher standard than the modern 22 carat. There are six necklaces, nineteen bracelets, three finger rings and an elaborate body chain. One necklace has a small Christian cross on the fastener and the body

Excavating the site of Roman and Early Anglo-Saxon activity beside Handford Road in Ipswich. Suffolk County Council Archaeological Service is uncovering the evidence on the former site of Firmin's works.
© Suffolk County Council Archaeological Service

Excavation of the Early Anglo-Saxon "sunken featured building" at Handford Road. The black area is the material that filled the cellar, of which two quarters have been excavated away.
© Suffolk County Council Archaeological Service

chain incorporates a solidus of Gratian (AD367-383). One bracelet carries the openwork inscription "VTERE FELIX DOMINA JVLIANE" meaning "Use this happily Lady Juliane". Other items included the solid silver tigress handle from a large flagon, the four elaborate gilded silver statuette pepper pots, seventy-eight spoons and twenty ladles, mostly in matching sets, as well as four silver wine strainers. One silver spoon does carry the name Faustinus, and a whole set of ten are inscribed Ursicinus, both common Roman names.

The last official coins represented in the hoard are the silver siliquae of Constantine III, minted in 407/8. Peter Guest in his study of the coins from the hoard[30] suggests that the silver from the clipped coins was probably used to make the good-quality copies of siliquae present in the hoard, which were of the same standard silver as the real ones. He thinks they were minted to increase the number of siliquae in circulation in Britain when real ones were in short supply. The clipping was done in a way that preserved the head of the emperor on the coin, which marked it out as a real Roman coin, and the silver content of the copies was consistent with the originals. This distinguishes the copies from a small group of forgeries in which a copper core was enclosed by a thin foil of silver, producing a "coin" with the minimum amount of silver but carefully made to look like the real thing in a laborious process that suggests the real coins were of significant value to be worth the trouble. He suggests the hoard might have been buried as late as 450 or 480, but I do not think we can tell when it was done. We can only say with certainty that it must have been some time after 408, as the issues of Constantine III provide a secure terminus post quem, the earliest possible date for their burial. He points out that some of the silver siliquae had been clipped several times, gradually reducing their size.

It seems that Roman coins remained in use for a considerable time after the end of official Roman government. Somebody in Britain, and possibly in East Anglia, was exercising considerable skill to keep a supply of acceptable coins in circulation. This was more than just casual use of left-over coins;

30 Guest, P.S.W., *The Late Roman Gold and Silver Coins from the Hoxne Treasure*, British Museum, 2005.

somebody was actively managing the currency to maintain a trading economy. While the silver coins seem to have been tipped into the box after all the other items had been carefully packed, the gold solidi were in groups and had perhaps been placed in bags.

Peter Guest points out that the gold solidi have a total weight of eight Roman pounds, and draws attention to four deep silver bowls, each weighing half a pound. As exchanges of gifts between wealthy individuals, starting from donatives given by the emperor himself, are recorded by weight rather than number of coins he suggests these represent four gifts of two pounds weight of gold, each presented in a silver bowl of half-pound weight. Perhaps this was how the owner received them, and he kept them ready for an occasion when he wished to make a gift himself. When the hoard was buried the time was probably not right for such gifts, so they were hidden in case better times returned. In the same way the owner might have felt it was not worth restoring the tigress handle to its flagon, but he tucked it in with the other reserve valuables in the hope it would be used one day.

Here we seem to have evidence of an individual who was among the wealthy upper class of Roman society in Britain. He was part of a world in which people exchanged gifts of high value to mark special occasions, and where it was

Above left: *One of three silver pepperpots from the Hoxne treasure, this one in the form of the head of an empress. Pepper was an expensive import from the east, bought in from outside the empire.*

Left: *The base of the pepperpot, showing the basic but effective mechanism that enabled it to be turned to sprinkle the pepper or to fill the pot.*
Both © Trustees of the British Museum

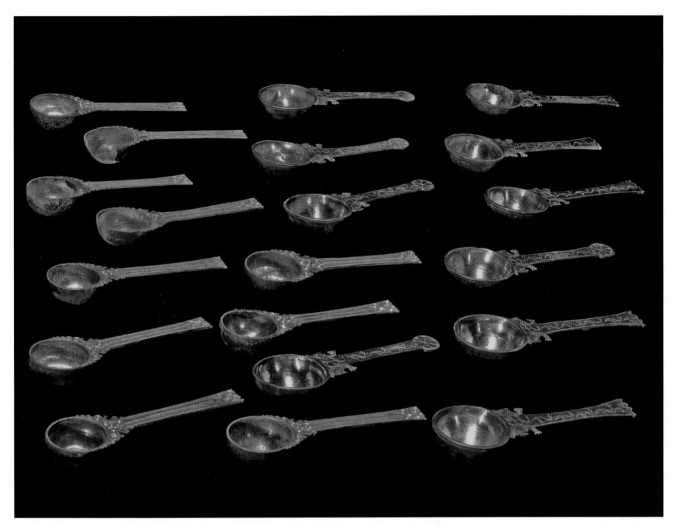

Silver ladles from the Hoxne treasure, in which there were ladles and spoons in sets of ten.
© Trustees of the British Museum

customary to provide lavish displays when entertaining guests. This is what we might expect of the owner of an estate large enough to feature by name as Villa Faustini, "the estate that once belonged to Faustinus", in the Antonine Itinerary. Perhaps it is not too far-fetched to suggest that the single silver spoon inscribed Faustinus, unfortunately a common name in the Roman world, might have been an heirloom from that previous owner. The presence of a full set of ten silver spoons inscribed with the name of Aurelius Ursicinus must make it very likely that he was the last owner of this treasure, and perhaps of the estate once held by Faustinus.

The total of coins alone in the hoard was 580 gold solidi and 14,630 silver coins, of which 14,565 were siliquae. A collection of 600 gold coins of similar date that had been buried at Clint Farm, Eye, was found about 1780, but the records tell us little about them. However in the second volume of the Proceedings of the Suffolk Institute of Archaeology it is reported that at a meeting held at Eye in 1854 "The Rev. C.R. Manning exhibited ten gold Roman coins found at Eye, Suffolk, in May 1781. Several hundred coins were found at the time, chiefly of the Emperors Honorius and Arcadius, in a leaden box; and near them were found some human bones." In the same volume Henry Creed recorded that "in 1781 a leaden coffer was turned up near the river on the Clint Farm by some labourers. It contained several

hundred aurei [presumably gold solidi] of the Roman emperors Valens &
Valentinianus, Gratian, Theodosius, Arcadius & Honorius. I have seen several
of these in the possession of a lady lately deceased and ten of them, in the
finest preservation, are now on the table being exhibited by Rev. C.R.
Manning."

It might be that both these hoards, and likewise the silverware at
Mildenhall, were entrusted to the care of the Genius Loci or some other local
deity, but not I suggest with the intention of consigning them to the ground for
ever. The owner or his descendants might always request them back from the
deity, perhaps in exchange for a suitable offering by way of thanks. The deity
protecting it in the ground performed the function of a modern banker and
was entitled to a fee.

On this occasion, as with other hoards found in modern times, the owner
and his or her heirs never did recover it. Whether they died without passing on
the details, forgot where it was buried or were physically prevented from
retrieving it we shall never know. Had the owner buried it because he feared it
might be stolen from his home? Was he removing the temptation to spend his
capital if it was available in the house? Was he putting it beyond the reach of
some new local magnate or ruler claiming the right to search his home and tax
or seize his property? In the uncertain world of the fifth and sixth centuries
any of these seems plausible.

Seen in this light we could be looking at the actions of somebody who
still believed the customs of life at the highest level in the Roman Empire
would be restored at some future date. He might have been living in a region
that was subject to the influence of the Angles rather than Rome, but he still
expected Roman imperial power to return, and he would be ready for it. He or
his family would be able to buy back their rightful position.

If that aspiration was thwarted, at least his gold and silver did not find its
way to the treasury that furnished the great burial ship at Sutton Hoo. We
might wonder how far that royal treasury did benefit from the wealth of the
neighbours of our Hoxne Roman as they fell under the authority of the new
Anglian rulers. If we assume that only a small proportion of the available
wealth was buried and never recovered, but that included the Hoxne Treasure,
the Eye gold coins and the Mildenhall silver, then a considerable amount of
gold and silver in coin, plate and other forms was kept in the homes of the
wealthiest of our residents. How much of it went to pay the new Anglian
warlords whose warriors replaced the Roman soldiers as guardians of this
land?

It is inconceivable that all the British abandoned their farms, but some
did not like the way things were going and took ship to Gaul, particularly
Brittany. Gildas says that some survivors of attacks by the Saxons "made for
lands beyond the sea; beneath the swelling sails they loudly wailed, singing a
psalm that took the place of a shanty: 'You have given us like sheep for eating
and scattered us among the heathen'."[31] The minutes of the Council of Tours
in 461 includes among its signatories "Mansuetus, Bishop of the British",
who is assumed to be bishop of the British settled in Gaul, unless he had
crossed the sea from Britain for the occasion.

Sidonius Apollinaris in 480 described the trial in 468 of Arvandus, the
Praetorian Prefect of Gaul, charged with treason for sending a letter
encouraging Euric, the king of the Visigoths, to attack the Britanni who had

31 Gildas, *De Excidio Britonum*,
chap. 25.

established themselves in the estuary of the Loire.[32] According to Jornandes their king Riothamus could mobilise a substantial army of 12,000 British soldiers in the middle Loire.[33] We have no means of knowing whether any of these Britanni had sailed all the way from East Anglia. Sidonius wrote to Riothamus in support of a man who complained that Britanni settled in Armorica (Brittany) were enticing away his slaves.[34] Sidonius thought his friend would make a good case but wondered whether he would get a fair hearing as he was a poor, humble, solitary rustic among the crowd of noisy armed disorderly men emboldened by courage, numbers and comradeship.

The Britons who stayed in East Anglia during those unsettled times might have understood the plight of this anguished Gaul. Sidonius' grandfather had been Praetorian Prefect under Constantine III, and he was Bishop of Clermont from 470 to about 483. He wrote a poem in praise of Avitus for putting an end to Saxon raiding in Brittany as Master of Cavalry and Infantry in 456.[35] He said the Armorican region was previously expecting the Saxon pirate who considered it sport to plough the British waters with hide ships, dividing the blue sea in a stitched boat.

In a letter to a Gallo-Roman naval officer serving Euric, king of the Visigoths, Sidonius describes him meeting on the Ocean the curved vessels of Saxons.[36] They give him the impression every oarsman in their crew is a pirate captain, as all at the same time give and receive orders, teaching and learning piracy. But they are the most dangerous enemies as they attack unforeseen and if spotted slip away. They are so familiar with the perils of the sea that when a storm lulls their enemy into a feeling of security but conceals their attack, they rejoice in the risks of attacking through waves and jagged rocks to secure surprise. When they set their sails to leave enemy waters they kill one in ten of their prisoners by drowning or crucifixion as a superstitious rite. This was how the Romans viewed the Saxon threat.

We have noted that in the Waveney valley at South Elmham St Margaret's a high proportion of Roman sites remained in existence throughout the fourth century. Various sites also produce metalwork and pottery of the early Saxon period and Middle Saxon Ipswich-type wares as well as Thetford-type wares, which take us right up to the Norman Conquest. This strongly suggests continuity of occupation, so perhaps the same families went on living in the area. At neighbouring Flixton were found two fourth-century Roman bronze coins, both of which had been drilled so that they could be strung and worn around the neck. These were found close to an Anglo-Saxon burial with sixth-century brooches and an unusual glass claw-beaker.[37] The beaker of green glass marks this as a high-status burial, and we have noticed that Flixton was a busy place in the Roman period. A single fourth-century coin, similarly drilled, was found at Thornham Magna close to the river. Clearly in the sixth century Roman coins were still being valued, although we cannot say whether they were worn as ornamental pendants or strung together as a safe way of carrying money. In either case it is likely that they were respected because they carried the portrait of the Roman emperor when the Wuffing royal family of East Anglia were proclaiming their descent from the deified Roman Caesar. The new rulers did not break all links with the past, as the traditional authority of the Roman Empire remained the point of reference for those claiming to be legitimate rulers of others.

While the rich kept their reserves of coins and their silver cutlery, at least

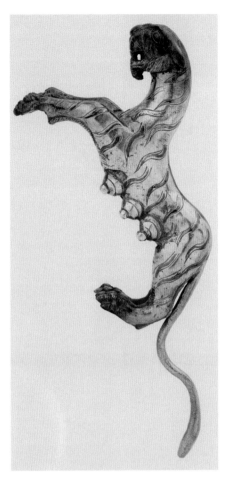

This solid silver tigress formed the handle from a jug for serving wine. Part of the Hoxne treasure, it appears to have become detached from its jug and been placed with the cutlery.
© Trustees of the British Museum

32 Sidonius Apollinaris *letter* I 7.5
33 Jornandes *Getica* 45.
34 Sidonius Apollinaris *letter* III 9.
35 Sidonius Apollinaris *poem* VII lines 369 ff.
36 Sidonius Apollinaris *letter* viii 6 to Naumatius.
37 PSIAH vol.37 (1991) "Archaeology in Suffolk 1990", p.268.

for a time, did the ordinary farming families continue for decades, if not longer, using the large number of pots and other "Roman" items in their cupboards? Did they still use "Roman" brooches to fasten their clothes, and perhaps use Roman coins when trading with their neighbours? If some of those pots and dresses lasted a long time it might have been another factor in the demise of industrial production, as the declining economy destroyed the purchasing power of most households. As things finally wore out it was the new Anglo-Saxons who dominated the market, so replacements were produced in their styles.

Not everybody stayed on their ancestral lands. Gildas told of some Britons emigrating before the emergence as leader in Britain of Ambrosius Aurelianus, whose parents had "worn the purple", and the battle of Mount Badon.[38] The latter is usually dated as about AD500, as Gildas said it was in the year of his birth, and he was writing forty-four years later. There is no reference in Gildas as to which were the "lands beyond the sea" to which they sailed, but this is generally assumed to be the origin of British settlement in Brittany (formerly Armorica), which seems reasonable. It does not mean this was the only destination, as Procopius, also writing in the sixth century, reported that Britain was occupied by three very populous nations: Angiloi (presumably the Angles of East Anglia), Frissones (presumably Frisians, from the modern Netherlands) and Britons.[39] He said that not only Britons but also some Angles and Frisians were emigrating from Britain to the continent. Perhaps this was because their defeat at Mons Badonicus had halted their expansion into western Britain. In these passages Procopius, writing in about AD553, calls Britain "Brittia" and Brittany "Britannia".[40]

This could be the source of a legend in Germany that some Angles from Britain landed at Haduloha, modern Cuxhaven, and were settled, outside the Frankish Rhineland, on land between the rivers Unstrut and Saal (later the canton of Engilin) where they became known as "Saxons".[41] These movements between Britain and the continent make it difficult to be sure of the significance of some of the archaeological evidence, if some continental Saxons might have spent several generations in Britain and very possibly in East Anglia. While it is tempting to suggest that emigrants to Cuxhaven might have sailed from East Anglia and those to Armorica and the Loire from western Britain, there can be no certainty. Once people had put to sea we cannot tell which way they headed or where they might have paused on their journey.

We have to remember that the sea was always a highway. It brought East Anglia particularly close to Frisia, that is, modern Holland, so it is not surprising that imported Frisian pottery was used by our early Anglo-Saxons and that Paul Blinkhorn sees Frisia as the origin of the design of the Ipswich Ware pottery of Middle Saxon times. Indeed he speculates that Frisian potters might have settled in Ipswich.

East Anglia has produced many early Anglo-Saxon cremation cemeteries and some inhumations with Anglo-Saxon grave goods alongside cremations ("mixed cemeteries"), but Tom Williamson has drawn attention to their absence from the Shotley peninsula and north Essex. Looking at his map it appears that the area without such cemeteries might reflect a reduced late-fourth-century territorium of the colonia at Colchester, so perhaps here a British population continued burying their dead as they had done before.[42]

38 Gildas *De Excidio Britonum* chap. 25.
39 Procopius *De Bello Gallico* VIII xx 7 and VI xv 4.
40 Thompson, E.A., *Classical Quarterly* vol.30 (1980), p.498.
41 Stenton, "*Anglo-Saxon England*" 3rd ed., Oxford, 1971 p. 7.
42 *Saxon* (the Sutton Hoo Society Newsletter) no.42 (2005).

The town seems to have gone into decline, perhaps just because it remained an enclave of Roman attitudes. Perhaps the valley of the Blyth, where the later Blything Hundred always appears to be a distinctive unit that did things in its own way, also kept its traditional customs. Notably its north and south boundaries are both marked by "Hundred Rivers".

Perhaps after the collapse of the systems of government imposed by the Romans over the territory of the colonia at Colchester and the civitas of the Iceni centred on Venta Icenorum, the area broke up into smaller units. Some might have been derived from the pre-Roman communities reflected in the later Blything Hundred and the Wicklaw of south-east Suffolk that possibly originated from the Iron Age community based on Burgh by Grundisburgh.

If Colchester remained the centre of a small Roman community, it is notable that while the great road into Norfolk, the Pye Road or A140, survived north of Capel St Mary and some other roads in Suffolk continued in use, all routes into the Colchester area seem to have been broken off. Presumably land communication between Ipswich and Colchester was unwanted for some time. Thus at a later date Ipswich people could still use the Roman route to Norwich, but a new link had to be forged south of Capel St Mary through Stratford as the route to Colchester, with an alternative via the lowest possible crossing of the Stour at Cattawade.

The focus of communities seems to relate to the waterways and valleys. Tom Williamson points out that in the coastal area of Suffolk known as the Sandlings it is only the soils of the higher ground that are poor quality known as "Newport 4". This soil created heathland, which would naturally be covered by trees. In early times men felled trees for timber, the open ground supported furze, heather and shrubs which provided fuel, thatching material and bedding, gathered by families living on the better soil lower down the valley slopes. Here they could grow crops and manage the heath as a place to graze animals, particularly sheep, which certainly in more recent times were moved down the slope at night to manure the arable fields. Land further from the rivers could be managed as woodland which might be coppiced as we saw in chapter 3, or used to pasture animals, particularly pigs. All animals had to be excluded from coppice woodland by a large bank with a deep ditch on the outside as they would eat the new shoots.

In wood pasture some trees might be pollarded by cutting branches above the browsing line of animals so they could grow again. Woods might be seen as dark, enclosed spaces and people no doubt welcomed returning home to their houses looking over the light, open waters of their rivers. As the soils of local valleys also vary in their quality, management of the landscape was an essential art for its inhabitants, demanding sophisticated local knowledge. It would be no surprise if new landowners, be they Roman, Angle, Saxon or Dane, chose to encourage the native British families to go on farming the land as tenants or as slaves. These indigenous workers would leave little trace on the archaeological record beside Roman villas and Saxon halls.

The inhabitants of separate valleys could communicate more easily by water than by land, and we should see rivers and the sea as the highways of this world and the focus for social groups. People have asked why the Wuffingas emerged as the royal family when their base was in a corner of the kingdom. Part of the answer may come from the very nature of this location.

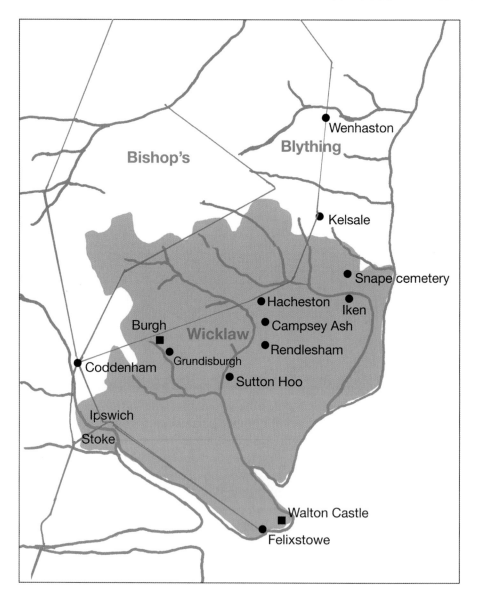

The Anglo-Saxon ring from the ship burial at Snape, incorporating a Roman intaglio figure to create a signet ring.
© Trustees of the British Museum

Perhaps when the Roman administration collapsed Colchester became the centre for a strong unit south of the Stour, which later became part of the kingdom of Essex. If the Wicklaw and the Blything retained some sense of identity from their time as independent sub-kingdoms before the Roman conquest they might accept different overlords, as would other parts of East Anglia. The Wicklaw group had the advantage of the Orwell, Deben and Alde estuaries with the port at Felixstowe and inland ports at Ipswich and perhaps Woodbridge (Kyson?) giving them the means to control trade between much of East Anglia and the continent. The ancestral Wuffings took control of an ideal power base from which to dominate the other groups and so create the East Anglian kingdom.

The north-east coast of Norfolk has no deep valleys offering sheltered anchorages, and small coastal communities depending on open beaches do not have the same potential for development. Beyond this lie the uncertain waters of the Wash, perhaps seen more as a route of access to western centres such as Exning and Ely, although the valley of the Babingley River is linked to St Felix. This western side of the kingdom was more remote from Germanic and Scandinavian contacts and closer to rival Mercia.

If the mouth of the Deben was free from the sandbanks that tend to make entry difficult today and the "Goose Fjord", as Sam Newton interprets Goseford, was a more open estuary, the valley was an attractive proposition. Although Ekwall says the name of the Deben is a back formation from Debenham, its likely meaning is *deep*, and this would be a plausible name for the river itself, with reference to either the depth of clear water or the deep-sided valley as seen from the water. Smaller ships would easily reach Rendlesham, just as larger ones sailed up the Orwell to Ipswich, then emerging as a trading centre.

One tributary of the Deben flows past the ancient enclosure at Burgh by Grundisburgh, which might still have been important to a British "constituency" in the kingdom. The territory that later became known as the Wicklaw was bounded by the Orwell and centred on the valleys of the Deben and Alde and their tributaries. We have seen that before the Roman conquest this might have been an independent kingdom allied to the Iceni. Did it reassert its independence as the Roman province disintegrated? Given good access to the Orwell, Deben and Alde, immigrants from Anglian lands would welcome an invitation to settle there.

Presumably the Wuffings emerged as rulers of the Angles and Britons here in the Wicklaw before spreading their power further afield. One of their

The massive ditch and bank of the Devil's Dyke near Newmarket that formed so impressive a barrier controlling access by land into East Anglia from the south and west. Presumably it was designed to protect the independent kingdom of East Anglia.

43 British Museum 1950.12.06.1.
44 Filmer-Sankey, W., *Snape*, EAA
95, 2001, p.195.

*At the Cranfields Mill site beside
the Wet Dock in Ipswich this trench
5 metres square revealed well
preserved timbers of the Saxon
waterfront facing the Orwell
2.3 metres below modern ground
level. This led to the large area
excavation that exposed the Saxon
timbers seen in the next picture.*
© Suffolk County Council
Archaeological Service

early kings might have been buried in his ship above the Alde at Snape in the
sixth century. His gold signet ring, now in the British Museum,[43] is a Roman
onyx intaglio engraved with the standing figure of "*Bonus Eventus*" (Good
Outcome) mounted in a gold setting which William Filmer-Sankey identifies
as a product of the Rhineland in the early sixth century.[44] He points out that
such rings were worn specifically for sealing documents and belonged to
kings or persons of very high status who were anxious to follow Roman or
Byzantine practice.

One is tempted to wonder if this might be the ring of Wuffa's father
Wehha, said to have been the first of the family to rule over the East
Anglian folk in Britain. The adoption of a practical Roman gemstone raises
the question of whether Filmer-Sankey is right to say there would have been
no documents to seal in sixth-century England. Of course no documents of
that age survive, but there is no compelling reason to see East Anglia as totally
illiterate just because it was no longer administered from Rome and
its new rulers were incomers. Gildas was writing good Latin in western
Britain at this time. Perhaps early Wuffing rulers did have occasion to seal
documents as they imposed their control over the mixed population of
Britons and Angles, while adopting some of the symbols of Roman style
government.

By this time we might suppose the communities of Britons and Anglo-

Excavation of a larger area at the Cranfields Mill site in Ipswich in 2006 revealed Saxon timber revetments and other structures. The wood was preserved because it had been waterlogged since Saxon times.
© Suffolk County Council Archaeological Service

Saxons who stayed in our region were fusing to become the folk of East Anglia under their own kings. As the Wuffing kings took control of the whole of East Anglia evidence suggests the base of their power was at Rendlesham, which Bede calls *vicus regius*, a royal town, and along the Deben valley. Presumably Rendlesham replaced the Roman market town at Hacheston two miles up the river beyond the *campus* at Campsey Ashe. A survey in Rendlesham is revealing a lot of activity in the Early Saxon period. Although there is also a scatter of Roman material, the archaeological evidence cannot tell how much of this was being used after 410 and it certainly includes coins pierced for hanging. Nor is there anything that has to be earlier than the end of the fifth century. Here archaeology is indeed confirming Bede's report. There is a story in the 1722 edition of Camden's *Britannia* that a silver crown weighing 60 ounces was found at Rendlesham in 1690 but was sold and melted down. Could this really have been a piece of the royal regalia?

Perhaps, just as a wealthy man had buried his treasures at Hoxne in the fifth century, the family of King Edmund buried the crown for safe keeping after the Danes beheaded their monarch in the ninth century. The Wuffings had a port on the Orwell at Ipswich importing continental goods and royal centres throughout the region, including Blythburgh and Exning. This new unity defied incursions by Mercians, Danes and the kings of Wessex, to outlast the end of independent kingship. Even in the late tenth century East Anglia was referred to as the "kingdom" of the earl Athelstan "half king". It was probably King Canute (Cnut of Denmark) who finally destroyed that power in the 1020s by dividing North Folk from South Folk along the arbitrary line of the Waveney and creating the separate Liberty of St Edmund, which later became the county of West Suffolk.[45]

We might wonder whether some aspects of Romano-British life survived

45 Lucy Marten, personal comment.

in East Anglia. Did Christianity continue among the local people without official recognition by the rulers and independently of the authority of the pope in Rome? Gildas complained that the British rulers of western Britain in his time failed to convert the leaders of the Anglo-Saxons in the east of the country. It was conversion of the rulers and imposition of central Roman authority and practice that St Augustine's mission brought to Britain in 597.

For Bede, writing his *Ecclesiastical History* in the eighth century, the authority of the Pope in Rome was central to his thinking, but at the end of the sixth century that authority was less secure, and one aim of the mission to Britain was to strengthen papal control. No emperor could claim to control an East Anglian kingdom from Rome, but the Pope in Rome could seek authority over its religion. Talking about the Irish church, Richard Fletcher points out that in sixth and seventh-century Europe there were many churches, not One Church but a many-mansioned Christendom.[46] He rejects the idea of a Celtic Church as the Irish churchmen professed their Roman allegiances, even though there were divergent practices.

The mission of Augustine set about ending such divergences in England, but this does not mean there was not a Christian Church in eastern England that remained loyal to what it saw as the ancient tradition of true Christianity. It might be significant that some churches dedicated to St Botolph can be linked to important areas of Roman activity, which might have retained a religious tradition. Botolph was famous in the seventh century for the high standards of his monastic community of Icanhoe, almost certainly at Iken on the River Alde. Surely this was the "hoe" (hill) of British Iceni whom Botolph expelled as "wailing demons". The church of St Botolph at Burgh by Grundisburgh stands in the substantial British enclosure occupied throughout the Roman period. The lost church of St Botolph at Thurleston outside Ipswich was close to the great villa complex at Castle Hill, Whitton, and Botolph's valley at Botesdale rises up to the pottery works of Wattisfield.

Many of our medieval churches incorporate reused Roman material. For example Bob Carr reports that when an area of external rendering fell off a wall at Wissington church near Nayland Roman tiles were revealed in a wall that is genuine Norman work, although much of the church was "improved" in 1853. The tiles in the internal arcades at Polstead church may be Roman, although there have been some later alterations or repairs, and some think they are all early medieval.

However, it is the outside walls of the chancel at Polstead that demand our close attention. The tile patterns in the exterior on all three sides of the chancel are unlike any standard Anglo-Saxon design. They suggest these walls are part of a Roman structure that has survived almost intact and simply been remodelled. I cannot claim to be sure and would like more evidence. Nonetheless, having suggested the unthinkable I would propose thinking on similar lines about the exterior of the massive tower of Great Tey church with its brick arches and about the chapel of St Peter's-on-the-Wall at Bradwell, which appears to be on the site of the gate to the Saxon Shore fort.

It seems strange to think of Bishop Cedd, whose men are unlikely to have been great stonemasons, knocking down a Roman building at Bradwell in order to build something remarkably similar. The remains of the brick arches at the east end can only be projected to form a double arch, not a triple one, making them amazingly unsuitable for the east end of a church,

46 Fletcher, R., *The Conversion of Europe*, HarperCollins, 1997, p.92.

assuming they would need a column in front of the apse and altar. It seems more like a conversion of a Roman gatehouse with a double carriageway. Perhaps some Roman buildings do survive, even if much altered.

When King Raedwald of East Anglia accepted conversion early in the seventh century without abandoning his traditional gods, did he already have a significant number of Christian Britons among his subjects? If so, this might have been an incentive to add the Christian god to the pantheon in his temple at Rendlesham. Even if Bede saw this as reversion to paganism, we might interpret it as the cautious introduction of another strand to royal worship. If there were British Christians in East Anglia in significant numbers before the time of Raedwald they have not left much sign of their presence. In western Britain we are able to see Christian burials because they are marked by inscribed stones, while our region made minimal use of inscriptions on stone even in the Roman period. In fact during the fourth century when Britain was part of a Christian empire the only clearly Christian cemeteries we have located are at Icklingham and Colchester, so given an accepted decline in population we should not be too surprised at the lack of evidence. Perhaps our strongest clue is the survival on the Norfolk coast of the place name Eccles, surely derived directly from the Greek for a Christian community.

If he was indeed buried in the great ship under mound one at Sutton Hoo, the pair of spoons with Greek inscriptions found in that great ship must

The north side of the chancel of Polstead church, with remains of tile arcading that looks like part of a surviving Roman building. The arcading is visible on the outside of all three walls of the chancel.

—————oOo—————

The Final Journey

Raedwald was dead. They dressed him as he would have chosen, in the fighting array of a Roman emperor. The gold and garnets glinted in the sunlight. They carried him to his ship. The mast had been removed to make way for a great open wooden chamber lined with bright fabrics. His standard flew at the stern. Solemn attendants carried down his weapons, and his cooking pots, even the great cauldron chain, so many valuable possessions. Silver dishes sparkled as a bard played a final requiem before placing the instrument near the king's hand. Edwin of Northumbria himself laid the great sceptre and the silver christening spoons in place. The line of his subjects, Angles and Britons, worshippers of Woden and of Christ, eased slowly along the quayside looking into the chamber. At last the ship was ready for its last voyage to the burial ground. After it was buried among the graves of his ancestors, the standard would be seen flying from the largest of all the mounds.

—————oOo—————

emphasise his Christian aspect. One of the spoons clearly carries the original name of Paul alongside a cross, while the other has been altered to read Saul in a different Greek script. Apparently two spoons were taken from a standard set inscribed with the names of leading disciples. The one bearing Paul's name was kept in its original form but the other was changed to read Saul. Presumably they marked the conversion of Raedwald as being as sudden and significant as the conversion on the road to Damascus of the anti-Christian Saul to become the Christian leader St Paul.

Whoever did this was certainly conversant with the Greek alphabet as used in the Christian Church, and we should not forget that Greek was the language of Christianity. The Bromeswell bucket, which presumably came from a grave in the "secondary" cemetery at Sutton Hoo, has a Greek inscription. The British craftsman who produced the square enamel escutcheons on the great hanging bowl was presumably working in a Christian tradition that was already established before the Kentish mission and might have continued unbroken from the late fourth century. This style of coloured glass enamel applied to bronze was an established tradition in Iron Age Britain long before the Roman conquest. Tom Plunkett points out that they show a large red cross against a white background represented by the oval shapes, and he has no doubt they are Christian.[47]

Presumably there was a Christian presence among the local population, even if they failed to convert their rulers until the mission from Rome influenced their contemporaries in Kent. Much else in the burial suggests Raedwald saw himself in the direct line of Roman imperial power as seen in the descent of the Wuffing family tree from Cassar ("Caesar") after Woden ("God"). Such a succession was familiar in Roman thinking, where it strengthened a new emperor's position if he could claim to be the adopted son of his predecessor, even if there was no blood relationship, and all but the very worst emperors were said to become gods on their death. Every Roman emperor claimed descent in this way from the deified Caesar, so the Wuffings saw themselves as continuing that tradition. The attitude continued into the later Middle Ages as the fifteenth-century "Roll Chronicle" documents the descent of Henry VI from Adam and Eve by way of Julius Caesar.[48]

Martin Henig singles out the sceptre as a link with the Romano-British past.[49] Sceptres were widely used in the Roman world and its naturalistic stag is in the Roman style. At the same time, being a large sharpening stone, it might also represent the king's power over metal, recalling Wayland the Smith. Many see the ornate shoulder clasps as derived from the finest type of Roman parade armour, being used to fasten the type of leather cuirass we saw on the Barking Nero. While the helmet shows clear links with Scandinavian traditions, the decoration with fighting figures, on horseback and on foot, can also be compared with that on the Roman cavalry helmet from Ribchester.[50]

Rather different but closer to home there is the gilded Worthing helmet from the River Wensum now in Norwich Castle Museum. The Romans clearly had their share of elaborate helmets. Raedwald was the mentor of Edwin of Northumbria and Bede tells us how he set out to be a ruler in the Roman tradition, including his use of a standard that was based on a Roman imperial prototype. Edwin probably had a major role in the funeral of Raedwald and might have influenced its classical aspects.

When we look at the wealth interred with an Anglo-Saxon ruler at Sutton Hoo we might recall the evidence of personal wealth in the hands of an East Anglian individual who buried his reserve wealth at Hoxne some time after the end of Roman administration. We could look back further to the Bartlow Hills, the Rougham tumuli or the elaborate burial chamber of the Iron Age ruler beneath the Lexden tumulus. Powerful men did accumulate great wealth in this region. Authoritarian rule from Rome had come and gone, but in East Anglia the new rulers buried objects as valuable and beautiful as the gold torcs of their Iron Age predecessors.

Edwin had been an exile at Raedwald's court and was befriended there by Paulinus, one of Augustine's team. Edwin as king of Northumbria became a Christian and welcomed Paulinus as his bishop. After Raedwald's death about 625 his son and successor Eorpwald adopted Christianity, but it was left

47 Plunkett, S.J., *Suffolk in Anglo-Saxon Times*, Tempus, 2005, p. 89.
48 Society of Antiquaries of London manuscript, MS 501.
49 Henig, M., *The Art of Roman Britain*, London, 1995, p.174.
50 British Museum PEE 1814. 7-5.1.

The design and const
above is Celtic. The p
for religious use. The
cross in the enamelle
used for Christian rit

Left: *This silver dish*
Mediterranean as it
underside of the dish

large hanging bowl from the Sutton Hoo ship seen
bowl is uncertain, but it might have held holy water
underside of the hanging bowl, above left, shows a
strengthening the possibility that it might have been
Trustees of the British Museum

on Hoo ship had been imported from the eastern
ntrol stamp of Anastasius, which can be seen on the
below. Both © Trustees of the British Museum

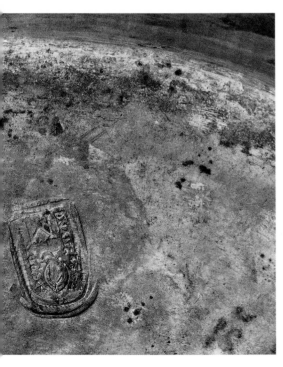

The silver spoons from the Sutton Hoo ship, showing
the names SAUL and PAUL in Greek letters.
© Trustees of the British Museum

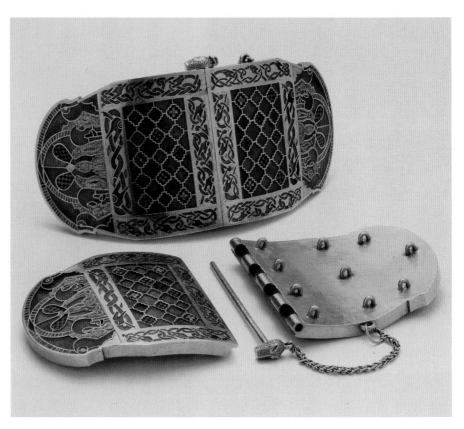

to Sigeberht as king of the East Angles some five years later to introduce a bishop to East Anglia.

Felix came from Burgundy by way of Canterbury to be installed at Dommoc, almost certainly Felixstowe, or rather the Roman fort of Walton Castle.[51] Presumably the Roman connection was seen as providing a proper setting for the Christian Bishop of the East Angles, while the Deben gave him direct access to the royal residence at Rendlesham. If the naming of Walton does imply a surviving British community, they received in Felix a bishop who had learned his religion in Burgundy from the Irish monk Columbanus, so stood in the British as much as the Roman tradition. The early holdings of the Priory of St Felix at Walton as listed in the inspection and confirmation of the charters of the priory by Edward III[52] include "the land late of Columbanus the priest". This suggests that at some much earlier date, perhaps before the Vikings destroyed Dommoc, a priest serving there took his religious name from the patron of his founding bishop. Was "Dommoc" derived from the Latin Dominus, meaning "lord" in the religious sense of "Our Lord", so being "Our Lord's House"? This seems to be the origin of Irish place-names derived from "Domnach" for "church".

Sigeberht also installed an Irish monk, Fursa, at a place Bede called Cnobheresburg, probably the Roman fort at Burgh Castle, although a good case has been made for the ditched enclosure at Burgh by Grundisburgh[53] which would make it part of the group of significant places in south-east Suffolk. If so, the East Angles saw their Christian leaders based in forts with British and Irish connections. Felix brought teachers to Dommoc from Kent, probably from Paulinus who was by then Bishop of Rochester, a town of Roman origin whose cathedral priory of St Andrew retained in Norman times

51 S E Rigold "The Supposed See of Dunwich", *Journal of the British Archaeological Association* vol.24 (1961), p.5, and "Further Evidence about the Site of Dommoc", *Journal of the British Archaeological Association* vol. 37 (1974), p.97.
52 Calendar of Patent Rolls 13 Edward III, 2,11.
53 Tom Williamson, *Sutton Hoo and its Landscape*, Windgather 2008, p.19.

Left: *One pair of the magnificent shoulder clasps from the Sutton Hoo ship, showing the elaborate decoration in gold, blue glass enamel and garnets. The underside shows how it was attached to a breast plate, probably of leather.* © Trustees of the British Museum

Right: *The interlocking wild boars on the shoulder clasp provide an example of the high-quality workman-ship found in the regalia that might have been worn by King Raedwald.* © Trustees of the British Museum

its links with Walton,[54] and with Alnesbourne[55] and its church of St Felix, Hallowtree, up the Orwell. Perhaps the conversion was stronger because the Roman tradition of Christianity survived among conquered British communities.

In a valley behind Combretovium, within the modern parish of Coddenham and beside the original direct road up the valley as shown on eighteenth-century maps by Pennington and Johnson,[56] somebody in Early Saxon times built a large hall and employed a goldsmith. On the summit of the hill opposite, within Shrubland Park, people were buried at that time, one woman in an elaborate bed. Her valuables included a gold pendant enclosing a coin of the Frankish king Dagoberht (629-639), and a silver coin of about AD700 was dropped in the grave. On the slopes below at least seven early gold shillings, "thrymsas", have been recovered with a metal detector, although even single finds of these high-value coins are uncommon. Can these signs of wealth indicate continuity of activity here from late Roman Combretovium to its early Saxon successor?

Without more evidence we cannot say for sure, but it looks more likely than not that there and at Ipswich there was not the dramatic break with the past that was once assumed. Excavations in London near St Martin-in-the-Fields in 2005/7 suggest a similar transitional scenario on the edge of Roman Londinium, with a burial made in a Roman stone coffin some time between AD390 and 430. A kiln for roof tiles was working between AD400 and 450. By AD650 a man's grave contained a glass palm cup, a silver finger ring and a hanging bowl with hazelnuts in it. That does still leave a two-hundred-year gap in the evidence to be explained, unless it is filled by new discoveries!

54 Fairclough, J and Plunkett, S.J., "Drawings of Walton Castle ..." PSIAH vol.39 (2000), p.450
55 *Domesday Book, Suffolk* ed. Rumble 1986 at 8.13
56 SROI: HD1467/1 to 3.

A decorated Byzantine bucket with a Greek inscription was ploughed up in Bromeswell parish in the 1980s. It presumably came from a grave in the "secondary" cemetery at Sutton Hoo, which was revealed during construction of the National Trust Visitor Centre. The decoration shows warriors fighting lions, and the Greek inscription can be read as "Lord Count, use this in good health for many happy years". Probably made at Antioch in the sixth century, it is another example of the Mediterranean links at Sutton Hoo. See Mango, M.M. et al. "A sixth century Mediterranean bucket from Bromeswell parish Suffolk," Antiquity 63 (1989), pp. 295-311.
© Suffolk County Council Archaeological Service

In East Anglia we can only assume that agricultural productivity and seaborne trade prospered throughout, dependent on the labour of local families who knew the potential of their land and braved the perils of the sea. If only we could recognise their descendants among the householders of Domesday Book, the census returns of the nineteenth century and our own electoral rolls, we might find true continuity.

One clue might be found in the large numbers of freemen recorded in Suffolk in the Domesday Book. This is very different from the typical structure of the midland counties, where a high proportion of the population were villeins subject to their manorial lords. Nobody has explained this feature of society, which must have originated long before 1066. Could it be that it was inherited from the Iceni and their associates in East Anglia? We have seen that before, and throughout, the Roman period East Anglians dared to be different. Their organisation of the landscape in the Middle Ages was also notably different from the highly regulated three-field system of the Midlands.[57] Much of the land was divided into individual enclosed fields, and we have already seen that some of them might have been created, or at least their general pattern had been established, even before the Roman roads were built. Perhaps some of the enclosed fields and the irregular open fields, which were the most common alternative in our region, had been laid out by British farmers long before the Roman conquest and were maintained by their descendants.

It seems that changes in these patterns might have been less frequent than continuity of use. There was no reason to alter ways of farming that suited the nature of East Anglian soil and climate just because new landlords came along. We are left to wonder how many of the subjects of King Raedwald were descended from families that had served Queen Boudica and prospered or suffered under Roman rule in between.

57 Bailey, M., *Medieval Suffolk*, Boydell, 2007, p.102.

Appendix

Some Roman roads in detail

1. Cambridge to Haverhill

The road from Cambridge to Haverhill past Wandlebury (Margary 34a) has been variously called Via Devana, Wool Street, or Worsted Street, but none of these are Roman names. It can be seen as part of a long-distance link between Colchester and Chester via Cambridge, Godmanchester and Leicester. It could also provide a link to the north-east, avoiding the Wash, via Longthorpe near Peterborough and/or Water Newton (*Durobrivae*). From Cambridge to Godmanchester, near Huntingdon, it is largely followed by the main road that is now part of the A14, the main route from East Anglia to the west and to the north. Margary traces the route from the Roman town of Cambridge in the Castle area via Bridge Street, St Andrew's Street and Regent Street.[1] This line continues as Hills Road which is a very direct line.

Margary records a road through Perse School fields about 100 yards west of Hills Road, with layers of chalk and gravelly earth 12-15ft. wide, which sounds narrower than the surviving main route and might be a second parallel road at this point rather than the main road. Hills Road near Addenbrookes Hospital might preserve evidence of a wide raised agger: house drives drop abruptly on the north and there is a slight drop on the south towards the hospital. Here the road changes direction sharply to leave the river valley and climbs as Worts Causeway (improved by William Worts in the eighteenth century – was this still the main road when he funded it?). As it rises there are good long-distance views over Cambridge. As the modern road curves to tackle the summit of a hill the Roman route appears marked by a hedgerow which could be the north side of the road, the carriageway here being destroyed by landscaping of the golf course. From that point the Roman road is well preserved, running on a single alignment as a green lane, with the agger generally about 33ft. to 36ft. wide and 1ft. to 2ft. high. Dewhurst observed the cutting of a gas main trench for ten miles in 1959 and recorded that only the first four and a half miles from here were really solidly constructed.[2] After this the road was less substantial. The agger was entirely of chalk dug locally, but further on some parts had a gravel surface 2½in. thick. I noted some years ago parallel lines in fields at some distance on either side just before the Wandlebury track from the Wandlebury hillfort enters, which might mark the ditches defining the road zone.

The stretch from Wandlebury to beyond Worsted Lodge is remarkably well preserved. At Worsted Lodge it crosses one line of the Icknield Way, now the A11, which appears to have been Romanised. Dewhurst noted that the road was laid at a lower level here to match the level of the Icknield Way. In a cross section near here the road was 42ft. between the ditches. He suggests the chalk dug from the ditches was rammed down to form the agger, here 3ft. 2in. above the topsoil. The agger was laid directly on the topsoil, then a layer of gravel was laid on top, brought possibly from a gravel pit a quarter of a mile to the north-east. When the A11 was widened in 1991 a section revealed that Worsted Street west of the Icknield Way was 11.5m wide with flanking ditches 2.5m wide and 1m deep. The agger was at least 1m high in three layers: thick turf laid over the ground surface, covered by rammed chalk dug from the side ditches and topped by at least 30cm of clean imported gravel. Some distance beyond Worsted Lodge one stretch on high ground appears possibly converted into a dyke with a high bank reducing the carriageway. Perhaps this was a post-Roman dyke across the general line of Icknield Way as it entered East Anglia.

1 Margary, I., *Roman Roads in Britain*, ed. 3, London, 1973, p.210.
2 Dewhurst, P.D., Proceedings of the Cambridge Antiquarian Society, vol. 56/57 (1963/4), p.42.

At this point on the Roman road from Cambridge to Haverhill, behind Wandlebury, only half the width of the agger is clear where it is still in use as a track. The other half has been covered by the undergrowth that grows quickly if unchecked.

According to Dewhurst the modern track is running in the north-east ditch of the Roman road at this point. Half a mile beyond Worsted Lodge he noted a layer of coal between the chalk base and the gravel topping of the agger. The green way continues towards Haverhill. Until the road crossing on the edge of Horseheath the road is well preserved, although the later part appears damaged by the gas pipeline as well as use by 4x4 vehicles. Alison Taylor in *Archaeology of South East Cambridgeshire* notes evidence of a Roman settlement beside the road as it approaches Horseheath. Excavation in the 1920s found substantial buildings, pottery, glass, tile, metal, and coins (second-fourth century). As the parish north of the road is West Wickham, the use of the Wickham name suggests the Horseheath site was probably a Roman market town. Also note Shudy Camps on the other side of Horseheath suggests this was a "campus" site. Bartlow Hills Roman barrow burials are not far away. Dewhurst noted that the road was not so heavily engineered east of Worsted Lodge and Brian Charge[3] therefore rejected the stretch from Worsted Lodge to Wixoe, declaring it more likely medieval or perhaps prehistoric. However I find the line convincing and suggest that this section is not so substantial because it runs on higher dry ground where there was no need for a solid agger with deep side ditches. It seems likely to have gone out of public use through Horseheath Park, so was probably less well maintained. The stretch from Cambridge to Worsted Lodge has survived in particularly good condition, so I accept that the contrast is marked and the section from Worsted Lodge to Wixoe must remain unproven even if very likely to have been the Roman route.

After crossing the Horseheath road the route is used by a farm access road of modern construction but apparently on the correct line, then becomes a footpath. The Roman road appears to have been cut by Horseheath Park and it is possible it remained in use through the medieval park, but was closed by eighteenth-century owners to create their private park, thus diverting the entire road route between Cambridge and Haverhill. It is lost beyond Horseheath Park, at the crossing of the road to Withersfield, but a corridor of overgrown ground appears to mark the route into Haverhill. Margary suggests it joins the main road about one mile west of Haverhill and continues through the town as the High Street. It goes on to Sturmer and the possible Roman town at Wixoe. Margary suggests it continued past Ridgewell via Great Yeldham and Sible Hedingham to Colchester. G E Fox, *Archaeological Journal* 1900, p.146, reports that a large cemetery, apparently with Roman pottery and glass, was found in 1759 beside this road between Withersfield and Haverhill "in a disused lane...near a rivulet under the wood by Haverhill Castle" (he quotes Coles MS BM MSS V 31, f92, 93). Walford, writing in *Archaeologia* in 1803, was confident

3 Charge, B. B., Journal of the Haverhill and District Archaeological Group IV.2 (1986).

that the road reached Haverhill through Ridgewell and Baythorne End and "thence by a broad and direct way crossing the road from Newmarket to Bourn-bridge goes up the hill towards Gogmagog".[4]

2. Peddars Way – Stanton Chare to Holme-next-the-Sea

North of Stanton Chare at Barningham Park the alignment of Peddars Way is marked by a hedgerow east of the farm with traces of the agger on the parish boundary. It crosses the Coney Weston to Thetford road east of Heath Farm and Margary traced it across arable with "clear belt of gravel and indications of a filled-in ditch". Is Chalk Pit Plantation near the line significant of a Roman pit dug for road material, as similar features are noted further up the road? Further north it is lost for a short distance but can be found in woodland before being marked by the edge of Knettishall Heath Country Park, where it is part of the "Icknield Way Path". Beyond this it is followed by the "Peddars Way national trail". The first section of the actual trail shows signs of the agger. The precise crossing of the River Little Ouse at Blackwater Ford is uncertain, although there are signs that the river is eroding gravel from the bank, which might be significant. Beyond here the trail makes a dogleg among ancient trees, including one very old large pollarded oak which might be a boundary marker at the corner of woodland and park. The path beyond appears to be east of the agger, which might be overgrown with shrubs and trees. Near the A1066 a deep pit beside the agger might have been dug to obtain material for the Roman road. Beyond the A1066 the road has been used as a tarmac short cut, now closed to traffic. The path appears to continue on the agger, but may diverge slightly east on the boardwalk in a wet area approaching the crossing of the River Thet, which is larger than the Little Ouse here, as there appears to be drier ground on the west. There is a significant divergence to reach the footbridge and a gradual return on the further slope to pick up the agger which is solid here. Margary records a section cut near the south bank of the Thet as a causeway 16ft. wide of rammed flint with gravel coating 2ft. 6in. thick at centre with an extension 4ft. wide on the east side. An area on the north side of the Thet crossing has produced sufficient Roman material to suggest the site of a small settlement or market town in Brettenham parish.[5] Further north across Bridgham Heath the agger is described by Margary as 36ft. wide and 1ft. high. In woodland on the western edge of the agger are two deep pits that look like Roman pits for roadmaking material. One revealed a fragment of early Roman pottery inside the top edge of the pit. The solid agger, which Margary records as 30ft. wide and 1ft. to 2ft. high, continues beyond the A11 and into the village of East Wretham/ Stonebridge.

After Stonebridge, beyond the houses on the right is a pit that might be a quarry pit for road material. A possible further "double" pit for material was noted on the right further up the Way near a crossing road, and large oak trees are conspicuous along the Way. The Peddars Way changes alignment slightly to the north-west at Galley Hill, where it crosses the road into the military range from Hockham. The path follows the apparent direct line of Peddars Way for a long stretch to just beyond the 97 grid line. At that point deep pits on either side of the Way look artificial. They make the space for the Way very narrow here. They could be very large quarry pits or an attempt at some date (possibly post-Roman) to control and restrict access along the Way.

North of this point the Way soon enters good arable farming land. Beyond the 97 grid line the path diverges from the Way, which appears to continue straight in woodland parallel to the path but on its right. The path then crosses the Way line, at which point there is no trace of the Way, but it could be picked up as a hedgerow with oak trees slightly left of the line marked on the OS map. The path follows a route that might be a branch road from the Way as it runs straight through Home Farm and onward. The path leaves this route to pick up a straight track which might be the Way itself as it continues the line of the hedgerow noted above. The path takes this line,

4 *Archaeologia* 14 (1803), p.61-74.
5 Brown, A.E. ed., *Roman Small Towns in Eastern England and Beyond*, map p.54.

which is probably the Way as far as the B1108, beyond which no trace is visible
where the line would run across fields between Threxton Church and Saham
Toney/Watton. Here it must cross the line of the Roman road from Caistor to Denver
via Ketteringham, Crownthorpe/Wicklewood and Watton High Street. The roads
cross in the area of the Roman market town at Threxton/Saham Toney/Woodcock
Hall, on which see the paper by David Gurney in *Roman Small Towns in Eastern
England and Beyond*, ed A.E. Brown, p.55. It lies in the valley of the river, which is a
tributary of the River Wissey. This is also the site of a Roman fort overlooking the
valley. This river valley appears as a rich farming area – arable fields above the water
meadows – as opposed to the heath-type land through which the Way passed to the
south.

North of Threxton the Way is inaccessible for some distance but is marked on the
map by several hedges on the correct alignment. The path follows a modern road
north from Little Cressingham and the line of the Way seems to be visible to the east
for several stretches as a hedgerow on the skyline. The path seems to cross the River
Wissey at much the same point as the line of the Way, but nothing appears visible on
the ground at this point.

Past North Pickenham, just beyond the disused railway bridge, a pit looks like
another possible source of Roman roadmaking material. Continuing north along
Procession Lane the agger seems to vary between 36ft. and 30ft. wide. In places deep
vehicle ruts cut through several inches of soil, which is probably the result of years of
decaying tree leaves, grass, etc., but there is solid metalling in the bottom of the ruts.
The course is lost beyond the deserted medieval village at Great Palgrave, so it is not
clear whether it took a straight line across Hungry Hill to Castle Acre or deviated
down the slope to a suitable crossing of the River Nar.

North of Castle Acre the line is remarkably straight and solid, with signs of a wide
agger in excess of 30ft. On Harpley Common it passes a number of mounds on high
ground which appear to be Bronze Age barrows. At one point (737334) it makes a
slight deviation to the east, going round a large pit which looks similar to some we
have seen as possible Roman pits for road material. This pit would be immediately
beside the straight line of the road, and there is no indication why the road makes this
one minor but notable deviation in a very straight stretch (is it a post-Roman
change?). The wide agger continues until it crosses the minor road from Fring to
Sedgeford. For the next section up a steep hill to Dovehill Wood and beyond to
Littleport the modern path is on the correct alignment, marked by field boundaries,
but the agger is not clearly defined. The road past the remarkable seventeenth-century
Magazine Cottage is convincing and on the correct alignment, but beyond the disused
railway crossing the precise line is lost for the first time since Castle Acre. After a
brief diversion the footpath reverts to the correct alignment on a field boundary until
it becomes a good stretch of agger apparently 45ft. wide (Margary places this wide
stretch near Fring but the conspicuous piece is just south of Ringstead).

The direct line continues in Ringstead as Foundry Lane. The line is then lost
across a large field, and the line from here to the sea is uncertain. Margary suggests a
field boundary past the old windmill and then a lane which is the parish boundary.
This lane is not straight, is restricted by ditches to about 15ft. wide, and varies
between sunken way and raised agger. It is conspicuously different from the
preceding stretch of Peddars Way, and I suggest it is almost certainly the Romanised
northern end of the Icknield Way, which otherwise seems to be lost at Ringstead. In
fact this line looks better as continuing the suggested line of Icknield Way from
Flitcham via Shernbourne and Sedgeford to Ringstead (Margary 333). Its behaviour
suits the idea of a Romanised prehistoric trackway, and this would be an equally good
explanation of the coincidence with the parish boundary. The more convincing line
for Peddars Way north of Ringstead seems to be that signposted by the highway
authority as "Peddars Way" but rejected by Margary and the modern long-distance
footpath. This is an open road to Holme-next-the-Sea on straight alignments with
slight changes on high ground. One happens where it crosses Green Bank, which has

been claimed as marking an Iron Age track running east-west.[6] The property boundaries on some stretches leave room for a wide agger, while the narrowings look like modern encroachments on a wide carriageway. The line continues as a trackway to the limit of the drained marshlands behind the coast.

If this interpretation is correct Peddars Way and Icknield Way terminate on the coast about a quarter of a mile apart and close to the Bronze Age feature known as "Seahenge".[7] Coastal erosion has removed all evidence of any possible harbour or other terminal feature, but the coast of Lincolnshire is clearly visible across the mouth of the Wash and any vessels entering or leaving that haven would have been clearly visible from here. There are reports of quantities of Roman material being found "a considerable distance" out to sea, and David Gurney estimates the Roman coastline was probably about two kilometres further north.

3. Colchester to Pakenham/Ixworth and Stanton Chare

It is most likely that this route out of Colchester was Margary 3c as far as the river crossing at Stratford St Mary. The direct alignment seems to be followed by the old A12 from Colchester to the top of Gun Hill at Langham. Here the direct line is cut by a steep drop that looks like the result of a landslip, and the modern road follows the eastern edge of this down to the bridge across the River Stour into the modern village of Stratford St Mary. The presumed Roman alignment beyond the landslip would cross open ground with very poor grass, of which the western fence might be the road line, but it then disappears in the private woodland of Langham Hall down the hill. The line reappears as a track on lower ground heading between a small stream

6 Robinson, B. & Rose E.J., *Norfolk Origins 2: Roads and Tracks*, Poppyland, 1983, p.10.
7 dated c. 2050 BC, *Current Archaeology,* 167 and 174.

This track within Knettishall Heath Country Park is probably based on part of the Roman agger of Peddars Way.

8 *Journal of Roman Studies* vol. 17 (1927), p.203.

and a hedge direct towards the River Stour, but is lost in new woodland short of the river, although its line places the river crossing just inside Stratford but close to Higham.

This is probably, but not certainly, the point described in 1927 as "at Stratford St Mary, where traces of the road that ran northwards from Colchester seemed to end, piles of an early bridge which crossed the Stour have been found and also a coin of Pius".[8] At the relevant point on the north (Suffolk) bank of the River Stour there appears to be a low causeway which becomes a track on the correct line, but this seems to be lost as soon as it leaves the low-lying land.

North of the river there is no sign of any road alignment towards Combretovium, but another alignment is apparent. This was first noted by Robert Malster and myself using a CD showing an aerial view of the whole county. Projecting the line of the causeway beyond the crossing leads north along Green Lane, which marks the parish boundary between Stratford and Higham (grid ref 043353). A possible short section of the agger is visible on the ground at a junction of trackways (about 041349) on the footpath from opposite Brook Farm to Higham Hall. This is on the edge of the terrace above the wide valley where the course of the Stour in Roman times might have been north of the present channel.

There is no trace in the fields either side of the modern road from Stratford to Higham, but two straight stretches of Green Lane apparently preserve an agger about 15ft. wide. The curving section that links the two stretches might, as elsewhere, be a Roman diversion to avoid a prehistoric burial mound, but there is no visible evidence

This part of Valley Farm's hard standing is probably based on the agger of the Roman road from Colchester to Pakenham and Stanton Chare, which is visible through the gate beyond, as can be seen in the photograph on the next page.

of this. Beyond a T-junction with the B1068 the line is continued by a straight field boundary, on or close to the parish boundary just east of Dewlands Farm. Evidence is lacking across the valley here (not helped by the presence of a golf course over part of the line) but the alignment would take us close to Barrow Hill (042387 – is there a barrow?). Disused pits close to the line south-east of Timber Hill Wood (042371) and just north of Barrow Hill could have been sources of road material. A new alignment from the high point of Barrow Hill is marked by a crop mark and then a track to the west of New Barn Farm leading north-by-east to two fields below the railway line.

The line is picked up some distance north of the railway line at about 045414 as a straight ditch on a field boundary which becomes a track along the western edge of an industrial area. North of the modern road the industrial works seem to be across the line, which is then followed by the lane to Valley Farm, but south of the farm it changes alignment slightly. The agger might survive beneath a hard standing in front of agricultural buildings, just north of which the agger about 12ft. wide with ditches on either side is visible in the grass of a small paddock. The line continues north as a bridleway touching the western edge of Beestons coach depot on the main A1071 from Ipswich to Hadleigh. There is no trace in the field north of the road, but the line would enter the edge of Wolves Wood. There is no certain trace in the wood but a ditch visible at the northern edge of the wood might mark the line.

North of the wood the house called Shooting Box (053444) stands on the agger, which is visible for a short distance south of the house as a narrow corridor used for

The stretch of Roman road heading towards Wolves Wood at Hadleigh is defined by the two dark lines in the field beyond the gate, resulting from differential growth over the hidden ditches on either side of the road.

Rattlesden church stands in the angle between two diverging Roman roads. That to the east (right) of the church takes a direct line to Woolpit and on to join Peddars Way. The one to the west (left) of the church heads directly towards the fort at Pakenham.

garden refuse and then overgrown before the line is lost across an arable field. North of Shooting Box the agger is marked by the modern drive past Frog Hall Farm, with one slight realignment to north-west. At the road called Aldham Street the modern lane to Elmsett is east of a group of houses that appear to be on the line of the road, which might be picked up by the lane or marked by an apparent strip of rough ground in the field beside the lane to Eleys Corner (050459). The general alignment continues on Corn Hatches Lane, although it makes an unexplained deviation to the east north of Corn Hatches house, perhaps to avoid a barrow or other existing feature, before returning to the line and running across the end of the airstrip of Elmsett Airfield near Poplar Farm. From here the lane wanders left as a minor road at 040468, while the line continues directly as a crop mark across an irregularly shaped field which lines up with the boundary of the next field going north.

It then picks up the modern road to Naughton running north-north-west to Naughton Church. Beyond the church it might be marked by a field boundary on the same alignment taking it through Nedging Tye, then by a field boundary west of Bush Farm before crossing the known Roman road from Bildeston to Barking (Long Melford to Combretovium) which survives here as a solid track about 15ft. wide. It is marked by a track on the field boundary north of the crossing but is then lost towards Wattisham Stone and past Hitcham, where it should join the known Roman road north to Poy Street and Rattlesden and on to Pakenham. It could do this by maintaining its alignment to a point on that road just north of Dale Farm, Hitcham, which is the southern end of the straight stretch of road.

Alternatively it could turn almost due west just before crossing the Hitcham to Cross Green road to reach a possible short stretch of agger surviving as an overgrown footpath with substantial ditches on a sharp bend of the road south of Dale House, Hitcham. Here it would meet a southward projection of the other road straight through Dale Farm and Dale House. Either route gives a good way across the high ground with minimum changes of gradient, but any evidence seems to be destroyed by the creation of prairie fields here. It might be worth checking the tithe maps as footpaths and field boundaries suggest traces of a rectilinear pattern that could be based on the road.

This would be a good route from Colchester to Peddars Way on the higher ground along the edge of the Brett Valley. It would be worth looking for any evidence of a Roman settlement or small market town in the Hitcham/Wattisham area as a predecessor of Hadleigh near this junction of Roman roads. One clue could be the name of Brettenham, which should be "settlement of the Britons", and Brettenham in

Norfolk is a Roman small town on Peddars Way. The Rev. Copinger Hill claimed that behind Hitcham White Horse at Brick House Farm there is a Roman road in a meadow at the foot of the hill.[9] Later he recorded much Roman material here associated with flint footings 2ft. thick just below the plough with one wall at least 52ft. long.[10] This and more recent finds suggest significant Roman activity associated with a substantial building here close to the southern end of the Roman road from Poy Street Green. Perhaps there was a settlement here related to the Roman road running south from Rattlesden, while the Roman crossroads might be causing some confusion as to the alignment of the roads at this point. It is possible that the road from Stratford was aligned just north of Hitcham to avoid wet ground and the steep valley there.

Continuing the route north at the crossroads on Cooks Green, near Pepper Tree Farm, Copinger Hill found a medieval reference to "Snayllishalestrete". The road is the hundred and parish boundary between Buxhall and Rattlesden north of Pye Hatch Wood. At one point he noted that in 1924 the steam plough was turning up great quantities of the road material at the headland, and further on a length had been robbed out in 1845 to make a new road parallel to the Roman one, leaving a hollow way. Both of these are familiar problems in tracing Roman roads throughout the region.

Before Louse Lane in a meadow he found the agger 15ft. wide, its camber of gravel over rammed stones rising to 18in. at the centre but tapering to 3in., with side ditches. The ford had setts. It continues as the road to Poy Street Green. At Poy Street Green Copinger Hill traced it "down Kempistone Hill into Rattlesden", where it crossed the Orwell stream.

In fact there seem to be two alignments out of Poy Street: one passes just east of Rattlesden Church, where local comment records a route straight up the hill towards Clopton Green Farm on the line of the straight road to Woolpit. A straight property boundary continues the line into Woolpit. This alignment appears to head directly for the southern end of Peddars Way at Stanton Chare.

Beyond Woolpit the route appears to be lost through Elmswell and Norton. The fact that the alignment survives immediately north of the parish boundary of Norton suggests the field pattern of Norton has been reorganised in a way that ignores the Roman alignment. Entering Stowlangtoft parish it is marked by the straight eastern boundary of Nine Acre Wood and the western boundary of The Spong wood – not the track through The Spong, which appears to be a more recent creation east of the apparent position of the Roman road. North of The Spong, at the crest of a valley, it makes a slight change of alignment to become the very straight track, about 25ft. wide with solid base, down to the road beside Street Farm. The alignment continues beyond the road as a solid access across a ditch into the park of Stowlangtoft Hall.

As it immediately disappears it was presumably destroyed by the landscaping of Stowlangtoft Park. Stowlangtoft Hall stands on or immediately beside the alignment, so the original Hall was probably built beside the road which was later closed to create the Park. North of the Park it is possible that the line is marked by a short north–south stretch of parish boundary (?Stowlangtoft/Langham) parallel to Kiln Lane, and the general line might survive as the lane past Wyken Vineyard and Wyken Wood. If so, a change of alignment here on high ground could provide a link to the projected line of Peddars Way beside Stanton Chare villa. A pit beside the track on the crest of the slope above Street Farm might have originated as a source of roadbuilding material for the Roman road.

The other route runs west of Rattlesden Church heading for the fort at Pakenham, although there is no trace on the ground between Poy Street and Mill Hill. It is defined from Mill Hill (a cottage now called Peddars Way!) as a straight track through Hill Farm, Drinkstone, to an apparent agger on Deadman's Lane. The line would continue just east of Drinkstone windmills on a line that appears to be heading for Pakenham (Deadman's Lane visibly heads directly towards the water tower behind Ixworth). This very straight alignment is picked up by a short length of track on the western edge of Tostock churchyard. If projected south this runs through the park of Tostock

9 PSIAH vol.18 (1924), p.211.
10 PSIAH vol.19, p 93 and 230.

Place, where there is no obvious trace, but it could have been lost in landscaping as the modern parallel road west of Tostock Place suggests a diversion of the road away from the park.

North of the railway at Tostock the alignment is followed by a straight stretch of the minor road from Tostock to The Dog at Norton. Presumably this is where Copinger Hill said the old foundation of the road was seen on the Norton side of the railway arch on the road to Stowlangtoft. He described the Roman road from Rattlesden "on up the hill towards Sadlers Hole Drift, past the mill on west of Woolpit to cross the main Woolpit to Bury St Edmunds road at White Elm". He thought it then diverged to avoid wet ground or mere, so went down to a house called Fox and Geese, then by the present road under the railway arch to Stowlangtoft, but this is probably the modern diversion past Tostock Place. About half a mile from Ixworth it follows a grass lane, Davids Lane and Woolpit Lane. This would be the route to the fort and town at Pakenham which was bypassed by the direct line to Peddars Way. Perhaps it was part of this road that Hamlet Watling noted in 1878 as "At Stowlangtoft another [paved road] may be seen in the direction of the places I have already given [Elmswell, Norton, Hunston]".[11]

Another road out of Colchester is Margary 322, which is clearly marked from Colchester to Great Horkesley, where it probably followed the modern road line to cross the River Stour at Nayland. It is lost from there presumably through Assington, and Margary suggests it continued on a different alignment by a track and hedge at Newton Leys which leads into the road to Great Waldingfield. From here it could have continued through Acton to join the road from Long Melford to Coddenham at the western edge of the "slough" curve.

4. Colchester to Westerfield via Mistley and Ipswich

This road, one of three heading north-east from Colchester that diverged after leaving the East Gate and crossing the River Colne, headed towards the presumed port at Mistley and a possible crossing of the Stour near Wrabness. It survives as a straight stretch of Bromley Road from Crockleford Hill TM033262. Its continuation is recorded as a crop mark over three miles, the existence of the road being confirmed by excavation at TM054275 as two adjacent roads of gravel set in clay.[12] One was 4.3m wide between ditches only 30-40cm deep; the southerly one was 2.3m wide between ditches 50cm deep and 1m wide. It was recorded near Lawford "20 paces wide" cutting through a ring ditch at TM09073000.[13] Air photographs show crop marks of parallel ditches for the road on this line up to Dairy Wood at TM112313 but not beyond.[14] Continuing this single alignment would bring it to the River Stour at Mistley Quay, which was probably a major Roman port with a deepwater anchorage.

Despite the lack of positive evidence it is possible that a branch road ran eastward from Mistley parallel to the Stour on a terrace in the fields above the shore, where a break of slope was observed at TM142314. Perhaps this continued until it could turn directly north to pass through Ragmarsh Farm just behind Wrabness, with the house standing on the agger. Directly below Ragmarsh Farm at TM156315 a shingle hard is sharply defined as a strip about 27ft. wide heading directly towards Graham's Wharf in Stutton (I am grateful to David Cleveland for pointing out this feature). It is possible that in Roman times the hard was an agger on dry land leading to a ford passable at low tide, or even a bridge equivalent to the modern crossing at Cattawade. The present occupier of the farm reports that his grandfather created the hard by tipping gravel, but it remains possible that he was putting a new surface on the solid remains of a Roman road. The river channel has been modified in recent times by extensive dredging for ballast and part of the hard is now covered with thick ooze. The suggested Roman port on the Stour has yet to be located, but was presumably somewhere between Mistley and Wrabness.

If the road did cross the Stour at Ragmarsh Farm it would reach the north bank at Graham's Wharf on Holbrook Bay. From here a straight field boundary and track lead

11 *Suffolk Chronicle*, 9 November 1878.
12 *Britannia* vol.7, p.342.
13 Kemble, J., *Prehistoric and Roman Essex*, Tempus, 2001, p.143
14 Philip Cunningham, personal comment.

to Crowe Hall Farm, continuing as Crowe Hall Lane into Church Road and so through Stutton village into Alton Lane. The line is broken today by Alton Water, and the Roman route is likely to have left the direct line to cross the Alton valley. It might be marked briefly by a ride through the edge of Crag Hall Covert and a short stretch of footpath that curves to create the new alignment beyond the Alton valley.

North of here the road was closed to protect Holbrook Park. Throughout the county Roman roads are frequently lost where the route was diverted around a park in the Middle Ages or more recently. On the north side of the park the likely line is marked by the very straight concrete track north from Valley Farm. This might preserve the Roman line, which continues as the road to Wherstead, although diverted slightly around the edge of Park Farm outbuildings. There is a significant Roman site about a kilometre to the east on the spur overlooking the Orwell above Redgate Hard, and a possible branch road here to Downham Bridge. The line continued through the edge of Wherstead Park to the modern road down Bourne Hill and straight across the old bridge into Wherstead Road.

This straight road continues as Great Whip Street to the ford across the Orwell that was still in use at the beginning of the nineteenth century. Perhaps both the waterfront quays and the ford were in use during the Roman period. From here Brook Street and Northgate Street form a remarkably straight line leading towards the Avenue through Christchurch Park, continuing as The Avenue and a field boundary into Ipswich School fields. There is evidence of Roman activity, including pottery and metalwork, at Westerfield, which might be the destination of this road. Roman pots, which might possibly have been cremation urns, were found here while digging sewerage trenches south-west of the railway and road.[15] There are also reports of Roman and pre-Roman metalwork being found. However, if the alignment is projected it joins the modern road to Henley at Akenham Hall Farm, and this straight road would take it on to join the known Roman road from Baylham House, Coddenham, to Hacheston near Henley Cross Keys.

15 PSIAH vol. 11, p.338 (misrecorded as Burlington Road).

Is this hard on the River Stour at Ragmarsh the remains of the approach to a Roman crossing point? More recently it was used as a loading point for barges.

5. Coddenham to Felixstowe

The road to Felixstowe probably left Combretovium along the modern track past Barham church, where some Iron Age and Roman occupation has been noted at the sand pits and near the church.[16] The track probably preserves the general line but has been affected by the pits and the steep hill north of the church. In 1949 Basil Brown cut a section north-west of Barham Church at TM136510, where he interpreted the ditches as evidence of a Roman road 24ft. wide running east with a coin of Domitian and Roman pottery in the ditch. However the evidence is far from certain, although such a road might continue as the Slade at Claydon. Then some field boundaries could possibly take it, still on the higher ground, to the surface of "grouted flints" recorded running north on the western edge of the villa site at Castle Hill, although these might just be the surface of a yard. This section remains very speculative.

Parts of Norwich Road and Westgate Street are laid over an ancient timber roadway which has not been dated but might have been used in Roman times. It is most likely that the modern route to Felixstowe up Bishops Hill follows the Roman road to avoid the awkward valleys on that side of Ipswich. During excavation of the Blackfriars it was revealed that Fore Street originally continued diagonally towards the town centre until it was cut by the first town ditch about 917. It was impossible to date this cobbled road, although it was respected by early tenth century buildings. Perhaps this was the Roman road from the Cornhill, going on to skirt the edge of the great bend in the River Orwell before climbing Bishops Hill and proceeding on the line of Felixstowe Road into Bucklesham Road. Excavation by Suffolk County Council in 2004 at Purdis Farm revealed a road that was used in late Saxon times. It could be part of a direct link between the first part of Bucklesham Road and the modern line of the Felixstowe Road at Seven Hills, Nacton. It was impossible to date its construction but a Roman road across this very dry heathland would not be heavily engineered. Perhaps this stretch went out of use when the Saxon settlement at Purdis Farm was abandoned. The Roman road probably continued from Seven Hills on the line of the old main road to Trimley, parallel to the new A14.

A branch road might be represented by Clapgate Lane, which once ran to Alnesbourne Priory. Possibly it crossed the Orwell by a ford at Downham Bridge. There was a solid floor under the river between Pond Hall and Redgate Hard which might be an artificial surface giving access to a bridge (could "Pond" be derived from the Latin *pons, pontis* = a bridge?). On the other hand it could be part of a Roman barrage to control the river. This would provide a link to the road between Wherstead and Stutton. The apparent similarity of the river crossings of the Stour at Ragmarsh Farm/Stutton and of the Orwell at Redgate Hard/Pond Hall suggest they were designed to create the shortest land route between the colonia at Colchester and the coastal port at Felixstowe. Alternatively they might both have been created as barrages to prevent hostile ships proceeding further up the Stour and the Orwell.

It has been suggested that the main road into Felixstowe should have run through Stratton Hall, where its line is given as Suffolk E on the basis of Stratton meaning "Street Village". One route here is now destroyed by a crag pit beside the access road to Levington Marina, but continues as a straight track through the farmyard of Morston Hall, although there is no sign of a link between Morston Hall and Trimley. However this track crosses a deep valley that would be avoided by the present road called Strattonhall Drift.

On balance the old A14 seems the most likely route and might have marked the edge of Stratton, so giving it its name. At Trimley it is most likely that the Roman line is the modern road through Trimley St Mary, since Great Street Farm presumably takes its name from the road. It appears in Domesday Book as *Mycelgata* in Colneis Hundred. That is surely Mickle Gata, the Scandinavian version of Great Street. At the boundary between Trimley and Walton it crosses the lane known as Spriteshall Lane, which marks the parish boundary. This lane and boundary continues over the road as a footpath which makes its way towards the Blofield Hall area of settlement on a

16 Martin, E., *Settlements on Hill-tops*, EAA 65, 1993.

The line of the Roman road from Colchester to Westerfield ran from the Ipswich ford up Brook Street and Northgate Street, through the site of the medieval North Gate and up to the Avenue through Christchurch Park. In this photograph the Avenue is busy with pedestrians on Ipswich Music Day.

coastal creek, which might mark a sheltered anchorage used before and during the Roman period.

It appears that the Roman road is cutting across an older pattern of tracks represented by Spriteshall Lane from Blofield, also Keepers Lane and Gun Lane, and probably Hawks Lane, although here we have to move a critical footpath to the opposite side of a rectangular field. This excludes Cordys Lane to Searson's Farm, so was it a Roman addition? These tracks are linked to a lane running via Candlet to high ground above the Deben marshes.

There is a change of alignment at Walton, but finds of Roman domestic pottery and oyster shells recorded by Samuel Wall in the Exeter Road area might mark a small settlement at a road junction, the other road being a link, marked by the modern Seaton Road, from the settlement at Blofield Hall. The route of the main Roman road along High Street keeps to the narrow corridor of high ground between the head of the streams flowing into the Deben on one side and into the Orwell on the other. In Felixstowe itself High Road runs pretty straight.

Before landscaping in the 1990s what appeared to be an eroded section of this road was exposed in the cliff face below the site of Brackenbury Fort, showing that it continued in a straight line beyond the present coastline. A nineteenth-century photograph of Priory Farm (now The Priory) shows a substantial road with what appears to be a raised agger at a time when it could only have led to a dead end on the cliff edge. It does not head for the Roman fort of Walton Castle, but could have been the original direct main Roman road to a sheltered port on the Orwell side of the lost headland on which the fort was built later. It is too high above the sea, but presumably dropped down to sea level in the area lost to erosion.

The line of Quinton's Lane extended to the east might have been a roughly parallel route leading later in the Roman period to Walton Castle itself. Just possibly the reference from the manorial court record of the Friday after 29 June 1473 that "John Pope tenant of the Lord of the old priory (veterem prioratum) ploughed up a way there" records the moment when the extension of Quinton's Lane leading to Walton Castle was ploughed up by the tenant as he created the field known as Great Long Dole.[17] A possible alternative route, slightly further north, would follow a footpath, now lost but shown on the 1902 Ordnance Survey map, from behind St Mary's Church, Walton, passing the site of Walton Old Hall to SS Peter and Paul Church at Old Felixstowe and then picking up the above ploughed-up way.

17 Davison, PSIAH vol. 33 (1974), p.146, refers to SROI: Felixstowe Priory Rolls 4.7.

18 Loughlin, N., in "Archaeology in Suffolk 1973", PSIAH vol.33 (1973), p.96.
19 PSIAH vol.31 (1970), p.185.
20 Plouviez, J. in Blagg, T. et al., *Excavations at ... Hacheston*, EAA 106 (2004), p. 87/88 and 107.
21 Steerwood, R., "A Context for Sitomagus", PSIAH vol.40 (2003), p.253.
22 *Suffolk Chronicle*, 16 November 1878.

6. Coddenham to Hacheston and Wenhaston

Much of the road from Coddenham to Hacheston (Margary 340) is under the modern road from Needham Market to Wickham Market, but the Roman route has gone out of use at both ends. A road to the east was sectioned within the scheduled area of the Roman town at Coddenham in 1973 and was said to be about 10m wide, with continuous side ditches containing early pottery and an iron brooch.[18] There was some evidence of a timber building and industrial activity beside the road.

Loughlin's excavation is said to have "located the main road leading eastward from the ford over the Gipping, presumably to fork eventually in the direction of the Dunwich [sic] and Hacheston settlements...the road was about 10m wide with continuous side ditches ...". Exactly where was this found? The line of the road to Hacheston is probably preserved by a straight parish boundary between Barham and Hemingstone starting inside Shrubland Park at TM131525 as far as 144525, then resuming as the Hemingstone boundary on Clay Lane at 160527, continuing to Ashbocking crossroads, where it changes line slightly. The modern road deviates to cross the valley at Otley. Here the Roman road was sectioned by Elizabeth Owles in 1968.[19] It had been noted that a cart track westward from Catshill Farm was on the alignment and this continued as a stony streak in the ploughed field. The excavation was carried out across the stony streak at TM21085433, revealing ditches 4ft. wide and 2ft. deep from the modern ground surface. The ditches were 25ft. apart and the gravel agger 8in. thick at the centre, but it was so greatly damaged by ploughing that it was impossible to determine the original thickness. The source of road material might have been a gravel pit a fifth of a mile away opposite the Crown Inn. Just beyond Clopton Corner at 234547 modern maps mark as "Roman Road" the straight road to Charsfield, but this appears misleading as the most likely line to keep the high ground into modern Wickham Market continues the alignment from Otley which reaches Highgate Farm at 254552. The line continues as Highgate Lane and this name is likely to be derived from "gata" for road, a Scandinavian form found elsewhere referring to Roman roads. This line is also marked by straight field boundaries at 280558. This is the most direct line to a crossing of the Deben at or near the modern bridge, leading to the Roman town at Hacheston Fiveways. Perhaps there was a branch road from Clopton Corner to Charsfield, which is thought to have been the site of a temple on the basis of many brooches, including various bird and dog designs, and a very fine decorated bronze figurine of a dog.[20]

From Hacheston there was probably a road running north on the general line of the A12 through Marlesford, but crossing Glemham Park past Little Glemham church and close to the Hall, where the modern curve looks like a diversion around the Park. The place name suggests that it crossed the River Alde at Stratford St Andrew, then perhaps ran via Friday Street towards Kelsale East Green, if we accept Rob Steerwood's suggestion that this was Sitomagus.[21]

North of Friday Street the A12 and B1121 could mark the line to a change of alignment at Bigsby's Corner to follow the western side of the valley of the River Fromus through Saxmundham. Here it is obscured by the town and the railway, but a possible line keeps west beyond the crossroads of B1119 behind the Bell Hotel and taking the western lane through the market area and west of the railway bridge rejoins the present road through Carlton. Then it runs close to the Fromus as far as the present bridge in Kelsale and up the straight lane to the church (Dennys Lane) which heads just west of the church tower. At this point it is less than a mile from the proposed site of Sitomagus. Hamlet Watling reported apparent Roman burials "immediately south of the present cemetery" at Kelsale.[22] From here the road is lost, perhaps destroyed by the plough.

Projected northwards the line soon crosses the presumed road from Needham to Kelsale which stays north of the Fromus valley to reach the proposed site of Sitomagus. Our proposed route to Wenhaston would continue north of Kelsale Place on the line of the modern track parallel to the A12, but keeping to the higher ground one field east of the modern road. This track makes a slight change of line and then picks up a track east of Yoxford village but on the western edge of Rookery Park, heading directly for the present crossing over the river Yox. Norman Scarfe sees this as the original Yoxford, and believes the stream would have been a much more substantial obstacle before the drainage works that included creation of the Minsmere Levels.[23]

It then follows the A12 again along the Darsham Straight, which originally continued straight through Thorington Park. At Thorington John Newman found Iron Age and Roman pottery at the quarry,[24] with a possible pottery kiln of the second to third century, adjacent to the line of the old East Coast main road, the predecessor of the A12 before it was diverted to create Thorington Park. John notes a dog-leg in the old road here which might avoid an existing Iron Age settlement. If so, it must have been a place of some importance. At Wenhaston Gilbert Burroughes has noted on an air photograph features immediately north-east of the point where the modern road crosses a tributary stream which might be quays or docks for small river craft.

At Wenhaston itself there is a large area of Roman settlement, presumably a market town overlooking the River Blyth. In Wenhaston village it is likely that The Street is the general line of the main Roman road. If so the north end probably followed a left fork in the modern road and headed for the river crossing at Mells (the Blyford Bridge crossing could be part of an older "linear" north-south long-distance route). It then ran through Holton to the straight Roman road from Halesworth to Bungay known as Stone Street (Margary 36, partly the modern A144) heading for a

23 Scarfe, N., *Medieval Suffolk*, Woodbridge, 1986, p.144.
24 PSIAH vol.37 (1992), p.389.

The valley of the Waveney at Bungay seen from the tower of St Mary's church. The Roman crossing point from Wainford to Ditchingham is marked by the large maltings in the centre of the picture.

Gilbert Burroughes and members of the Suffolk Archaeological Field Group excavated a trench across the line of the Roman road from Combretovium to Venta Icenorum where the A140 now bends away from it on the slope to the river crossing at Stoke Ash. The trench at Stoke Ash revealed a complicated story, probably the result of changes to the road line and later erosion of the surface. One of the ditches beside the road is visible here and some of the gravel seems to have washed into it. On the right Jude Plouviez and Gilbert Burroughes are looking at possible remains of a damaged road surface towards the middle of the trench.

25 Hartley, K. & Gurney, D., *A Mortarium Kiln at Ellingham, Norfolk*, EAA Occasional Paper 2. (1997) page 1.
26 cf. NAHRG Quarterly 61 (March 2006).
27 Robinson, B. & Rose E.J., *Norfolk Origins 2: Roads and Tracks*, Poppyland, 1983, road 19.

crossing of the River Waveney at Wainford, on the boundary between Broome and Ditchingham. Here there is evidence of a settlement, including the manufacture of pottery.[25] From Ditchingham a road continues north through Woodton (B1332), where it is named "Stone Street" on Faden's eighteenth-century map of Norfolk, and through Brooke. Faden also shows as "Roman Road" the B1135 through Hempnall towards Tasburgh,[26] which might be a branch road. From Brooke the main road appears to proceed northwards through Poringland (ignoring Caistor-by-Norwich), across the River Yare from Trowse to Thorpe, climbing the hill at Thunder Lane on a direct line to the town at Brampton.[27]

There was probably a direct road from Kelsale East Green picking up the alignment of the Weybread Straight (Margary 35). The straight route through Peasenhall to Needham crosses Margary 34b at Peasenhall. From the proposed site of Sitomagus the first stretch is lost as far as Peasenhall, probably because it would have been destroyed when the Bigods created their great deer park in Kelsale. The road runs north-west from Peasenhall as Heveningham Long Lane, and further stretches on the same alignment are marked by roads and tracks. It is lost crossing the River Blyth, but it resumes directly as a lane north of Ubbeston Hall, until lost in a small valley at Cratfield.

It is then soon resumed as parts of Tongs Lane, which appears as a solid agger about 16ft. wide near Silverley's Green but defined by deep ditches that might encroach on the original road. Although obstructed by a modern house at Silverley's Green, it immediately forms the straight road to Little Whittingham Green, but is then lost across open ground and valley until it forms the Weybread straight. It appears to aim for a crossing over the River Waveney to the known settlement on the Norfolk bank at Needham. There is no sign of a road beyond Needham, but if continued it would join the A140 at Pulham St Mary or Long Stratton. However, it may be that it was part of the boundary system attributed below to the road from Long Melford to Peasenhall, so only ran in solid form as far as the Waveney.

7. Stoke Ash to Icklingham

From the White Horse crossroads going westwards it is possible to suggest a line that diverges slightly north of the modern road to Thornham so that it passes through Street Farm in Thornham Magna and on by a bridleway in a straight alignment to join Clay Street. This line continues as a field boundary to Jims Wood, is lost briefly and then picked up by the parish boundary of Finningham as it is crossed by the railway. It is marked by pronounced bends in two roads north of Finningham village and continues as field boundaries and a footpath to Westhorpe Hall. There it changes alignment to run through Westhorpe village, where the modern road is on the agger, which continues as the start of Overhill Lane, where it appears to survive as a garden feature.

After a short break up to the Hartismere Hundred boundary (Hundred Lane) it seems to be followed by the boundary of Walsham-le-Willows. This is marked by a line of footpaths and boundaries, including Madge's Lane, on the border with Badwell Ash. Here Audrey McLaughlin and Rob Barber showed me surviving sections of "Precession Waye or Peddars Waye" as recorded by a survey made in 1577.[28] The use of "Peddars Way" is not always significant but I regard it as support for this being a Roman road adopted for the parish boundary. It survives as a track south of Crownland Farm, and beyond Low Barn a deep ditch is probably the line of the road's ditch. Beyond the modern road the boundary crosses damp ground but could still be the Roman line until it turns sharply north short of Hillwatering Farm. If the line is projected it might survive as disconnected field boundaries and a short track into Kiln Lane. There it crosses the alignment of Peddars Way from Barningham Park past Stanton Chare. From Woodstreet Farm a straight stretch runs as Crown lane into the centre of Ixworth, but this might be misleading as a geophysical survey of the villa site south of this road shows the orientation of Roman field boundaries does not match the road.

A possible second road heading more directly to the Pakenham fort would diverge where the boundary crosses Badwell Road to pick up a footpath just south of Langham Old Rectory, then by woodland tracks, a field boundary and a lane to Baileypool Bridge to reach Pakenham via Grimstone End. It might continue as Thieves Lane, Cutters Lane and Heath Lane to the road found on Queach Farm.

An east to west road (Suffolk A) crosses the fort at Pakenham (Ixworth) and this might be part of the wider system. A road west of Ixworth was recorded in the nineteenth century near Puttock's Hill on Queach Farm in Pakenham (not far from Red Castle Farm where there was a Roman house with a mosaic floor).[29] The road had a gravel surface ten yards wide and about a foot thick at the crown. It was traced running east to west over three fields at the back of cottages and has been located more recently on aerial photographs. Presumably this is "the remains of a paved road ... discovered leading in the direction of Icklingham and Cambridge, and plainly visible for a considerable distance" noted by Hamlet Watling in 1878.[30]

The road has been cut by Ampton Water but the line can be traced through Ingham village. In Ingham east of the A134 a track behind a new house is marked by two oak trees just north of the dotted line on the OS map. On the west side of the A134 another oak on the southern boundary of "Full Oak" continues the line along the north boundary of modern housing. This line could pick up the road to Brockley Corner and beyond that straight to Brick Kiln Cottage. Here it is lost, perhaps because the water meadows were included in the park of West Stow Hall. It continues as the forestry track from Forest Lodge to Wideham Barn, a solid agger which continues straight on where the modern path deviates to the north just east of Wideham Barn. The agger, now overgrown, continues as the boundary between forest and field until it crosses the Icknield Way, bringing it close to the Roman town. At Icklingham itself a short length of road was identified from the air and found to be 24ft. wide.[31] More recently its line through the Roman town has been plotted from air photographs and geophysics.

28 See map in *Towards a Landscape History of Walsham le Willows, Suffolk*, EAA 85, 1998.
29 Warren, J., "Antiquities found at Ixworth", PSIAH vol.1 (1849), p.74-8.
30 *Suffolk Chronicle*, 9 November 1878.
31 Goodburn, R., "Roman Britain in 1977", *Britannia*, vol.9 (1978), p.448.

Index